EIGG

THE STORY OF AN ISLAND

Scotland

A person belongs
In as much as they are willing
To cherish and be cherished
By this place
And its peoples

Alastair McIntosh
Love and Revolution

EIGG

THE STORY OF AN ISLAND

Camille Dressler

BIRLINN

This edition published in 2007 by
Birlinn Limited
West Newington House
10 Newington Road
Edinburgh EH9 1QS

www.birlinn.co.uk

Reprinted 2014, 2016

First published in 1998 by Polygon, Edinburgh

ISBN: 978 1 78027 450 8

British Library Cataloguing-in-Publication Data
A catalogue record for this book is available from the British Library

Typeset by Hewer Text UK, Edinburgh
Printed and bound by Gutenberg, Malta

CONTENTS

LIST OF ILLUSTRATIONS
AND PLATES

CHAPTER ILLUSTRATIONS

PLATES

ACKNOWLEDGEMENTS

I would like to pay tribute to the memory of Hugh MacKinnon, whose recordings are one of the archive treasures in the School of Scottish Studies in Edinburgh, to Duncan Ferguson who had the foresight to write down his extensive knowledge of his native island, and to Duncan and Katie-Ann MacKay, Mary Campbell, Marybel MacDonald, Gordon Campbell and Dr MacLean in whose company I spent many pleasurable hours discussing the island's past. I am also particularly indebted to Katie and Dougald MacKinnon, Angus MacKinnon, Dolly Ferguson, Morag Campbell, Peggy Kirk, Allie MacDonald, Ann Campbell, and Mary-Anne and Catriona Campbell, who shared their traditions with such great willingness over the years. Without their knowledge and help, this book would not have been been possible at all. Sadly, many of them have now gone too. Many thanks to everyone else on Eigg, particularly Maggie and Wes, Davey, Bean, John, and my family, of course; Brian, for his help and support, and our children, Felicia and Brendan, for their patient understanding. Thanks also to Jude Devereux, Doreen Jones and Daniel Morgan, to Alice Stoakley for copy-editing, to Rob, Caroline and Mandy for their photographs, to Ian Fisher, Steve Boyle and his team at the RCAHMS, to Michael Butler for the use of the MacPherson family sketchbook, to Noel Banks for the M.E.P. diaries and to Dr Margaret MacKay for the use of the Eigg material in the School of Scottish Studies.

ACKNOWLEDGEMENTS FOR MAPS, PHOTOGRAPHS
AND ILLUSTRATIONS

Maps: Map 1: reproduced by permission of the Trustees of the National Library of Scotland. Maps 2 and 3: Caird Design, Isle of Eigg.

Plates: 1: Mairi Anna Birkeland-Clyde. 2: Drawings by Ian Scott, Crown copyright © RCAHMS. 3: *Proceedings of the Society of Antiquaries*, Edinburgh, vol. 12, p. 588. Cover photograph, 4, 25, M.E.M. Donaldson, Scottish Life Archive, National Museums of Scotland., 6: Banff Collection, Crown copyright © RCAHMS. 8, 9, 10: reproduced by kind permission from the Gargunnock Charitable Trust, Crown copyright © RCAHMS. 16: Murray of Hawick, Crown copyright © RCAHMS. 27: Crown copyright © RCAHMS, 52, 53, 55: Iain MacGowan. 54: Rob Blom van Assendelft. 55 and back cover insert: Mandy Wragg. 57: Caroline Frances-King. 59: Paul Reid. 61:Wayne Wilson. 63, 70, 72: Scotsman Publications Ltd. 64: Les Parker. All other photos, Isle of Eigg Archive collections: 6, 19, 31, 32, 33, 39, 42,

45: Barbara Barrie Collection. 7, 47, 49: Peggy Kirk collection. 11, 40: Janet Macdonald collection. 12, 13, 14, 29, 35, 36, 38: Chrissie Oliver collection. 15, 17: Ishbel Anderson collection. 18, 37: Duncan Ferguson collection. 20, 21: Wheelan collection. 22, 23, 26: Catherine MacLean collection. 24, 34, 44, 51: Dressler collection. 30: Duncan MacKay collection. 41: Iain and Myrtle Campbell collection. 46, 48: Iain Campbell collection. 50. 58: Marie Carr. 60, 62, 66: IEHT. 67, 68, 69: Camille Dressler. 71: Kathleen Smith.

INTRODUCTION

Islands have always been the focus of desire. They invite yearnings and dreams, some more conspicuously so than others. Eigg is perhaps one of these, dominated by An Sgurr, that archetypal promontory, which an old island saying has turned into a metaphor of permanence: '*Bidh an Sgurr an sid 's bidh mis an seo*' – the Sgurr will always be here and so will I.

The Sgurr, that mile-long ridge of columnar basalt, is the backbone of the island, yet underneath lies the fossil remains of the pine forest which once grew on the side of an ancient river bed. This is only one of the many paradoxes which Eigg has to offer. Spawned by lavas erupting along fissures cracked open as the Atlantic formed, covering the shallow estuarine laguna where plesiosaurs used to wallow, the 7,400-acre island is half 'speckled mountain', half fertile green slopes. Its south side, all high cliffs gouged out into 'geos' and caves, is the domain of otters and sea-birds. Above, the mountainous terrain is Golden Eagle territory, its lochs sheltering the rare red-throat diver in its breeding season. Then, beyond Bidein Boidheach, where the Sgurr ridge ends in the sheerest cliff, the coastline curves into the wide sweep of Laig bay, soft folds of arable land rippling down from a great amphitheatre of crumbling basalt cliffs colonised by shearwaters. This is Cleadale, looking to the west, where the hay meadows vindicate every summer Eigg's reputation as 'the island of flowers', as the naturalist Seton-Gordon called it. From Laig's pounding surf to the Singing Sands, where the dry quartz grains emit a shrill sound when crushed underfoot, a fantastic sandstone landscape sculpted by the sea fringes the crofters' fields. Then, from the north end all along the eastern coast, steep rock-strewn slopes plunge down from the flat moorland plateau of Beinn Bhuidhe, a desolate area of bogs and heather where rare alpine flora can occasionally be found, until a succession of rocky outcrops allow a gentler descent towards the green fields of Kildonnan. There, sandy coves and muddy flats fringed by hazel-covered slopes lead to Galmisdale Point and the pier, sheltered by numerous reefs where seals live and play without paying attention to the comings and goings of the island's flit boat as it meets up with the Small Isles ferry four times a week, when the weather permits.

About eighty people inhabit Eigg now, yet at one time the island population numbered five hundred. It is the story of these people and of those who have succeeded each other since the earliest times which is inscribed in the landscape. Cairns and crosses, snaking earthen dykes and straight croftwalls, mounds engulfed by heather and townships in ruins make a powerful memoryscape, each place name 'the writing of human activity, of personal and collective experience'.[1] At one time, not so long ago, when every corner of Eigg had its stories and legends, the land was an open book for all to read. Oral tradition was constantly at work to pass on the island's unwritten history, foster the feeling of kinship with a land with which people felt intimately connected, and engender a sense of continuity through the many changes the island has known. Today, thanks to some outstanding tradition-bearers, enough pages remain for the next generations to discover what gave the island's past its unique flavour.

In that respect, the story of Eigg is also the story of a culture's survival against the powers of the day. From the fierce struggles in clan times to the bleak periods of famine and emigration, through to the modern-day fight to maintain a viable crofting community, the island has always been a microcosm of Highland history, as recent events have proved only too well. The community has acquired at long last a stake in its own future, halting and, it is hoped, reversing the movement of depopulation and exile which has slowly bled it of its strength.

Today, a new sort of *Gall* has come to the land of the *Gaidheal*. I am one of them, a French person with a complicated story of dispersal in my parentage, who arrived on Eigg seventeen years ago and found in the Hebridean tradition of hospitality to the stranger something so warm and congenial that I put my roots down there. I anticipated little then of the hardships and turmoil of the past few years, but looked forward to participating in the island's renewal. For myself, and the other people who chose to make the island their home, the challenge was – and still is – to give our children, the new generation of 'native islanders', a chance to play their part in the island's future. To this end, it seemed that a knowledge and understanding of the past was essential to complete that sense of belonging which islands generate.

This is how the idea of this island chronicle was born. It came into being through the listening and collecting of oral accounts which the islanders gave of their lives and traditions. It now includes the process undergone by the community in the last twenty years. The raising of a great pillar of Sgurr stone, lying almost forgotten, nearly buried by centuries of slow growth, is a symbol of this new awareness of a collective history, for it now commemorates the Eigg community buy-out. They'll be telling stories about it for years to come.

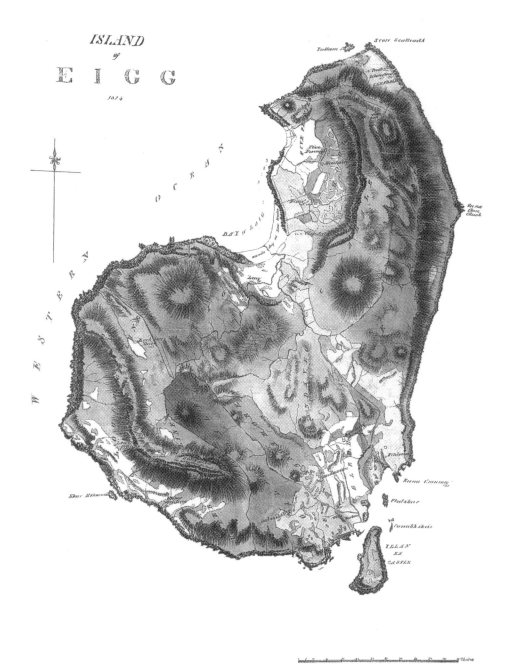

Map 1   Map of Eigg from 1824 ordered for the sale of the island by Clanranald, after William Bald

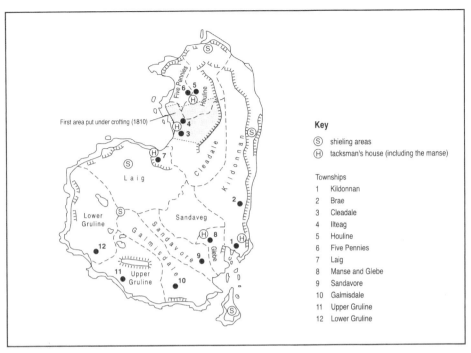

First area put under crofting (1810)

Map 2 The farms and townships of Eigg before crofting was introduced

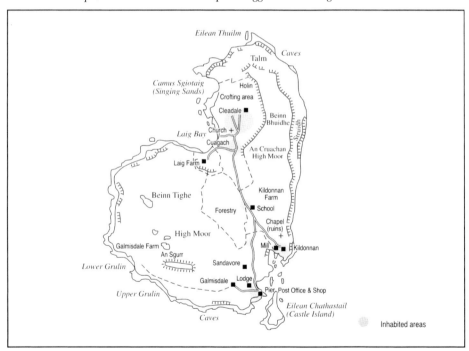

Map 3 Eigg today

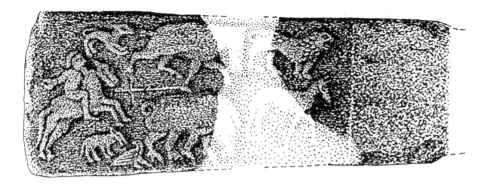

Chapter 1

ORIGINS

A FEW STONE FLAKES

Sometime around 5000 BC, a few stone tools were abandoned on one of the grassy slopes tumbling down from the Corravein. There they lay undisturbed, inches of peat growing slowly over them until a forestry plough finally brought them to light again: a core of stone yet to be worked, a handful of blades and scrapers fashioned out of Sgurr lava and Rum bloodstone. This small find told of the presence on Eigg of Scotland's first inhabitants, the fisher-hunters of the Mesolithic Age. Beckoned by the great basaltic ridge of the Sgurr on their migration along the coast, they came to Eigg in their boats of skin and bark and found it a hospitable place. The shore had fish and shellfish in abundance, the cliffs teemed with sea-birds whose nests could be robbed in the spring and there were seals and otters to hunt. Hazel trees grew thickly in the far milder climate, holding the promise of a rich nut harvest every autumn. There were other riches too, like the small cowry shells whose shape, evocative of the mysteries of birth, made them greatly sought after for ritual decoration, or the glassy pitchstone from two intrusive seams, black like contorted coal, at Rubha na Tancaird. It was precious for tool-working, almost as good as bloodstone, a dark green agate spotted with red, which could be found in greater abundance on the neighbouring island of Rum, a few miles north of Eigg. It was there that more telling evidence was found about the fisher-hunters' life: the remains of their tool-working camp indicate that their gatherings were great convivial occasions where they consumed venison and hazelnuts in vast amounts and drank them down with a potent brew made out of honey, heather and meadowsweet.[1] Little else is known about the lives of these first inhabitants except that nature was kind to them and that they revered her for her bounty.

QUERNS AND CAIRNS

By 3000 BC, the neolithic colonisation had reached Hebridean shores. Adventurous chieftains of Iberian origin took over the fisher-hunters' territories, leading a new people armed with strange weapons of polished stone. They settled on Eigg's near-empty shores, building stone and turf huts where the deerskin tents of the fisher-hunters had stood for a brief time each season.

Eigg's fertile glens and valleys were sown with primitive cereals like bere or black oats. Pens were built for goats and sheep of an ancient soft-fleeced breed not unlike the Soay sheep, and cattle were led to graze in the hills. Milk and meal were now the staple food, the grain parched after harvest and ground in hollowed-out stones – the most primitive of querns – before it was boiled into porridge or baked in unleavened bannocks, a way of preparing food which was to last for millennia.

Thus started an era of intense growth, the neolithic farming revolution benefiting from the warm and moist Oceanic climate. During the next thousand years, a sophisticated culture developed, linked by the Atlantic sea-routes to settlements on the continent. Worshipping nature for her fecundity was no longer enough; she had to be controlled and harnessed in order to maintain the necessary cycle of growth. The sun's course through the sky was observed carefully and recorded in complex megalithic structures to ensure proper sowing and harvesting times. Recently rescued from near-complete burial by the surrounding vegetation, two huge Sgurr pillars may have fulfilled such ritual and calendar functions on Eigg, although the landscape itself could have been used: the sun sets on the peaks of Rum in midsummer, behind Beinn Tighe in midwinter.

It was in their concern for the dead that people left their most conspicuous mark. Their burial mounds can be found all over the island, always in view of the sea, and in the midst of rich arable land. Two of these mounds were opened in the mid-nineteenth century, when their stones were plundered for road-building, much against the islanders' wishes. (These mounds were believed to be the dwellings of the *Sidheanan* – the people of the underworld – and it was thought that bad luck would befall those who dared to disturb them in any way.) In Sidhean na Cailleich, the mound of the Hag, overlooking Laig bay, two stone cists were found, one of them yielding a beautiful axe-head of polished basalt identified as coming from Rathlin Island, off the coast of Antrim, from where such axes were exported in vast numbers. This find elicited a little more care in the opening of a second mound at Kildonnan which was supervised by an antiquarian friend of the island proprietor. He was able to note that it was perfectly circular in shape and carefully built of five alternate layers of beach pebble and gravel. In its midst, a single stone cist was found containing a little dust and a few fragments of charred bones.[2]

The two mounds spanned the neolithic period in their style and contents: they housed the remains not of mere commoners, but of leaders of the community, chieftains whose death was accompanied by rituals which went from simple burial in the early neolithic period to preliminary cremation later on. The mound of stones erected on top of the cist was the outward symbol of the temporal power exerted by the chieftain in his lifetime – the axe found at Laig would have been a prestige object denoting rank – as well as of the supernatural power which he acquired after his death. It became a place of mediation between the living and the dead, where the protection of the departed leader was invoked after his transformation into a tutelary ancestor enjoying everlasting life in an afterworld of plenty. It is from such ancient roots that the belief in the underworld of the *Sidheanan* would have originated, as well as the enduring custom of circling mounds sun-wise to show respect and avert bad luck.

Towards the end of the Neolithic Age, around 2300 BC, new influences found their way to Eigg, coming from the East this time, following the trade route for amber and jet which its chieftains coveted for their personal adornment. The use of a new type of arrowhead became prevalent and the Rum bloodstone was once again in great demand for their manufacture. The delicate barbed and tanged arrowheads were traded all along the coast from Wester Ross to Ardnamurchan. (Turning up under islanders' ploughs many centuries later, they were believed to be the magical arrows of the *Sidheanan* and were kept as good-luck charms.)

The trade routes soon brought the first metal objects, gold ornaments and then copper and bronze weapons from the continent. Unfortunately the advent of the Bronze Age, towards 2000 BC, was to signal the decline of the cairn-builders' culture as the climate gradually changed from the warm and moist of the Oceanic period to the cold and wet of the Sub-Atlantic, which we still endure to this day. The increased frequency of storms and wet weather prevented grain from ripening, the shrinking of resources causing populations to dwindle. Oak and pine started to die and it did not take long for their tree stumps to be buried under the rapidly growing peat which covered over so many remains of these distant times. High up below the Sgurr and the lochs, on the high moorland plateau above Laig, tantalising stone structures can still be traced amongst the deer grass in the middle of former peat grounds.[3] On the south side of the Sgurr, grave mounds have been recently discovered, their entrance guarded by stone pillars which have long fallen on their side, recalling old forgotten legends telling of giants' graves.

THE COMING OF THE CELTS

By the end of the Bronze Age, a new people arrived on the shores of Eigg: the Celts had started their restless expansion towards the west. The first wave, reaching the islands by 600 BC, were the Goidels whose characteristic language was to form the basis of Irish and Scottish Gaelic. They brought with them a culture deeply coloured by their nomadic cattle-rearing life in the steppes of Central Europe where their distinctive art had evolved, combining religious motifs of the Bronze Age with Greek foliage ornamentation and Eastern animal art. They had also adopted the striking Scythian custom of tattooing mythical beasts and symbols on their skin to confer magical power and protection, a custom which would earn their descendants the name of Picts, or painted people, from the Romans who, according to Herodotus, marvelled that they went about partially naked to prevent the brilliant figures painted on their bodies from being hidden.

The new colonisers easily adapted their pastoral economy to Highland conditions, introducing the semi-nomadic lifestyle of taking the cattle into the hills each summer, ingeniously transforming their yurt-like tents into circular stone dwellings, the astonishing wheelhouses. Their short-horned cattle thrived on island pastures, and the people ploughed the machair with barley and oats which tolerated wetter conditions. Hunting ducks, geese and deer, they supplemented their fare with fishing, whaling or plundering. However, their bronze weapons were no match for the superior iron swords and spears which a second wave of Celtic invaders brought with them around 200 BC. In their turn, these offshoots from the war-loving tribes who sacked Delphi and threatened Rome found Scotland ideally suited for settlement by their piratical cattle-owning aristocracy.

Eigg, like other islands and coastal regions, offered an ideal combination of farming and pastoral land with immediate access and control of the waterways. But the new territories had to be protected by building fortifications on every promontory overlooking a landing place, and Eigg was soon circled by a ring of duns, or stone fortlets. At Galmisdale Point where the jetty now is, the Iron Age invaders made clever use of an intrusive basalt dyke to which they added a semi-circular wall, the remaining boulders of which were unfortunately disposed of when sheds were built on that site in the 1930s. At Kildonnan, they used the small peninsula of Rubha na Crannaig which juts out to protect access to the bay of Poll nam Partan. A low, turf-covered circular wall is all that is now left. Above Laig, 'an Dunan' at that time would have dominated a shallow estuary now well above sea-level. Further along, 'Dunan Thalisgeir' at the north end of Beinn Bhuidhe would have commanded an outstanding view over the sounds of Sleat, Rum and Soay. Nothing remains today of any fortification, the cliff edge constantly crumbling from erosion, but the site was still used as a look-out in clan times: 'there is a Dunan Thalamh Sgeir on Rubha an Dunan on Skye and Dunan Thalamh Sgeir on the island of Eigg', told a nineteenth-century islander. 'One can be seen from the other, and when a fire was seen on one, the other could respond. There was always a watchman on the dun day and night and if he fell asleep, he had to die, death by hanging. The baillie had to ensure that the watchman did not fall asleep or doze; and that watchman was called the Gocaman, after the wee bird that follows the cuckoo.'[4]

The Sgurr itself, its pitchstone crag rising 400 ft from the hills below, seems to have been used as a place of ultimate refuge, the thick wall barring its only access enclosing about nine acres of ground. But other structures nearby were of a less defensive nature, like the artificial island which was built out of pitchstone blocks in the middle of Loch nam Ban Mora, the largest of the three lochs which lie below the Sgurr. The small crannog, about 9 ft in diameter, is said to be linked to the shore by a submerged causeway which, tradition relates, could only be used by a race of women of supernatural proportions. The legend goes that they were so tall that only they could step from one stone to another without any difficulty, and that the loch is named after them, the Loch of the Big Women. There is a strong pagan flavour in that tale, given that the Celts had a special respect for lochs, burns, springs or pools as embodiments of their goddesses, and often threw ritual or votive offerings – ornaments or weapons – in honour of the deity believed to inhabit them. The bronze penannular brooch which was recovered from the Laig burn during drainage work in the nineteenth century may have been such an offering. That burn was certainly believed to be haunted by a guardian spirit, a shape-shifting Cailleach, an old woman who would sometimes appear with a bull's head, and was also associated with the mound called after her; whilst it was a much gentler spirit, the 'Gruagach', that supernatural water maiden, who was thought to inhabit a pool in Cleadale. Maiden, mother and old woman were all manifestations of the Celtic Mother Goddess, who was also believed to be embodied in the land itself. Indeed, Eigg's Gaelic place-names echo from the memories of a time when features of the land were described as parts of her body: head, back, shoulder or hip-bone – Ceann, Druim, Guala, Cruachan – when land had to be nurtured and placated through ritual ceremonies which took place in the round of festivities from one end of the year to the next, led by tribal leaders who had mystical as well as temporal powers, their role being to make the land fruitful and to be a guarantee of plenty, prosperity and security.

Maintaining the fertility of the land would have been of prime concern to Eigg's Iron Age inhabitants, for the sizeable number of their oval or circular huts, spread in clusters all over the island, suggests that it supported a relatively dense population. They had superior agricultural implements fashioned out of bog iron in lieu of ore, which allowed them to produce the surplus barley which made the Hebrides famous for export in Roman times. Iron was very important for the Celts, who considered it a sign of wealth, yet not as much as the possession of cattle. Cattle was the currency at the base of their economy, on which everything depended, even honour and freedom, status and bloodprice.

Celtic society was based on the ownership of cattle: to be a freeman was to be an 'Oc Aire' or cow-lord, who had the right to attend the tribal assemblies, owed military service to the chief and paid three cows in annual rent. The minimum of land required to be a cow-lord was seven 'cumals', a cumal being the amount of land supporting three cows and their followers. Below the cow-lord, there was a caste of sub-tenants who were not free, but could nevertheless acquire higher status by leasing cattle from freemen. Above the cow-lord were the tribal elite of craftsmen, erudites and warriors, these enjoying a high but precarious status which had to be constantly preserved with valorous feats measured by the number of severed enemy heads, for the glory of being allowed the 'hero's portion' at the chief's table. At the top of this pyramid was the chief, who dispensed cattle and land and received in exchange a levy from each man in the tribe in the form of various food levies, provision of labour and military service, a system which was to form the basis of clan organisation and give it its essential characteristics.[5]

With cattle reiving the way to acquire honour and wealth, the heroic ethic which dominated tribal life occasioned endless reassertion of status and claims of redress for real or assumed wrongs, causing a state of endemic warfare. Yet as tribal kings were linked to the overkings of the seven provinces of Celtic Scotland and their high king by a complex system of bonds of allegiance and treaties, these warring tribes shared a common culture which was strong enough to bind them into the Pictish confederation which repelled the Roman invaders and evolved into the more state-like society of Dark Ages Pictland.

THE AGE OF SAINTS

Thus, by AD 600, Eigg found itself on the southern border of Pictland, with the land of Ardnamurchan as its only buffer against the expansionist ambitions of Dalriada, the Argyll kingdom originating from a colony of Antrim settlers and ruled by Ulster princes driven from Ulster by dynastic pressure. Their kinsman, Columba, had obtained leave from them to set up his monastic community on the island of Iona, whose geographical situation made it an ideal base for his mission to convert Pictish Scotland to Christianity. Yet if tradition asserts that the saint visited Eigg and Canna in the course of his travels, banishing all snakes and toads from the two islands, and blessing the well in Cleadale which is called after him, Tobar Chaluim Chille, it was not him, but Donnan, a Pictish saint, who is credited with the conversion of the people of Eigg to Christianity.

Donnan was said to have visited Columba in Iona before coming to Eigg to ask him for the honour of becoming his *anamcara*, his soulfriend – soulfriends in the Celtic church offered each other spiritual guidance and opened their hearts in confession, giving each other strength and insight – but Columba told Donnan that he would not need his soulfriendship. Drawing on his famous prophetic powers, he foresaw instead that Donnan's fate was not to be the 'white martyrdom' of the hermit seeking solitude away from the world and enduring privation, but the 'red martyrdom' of those who were to face a violent death.[6] Donnan was certainly risking his life in venturing into a territory where Pictish chiefs already felt threatened by Dalriadic ambitions. But it may be that Columba was not so happy to see a rival missionary in his sphere of influence. Yet, the teaching of St Ninian's monastery in Whithorn in Galloway where Donnan had received

5

his training was very close to that of Columba's. Both derived their form of monasticism from St Martin of Tours, the fourth-century legionnaire convert whose ideals were modelled on the Eastern fathers of the church and adapted more easily to the tribal nature of Pictish and Irish society than the more hierarchical Roman church. Martin had preached self-imposed exile to his missionaries in Gaul, who would wander with their staff and bells to proclaim the glory of God and seek the place of their resurrection in isolated places, where, after much fasting and self-chastening, they would gather round them a *muinntir*, a family of monks to create a self-supporting community dispensing preaching and prayers for the surrounding lands.

Donnan, who had already established religious communities in Northern Pictland, is said to have arrived on Eigg with twelve companions. Crossing over in their skin coracle, they may have first sought shelter in one of the island's caves which, according to the Irish tale of mad Suibhne,[7] was named after the saint. From this eremitic retreat, Donnan would have gone on to preach to the islanders, perhaps at the place called Leac a' Ghuidal, the stone of the pulpit, along the coast from Rubha na Crannaig on the eastern side of the island. The message that he would have preached was that nature in all its entirety, including human beings, was part of a single immense whole to which religious man turned and sang his gratitude. It was the triumphant aspect of Christ rather than the suffering one, as in the Roman church, which was emphasised. With the veneration of Mary, it combined well with the Celtic worship of nature as the dwelling of the gods and goddesses, and was readily accepted.

The land given to Donnan to set up his *muinntir* was on the fertile land overlooking the sea down from the slopes of Beinn Bhuidhe, near the burial mounds which had already made it a hallowed place for former generations of islanders. It is said by tradition to have been built not far from a well sanctified by Donnan himself, which was known as 'the well of Donnan's altar'. The monastery would have consisted of an oratory and cells built out of wood and wattle which served as refectory and sleeping quarters within a circular enclosure marked by a wall which separated it from the surrounding land, taking it 'out of the world'. A thin sandstone slab now marking a grave within the ruins of the existing chapel is thought to be the cross which would have marked the centre of the monastery as that place out of the world, its equal-armed 'cross potent' representing Christ as the glorious sun. At each of the cardinal points, other crosses would have stood, marking them as preaching places: the areas known as 'Crois Mhor' and 'Crois Bheag', where crosses once stood according to tradition, may thus have indicated the monastery's east and west boundaries. They may even have been the two early 'Tau' crosses recovered from the churchyard at Kildonnan, which attest to the Eastern influence on Donnan's teaching.[8]

The monks of Donnan's *muinntir*, who soon numbered fifty-two people according to the Irish Annals of Tighearnac, would have lived a life of prayer and learning, eating one meal a day, wearing a plain garment of coarse white wool which was their cloak in the day and their blanket at night. They would have tilled their fields, taken care of the sick and the dying, prayed and celebrated the feast days of a new calendar. But tradition and religious annals recorded that the establishment of a monastery on Eigg was not welcomed by the ruler of the island, the Pictish Queen of Moidart in whose territory Eigg was included and which was reported by Columban chroniclers as keeping such pagan practices as observing Beltane rather than Easter and worshipping serpents. Yet it was as much the power and influence of the new monasteries as the new beliefs which were feared and resented by Pictish chieftains.

Legend tells that from her dun in Glenuig, the Queen of Moidart ordered the monks to be killed: 'I am keeping herdsmen to herd my milking cattle on the face of the Corravein, not to be herded themselves by a monk'. When the newly converted islanders refused to obey her orders, she flew into a red-hot rage and sent her own warrior women over to Eigg. They came upon Donnan and his monks as they were singing mass in their oratory on 17 April 617, but the saint beseeched them to wait until they had finished their prayers. As they left the church, Donnan and his monks were beheaded one after the other, their bodies were piled up and burnt: Columba's prophecy had come to pass. But the story did not end there, for the legend tells that at midnight, lights appeared where the bodies had lain and unearthly voices were heard chanting Donnan's death croon, bewitching the warrior women who found themselves compelled to follow the lights as they led them towards Loch nam Ban Mora below the Sgurr, where they finally rested above the little island in the middle of it. One by one, the warrior women entered the dark water, their eyes fixed on the lights, oblivious to the submerged causeway until each of them drowned in her turn.[9] The Loch of the Big Women had claimed them as its own and from then on the big women merged with the warrior women in the island tradition, so much so that the islanders came to call their island after them whilst at sea, using the name of Eilean nam Ban Mora, the Island of the Big Women, as their sea-kenning for Eigg.

The site of Donnan's monastery became all the more important for the presence of the saint's ashes and bones. The islanders gave Donnan the kind of burial which was reserved for chieftains, and placed his remains in a mound which was still known as Cnoc Dhonnain in the early nineteenth century. A chain of crosses was also said to have spanned the island, converging on Donnan's burial place,[10] but it was not until the seventeenth century that the site was investigated by Martin Martin. It exposed to view a large sepulchral urn containing human bones, consisting of a large round stone which had been hollowed out, covered with a thin flagstone. Martin Martin also noticed a narrow stone passage under ground a few paces north of the urn, and wondered why there were no skulls amongst the bones, at which one islander hazarded the guess that the heads had been cut off with a two-handed sword and carried away by the enemy![11] The urn was buried once more and exposed again in the early nineteenth century when a ploughman for the farmer in Kildonnan levelled the mound. It remained exposed for a long while, and it became a tradition to pray to the saint for fair wind by taking the lid off. The farmer, MacDonald of Balranald, did not approve of disturbing the saint in this way and alleged that bad weather always followed.[12] But Donnan eventually stopped answering prayers for wind after some Skyemen who had been becalmed on Eigg took off the 'Leac Dhonnain' to get enough wind to return home and neglected to put it back into place. The urn was eventually buried again and its place is said to be marked by a large oblong pebble, which was also found in the mound and venerated as St Donnan's pillow. In olden days, an area the size of a grave was left unploughed around it as a mark of respect.

It was perhaps Baithne, Columba's disciple and kinsman, who sent abbot and monks to Eigg to re-establish a religious community. He is said to have often visited the island, being occasionally detained on Eigg by storms, and the cult of Columba soon became as important as Donnan's on the island. The well blessed by him was said never to run dry, the number of rivulets trickling down prophesying the fate of the children baptised with its water, the drinking of which always ensured good luck. 'May our share of Colum Cille take us safely across', the island fishermen would still say many centuries later. Under abbots whose names have been preserved in religious annals – Berchan, Congalach, Conan, Enan,[13] Donnan's monastery developed in strength and influence, fostering a spiritual tradition which was to outlive the Columban church itself and flourish in the poetic expressions of faith which so impressed nineteenth-century folklore collectors. Holy men and women were said to have embraced contemplative lives in cells below the Sgurr or facing the sea in Grulin,[14] in Gleann Mhartin on Muck, in a cave on Rum or at Sgor nam Ban Naomh on Canna. Yet by the time the death of Oan, 'princeps' of Eigg, was recorded in the Annals of Ulster for 724, Roman observance had been imposed and the Celtic church of Donnan and Columba had been condemned as heretical.

Eigg was now the site of a wealthy monastery under royal patronage[15] and it was in the hands of a Pictish lord powerful enough to have commissioned the beautiful carved cross slab which was found in the Kildonnan graveyard at the beginning of the twentieth century. The cross was no prayer marker or monastic boundary but a votive offering from a prominent nobleman seeking salvation by commissioning such a work of art, executed by Pictish craftsmen reacting imaginatively to Northumbrian influences introduced at the royal court. On one side the magnificent cross in interlacing with underlying key-patterns glorifies God, whilst on the other the secular patron is depicted in the noble pursuits of hunting and riding: a horseman flanked by a bird and a hunting dog pursues a boar and a deer, the whole scene deeply incised with another cross to further implore Godly favours.[16] As the century wore on, monasteries and saints' shrines became more and more richly endowed by their secular patrons, the nobility of Pictland or Dalriada. Beautiful silver reliquaries were commissioned, mounted with precious stones. Craftsmen fashioned exquisite covers and mounts for psalters and holy books which became renowned far and wide. By the end of the eighth century, these riches were to attract the attention of a piratical people who cared little for religion but much for gold and plunder.

THE NORSE COLONISATION

'From the fury of the Norsemen, deliver us, oh Lord', chanted the monks as Viking bands descended on them, repeatedly devastating Iona, Eigg and any other unprotected island monasteries in the path of their southbound vessels. In their hit-and-run raids, the Vikings sought to overcome all resistance by burning and pillaging, coming back to exact tribute from terrified populations whose surplus wealth they creamed off, leaving them enough time to re-establish themselves before raiding them again, taking hostages to ensure compliance.

The Vikings' devastation of the Hebridean, Highland and Irish coasts was the outcome of a peculiar population explosion which found no other outlet under the Norwegian system of land tenure than precipitating well-led bands of warriors on such piratical, land-raiding and slave-trading expeditions. Capturing Picts and Dalriadic Scots became a very lucrative business once a trading post was established in Dublin for the Norse slave trade, and smaller islands such as Eigg were amongst the first to fall under Viking control, used first as summer bases for mainland raids, then as permanent settlements.

With Norse territory soon extended from Shetland to the Isle of Man, divided into two parts north and south of Ardnamurchan, the Nordreys and the Sudreys, early Viking raiders were soon followed by aristocratic Norse colonists in the ninth century when internal problems in Norway spurred the emigration of discontented chieftains, as shown by archaeological evidence from the rich grave goods found on Eigg and other islands in the Inner Hebrides.[17] The excavation of two Viking graves at Kildonnan by nineteenth-century antiquarians in what appears to have been re-used prehistoric cairns produced an assortment of weapons and implements – fragments of iron sword, belt clasp, iron knife, axe-head and spear-head, sharpening stones, part of a sickle, amber and jet beads, a silvered thistle brooch – indicating the burial of pagan warriors well equipped for the heroic afterlife in Valhalla, the dwellings of the gods, reserved for those who had a glorious death in battle. The richest find of all was made earlier, in the 1830s, when an islander, Allan MacKay, levelled a hillock in Dail na Sithean, the field of the fairy mound, halfway between the island burial ground and the rocks to the east. It yielded a magnificent sword, its long iron blade soon crumbling away but its hilt perfectly preserved, cast in bronze ornamented with plates of silver and gilding fastened by engraved rivets. The sword, which was probably made in Scandinavia, was found with a few thin plates of bronze and part of a buckle – what was left of a sword belt – a sharpening stone and what seems to have been the remains of a large bronze vessel.[18] A sword such as this would have been the pride of its owner, its blade engraved with the rune of Tyr, the god of war, and held so sacred that oaths were taken on it.

The Norse colonisers quickly imposed their language on the local population, drawing on their stock of place-names from their homeland for the naming of the new settlements in an environment which was in so many respects similar to the one they had left behind, for as a sea-faring people they had at their disposal a rich vocabulary of topographical and maritime terms. As a result, two-thirds of the island's place-names are of Norse origin, with coastal features issued with descriptive names such as 'Bogha na Bricenis', the tidal rock of the sloping headland; 'Laig', of the bay of the pounding surf; or 'Grulin', the stony place, an apt description since it is littered with erratic boulders from the Sgurr. The name of the island itself, Eilean Eige, is derived from the Norse word for notch.[19]

The dearth of homestead names on the island (they occur in much greater number in the Outer Isles or Skye) hints that only one or a few aristocratic colonisers would have taken over the island farms as opposed to a number of freemen carving the island between themselves. Names ending in 'dalr', dale, pasture land in Old Norse, such as Cliadal – the cliff pasture; Galmasdal – the pasture of the roaring surf; Cnoc Smeordail – the hill of the butter pasture; indicate that the Norsemen took over the farming land, marrying into a few dominant families and reducing the rest of the population to slave status, providing them with a pliable labour force. The island farms would have provided them with sufficient resources to allow them to live as farmers for part of the year, and traders–raiders for the rest of the time. The two boat stems which were found on the island – in a peat bog where they were probably deposited to season – showed that the Norsemen had brought with them the skills necessary for carrying on the building of their longships, whose incomparable manoeuvrability gave them such a superior advantage over native vessels. Carved from a single piece of timber, one of the stems compares closely to similar pieces found in Scandinavia: all have the same V-shaped cross section and the six stepped edges on each side to which the strakes would be attached with clinker nails.[20] The place close to where the stems were found is locally believed to have been at one time a landing place, for the rockface which juts into the boggy meadow is called 'Sron na Laimhrig' – the point of the landing – another Norse name. It would have at one time overlooked a shallow lagoon at Laig, where the Norsemen could have taken their ships quite a way inland for wintering.

The wealth derived from trading meant that each island had to be assessed for taxes: each homestead paid a penny in tax and contributed to a naval levy. This was paid to the Norse overlords who had succeeded in establishing a remarkably democratic from of government where all freemen had a say through representatives sent to the All-Thing, the yearly gathering in the Isle of Man whose king gradually imposed himself as ruler of the Norse colonies. Thus land came to be measured in units of pennyland (about four acres), ounceland and merkland, measures which were derived from an Irish coinage based on the Anglo-Saxon penny. These measures were to survive long after the Norsemen were gone: today, the crofters' common grazing still bears the name of 'Cuig Peighinnean', Five Pennies – a name which would have originally designated a Norse farm unit.

Living in style because of booty and trade, the Norsemen on Eigg would have built themselves great big rectangular halls on the traditional Norse model which replaced the circular corbelled houses of the Celts and were to become the dominant architectural pattern in the islands. In these long houses, feasting took place at key festivals of the year: saga men told their stories and the scalds their poems. They told how the world was originally created out of ice and fire, with Jøtunheim as the home of giants always ready to sally forth and raid the land of the Gods. To their poetic imagination, the neighbouring island of Rum was like that desolate mountainous land where the giants dwelt, and they named its peaks after their own mythology. They saw in the shape of a lochan near Laig the footprint of a giant who battled with another, strewing gigantic boulders on the land, picking up a rock as his limpet hammer and dropping it at Grulin where it was named after him, Clach Thusthasdail, Husdal's stone. They told that another giant, Hasdal, fashioned the little island guarding the entrance to Eigg.[21] Hasdal is said to be buried with the giant Nuallan at the place where they fought to the death, two stones marking their grave. Nuallan, after whom that place is named – Cnoc Nuallan – has a Gaelic name, the story hinting at the mythologising of the conflict between Norse and Gaels. Like their place-names, the Norsemen's myths were readily absorbed and transformed by the culture they had colonised.

However, as the incoming chieftains married freely within the local aristocracy, particularly in the Sudreys, a reverse process of gaelicisation had started as early as the ninth century, producing a new people with a distinctive identity, the Gall Gaidheal – the foreign Gaels – who finally succeeded in challenging Norse supremacy in the islands. When Somerled, the son of a Norse princess and of a dispossessed king of Argyll, defeated Godred, the tyrannical king of Man, in 1156, a new independent kingdom was born which owed allegiance to the King of Norway and had close dynastic links with Ireland. It looked with contempt at a Scottish crown which had turned its back on its Celtic heritage and was increasingly dominated by Anglo-Norman feudal lords. From then on, the history of Eigg would be closely linked to the fate of that kingdom and to the whole issue of the survival of a Celtic culture in the west of Scotland.

EIGG AND THE LAND OF GARMORAN

From the twelfth century onwards, the isle of Eigg found itself included in the land of Garmoran, the territory situated between Ardnamurchan and Glenelg, the 'Rough bounds' of Moidart and Knoydart. It also included Rum, whereas Muck and Canna were counted amongst the church lands held by the Bishopric of Man and Sodor. Once the portion of Angus, the youngest of Somerled's sons, Garmoran was soon appropriated by Ranald who came to rule the Isles after his father. After Ranald's death, it went to his youngest son Ruairi, who proved to be a zealous partisan of the Norse interests in the isles. But the time of the Norsemen was over, and the kingdom of the Isles found it hard to keep its independence when the Hebrides were ceded to the Scottish crown after Haakon's final defeat in 1266. Ruairi's son obtained confirmation of his possession of Eigg and Garmoran by royal charter, Alexander III imposing baronies and sheriffships in the place of the old Norse land divisions. The War of Independence saw his descendants siding with Robert the Bruce, with Christina, the heiress of the MacRuairis, lending men silver and shelter whilst her half-brother Ruairi fought at Bannockburn. But like the other island chieftains, their reward was to be issued feudal charters for their lands. Robert the Bruce was too sharp not to use this victory as an occasion for imposing vassalage ties on these dangerously capable allies. Ruairi, in whose favour his sister Christina had resigned the greatest part of Garmoran, thus obtained a charter for 'the six davoch lands of Eigg and Rum',[22] whilst as the king's vassal, he was in turn held 'for the service of a ship of 26 oars with its complement of men and victuals for the king's army and on due warning'. Obtaining the patronage of the church of Kildonnan as well as Eigg and other lands was certainly quite lucrative, as Ruairi would have collected the church teinds for the new Scottish bishopric of the Isles – the Norse bishopric of Sodor had hitherto received a third of all the teinds of Eigg – and kept a proportion as his own portion,[23] the church being once again part of the strategy of royal control as in earlier times. But support for the king was to cost Ruairi his life and that of his two sons. Thus Eigg, Garmoran and the rest of the MacRuairi lands passed on to Ruairi's daughter Amie, who brought them as dowry on her marriage to John of Islay, Lord of the Isles, in 1337.

With Garmoran, the Uists and soon Harris and Lewis under his control, John of Islay was as powerful as he could be. Yet his ambitions were greater still and he repudiated Amie for a more rewarding alliance with the King of Scots' daughter. Bringing to his court in Islay all the bards, musicians and learned men of Gaeldom, John of the Isles now ran the lordship as a semi-independent state with its own government issuing its own laws and charters, trading freely with France, England and Ireland, counting on the impressive fleet of galleys and the considerable amount of men which the clan organisation put at his disposal. The great cross of blue schist incised with a tree of life which now stands at Kildonnan after marking the grave of a MacKinnon chief in Iona is a testimony to the artistic achievements of that period.

Towards the end of John's life, it was to be Ranald, the second of his two sons by Amie MacRuairi, who ruled the islands as Steward of the Isles. When his half-brother came of age in 1380, he chose to relinquish the lordship to him, 'contrary to the opinions of the islemen', told the clan chroniclers. The ceremony took place on Eigg instead of Islay as was customary, for the island occupied a central place in the midst of Ranald's territories, Robert II confirming in 1373 the charter he had received from his father for the lands of Garmoran. The nobility of the isles converged on Eigg to witness the elaborate investiture ceremony which was followed by several days of feasting. In front of the Bishop of the Isles accompanied by seven priests, Donald of the Isles became *Buachaille nan Eilean*, the shepherd of his people, and swore to protect and lead them, symbolically placing his foot on the carved footprint of the inauguration stone used by his ancestors to denote that he would follow in their footsteps.[24]

This meeting of the island chiefs on Eigg was not to be the last in the history of the island, for Ranald was to be the founder of one of the most important – and most belligerent – branches of clan Donald, the MacDonalds of Clanranald, in whose possession the island was to remain for the next 440 years.

11

Chapter 2

EIGG AND THE CLANRANALDS

RAIDS AND REBELLIONS

The first description of Eigg, in the Dean of the Isle's account of 1549, is of a 'Gude mayne land, with mony solenne geis, very gude for store, namelie for sheip, with ane Paroch Kirk and ane heavin for hieland galayis'.[1] It was no wonder that the preceding century had seen the Clanranalds fending off rival claims to Eigg and Garmoran, notably from the MacDonalds of Sleat. Forty years or so later, Dean Monro's description was confirmed by a 1593 report on the Hebrides ordered by the Privy Council. Eigg was described as 'ane Ile verie fertile and commodious baith for all kinds of bestiall and corns, specialle aittis for eftir everie boll of aittis, sawing in the same ony yeair will grow 10 or 12 bollis agane'.[2]

Sixteenth-century Eigg would have been divided into a number of farms, the largest being allotted by the chief to his close kin, and the smaller ones being shared between groups of tenants with more distant kinship ties. The gentry of the clan – the Daoine Uislean – paid only a nominal rent, a few heads of cattle for the larger farms, a sheep and some hens, grain, butter and cheese for the smaller ones. The real rent was the number of fighting men who occupied and worked the land, ready to follow the chief's kinsmen to war. The thirty merklands of Eigg could thus raise sixty men 'to the weiris',[3] indicating a population of around 300 on the island.

The clan system was indeed such an effective military organisation, bonded by kinship and unswerving loyalty to the person of the chief, that at the height of its power, the Lordship of the Isles had been able to muster 10,000 men to further its territorial ambitions on the mainland. Unfortunately, the political acumen of its leaders had not been in proportion to these ambitions which posed an all-too-real threat to the Scottish kings. Using every means at their disposal to curb and destroy the Lordship's power and independence, they had finally managed to abolish it in 1493, after a long and bitter struggle which pitted the clans against each other. From that time on, a period of anarchy and turmoil ensued as the chiefs embarked on numerous attempts to restore the Lordship as the islands' rightful government, fighting all the while to protect their territories from rival clans or from feudal overlords imposed on them by the Crown.

With Clan Donald continuing to regard the leadership of the isles as its hereditary right, Clan Ranald became involved in each attempt at restoring the Lordship. The 4th chief had actually conducted a successful raid in Ross-shire which brought him a booty of 600 cows, 1,000 sheep and 600 pounds of food before he was caught, tried and executed for treason against the king, a fate which also befell his son. Rebellion against the Crown was judged by the clan to be its leader's duty so that when Dugall, the 6th chief, chose instead to back the two hated agents of the Crown, Argyll and Huntly, he met with a violent end at the hand of his own clansmen in 1520, his sons were barred from the succession and the leadership passed to the Moidart branch of the clan. However, the new chief, John of Moidart, did bestow on Dugall's dispossessed sons nine of the thirty merklands of Eigg as well as the land of Morar he had acquired with the chiefship, so that from then on their descendants, who were to play a large part in the history of Eigg, were to be known as the MacDonalds of Morar. As to the remaining twenty-one merklands of Kildonnan and other lands on Eigg, John of Moidart managed to obtain confirmation of his ownership by royal charter in 1534,[4] during one of the rare periods when 'that notorious robber' and 'auld enemy of the realm of Scotland' was not playing 'foul and monstrous pranks' on the king's forces. Indeed, by 1543, he was involved in the next major attempt to reinstate the Lordship of the Isles when Donald Dubh, the direct heir to the title, made his second bid for freedom after forty years in prison. Occupying a strategic place at the centre of Clanranald territories, the isle of Eigg was thus chosen for the gathering of seventeen chiefs into a Council of the Isles which nominated Donald Dubh as 5th Lord of the Isles and struck a promising alliance with King Henry VIII, agreeing to acknowledge him as overlord in exchange for gold and support. But Donald Dubh's death from fever in Ireland, where the force assembled counted no fewer than 8,000 men and 180 ships, put an end to these ambitions. Accused of treason for his role in organising the rebellion, John of Moidart was made an outlaw, but neither the attacks on his lands by Gordons and Campbells on behalf of the Crown nor the revocation of his charters by Mary of Guise had any effect on him. His skill in manoeuvring through the quagmire of sixteenth-century politics earned him great praise in lengthy elegies by the MacMhuirich, his hereditary poets, but of his successor Allan they had little good to say, for it was under his leadership that Eigg was to suffer one of the worst episodes of its history.

THE MASSACRE OF UAMH FHRAING

Without the institutions of the lordship to ensure that justice was carried out in accordance with Gaelic law, which was administered by brieves in each district with the possibility of recourse to the Council of the Isles, revenge and counter-revenge spiralled out of control as every clansman adopted his chief's quarrels as his own, bound by the absolute loyalty which was demanded of him. Six full-scale feuds tore the islands apart during the sixteenth century, the feud between the Clanranalds and the MacLeods of Harris being one of the longest and bloodiest of them all.

A quarrel at a chiefs' gathering in Mull, when Clanranald implied insultingly that the MacLeod genealogy was tainted by its Norse origins, was allegedly the origin of the feud. Enmity deepened when the two clans found themselves on opposite sides at the battle of the Bloody Bay. Fuelled by territorial disputes over the north part of Skye, the feud raged on, kindled anew when Allan of

Clanranald repudiated his wife for another, an unforgivable insult to the honour of her father, MacLeod of Dunvegan.

According to MacLeod historians,[5] the escalation in violence occurred when the entire crew of a Clanranald galley, driven ashore in Harris by a storm, were beheaded by their MacLeod host – who presented the heads on a rope to the governor of the island. In reprisal, a MacLeod birlinn was captured and its thirty-six men – including an illegitimate son of the chief of Dunvegan – were thrown into a Uist dungeon and starved to death. Consequently, when bad weather forced a MacLeod galley to seek shelter in the lee of Eigg, the crew decided against landing on the island but took refuge on Eilean Chasteil, off the coast of Galmisdale. Led by a MacAskill and a foster-son of Alastair Crotach, the chief of Dunvegan, the thirty men helped themselves to a few cattle which they proceeded to roast, molesting the girls who were looking after them. But as they were enjoying their dinner, the inhabitants of Eigg descended on them and massacred the entire crew, except their leaders. For them they reserved a slow and painful death: their legs and arms broken, the two men were set adrift on the sea in a boat without rudder or oars.

But what the MacDonalds did not count on was that, carried by the currents, the boat drifted all the way back to Dunvegan. When he heard what had happened on Eigg, Alastair Crotach vowed not to change his clothes until he had taken his revenge on every soul on the island. With his son Uilleam, who was no less outraged by the treatment his foster-brother had received, he set sail immediately for Eigg at the head of a force of several galleys full of armed men. As soon as the galleys were sighted, the inhabitants of Eigg knew what was in store for them and took to their traditional hiding place, Uamh Fhraing, the cave on the south side of the island which once gave shelter to St Donnan, to sit the raid out. The cave was an ideal refuge, deceptively spacious inside, but with an entrance concealed by a waterfall and small enough to be easily overlooked.

Landing on Eigg, the MacLeod revenge party conducted a thorough search for three whole days. They did not find a soul save one old woman at the north end of the island who had not bothered to hide because she was too lame to walk. They tried to make her tell where the rest of the islanders had gone, but the obstinate old woman would always answer in the same way: 'If it comes through my knee, it can't be helped but it shall not come through my mouth'. They burned her house and destroyed her crops, but still she would not tell. She taunted them even more: why, she had a home under every rock and she had all the cockles of Laig bay to eat if she wanted. Enraged, the MacLeods ploughed the sands in the bay – to this day, there are no shellfish to be found there, maintains tradition – but undaunted, the old woman laughed at them: she could live, and live well at that, on the dulse of the rock pools and the watercress of the well in Hulin![6] The raiders gave up in the end, persuaded that the islanders had taken refuge on another island, and left under her curses: 'Humpback is the heir of MacLeod today and as long as dry straw will burn, many a hump and a crook there will be in the clan hereafter!' shouted the old woman as they made their way to their galleys.

Meanwhile, the islanders, who had spent three days in the cave, thought it safe enough to send a scout outside. But it was a cold spring day and there had been a fresh snowfall in the night. No sooner had the MacLeods rounded the south side of the island on their way back to Dunvegan than they spotted the scout against the snow. They turned straight back and had no difficulty in finding the cave even though the poor scout had taken the precaution of retracing his steps backwards. The MacLeods decided to smother the islanders in their refuge and set about diverting the waterfall in front of it, piling up at the entrance all the heather and thatching they could find. Just as they were about to set fire to it, Alastair Crotach hesitated: willing to show some mercy, he wanted to let the women and children go unharmed, but his son Uilleam was unmoved: he would only spare one life, the life of the Eiggach who had been merciful to his half-brother when he had starved in Clanranald's dungeon. The man asked if he could bring his son out with him but Uilleam would not even allow this, so he preferred to perish with the rest. Once again Alastair Crotach hesitated, deciding to ask for God's judgement: they would wait another six hours and if at the end of this delay, the wind blew away from the cave, the islanders would be spared. But the wind rose and blew towards the land, sealing the islanders' fate. The chief sailed away, leaving his son to set the blaze alight, a deed for which he was known as 'Uilleam of the Cave' for ever after. Thus perished the entire population of the island, save the old woman in Hulin.

> Sad is the climbing
> E ho a ho sad is the climbing
> Hi hoirean o sad is the climbing
> E ho a ho sad is the climbing
> Sad is the climbing

sang a Uist poet who so grieved at the thought of the island bereft of all life that he was moved to compose this song which was to be preserved in the oral tradition of Benbecula.

> Distant is the view that I can see
> I can see Rum and Eigg and Islay
> Where MacLeod has wrought destruction
> He has slaked his thirst in bloodshed
> I see Barra low land lying.
> I see Uist of the bountiful people
> Where they keep the feast of St Michael
> Hi Hoireann o
> Who will be mirthful
> Who will carry the slender gun
> Sad is the climbing,
> E ho a ho, sad is the climbing.[7]

Yet the Eigg massacre did not signal the end of the feud between the MacLeods and the MacDonalds. As new people from other parts of Clanranald lands came to settle on Eigg – MacKinnons and MacQuarries as well as MacDonalds – revenge was taken at the first opportunity: some Uist MacDonalds descended on Skye to set fire to a church full of MacLeods at Trumpan and all those who tried to escape were killed, save one old woman. But the MacDonalds' luck turned when the MacLeods unfurled their famous fairy flag, and they were all killed, their bodies piled against a stone dyke which was overturned on them, hence the name of that battle, Blar Milleadh Gàraidh – the battle of the spoiling of the dyke – which finally put an end to the conflict. The feud had been so long and bloody that an aura of legend inevitably grew around it. It was said that long after peace was restored, the ghosts of all who fought each other during that time carried on the fight once a year. 'One man was tending his sheep one night to protect his lambs from foxes, near Loch Eynort Church when to his horror, come midnight, he saw all the graves in the churchyard open and a host of warrior spirits emerge from them. They all had wings with which they soared to the sky. Two of them seized hold of him and rising to the air, they carried him with tremendous speed over moon-lit land and sea until they reached a great expanse of machair in Lewis. There he saw the ghost warriors form a great ring and he realized that this was a meeting of the two ghost armies of the MacDonalds and the MacLeods who had come to fight their feud once again. And he was the man who was to fight on behalf of the MacLeods for he was the only mortal amongst them and the MacDonalds ghosts had also brought a man. They were both made to fight each other in the middle of the ghostly ring until the first light of dawn. Then the two mortals were taken back to where they were found the night before and each ghost went to his respective grave.'[8]

The exact date of the massacre remains a subject of controversy. According to the 1593 report on the Hebrides which dated the massacre to March 1577, 395 people were alleged to have been killed.[9] Its author, a Campbell and therefore no friend of Clan Donald or Clan Leod, cited it as an example of Highland barbarity, yet he failed to mention the equally cruel events – more accurately documented – which befell the island some years later. However, by 1577 Alastair Crotach, who is held responsible for the massacre in the Campbell report as well as in oral tradition, had been dead for thirty years, his son Uilleam for twenty-five. Meanwhile the battle of Blar Milleadh Gàraidh following the avenging raid on the MacLeods was supposed to have been fought around 1530!

In the light of these contradictions, what is certain is that the skeletons of the suffocated islanders were left undisturbed in the cave which had become their mass grave. A good two hundred years later, the minister of the Small Isles parish commented on their remarkable state of preservation and reported about forty skulls left. Many more skulls had disappeared by the time Hugh Miller saw them in 1846: 'We came upon heaps of human bones grouped together,' described Hugh Miller. 'They are of a brown earthy hue, here and there tinged with green, the skulls with the exception of a few broken fragments have disappeared . . . Enough remains to show that the hapless islanders died under the walls in families, each little group separated by a few feet from the other . . . Beneath every heap are the remains of a straw bed largely mixed with the smaller bones and occasionally fragments of englazed pottery and various implements of rude housewifery.'[10] The small number of skulls left was the result of a macabre vogue for collecting them which had been set by Sir Walter Scott after his visit to Eigg in 1814, which finally caused the parish priest to have the bones taken for burial in hallowed ground at Kildonnan.

A SECOND MASSACRE ON EIGG

No sooner had the feud with the MacLeods finished than the clan found itself embroiled in another bloody conflict which came about through the marriage of Donald, the 9th chief of Clan Ranald, to a MacDonald of Islay whose family was at war with MacLean of Duart over the island of Iona. The 'great MacLane' had obtained a Crown charter for the island and, in the zeal of his recent conversion to Protestantism, had allowed wanton destruction to take place: the abbey library was burnt and the 360 crosses marking kings' and chieftains' graves – beautiful carvings representing one of the great artistic achievements of the Lordship of the Isles – were broken and dispersed, used as ballast for highland galleys. This fuelled the enmity existing between Clan Lean and Clan Donald since the failure of Donald Dubh's rebellion in Ireland, so that the chief of Clanranald entered the feud only too readily and invaded the MacLean lands of Coll, Tiree and Mull, carrying off a great spoil.

MacLean of Duart plotted a spectacular revenge. In exchange for providing food for the *Juan de Sicilia*, a galleon stranded in Tobermory after the defeat of the Armada, he commandeered the services of a hundred Spanish soldiers. In November 1588, 'accompanyed by a grite nawmer of thevis broken men and sorners of the Clannis, besydis the nawmer of ane hundred of Spanyeartis' he then came 'to his Majesteis proper ilis of Canna, Rum, Eg, the island of Elenole, and after they had scorned, wracked and spoilled the saidis hail illis, they tressonablie raised fyre and in maist barborous, shameful and creull maner, brynt the same illis, with the haill men, weimen and children being therintill, not spairing the pupillis and infantis . . . About aucht or nyne scoir of sawles, qha escapit the fyre was noch sparit by his bluidie sword.'[11] As inconceivable as it seems, Eigg lost its entire population for the second time in the century. Rum was devastated in the same way, as its people still followed the Clanranald chiefs even though it belonged to the MacLeans of Coll, and the church lands of Canna and Muck were not spared either. The Crown authorities accused Lachlan MacLean of atrocities 'the like barbarous and shameful crueltie has sendle been herd of amangis Christeanis in ony kingdome of age' but it seems that, were it not for the presence of foreign soldiers, the massacre would have probably gone unpunished. The Crown was in fact only too happy to let the clans decimate each other, but Spain was at war with Elizabeth I and King James VI was well aware of his position as her only heir. Lachlan MacLean was prosecuted for treason by the king's advocate but somehow was allowed to escape from Edinburgh Castle, forfeiting his bail. The following years saw him help Elizabeth I in her conquest of Ulster and succeed in intercepting the force led by Clan Donald to rescue their kinsmen in Ireland who were resisting the forcible 'planting' of Ulster by English colonisers.

It was, in fact, to emulate Elizabeth I in her Ulster policy that James VI, who viewed the Scottish Gaels as 'a wild and unruly race' who ought to be extirpated from the land, had commissioned the 1593 report on the Hebrides mentioned earlier – to establish their resources prior to their intended 'plantation'. In 1598, an Act of Parliament was passed to bring 'civilitie' and 'policie' to the restless natives of the isles, the first target for colonisation being feud-torn Lewis where the least resistance was expected. For 10,000 merks, twelve nobles from Fife bought in 1601 the right to 'plant' the island and exploit its resources for the good of the Crown, with a special recommendation to 'rute out its barbarious inhabitants, void of religion and humanities'. The effect was immediate: a truce was called between the feuding parties and the help of the chiefs of Clanranald, Sleat and Barra was successfully enlisted to fight the colonisers. Against the reward of Eigg, Rum, Canna, Uist, Barra, Raasay, Scalpay and St Kilda, Huntly was finally instructed to 'specially undertake and bind himself to extirpate and rute out the Captain of Clanranald and his whole clan, and their followers within the isles of Moydert and Knoydert and also Macneill of Barra and his clan and the whole of clan Donald of the north'![12] But by 1605, the colonisers had been driven out and Clanranald had yet to be extirpated from his land.

It was at that time that many MacLeods took refuge in the territory of their former enemy, and, according to tradition, this was how there came to be a line of MacLeods on Eigg. The story was that a MacLeod made his way to the island, landing on the deserted eastern side. There he lived, surviving on shellfish, sheltering in a sort of cave amongst the jumble of rocks in Struidh not far from the summer shielings, which came to be known as 'Uamh a' Chloinn Diridh' – the cave of the ascending slope – although few would know it today. In the summertime, a girl from the farm on the other side of Beinn Bhuidhe came to the shieling with her cattle and she found him, grew fond of him, and kept coming back to see him in secret, long after shieling time. When her father, 'Tuathanach na coig Peighinnean' (the tacksman of Five Pennies farm), found out that the man she was seeing was a MacLeod, he was ready to kill him there and then, but his daughter got the better of him, the two were soon married and from them are descended all the Eigg MacLeods.[13]

THE LAST BID FOR THE LORDSHIP

With the failure of his 'plantation' of the islands, King James VI, now James I of England, took measures to deal with the irrepressible chiefs. Imposed by stealth in 1609, the Statutes of Iona were calculated to ensure their disarming in the short term and their submission in the long term. All aspects of clan life which appeared most at odds with the rest of the country were covered in an attempt to bring the clans in line with mainstream culture. Since feuding was largely blamed on the idleness and drunkenness of the chiefs, imports of wine and brandy from France or Spain were declared illegal and subjected to heavy fines, and consumption was restricted to three tuns a year. Since the nobility of the clans was seen as a body of idle men without lawful occupation whose interest in warfare prevented the improvement of the country, measures were taken to restrict the chiefs' considerable entourage to a fixed number. 'Sorning' – the provision of free hospitality and food which had a central place in the complex system of obligations and renders of Gaelic clan law – was also banned. Exchange of goods and foods without money in a society ruled by kinship was an alien concept for legislators used to relationships of economic dependency within the Scottish realm. Inns were to be built throughout clan lands, the chiefs were to reside in one place, build 'civil and comelie houses', and take farms into their hands so that they 'might thereby be exercised and eschew idleness'. Bards and musicians, who had traditionally lived on free hospitality, were assimilated to the status of mere vagabonds and beggars and, like them, put into stocks and expelled from the land, when previously it had always been their right to wander freely within clan territories and to claim lodgings and a portion of food at the table unless their host could defeat them in a contest of wit or music. To prevent the educated class of Gaeldom, trained in history, genealogy and the art of poetry, from earning their living amounted to a direct attack on a culture which had to be suppressed. To that effect, the Privy Council actually planned the establishment of schools to promote the replacement of Gaelic with the 'language of true religion' and imposed that every gentleman of the clan worth sixty cows sent his eldest son or eldest daughter away to be educated in English.

As security for the proper execution of the statutes, the chiefs found themselves obliged to send a few kinsmen to Edinburgh each year as hostage for their good behaviour, and to enter into bonds which obliged them to keep to the law under the threat of severe financial penalties. As a reward for their 'cooperation', the chiefs were given new charters to their lands. Amongst other title deeds, the captain of Clanranald recovered his title to the twenty-one merklands of Eigg and obtained a charter for the remaining nine titles which were given to his Morar kinsmen. The Crown had now the chiefs firmly established as her feudal vassals, and, to retain their title deeds, the chiefs were forced to toe the line since the Statutes of Iona obliged them to become the guarantors of each other's good behaviour. Clanranald was urged more than once to behave with restraint by other chiefs who, like him, had to pay a heavy caution and appear in front of the Privy Council every summer. Peace was established in the isles as the chieftains' coffers emptied.

Yet there were still a few chiefs who were not bound by such conditions: those in Clan Donald who had lost everything, who had no land left from the growing encroachment by the Campbells and were reduced to a life of piracy. The dispossessed MacDonalds of Colonsay under the leadership of Coll Ciotach – Coll the left-handed – had now taken over the island of Muck as their base, and it was only natural for them to support another dispossessed chief, James MacDonald of Dunnyveg, the last direct descendant of the rulers of the Isles. Escaping from his Edinburgh prison in 1625 with a price of £5,000 on his head, he joined forces with Coll Ciotach. Together, they planned an attack on Islay to free it from the Campbells and thereby restore the Lordship. For a second time, Eigg was chosen as the starting point of the rebellion.

MacDonald of Dunnyveg was received on Eigg with the honour due to his position: Coll Ciotach and his men 'went round him onis, and in the nixt going about salutit him with their wolley of schoittis, and continowit sua shuitting and enviring of him for the spaice of half ane hour and therefter, com to him enerie man, particularlie chapping handis'. ('Enviring', sun-wise circling, was the traditional way to show honour, whilst 'chapping' was the Gaelic way of 'swearing obedience and to live and die in the service of the chief'.) Numbers swelled with the arrival of another 150 men from the surrounding islands, and preparations were made for the raid on the Campbells. 'Upone the morn thai conuenit all the hail bestial, horse and ky, to one place, quhilk they thocht to have slayne all. Bot opone better aduysement thei slew onlie ane number of ky for meat quhilk thei carryit immediatelie to thair boittis and thairefter tuik the sea to the number of thre hunder men of all'. Coll bringing two galleys to the number of boats James had got in Ardnamurchan and stolen from other parts.[14]

The expedition sailed on to Kintyre, gathering numbers and support, and finally reached Islay where the Campbells were waiting for them. They had destroyed the council stone in Loch Finlaggan, broken the stone of inauguration and thrown it in the loch, as a sign that the last challenge for the Lordship was but a futile gesture. For they were also vastly superior in numbers as, in compliance with the Statutes of Iona, the chiefs had been forced to supply the Campbells with men against the rebels: much against his will, Clanranald himself had had to provide fifty men. The outcome was predictable: the rebels were slaughtered, Coll Ciotach was forced to surrender and the last pretender to the Lordship escaped to finish his life in exile in Ireland and Spain.

BLACK CATTLE, WHISKY AND DEBTS

By the seventeenth century, as peace and order were finally imposed on the islands and life was no longer constantly disrupted by demands of armed service, people were able to enjoy a modest prosperity based on cattle exports. One consequence of the Union of the Crowns had been to open the Highlands to the southern markets, and the region's black cattle, slow to mature but very hardy, were proving a valuable asset. Highland society now experienced a gradual change from a subsistence economy to a more commercial one.

As trouble subsided, the chief's kinsmen and lieutenants became in effect his estate managers. Cadet sons were often given holding of a 'feu', a form of land tenure giving permanent tenure in return for the payment of a yearly duty. Other kinsmen were given the tack, or the lease, of a farm on terms which involved payment of 'grassum', or right of entry, and rental in cash rather than kind, as well as military service. These tacksmen farmed part of that land with their servants and rented the remainder to subtenants, who paid a rent to the holder of the tack, which generally exceeded what he paid to the chief. Labour was provided by farm servants and landless cottars who were allowed enough grazing for a cow as part of their wages. Many of the smaller farms were also held by joint-tenants who shared the payment of rent directly to the chief through his baillie, who was usually the most important tacksman of the area. However, farmland was still divided into rough grazing, outfields and infields. Infields – the arable ground surrounding houses – were intensively cultivated with oats and bere, whilst outfields provided close-at-hand grazing. More oat-crops were raised on the outfield which was used in rotation: a temporary dyke was built over a chosen area and used as a fold for the cattle which manured the land for a future crop, whilst other areas were laid fallow after cropping. Both outfields and infields were divided into strips of land which were reallocated each year between all the tenants in order to ensure that each received an equal share of good land and bad land. This 'runrig' system, derived from a Norse form of communal farming associated with shared rights to the seaweed on the shore or the birds in the cliffs, was not only very egalitarian in essence but could cope with a dearth of arable patches whilst being geared to the production of cattle. Cattle husbandry, to which the clanspeople devoted most of their time with great skill and knowledge, had always been the mainstay of Hebridean agriculture, and in an unpromising climate it had actually achieved a relatively successful balance between the needs of people and the availability of resources. The result of that success was that more and more dealers from the south came to buy the cattle taken to the autumn trysts, the most famous of which were those of Crieff and Falkirk where 20,000 beasts could be sold for fattening in Lothian or East Anglian pastures before reaching London.

On Eigg, cattle were gathered in early summer, the tacksmen buying stirks from lesser tenants, and were then taken to the mainland. It was difficult for island tacksmen to hire their own drovers to take their cattle to the trysts, like mainland farmers did, and they found it more convenient to sell their beasts to private dealers who went round the Hebrides – making a handsome profit when the beasts were sold later – a fact which was to occasion much complaint in the eighteenth century.

The cattle economy also produced a surplus of butter, cheese and cured hides, which, in the better years, were sent by the boat-load along the coast to Glasgow, procuring extra meal and whatever luxuries were to be had in the islands. In bad years, as no winter fodder was grown at all, the weakened cattle could die in great numbers, especially if a wet spring followed a hard winter, although there were always the hardier goats to see the year through. This meant that every year at the onset of winter, the farmers had to assess the number of cows that could be maintained alive through the cold season, and slaughter the rest for salting down.

The Statutes of Iona had classified anyone owning sixty cows as belonging to the gentry of the clans. This was exactly the amount of 'tocher' or dowry brought by an islander, Katherine nigh'n Allein, on her marriage to a Kinlochmoidart gentleman, receiving from him in exchange 1,000 merks in liferent. She was the daughter of the tacksman of Knockeilteach on Eigg, a MacDonald of Morar and kinsman of Clanranald.[15] As in earlier times, cattle was tangible wealth, and tacksmen prided themselves on their great herds of cattle. The last happiness enjoyed by an old tacksman, who had been retired to Eigg after many years on Skye as baillie for the MacDonalds of Sleat, was to count his herd. Whenever Mac Roy 'ic Dhomnuil Ghuirm could rise from his bed, he would make his son take him out and sit at the door of his house. There he would have all his cows made to pass in front of him so that he might count them. And when he had counted them once he made them pass again in front of him, and again, so that he might count them twice more. His last preoccupation as a man of wealth was now to have a funeral worthy of him. Feeling his end near, he asked his son to make sure of a proper funeral and send for the men of Moidart. 'It is now the winter season,' said his son, 'and should you depart when the weather is so coarse, I need not send beyond Skye.' The old man angrily replied: 'You MacLeod fool! You must have the Moidart men at my funeral or else who will be there to render my burial memorable by knocking down with their sticks and wounding with their dirks? If the Moidart men are not there, I shall pass away without anything to mark the occasion, any more than if I was a poor destitute Baloch! When I was in charge of the funeral of the tutor of MacDonald, no less than three men were killed at the burial ground and many others were severely wounded. This was caused by the abundance of drink that I distributed among them and whenever I think of it, I am proud to have had the management of that funeral. So my son, let it be said that still more took place at my funeral by your good management and that is the only request I have to make of you!' But his son had other ideas and there were neither wounds nor death, at his father's funeral.[16]

A funeral was indeed a big affair: it generally lasted a good three days, people coming a day before and staying a day after the funeral. The whole time was spent drinking and eating plentifully. In any case, it was an honour to have a funeral attended by the men of Moidart, who were praised throughout Clan Donald lands for their warlike behaviour. As for the casualties which were likely to happen, they only denoted the wealth and generosity of the host since it meant that spirits and wine had been served in abundance. The Statutes of Iona could fine the islanders for procuring contraband wine but they could not change Gaelic cultural habits overnight. The clans had inherited a feasting tradition from their Celtic and Norse ancestors which was not likely to disappear so easily.

Whisky was in fact flowing so freely by then that Hebridean people were said to have consumed on average a quart of it a day! The popularity of the home-made aqua vitae had soared rapidly after the Statutes of Iona restricted imports of foreign brandy but allowed the distilling of local spirit. Moreover, when the chiefs no longer accepted oats or barley as part-payment of rent, whatever surplus grain remained was promptly turned into alcohol. Whisky was not only drunk at all convivial occasions, it was also the first drink that any well-bred gentleman would gulp in the morning. In the damp climate of the islands, it was thought of as preventive medicine, the islanders having in fact a prayer for the preservation from any ailment it could not cure. In the space of a few decades, *uisge beatha*, the Highland *eau-de-vie*, had become the traditional drink of the whole population without distinction of class.

If black cattle and a generous supply of whisky meant wealth, there was actually little money circulating in the islands. Most transactions were conducted by way of bills of exchange supplied by drovers and merchants. A fairly typical transaction involved a merchant's agent, J. Munro, collecting money for ale and beer on behalf of an Edinburgh company, who was given a bond for £66 16s Scots by a servitor of MacLeod of Dunvegan, who was in turn given surety of the bill by Clanranald, on behalf of a Dugald Mac Ean 'ic Alister, of Grulinacrach on Eigg![17]

Money was in more than short supply for the chiefs in particular, for the amounts demanded by the Privy Council as a caution for peace in the islands had put a considerable strain on them, notwithstanding the expense of travelling to Edinburgh each year to appear as was required. It seems that Donald, the 11th chief, who was summoned before the Council on 10 July every year, had often forfeited his caution of 5,000 merks, because the accumulation of his fines put his son, the 12th chief of Clanranald, in dire financial straits. This was at least his excuse for getting involved in piracy or claiming salvage on ships which went aground on his coasts, helping himself to five butts of wine, eight casks of herring and 300 double ells of plaiding in a ship captured on Barra Head. But this was obviously not enough to make him solvent, for he found himself obliged to borrow money from Donald Gorm of Sleat, giving him in exchange the superiority of Benbecula and South Uist in wadset, a form of mortgage common at the time under which the creditor had the occupation and the produce of the land until the loan was repaid.

Failing to repay his loan, the 12th chief was eventually taken to court, and Donald Gorm obtained in 1622 the superiority of all his debtor's lands including Eigg, as compensation for sums in arrears. Sometime later, Donald Gorm had indebted himself to the Earl of Argyll, and, to clear his own debts, he passed on the superiority of Clanranald's lands to the latter, who had already acquired the rights to Canna from the Bishop of the Isles when the chief neglected to pay his teinds for the island. This was soon confirmed by Royal Charter, and Clanranald, who had not so long before boasted of his proud independence, ended up paying rent for Eigg and his other lands to his hereditary foe. This uncomfortable situation was made even worse by the constant scrutiny of the Synod of Argyll, the Protestant assembly in the Campbell territories, which was forever denouncing Clanranald and his tenants for their popish idolatry and demanding their punishment.

EIGG, A 'POPISH' ISLAND

The spread of the Reformation in the islands had been hindered by the lack of Gaelic-speaking ministers. Eigg was finally attached to the parish of Sleat in the presbytery of Skye in 1624, but the minister, Neil MacKinnon, had no converts on the island. This did not prevent him from coming regularly to the island, where he had some relatives, to collect the church teinds which were due to him by law. It was at that time, however, that a new Catholic mission was sent from the Irish Franciscan college in Paris when it became known that rebellious chiefs in the west of Scotland, like Clanranald for instance, still retained their Catholic faith. When Fr Cornelius Ward arrived on Eigg in August 1625, accompanied by gentlemen of the chief of Clanranald's household, he was the first priest to have set foot on the island for eighty years. Out of the entire island population, only one old woman could remember having heard mass in her childhood. The island church, rebuilt at Kildonnan by Allan, the 9th chief, in fulfillment of the vow his father had made to build seven churches throughout his lands, had never been roofed.[18]

The islanders were at first cautious in their welcome: a message was sent to Ward that they would wait until he said mass before they would pronounce themselves true Catholics. Ward, who came from a bardic family from Donegal and could speak to the islanders in their own language, complied with their wishes and went on to explain the meaning of the rituals of mass and the power of holy water. The islanders, still not entirely convinced, made him swear on the

Bible that what he said was true before they would believe him, but the Franciscan re-converted 198 islanders in the end, including the island's gentry, and baptised sixteen people during the eight days of his stay on the island. The only family who refused to be won over was the one related to Neil MacKinnon, the minister from Skye.

When news of what was happening on Eigg reached him, the minister immediately set off for the island with a party of soldiers to capture the priest. But the recently converted islanders threatened him with his life if he and his men did not withdraw on the spot. Infuriated, the minister assured them of a swift retaliation on the part of the authorities. Allan of Morar, Clanranald's baillie on the island, fearing the threat might only be too real, managed to placate him by giving his word that he would still be paid his teinds, on condition that the priest and the island were left alone. This arrangement was finalised when Allan received confirmation of his lands in Grulin in August 1630 and undertook at the same time to collect the Eigg teinds and 'furnish the elements of bread and wine for the celebration of communion in the churches of the said lands'.[19] Before Fr Ward's departure, the islanders asked him to consecrate their church as a place of worship, but as he was not empowered to do so – to their regret – they used it as their burial ground: adults were buried inside, infants in a place reserved for them along the walls. No Protestant was allowed at their burials.[20]

Following Fr Ward's success, new missions were soon sent to the Highlands. Catholic priests travelled freely throughout Clanranald territory, moving from one locality to the next to avoid capture, and would sail to Eigg and celebrate mass in a large and spacious cave on the south side of the island, close to the Massacre Cave, Uamh na Chrabhaidh, the Cave of Worship (renamed Cathedral Cave by Victorian visitors), where a convenient ledge of rock served as an altar. This did not mean that the islanders had given up their traditional religious observance: Mary, Donnan and Martin continued to be venerated, and the mounds which were dedicated to them were circled sunwise as a sign of respect. It seems in fact that priests took great pains to integrate the islanders' old beliefs: Martin Martin was to report in his description of Eigg that one Father Hugh had consecrated a well which the islanders had held since in great esteem, believing it to be a great cure-all. 'He obliged all the inhabitants to come to this well and then employed them to bring together a great heap of stones at the head of the spring, by way of penance. This being done, he said mass at the well, and then consecrated it: he gave each of the inhabitants a piece of wax candle which they lighted, and all of them made the Dessil, of going round the well sunways, the priest leading them: and from that time it was accounted unlawful to boil any meat with the water of this well.'[21] It looks very much as if the priest found the islanders guilty of a cult to a Gaelic saint unrecognised by Rome, like St Donnan for example, and that he sought to replace him with one who was fully canonised, using the islanders' sunwise ritual and making the ceremony an annual occurrence on 15 April, as this date was indeed very close to the traditional feast-day of St Donnan on 17 April. Perhaps the priest was also aiming to supplant another well, in the township of Five Pennies, which was reputed 'efficacious against several distempers': Martin was told that 'it never failed to cure any person of their first disease, only by drinking a quantity of it for the space of two or three days, and that if a stranger lie at this well in the night time, it will procure a deformity in some part of his body, but has no such effect on a native and that they say hath been frequently experienced.'[22]

Meanwhile, worried about the oppression suffered by Catholics in Ireland, Clanranald was quick to grasp the possibility of support that the arrival of the Franciscan mission could imply and sent a message to Pope Urban VIII suggesting that with four ships, weapons for their 7,000 men and the support of the Catholic states, Clan Donald could easily restore the Catholic faith in the whole of Scotland, 'all the Gaelic-speaking Scots and the greater part of the Irish chieftains [being] ready to begin war each in their district for the glory of God'.[23] This plea for a Gaelic crusade – amply justifying the Crown's fears about the clans – failed to move the Pope. John, the 12th chief, resigned himself to becoming a nominal Protestant, as Episcopalians generally were, and arranged to pay no more than a third of the teinds of Eigg and other lands within his territory.

MORE TROUBLES IN THE ISLES

Unsurprisingly, when civil war broke out in 1642, Montrose did not find it hard to win support for the Catholic King from Clanranald and other MacDonald chiefs. It was in fact the ideal opportunity for Clanranald to try and break free from the Earl of Argyll's shackles and pay off old scores. As Clanranald rose, the men of Uist, Eigg, Arisaig and Moidart were summoned for war and raided Sunart of all sheep and cattle to feed the campaign. Swelled by an Irish contingent from Antrim, the Highland army defeated the Protestant forces, successfully attacked the Campbells in their own territory, and set about reconquering Kintyre, Islay and Ulster. Unfortunately for them all, the early demise of Montrose's army was to lead to the islanders' defeat. Undeterred, the 12th chief carried on with his continued defiance of Argyll and the Covenanters until peace was restored, to the extent that the Synod of Argyll, whose demands for payment of church teinds he ignored, even considered asking Cromwell to deal with him! But the cost of war had added to his financial burden, and by the last decade of the century, his son, Black Donald of the Cuckoo, found himself in dire trouble for failing to pay the 10,000 merks owed to Rory MacLeod of Talisker who now held Eigg and other Clanranald lands in wadset. Black Donald of the Cuckoo had quite a reputation in his time: his arbitrary use of the Cuckoo (the gun which never left his side), and the more than summary justice he dispensed with it, led to a belief that he practised the black arts, hence his soubriquet. He was rumoured to have sold his soul to the devil and to be followed wherever he went by a giant toad, his supernatural familiar. The story was often told on Eigg how the devil himself came to claim Black Donald's soul as he was dying on the isle of Canna and how he was foiled by the prodigious strength of young Ranald MacDonald of Cross, who alone was courageous enough to stay by his chief and prevent him from leaving his deathbed to answer the devil's summons.

In sharp contrast to his father, Allan, the 14th chief, was said to be one of the most accomplished Hebridean gentlemen of his generation. After travelling extensively in Europe, he had set up home in Ormiclate, South Uist, where his castle, designed by a French architect who had brought his own masons from France, took seven years to complete. Surrounding himself with bards and poets, Allan lived there for another seven years, keeping state and dispensing hospitality as in those heroic days praised by the clan poets. But Ormiclate Castle was also a centre of Jacobite influence, as Allan followed his predecessors in their opposition to what they saw as a political and religious bondage against which the Catholic Stuarts now appeared to be their only hope. When James II was overthrown in 1688, Allan and the other chiefs did not fail to rise in his support against the Protestant William of Orange. Unfortunately, their initial victory at Killiecrankie in 1689 was followed by a disastrous rout at the hands of the Cameronian forces.

Repression swiftly followed, forcing the chief of Clanranald into exile in France and ultimately culminating in the massacre of the Glencoe MacDonalds in 1692. However, immediately after Killiecrankie, the Crown's strategy was to overawe the rebellious Hebrideans with a show of strength, and two frigates with 606 soldiers on board were sent on patrol around the islands in 1690.

Eigg might have been overlooked by the Cameronian forces in spite of Clanranald's involvement in the rebellion, if it had not been for an unfortunate incident on Skye. A boat from Eigg had gone to Armadale, the nearest port of call, on some errand or other, perhaps to get some meal, and the islanders had naturally stopped at the inn. But the *Dartmouth*, one of the Navy ships with Cameronian forces on board, was also anchored in Armadale, with the infamous Captain Ferguson at her command, and some of her soldiers were ashore. The islanders became involved in a brawl with the soldiers of the frigate which resulted in the death of one Cameronian. Retaliation was immediate: Ferguson ordered the *Dartmouth* to set sail for Eigg where he landed his soldiers at Kildonnan and let them take their revenge on the islanders. After burning and pillaging the island, the soldiers carried on board one of the island girls and kept her one night and one day before sending her back ashore with her beautiful hair all shorn.

The islanders then realised that the prediction made by the island seer four years before had finally come to pass. Since 1685, this seer, who lived at Kildonnan and 'foretold of things that were afterwards accomplished on several occasions', had been warning the islanders that he kept having visions of dreadful happenings on the island. 'He frequently saw the apparition of a man in a red coat lined with blue, having on his head a strange sort of cap, blue "with a very high cock on the fore-part of it", who was kissing a comely maid in [his] village and had concluded from his vision that a man in such a dress would either debauch or marry the girl.' The islanders had refused at first to take the prediction seriously and the story of the seer's unlikely vision was told as far as Skye, where, according to Martin Martin, everyone laughed who heard it, 'it being such a rarity to see any foreigner on Eigg, and the girl having no thought of going anywhere else'.[24]

The subject of second sight fascinated Martin Martin's contemporaries, theologians wondering if it existed at all or whether it came from Heaven or Hell, so that the Eigg prediction and its outcome were widely publicised at the time. Martin Martin mentioned it and John Fraser, minister of Tiree, published his own eye-witness account to add to the debate in a tract entitled 'Deuteroscopy, or a Brief discourse covering the second Sight'. According to him, the seer had told the whole island after mass one Sunday in the year 1685 'that they should all flit out of that Isle and plant themselves somewhere else because that people of strange and different habits and arms were to come to the isle and use all acts of hostility such as killing, burning and deforcing of women: finally, to discharge all that the hands of an enemy could do, but what they were or whence they came he could not tell. At first there was no regard had to his words,' remarked John Fraser, 'but frequently thereafter, he begged of them to notice what he said, otherwise they would repent it when they could not help it, which took such an impression upon some of his near acquaintance that several of them transported themselves and their families, even then, some to the isle of Cannay, some to the isle of Rum, fourteen days before the enemy came thither, under the command of one Major Ferguson and Captain Pottinger, whilst there was no word of their coming or any fear of them conceived. In the month of June 1689, this man fell sick, and Father O'Rain came to see him in order to give him the benefit of absolution and extreme unction, attended with several inhabitants of the isle, who in the first place, narrowly questioned him before his friends and begged of him to recant his former folly and his vain prediction; to whom he answered that they should find very shortly the truth of what he had spoken, and so he died. And 'within fourteen or fifteen days thereafter,' the minister added, 'I was an eye witness (being a prisoner of captain Pottinger) to the truth of what he did foretell; and being beforehand well instructed of all that he had said, I did admire to see it particularly verified; especially that of the different habits and arms, some being clad with red coats, some with white coats or grenadier caps, some armed with swords and pike and some with sword and musket.'[25] The final outcome of the story, reported by Martin Martin, was that the girl who had been so ill-treated married afterwards, 'her misfortune being pitied and not reckoned her crime'.

THE LAST PROTECTOR OF THE MEN OF ARTS

Meanwhile, whilst their chief was fighting in Louis XV's army, the islanders found themselves paying rent to Rory MacLeod of Talisker who still held the island in wadset, Clanranald having remortgaged the island for an additional 27,000 merks before his departure for France. Campbell of Argyll – now elevated to dukedom – was still Clanranald's superior for Eigg and Canna, and his power was now so complete that he could employ the army to collect his rent: a commission for the uplifting of the rents of two islands was granted in 1696 to a lieutenant David Calder, whose regiment now occupied Castle Tioram, Clanranald's ancestral home.[26] The duke of Argyll was also a staunch Presbyterian and this was another source of discontent in Jacobite lands, for the restoration of Presbyterianism meant the abolition of the Bishopric of the Isles which, in the government's calculations, would finance parochial schools and thus speed up the rooting-out of Gaelic in the Highlands and Islands. In these conditions, the union of the Scottish and English Parliaments in 1707 whipped up discontent and Jacobite fervour to such a pitch that another rising was attempted in 1715. Once again the Highland clans were asked for their help in spearheading the movement. Allan of Clanranald, by then the recognised leader of Clan Donald, returned from France to take part in the restoration of the Stuart heir and, according to the tradition of South Uist, the chief and his brother went personally around the islands to muster help from their people. On Eigg, for instance, he borrowed funds from the tacksman of Laig to help finance the rebellion: Lachlan MacDonald II of Laig was indeed quite well off since he also held the bailliery of Canna where he was the largest land-holder, and he contributed 17,000 merks to the campaign, a considerable sum of money at the time.

Among the men who eagerly followed Allan in the rising was one of his kinsmen, Iain Dubh Mac Iain 'ic Ailein, 'John MacDonald of the Black Locks', from the Benbecula branch of the clan, a staunch Jacobite and a well-known poet, who held the tack of Grulin on Eigg. Iain Dubh's compositions included many songs in praise of Clanranald and the Highland clans, and his rhetorical skills gave him a far from minor position amongst his lettered contemporaries. His satirical *Trod nam Ban Eiggaich* – the fight of the Eigg women – wittily described the sharp-tongued women of Eigg and the troubles caused by their gossip; and his tribute to Lady Penelope, Clanranald's wife, compared her to Ulysses' wife in a clever use of classical imagery. But the poem for which he was most famous was his *Bruadar mo Chor na Rioghachd* – 'A Dream about the State of the Nation' – in which he wishes to see Queen Anne, 'that borrowed sow', rent apart by deer hounds. In spite of his Jacobite fervour, his poetic vision prophetically anticipated the hardships lying ahead:

Siege set to our towns,
And many quietly captured,
The cannon volleys
Smashing limbs before us,
The cries of weans and mothers
And their men in prison.[27]

The Jacobites did indeed meet with a crushing defeat at the battle of Sheriffmuir in 1715, and its effects were disastrous. Hundreds of prisoners were transported as slaves to the West Indian plantations, and those chiefs who were involved in the rebellion were forced into exile to save their lives, their land forfeited. Allan was not amongst them for he was killed on the battlefield of Sheriffmuir, not yet 30 years of age. Whether or not Allan had a premonition of his fate, on his departure for war he ordered that Castle Tioram be set on fire and from the surrounding hills, he sat watching the flames destroy his ancestral home. The night of Sheriffmuir, his own beautiful castle in Ormiclate burned to the ground.

If Allan's widow had not intervened, urging her own brother to purchase the forfeited estate, the Clanranald lands would have been lost to the Duke of Argyll who could have claimed them as superior. As it was, in 1727, the lands were handed over to Allan's cousin, Donald MacDonald of Benbecula, who became the next chief, Allan's brother dying in Paris without heir. The passing of Allan, the 14th chief, was much lamented by the clan: 'The water is frozen despite our summer's sun, no fruit is found in the wood, no produce is driven by the wave', sang the MacMhuirich poets, echoing the ancient belief that the well-being of the land was linked to the person of the chief. But the lengthy elegy composed in his honour regretted more than the passing of a charismatic chief. It grieved for the loss of that hope for a Gaelic cultural renaissance which Allan had managed to kindle in the islands.

Chapter 3

THE END OF AN OLD ORDER

BLOOD PUDDING, *FACHACH* AND POTATO

If the seventeenth century had seen the introduction of the clans to a commercial economy, the eighteenth century was to see financial pressure effect the transformation of their leaders into commercially minded landlords. Already Allan, that lamented chief, had led a life in sharp contrast to his father's, his social ambitions marking him as a man used to living in a more monied environment. His successors would be the same, their situation aggravated by the political events of their time.

Yet at the beginning of the century, whilst the Clanranald chiefs lived in Paris, their kinsmen, the gentry of the clans, still led the life of patriarchal cattle farmers. They composed poetry and played the harp and the violin, but they led a very simple life devoid of many luxuries. The 1718 survey of Eigg, when the Clanranald estates were briefly included in the list of forfeited estates after the 1715 Rising, gives the first details of the island rent roll.[1] The island was divided into eight tacks: Grulin, Galmisdale, Sandavore, Sandaveg, Kirktown (as Kildonnan was called in the eighteenth century), Laig, Cleadale and Hulin. Apart from Laig, Kildonnan and Grulin, and excepting Knockeiltach which was owned outright, all these tacks were held in joint-tenancy. Lachlan MacDonald II of Laig paid a reduced rent on account of the loan which Clanranald had still not repaid: 35 merks instead of 185 merks a year. Being the largest tack with its 20 pennylands, Kildonnan had the highest rent, 500 merks. Sandavore, Hulin and Cleadale were worth between 100 and 120 merks, whilst the rent for Grulin was reduced on account of 'the badness of the land'. Sandaveg, split amongst eight tenants, and Galmisdale amongst six, were worth 200 merks each, the tenants of the latter also having to contribute three sheep a year. In total, the island's twenty-four tenants provided Rory MacLeod of Talisker with a revenue of 1,155 merks a year for a wadset worth 27,000 merks.[2] Renewed ten years later, the wadset would bring Clanranald another 25,000 merks.

If they had depended solely on the return of the land and not also on cattle, many tenants would have found very it hard to meet their rents: a special mention was made of the two tenants of Sandavore who were not in arrears. Even though the island was described as having eight ploughs, or eight ploughing teams, one for each tack, these were fairly inefficient so that tillage was mostly done by hand, using the *cas chrom*, the foot-plough inherited from the Norsemen. This was very labour-intensive but it meant that every awkward corner of land could be cultivated and that the return on land cultivated in this way was much higher. A lot of effort went in the manuring of the ground: creel loads of dung and seaweed were applied to the infields as well as to the cultivated patches higher up in the hills. Seashells were added to the dung-hill, and lime was burnt to increase the fertility of soil. Cattle were also made to move round the infields, kept in by temporary hedges made out of hazel sticks planted in the turf walls, so that the ground was further enriched after harvest. However, since bere and oats were grown without fallow and since the climate was expected to be bad at least one year out of three, the islanders rarely managed to grow more than seven or at best ten months' supply of oatmeal and beremeal. Any profit left over from cattle sales after paying the rent was spent on getting an extra supply of meal, although a certain amount could also be obtained in exchange for surplus butter or cheese.

Every year a temporary famine was experienced before the next harvest was ready. Spring was a time of dearth, and numerous shieling songs featured a milkmaid sending greetings to her lover, telling him that 'she had got over the winter', got through the springtime and reached 'the milky summer into autumn, time of reaping'. There was, nevertheless, an age-old method for eking out the last supplies of corn when the bad season drew to an end: the islanders bled their cattle and mixed this blood with meal to make a kind of blood-pudding. And to this day a narrow pass at the top of the Laig cliffs bears the name of Cachalaidh Dearg – the red gate – for it was there that the Laig cattle were taken to be bled. There was not really any alternative source of food to dairy products and cereals produced at the time in the islands. According to Martin Martin, Hebridean people could live and work on a diet which mostly consisted of frothed-up milk and whey, and yet their longevity was proverbial! The cultivation of vegetables was virtually unknown, although kailyards had been introduced by the mid-seventeenth century. Certainly travellers were able to report a few years later that Hebrideans were still strangers to any kind of vegetable food.[3] This was not entirely true, for many species of wild plants were harvested throughout the year, as Martin Martin recorded in his description of the islands. Greens like spring tansy, young nettles, sorrel and wild garlic were eaten in the spring for their blood-purifying qualities. Scurvy grass and watercress were very much appreciated, whilst the wild carrot was harvested in autumn and played an important part in the Michaelmas festival. Two other popular roots were *brisgean*, the tuber of the silverweed which to this day grows in profusion on every patch of wasteland, and *braonan*, the knobbly nodule of the earth-nut which was chewed for its pleasant flavour reminiscent of liquorice – it was sometimes used as a flavouring for spirits – and had the advantage of dimming hunger. There were of course all the wild berries in summer and hazelnuts in autumn. Seaweed was also widely used for food and medicine, like dulse, carrageen and tangle which were boiled and eaten with butter for all kinds of afflictions. In fact, there was little point in cultivating anything at all, when there were so many useful wild plants, and so many shellfish and sea-birds for the taking, as an elderly inhabitant of Rum told eighteenth-century visitors. If the sea was *cuile Moire*, Mary's treasury, the shore proved to be equally generous to the islanders, especially in times of dearth. When there was not much meal left, the shore was ransacked for mussels, cockles and razorfish, whelks and limpets.

'*Air sealbh bhairneach*', 'for abundance of limpets', said the gatherers, throwing their limpet-hammers behind them after a day's gathering, to be assured of more shellfish the next day. The sea-birds were also there for the taking: seagulls were robbed of their eggs in the early spring; gannets were caught by a device which exploited their voracity: a herring would be fixed on a plank of wood sunk just below the water, and the gannet diving for it would stun itself to death on the wood. Beltane, 1 May, marked the beginning of the fowling season on Eigg as on Rum, where the hunting of Manx shearwaters was reported by Dean Monro in 1545. The islanders climbed the cliffs to catch the handsome black-and-white birds, which since time immemorial have laid their single eggs in burrows at the top of the Cleadale cliffs. Eigg people used to catch both adults and young bird, which became so fat from their nightly feedings that the shearwater's name on the island was *fachach*, fatling. They were either boiled or salted down for later use, and the islanders were so partial to their taste, less oily than cormorant or shags and more like veal, that in time the name *fachach* became the islanders' soubriquet. They did not mind it; on the contrary, they took a certain pride in it, saying that no islander was a true Eiggach who had not eaten a *fachach*.

By the middle of the eighteenth century, however, influences from agricultural reformists from the south had made their way to the Hebrides. Like other chiefs inspired by the 'Honourable Society of Improvers in the Knowledge of Agriculture' founded in 1725, the 15th chief of Clanranald made attempts at improving farming methods on his lands. First of all, the growing of hay for the cattle's winter fodder was encouraged, and with it the building of earthen dykes to enclose and protect hay fields from cattle depredations. The cultivation of rye after barley was introduced in the crop rotation to combat the impoverishment of the soil brought about by that cereal: it is echoed in the place-name Lageorna which means rye-field. But the introduction of the potato was the most far-reaching innovation. Clanranald is credited with being the first chief to have had it planted in the Hebrides, starting its cultivation in South Uist in 1739, from where it spread to the other islands. According to tradition, the people of South Uist declared at first that their chief could perhaps force them to plant it, but that he could not force them to eat it. Soon enough, though, Hebrideans came to appreciate the *buntata* as a food which was easy to grow and had a higher return than cereal crops, so much so that the potato ultimately came to replace meal as a staple of life.

With the potato also came a new method of tillage, which helped to reclaim the worst lands. Pieces of sloping ground were chosen so that the soil would drain naturally and were spread with seaweed. Then ditches were cut about 5 or 6 ft apart and the soil from the ditches was turned over the seaweed so that there was a good covering of earth where the potatoes were planted. This flaying of the ground gave the method its name of *fianneagan* which was absurdly translated into 'lazy-beds'. The characteristic corrugation left by that method on every slope on the island attests on the contrary to the tremendous effort which people deployed in order to feed themselves!

THE RELIGION OF THE YELLOW STICK

It was not only the region's agriculture which was thought far too primitive, but every other aspect of life including education. The 1715 Rising proved only too well that the west of Scotland was 'imperfectly reformed', and the Society in Scotland for the Propagation of

Christian Knowledge (SSPCK) set about to remedy this state of affairs, with renewed support from its wealthy Lowland founders as well as the government. In 1725, it decided to send a special missionary to teach the four islands of Eigg, Rum, Canna and Muck their duty to God, King and country. Even though the owner of Rum, MacLean of Coll, was a staunch Presbyterian, like MacLean of Muck, a kinsman of his, who made his policy never to allow any priest to set foot on the island, the Small Isles were still a Catholic stronghold. This state of things was suddenly altered when, that same year, MacLean of Coll decided to pay a visit to Rum where one of his children was being fostered according to Gaelic custom. He arrived on the island accompanied by a Presbyterian preacher. But the child's foster-mother was a Catholic, and she was far from shy about her religious beliefs. When she saw the preacher who accompanied MacLean of Coll, she left the chief's presence at once, ostensibly followed by another person in the company, also a Catholic. MacLean flew into such a rage at this affront that he ran after them and, catching up with the man, proceeded to beat him severely with his gold-tipped cane, shouting at him: 'get back to the Kirk you rascal'.[4]

After this incident, most of the 152 inhabitants of Rum judged it prudent to change their religion and adopt the 'religion of the yellow stick' as people on Eigg and the surrounding Catholic areas now called it (an irony that the good Dr Johnson failed to understand, speculating that Gaelic may not have had a word for gold or for cane). Unsurprisingly, the two SSPCK teachers finally sent to the Small Isles met with unequal success, especially as parents on Eigg and Canna had turned MacLean of Coll into a bogey to frighten their children into behaving. There were only ten Protestants out of 340 islanders on Eigg, and the few scholars attending the SSPCK school advanced 'quite slowly'. Some were reading and writing tolerably well, but were often taken out of school on account of their parents' poverty. Eigg was certainly in dire need of education since no one apart from the tacksman of Laig had been able to sign his own name on the 1718 survey of forfeited estates, but the SSPCK's use of the Protestant Resolution as the only textbook beside the Scriptures met with little enthusiasm. Attendance soon dropped so low that it was decided that the schoolmaster on Muck would serve Eigg by turns, until the island was given up altogether, its inhabitants being 'much addicted to popery and under the management of priests and the awful power of Popish chiefs'.[5]

By that time, the Clanranald lands had indeed become a place of refuge for harassed Catholics and staunch Jacobites. It was therefore natural for those inhabitants of Rum who had refused to convert to the 'religion of the yellow stick' to turn to the chief of Clanranald and appeal to him for some land on Eigg. Among the refugees from Rum was a Lachlan MacQuarrie who settled in Grulin. He is remembered in the annals of Eigg as the grandfather of an outstanding piper, Donald MacQuarrie, of whom more will be told later.

THE YEAR OF THE PRINCE

With the Catholic religion under attack, Jacobite feelings once again came to a height in the west, as in the rest of Scotland where it was felt that the Union of Parliaments had brought little benefit to the country. The time seemed ripe for Charles Edward Stuart to try and reconquer the crown for his father, the unlucky Pretender of 1715. Yet it was a rather cold reception that was given to 'Bonnie Prince Charlie' in the Western Isles. When he arrived in Moidart in July 1745 after landing in Eriskay, he did not meet any more enthusiasm from 'Old Clanranald', who, like the rest of the Hebridean chiefs, was doubtful about the success of a new rising, especially as the Prince arrived without a great deal of armed support. But 'Young Clanranald', his son, was less level-headed and soon rallied to the Prince's cause. With his kinsmen Kinlochmoidart, Glenaladale and Glengarry, he raised the Jacobite standard at Glenfinnan and was given the honour of commanding the right of the frontline when the rebellion set off. A contingent of forty Eigg men, under the leadership of the tacksman of Laig, swelled the Clanranald ranks to 250.

The campaign started well with the Jacobites proclaiming James Edward Stuart king at Perth in September 1745. It looked then as if the Gaelic prophecy, well known at the time, that the western clans would rise to power again, might yet be fulfilled. But although it lasted almost a year, the rising ended in inglorious defeat for five thousand dispirited clansmen in April 1746 at Culloden. Earning himself the infamous nickname of the 'butcher of Culloden', the victorious Cumberland ordered that no quarter be given to the defeated Jacobites. His soldiers were sent to hound the survivors, pillage their lands, burn their houses and sell their cattle to any Lowland buyers. The rebels had come alarmingly close to success and had to be crushed without hope of ever gathering strength again.

The army's hunt closed in on the coast where Bonnie Prince Charlie was now awaiting a chance to escape back to France. From Moidart to Knoydart, Clanranald country was ravaged whilst the Navy patrolled the islands incessantly, hoping to catch any of the fleeing officers if not the Prince himself. Although his father had already been taken prisoner and gaoled in London despite his lack of involvement in the rebellion, Young Clanranald managed to evade capture by sheltering briefly on Eigg. A few days after meeting with the Prince, urging him to spend the last of his gold to alleviate the people's sufferings, he succeeded in landing on the north end of the island without attracting the Navy's notice.

Tradition has it that Young Clanranald of the '45s sheltered in one of the caves which open among the red volcanic pillars of Sgorr Sgaileach, and to this day it is called Clanranald's cave, Uamh Mhic 'ic Ailein, the Gaelic using the chief's patronymic, 'son of the son of Allan'. In this dank, dark place – Sgorr Sgaileach means 'the promontory of the shadow', for the shade it casts never allows the rocks to feel the sun – Clanranald ordered his ghillie to bring him a turf to rest his head on instead of the hard stone the man had already provided. The ghillie, Iain Ruadh, a MacLennan from South Uist, full of the Culloden gloom, expressed his surprise that his chief might be 'so fond of ease, when a stone should be enough for the head that may roll in the morning'![6] The threat was only too real: Kinlochmoidart, Clanranald's kinsman, had been caught and hanged in Carlisle and his head was on display at the city gates.

In spite of Iain Ruadh's misgivings Clanranald successfully escaped to France, and before leaving sought to reward his ghillie with the offer of Sandavore farm rent-free for the rest of his days. But the South Uist man was decidedly outspoken, for he told the chief that he would rather have 'a cow's grazing at Kildonnan than that "scrappy, useless place" of a farm'. He was given what he wanted, and there is a good chance that his choice may have been influenced by the close proximity of the island's inn, for Kildonnan was now the island 'change-house'. It is said that on his way home in high spirits from the inn at Kildonnan, Iain Ruadh would pause, shouting and waving his stick, either to challenge the dead to come and fight with him or to admonish them to keep quiet.

The story was also told on the island of how Iain Ruadh was finally awarded a pension of one shilling a year, some years after Culloden. To collect his shilling, he had to walk to Edinburgh and back, sleeping in haysheds and attracting as little notice as possible, for islanders were considered suspect for a long time after the rebellion. One time he stopped for a rest at a Perthshire farm. The farm servants, busy at the harvest, noticed the stranger who was brought in front of the farmer. By an extraordinary coincidence he was the very same man whom Iain Ruadh had saved from certain death during the battle of Falkirk. Regardless of the fact that he belonged to the Hanoverian troops, the islander had dragged the man, severely wounded in the leg, to the shelter of a wall, off the battlefield and out of harm's way. The man, who was still lame from his wound, gave him the most cordial reception, and from then on Iain Ruadh always stopped there on his way to the city of Edinburgh.[7]

Other Culloden veterans were not to be so lucky. As the prince was biding his time before embarking on a French frigate for a life of exile, the Navy was scouring the islands and laying them waste. Eigg was not overlooked: Captain Duff landed on the island to oversee the execution of the Disarming Act. The inhabitants were called to one place and told to deliver all their weapons at their peril: a few were delivered, a receipt was obtained and the islanders thought themselves out of danger. But a few weeks later, Duff came back, this time with Captain Ferguson on the *Furnace*. The latter, who had earned his nickname of Black Ferguson for his cruelty, had just dealt with Canna: his soldiers had been given leave to rape and pillage, and had slaughtered half of the island cattle under the pretext of getting supplies. When he complained that the beef had gone off and ordered it to be thrown in the sea, preventing the islanders from salvaging any for food, the rest of the cattle had been rounded up – most of it belonging to John MacDonald of Laig whom he knew to have been in the Prince's army – and another sixty beasts had been slaughtered. Ferguson and Duff were now looking for Captain John MacDonald, Kinlochmoidart's brother, whom they suspected of hiding on the island.

'The islanders stifly denied the doctor to be there with their knowledge,' related Alexander MacDonald, the famous Moidart poet, to Bishop Forbes from eyewitness accounts which he took down whilst residing on Canna after Culloden. 'With this [the captains] sent about a 100 men, divided into small corps, in search of him. One Mr Daniel MacQueen, minister of the gospel at the Isle of Rum, happen'd to be then at Eigg, and was both agent and interpreter 'twixt the inhabitants and the ennemie. He, Mr MacQueen, well knew the very place where MacDonald was hiding himself, and understood by reason of the narrow scrutiny they were resolved to make after him, they would fish him out. Therefore, he goes himself in person where he was, and, after explaining him the danger he was under, prevailed upon him to surrender. Accordingly he did. He was first well us'd. But behold the unluckiness of the poor Eigg people; for one of the party that was traversing the country back and forward, found out so many stands of arms that they reserved for their own use. Captain Ferguson did not seem to be much disobliged at this; but reflecting that notwithstanding what they had already delivered, they still reserved their full compliment. However, he bespeaks Captain MacDonald, the doctor, and earnestly desires him, for the poor people's own safety and good of the country, he should call them all and perswad them to come in, with their whole arms of all kinds, and that he would give them full protections for both their persons and effects that would save them against future danger: otherwise, if they should not come heartily . . ., he woud immediately cause his men burn all their houses, destroy all their cattle and carry the whole men away. Mr MacQueen advises Captain MacDonald to send for the men for the remainders of the arms in the terms spoken by Ferguson. He sends dozen of lads for them. They were seen comeing in a body.

Immediately Ferguson ordered Captain MacDonald to be seiz'd upon and made prisoner of, brought into a house and confin'd theret for ane hour. The men laid down their arms, such of them as had any. The few old people that came among them were picked out and dismissed home. Then, Captain MacDonald was brought out of the house, was stript of all his cloaths to the skin, even of his shoe and stockins, brought upon the *Furnace*, barisdall'd in a dark dungeon. And to the poor people's additional misfortune, there was a devilish paper found about him, containing a list of all the Eigg folks that were in the Prince's service. Then that catalogue was read by their patronimicks in the name of giving the promised protection, which ilk one answered cheerfully, and was drawn out into another rank, so that there were noe fewer than 38 snatched aboard the man of war, were brought to London from thence transported to Jamaica where the few that lives of them continue slaves as yet. Many of them dyed and starved ere they arrove at the Thames. The most of them were married men, leaving throng families behind them. They slaughtered all their cattle, pillaged all their houses ore they left the isle, and ravished a girl or two.'[8]

Alexander MacDonald was right: nearly half the islanders had died of fever and starvation before arriving in London. Of the eighteen that survived the journey to be tried, sixteen were found guilty and sent as slaves to the Jamaican plantations. Only two men were set free to return home, one of them a John MacDonald, farmer in Cleadale.[9] The *Furnace* had hardly left when General Campbell landed on the island, still looking for the Prince. There was nothing left to pillage or burn but John MacDonald of Laig, the island baillie, was made prisoner and taken away to London in his turn. The next soldiers to arrive on Eigg were French and were looking for the Prince too, but he was long gone by then. The money they brought to distribute in the Highlands and Islands was meant to support whatever rebellious feelings were left, but it was mostly used to stave off famine in the devastated country. Tradition states that one cache of arms was still hidden on the island, the weapons carefully greased and wrapped in cloth or leather to preserve them for another day of battle, buried on Beinn Bhuidhe at the place where five sounds can be seen, but they are yet to be found. They were never needed again, although ardent Jacobites like Alexander MacDonald, better known as Alasdair Mac Mhaighstir Alasdair, tried their best to keep the Jacobite flame alive. Amongst the many rousing songs Alasdair composed, when Culloden was still believed to be only a temporary setback, was a waulking song, 'Morag', a thinly disguised incitement to rise again for Bonnie Prince Charlie, which was widely sung on the islands.

Many a sweetheart has Morag
Between Morvern and Arran . . .

Every man in Uist and Moidart and
Arisaig of the green birches

In Canna, Eigg and in Morar
The bold band, the race of Allan.[10]

But not even Alasdair's considerable poetic talent could manage to rekindle the ashes of the rising: the year of the Prince was definitively over. The reality was that King George I and his government had felt so threatened by the rebellion that they decided once and for all to put an end to the Jacobite threat in Scotland. Cumberland had actually proposed to have the Jacobite clans in their entirety transported to Jamaica. It was resolved instead to implement measures which were to destroy the power of the rebellious chiefs by attacking the very fabric of clan life and breaking the people's spirit. The Disarming Act of 1746 was thus followed in 1747 by the abolition and proscription of the 'Highland garb': considered to foster the Gaels' warlike spirit, the wearing of kilt and tartan was now punishable by imprisonment and transportation. Considered an instrument of war, the bagpipes were also proscribed: playing them incurred the death penalty. Strict observance of the Acts was to be ensured by constant military patrols.

The chiefs involved in the rebellion saw their lands forfeited and given over to factors who were brought from outwith the Highlands and Islands so that they would feel no ties of loyalty to either tenants or chiefs. In this way it was calculated that the bonds which existed between landlords and tenants would eventually break. More extreme suggestions were even made, such as buying and sequestrating these lands and colonising them with Protestants from the south. At the same time measures were taken to end the independence of the clans once and for all. The chiefs saw their status reduced to that of mere landlords by an Act of Parliament which abolished their right of heritable jurisdiction. This meant an end to the chiefs' rather questionable power over their followers, but also the end of what had been a system of local government. This greatly angered the chiefs who had remained loyal to the crown, although they at least received some monetary compensation for their loss, unlike the attainted chiefs. This liberation of the common man from the power of pit and gallows, as it was called in the south, served its intended goal. It ensured the disintegration of the clan organisation by severing the relationships between each level of the clan's hierarchy. Its officers were turned into tenant farmers who for the most part did not even have a lease for the land they occupied, and its common soldiers into people who no longer had the rights to the land they had acquired through generations of armed service. This was to cause dramatic suffering in the 150 years to come.

FOR THE GOOD GOVERNMENT AND IMPROVEMENT OF THE COUNTRY

In the first decade after Culloden, the island slowly recovered from the effects of the Hanoverian repression. The islanders dyed their tartan plaids and cut them into breeches, nurturing like other clansmen dark thoughts about 'the Butcher Cumberland'. But any thoughts of revenge were probably dampened by worry about the fate of the men taken away and the rebuilding of their lives. Indeed, when David Bruce, the Surveyor of the Forfeited Estates, came to inspect Eigg in 1748, he found the island in a sorry state, much depleted by the war and Ferguson's expedition. The tacksmen and tenants of Grulin, Galmisdale, Sandaveg, Cleadale and Hulin were either dead, rotting in prison-hulks on the Thames or transported to Jamaica like the tacksman of Kildonnan. MacLeod of Talisker still held the island in wadset (apart from the farms of Laig and Knockeiltach), and Kildonnan was leased to a new tacksman who also acted as his factor. For this office, Lachlan MacLean was paid 100 merks a year and was in charge of the collection of rents and 'public burdens' which went towards the minister's stipend and the schoolmaster's salary.

The newcomer was one of only two farmers to have a proper lease in 1748, paying 1,000 merks a year for Kildonnan. The other was the tacksman of Laig, John MacDonald (III of Laig), who paid the comparatively low rent of 215 merks a year for his six pennylands of Laig and 75 merks for the three pennylands of Sandaveg he now rented. This low rent was certainly on account of the money still owed by Clanranald, and it was probably for that reason that he was also exempted from those public burdens which had to be paid by all the other tenants. Compared with the twenty-four tenants listed in 1718, there were hardly any people left to be surveyed: only the four joint-tenants of Sandavore, who did not have a lease for their land but paid 100 merks a year for it as well as a sheep each or 2 merks.[11]

The last survey of Eigg in 1718 had recorded yearly rents of 55 merks for Sandavore and 500 merks for Kildonnan. Rents had therefore doubled in the space of thirty years, without any noticeable change in the island's economy. The rise reflected the rising price of cattle and the growing pressure exerted by the landlord on his tenantry. There certainly was no other 'industry' than cattle-rearing, as David Bruce was able to ascertain after questioning the island's ground officer, Donald MacKinnon, who could only answer in the negative to the surveyor's exhaustive list: no dovecots, no connie yards (rabbit yards), no orchards, no coal, salt or lime quarries, no woods nor fisheries. The surveyor had two good reasons to conduct such an enquiry. The first was that it was his brief as the government's agent to promote industry and manufacture in order to reform the Highlands. The other was that he had in mind to take over the factorship of the Clanranald lands where lead mines had just been discovered in Strontian.

However, the chief of Clanranald had managed to escape forfeiture of his lands – which should have gone to the Duke of Argyll by virtue of his superiority over him – because of a fortunate mistake in the Bill of Attainder of July 1746 where Ranald, 'young Clanranald', was wrongly named Donald. After successfully arguing his case in court, his lands were taken out of the list of forfeited estates in 1749 and put in the hands of his father, Old Clanranald, who had not taken part in the rebellion. By that time, Clanranald was only too glad to lease them to David Bruce for nineteen years. His kinsmen's advice had been to regard the surveyor with caution, but this arrangement suited the chief well enough, for he was still in disgrace for his role in the rising and, preferring to live in France where he served as a high-ranking officer in the royal army, he needed the money badly, his finances being in a sorry state after the rising and a legacy of debts inherited from his mother.

By offering David Bruce the management of his lands, Clanranald was playing right into the government's hands. The brief of factors like Bruce – foreign to the Highlands and their Gaelic traditions – was to reorganise estates along the commercial lines prevalent in the south and to 'civilise' the Highlands by introducing industry and improved agriculture. This was exactly the result sought by the impoverished chief. Indeed, after Culloden, it was no longer the number of his clansmen that provided a chief's grandeur but the urban lifestyle which money raised on his estate could provide. By the end of the century, three-quarters of Hebridean chiefs would become absentee landlords, with more cattle and sheep on their estates than people.

Now that the lucrative cattle trade was flourishing again, money could easily be obtained by raising the land rents. The southern markets were eager for more of those famous black Kyloes bred in the Highlands, which were to become the main source of beef in the British Isles by the end of the eighteenth century. However, there was one main obstacle in the way of increased profits: the people who occupied the land. At the top of the social scale, tacksmen had been accustomed to paying a relatively low rent for their farms because of the military service they provided for the chief. They believed that this verbal arrangement known as *duthchas* – 'kindness' to the land – was enough to give them an inalienable right to a land they considered as much their inheritance as the chief's. But now that chiefs were no more than landlords, all concept of their kindred's interest in the land was cast aside: all that mattered was whether the tacksman had a lease and whether that lease was drawn on a commercial basis. And tacksmen were a hindrance to progress since 'they were usually more concerned to keep up a host of unproductive dependants and retainers than to cultivate habits of industry and thrift'.[12] If they showed no signs of adopting the methods of agriculture recommended by the new factors, they could be replaced by tenants who could offer more rent.

At the other end of the scale, the 'commoners' who held the land in joint-tenancy or were the tacksmen's subtenants were criticised for their lack of ambition which led them 'to be satisfied with the bare necessities of life which they could procure themselves'. Such was the conclusion of the 1764 report on the Hebrides compiled by a government official, Dr Walker, who had found Eigg, for example, 'tolerably fertile but full of idleness'.[13] However, in his largely self-sufficient economy, when cattle provided food, drink, utensils, tallow for candles, heat, footwear, leather for bagpipes and money to pay the rent, which islander needed more than the few luxuries that trading of cattle could procure? Strangers to the clan system often failed to understand the close-knit structure of Gaelic communities where whatever money was obtained from agriculture was immediately redistributed at the level of the extended family so that more could subsist. They did not understand the judicious use which Highland people – as experienced pastoralists – had always made of summer and winter pasture and criticised them for not growing any winter fodder. They blamed runrig agriculture for impeding production and discouraging people to improve or manure the land more than their neighbours.

In this new ideological climate, it was hardly surprising that Clanranald decided to 'improve' his estates as soon as the leases which Rory MacLeod of Talisker had given out whilst holding Eigg in wadset had run out. By 1760 David Bruce's land management had brought enough profit to Clanranald to redeem that wadset and regain control over Eigg. One of his first measures was to have a corn mill built on the island. It was built near a convenient waterfall in Sandaveg but was eventually relocated to Kildonnan after much engineering work was done to channel enough water to ensure a constant supply. This was a rather unwelcome innovation from the islanders' point of view since they had to pay multures – mill dues – to have their corn dried and milled instead of doing it themselves at home using their own querns of Lochaber schist. But Clanranald was not only looking for a new source of revenue, he was also intent on stopping the traditional method of 'gradaning', considered wasteful by eighteenth-century improvers. Gradaning, parching of the grain by burning the husk, had enabled the islanders to grind and bake their corn within hours of reaping, but it did give a certain taste to the grain which was now considered undesirable since corn still formed part of the rent paid to the chief.

A seventeen-year tack for the new corn mill (and for another built in Ardnafuaran in Arisaig) was given in 1763 to Donald Frazer, a former lieutenant from the Argyllshire militia, now innkeeper in Arisaig. The same Donald Frazer was to rent the farm of Upper Grulin for sixty-three years after paying '40 pounds as "grassum" to obtain the lease in preference to others', a condition of the lease being that 'he rid the tack from all wedsetters, tacksmen, tenants and subtenants'.[14] This was a taste of things to come: those who not only offered to pay more but were prepared to clear the land of smaller tenants were clearly favoured. Clanranald was not so inclined to give such long leases. In 1761 he had given a thirty-year lease for Laig to John MacDonald IV of Laig, and a ten-year lease for part of Sandavore and the island's changehouse to a kinsman, Ranald MacDonald from Arisaig, who had paid him grassum in advance. But the rest of the eighty-eight families recorded on the island by Dr Walker were not treated so favourably. Many of them were experiencing difficulties, like the two widowed sisters of John MacDonald III of Laig, tacksman of Laig, Ann and Mary MacDonald, whose lands in Cleadale reverted to the chief in 1756 when they had to renounce the tacks previously held by their husbands. As to their neighbour, Allan MacDonald, V of Knockeiltach, his debts became so pressing that he found himself obliged to sell his lands (four pennylands in Hulin and Cleadale and the three pennylands of Knockeiltach which had been in the hands of this ancient branch of the Morar MacDonalds since 1610) to Clanranald in 1761 for 5,000 merks, the chief undertaking to pay his most urgent debts. But when Allan of Knockeiltach or John of Laig's two sisters sought to rent some of their former land back, neither of them managed to obtain more than the short leases which the chief finally distributed in September 1765.[15]

These seven leases were almost identical in content and concerned about half the island population: the fourteen tacksmen and twenty-one joint-tenants of Hulin and Five Pennies, Cleadale, Knockeiltach, Sandavore, Galmisdale and Lower Grulin. There was no mention of the anonymous sub-tenants, cottars, servants and other dependants who comprised the other half of the population. The leaseholders were given licence to 'occupy, possess and enjoy their shares of land without any troubles or molestations whatever' for four years. Then, they were to 'remove themselves forth from the said lands without any previous warnings or proceeds of law under the penalty of one year's rent or their possessions'. Any contravention of the terms of the agreement by the Cleadale tenants would break it, and in Lower Grulin, any breach of the regulations enacted by Clanranald or his baillie 'for the good government and improvement of the country' would be liable to a 200-merk fine.

Old island families like that of Allan MacDonald now leased four pennylands in Hulin and three in Knockeiltach with six other tenants, including Mary MacDonald, or Ann MacDonald her sister, who now rented the ten pennylands of Galmisdale with seven other tenants. They were also newcomers, like Ranald MacDonald from Glengarry in Five Pennies, Lachlan MacKinnon and his son Hector from Skye in Cleadale, or the new parish minister, Malcolm MacAskill. The rent varied from £2 a pennyland in Cleadale to £2 8s in Lower Grulin but each lease also included rent in kind: one boll of 'good and sufficient' oatmeal per pennyland – about an eighth of the yearly production – with half a stone of butter, one stone of cheese, three hens and a wedder each year. In addition twelve days of carriage were expected of each named tenant and the performance of necessary services such as statutory labour, as well as payment of multures and public burdens.[16]

A few additional clauses were thrown in for good measure. First, all the lease-holders were to build new march dykes out of stone. This was an important undertaking since boundary dykes had hitherto been built out of turf and were forever crumbling, allowing cattle to go astray and causing endless trouble between farms. This would have been especially good news for young cowherds as the custom was to give them a sound thrashing on the site of the boundaries so that they would never forget where these were! To this day, the remains of these march dykes can be seen snaking their way throughout the island, a tribute to the islanders' labour. The lease-holders were also under obligation to sow a peck of linseed in each farm and pay the chief back in yarn or money. This was intended as an encouragement to grow flax as a cash-crop for the developing Scottish linen industry. But this attempt was short-lived compared with another rising industry: the manufacture of kelp out of seaweed which had spread to the west of Scotland from the north-east. Since the tacksmen of Laig, Galmisdale and Knockeiltach had already started producing the valuable alkali, Clanranald now demanded ten shillings per ton of kelp produced and another ten shillings for carriage on his vessels. He also included a provision to oblige each tenant to use the new corn mill. Compulsory thirlage to the mill of Eigg was obviously an answer to the islanders' lack of enthusiasm for this additional burden.

Tradition reports that in the end Clanranald had to resort to intimidation for the islanders to comply, and send his factor to break every single quern on the island. But when the factor arrived at the door of one Cleadale man famous for his strength, it was his turn to be intimidated. The factor was scared away and the man was never bothered again, although the rest of the islanders had to bring their grindable corn to the mill.[17] It is an ironic symbol that two of the querns that have survived with their broken upper halves adorn the Lodge terrace today.

EMIGRATION IS IN THE AIR

Whilst Clanranald was distributing leases to his tenantry, tales were circulating in the west about the British colony in North America and how land there could be obtained easily for prospective settlers. This was an unforeseen consequence of the British government's colonial policy. It soon realised that the Highlanders' 'warring skills' could be put to good use for its own ends. The proscription of the Highland dress was lifted for those who enlisted, and chiefs who could muster their men once again, this time in the government's name, were rewarded with lands and titles. Since 1757, a dozen regiments had been raised in the Highlands to fight the government's colonial wars in Canada and North America, men who had fought on opposite sides at Culloden often finding themselves brought together in the same regiments. This was much deplored by some tacksmen who thought 'it an immense Delusion for the People to think of the Army or the East and West Indies for their Offspring, or indeed any sort of roaming and adventurous line: nine out of ten perish: that Industry, which is equally necessary abroad, might if they could be reconciled to it support them equally at home without the risks, what Shoemaker, Tailor, Watchmaker, Sadler, Hatter etc, etc may not if he is capable and industrious, make equal to the half pay of an idle spendthrift Lieutenant or even a mighty Captain'.[18] However 'roaming abroad to other Nations in quest of a miserable subsistence by the Sword' was far more attractive to most Highland men than the occupations described above, especially as those who survived the Canadian and American campaigns found themselves rewarded by grants of lands in those colonies. Word soon spread that a new life could be had overseas, free from rack-renting landlords.

Tacksmen confronted with the harsh terms of their new leases dreamt of recreating clan life as they had known it on the other side of the ocean. There was also a sense of adventure, as with 'Spanish John', a Knoydart tacksman whose roving disposition made him opt to leave his native country for America. This was perhaps what also motivated John MacDonald of Laig to follow his Morar kinsman into the army, giving up his thirty-year tack in 1765, when it was leased to his relative, Janet MacDonald, for four years only. For others like the Captain of Glenaladale who acted as Clanranald factor in the 1760s and was therefore well placed to witness the difficulties experienced by the tenantry, it seemed the only alternative in the face of evictions and rising rents. For him, it was better to try and transplant whole communities together. Another decisive factor towards emigration was a religious one, Catholic bishops supporting the idea of establishing Catholic communities abroad, free from persecution. Funds started to be raised in Edinburgh and throughout the Highlands to sponsor the movement of emigration headed by Glenaladale.

The fact was that a Presbyterian chief like Colin MacDonald of Boisdale, Clanranald's cousin, had harassed his Catholic tenantry in South Uist to such an extent that in 1769, rather than being evicted if they refused to give up their religion, 100 tenants chose emigration to Prince Edward Island in Canada. Rumours that Lochboisdale, who openly declared that the country would be better off if a third of the population went abroad, was to take over land in Arisaig and Eigg strengthened many islanders' determination to leave: Clanranald's tenants no longer felt that they could depend on their chief or his family to ensure their freedom of worship. As a result, several of Clanranald's tacksmen started to recruit actively among their fellow clansmen for emigration to Nova Scotia, one of them being the tacksman of Laig. He would have had little trouble in gaining support for emigration on the island, as its population was now reaching its highest peak ever, with 501 inhabitants recorded in 1768 by the island minister, Malcolm MacAskill. Tenants had to subdivide their land to accommodate their grown-up children to such an extent that it was becoming harder for everyone to meet their rents when even the tacksmen themselves were impoverished. Many decided to sell what cattle they had to gather the necessary capital for emigration, so that when the leases granted in 1765 expired, few sought to renew them. They followed the tacksman of Laig overseas as their forefathers had traditionally followed him to war. The Eigg emigrants were among the 'flower of Clanranald', the tacksmen who followed Glenaladale in self-imposed exile to Canada with 214 oppressed tenants from Moidart, Arisaig and South Uist. In their midst were most certainly the two Galmisdale subtenants whose rent he had paid since 1765.

The American War of Independence, which started in 1775 and lasted for a decade, momentarily halted this tide of emigration, only for it to start with renewed vigour later on. In the meantime, old and new tacksmen on Eigg struggled on to face the new conditions which were imposed on them. Many of them were such colourful personalities that the details of their lives have come down to us in the memories of people whose families had served them faithfully. If the chiefs no longer commanded the islanders' respects, at least the tacksmen did.

Chapter 4

THE LAST OF THE TACKSMEN

MAIGHSTIR CALUM AND HIS FAMILY

Malcolm MacAskill was the first parish incumbent to reside on Eigg. Previously included in the parish of Sleat, the four islands of Eigg, Muck, Rum and Canna had only become a parish in their own right in 1740. Since then, Donald MacQueen, the first minister of the Small Isles, had resided on Rum where the ceremony of his presentation had been carried out, since it was the only island apart from Muck which had a sizeable Protestant congregation. The minister rarely ventured to Eigg or Canna, but his yearly stipend of 842 merks was nevertheless paid – somewhat irregularly – by all the heritors in the parish: Clanranald, MacLeod of Talisker, Allan MacDonald of Morar, John MacDonald of Knockeiltach as well as Hector MacLean of Coll and Lachlan MacLean of Muck, most 'being in Low circumstances and much burdened by debts'. Yet the minister found his stipend too small for defraying his charges: he needed four servants to ferry him from one island to the other, and found it very difficult to find lodgings, 'such lodgings as he can be provided with being at best but one of the small huts they built for their Cattel, and he is still worse accommodated than the poorest servant in his Paroch'.[1]

It was not until some years later that an official decree appointed the glebe of the parish to be assigned out of the wadset lands of MacLeod of Talisker at Kildonnan on Eigg, where a new church would also be built. When Malcolm MacAskill arrived as the new minister of the Small Isles in 1757, he accordingly took residence on the Braes of Kildonnan at a place called 'Tobhta Dhugaill'. Not only was the minister farming that part of Kildonnan appointed to him as a glebe, but with the farm of Galmisdale leased to him after the departure of its occupants to the New World for the time of his incumbency and the eight pennylands of Sandaveg and five pennylands of Sandavore, for which he was given a thirty-year lease, he could now be considered one of the most important tenants on the island.

Malcolm MacAskill is remembered in the island tradition as Maighstir Calum. Descending from that old Norse family who had held high office with the MacLeods of Dunvegan as hereditary Watchers of the Sea, the MacAskills' ancestral home was at Rubha an Dunain near Talisker in Skye. Maighstir Calum had inherited from his forebears a forceful temperament as well as great physical strength. From his early missionary days in Glenelg after graduating from St Andrews University, he had earned the nickname of *am ministeir làidir*, the strong minister. He certainly deserved it, for he had never stopped wearing the kilt in spite of its proscription, and went about clad in the ordinary tartan used by mere shepherds. That was how he saw himself, as a 'shepherd to his people', and he certainly cut a more charismatic figure than most of his fellow Episcopalians. He also earned quite widespread fame in his staunch defence of 'second sight' at a time when it was generally thought by ministers to be a pagan superstition or, even worse, a proof of association with evil powers. His arrival in the parish heralded at last an era of religious tolerance and even harmony between the Protestant and Catholic congregations in the Small Isles. He was on excellent terms with the priests who resided on Eigg, who were often from the same tacksman background as himself and well-educated men who had studied in Douai or Valladolid.

The minister was married twice. From his first wife, a MacLeod from Skye, he had two children, and their daughter was to marry John MacLean, a tacksman on Muck related to the Coll family, *Fear na Cornaig*, as he was known in the Muck tradition. It was said that both the groom and his best man, Donald MacAskill, the bride's brother, were equally matched in size, both being 5 ft 11 in, impressively tall for their time. Maighstir Calum's second wife was Mairi Nighean Eoghain, a natural daughter of Hugh MacLean XIV of Coll. Like many women of her rank, she was an accomplished poet and singer, well versed in her native language and possessing that quick vein for poetry which to many foreign visitors seemed so particular to Gaelic people. 'Her house was always full of rhymes and songs', as her granddaughter remarked to her own daughter, the pioneering folklorist Frances Tolmie. 'A great event was to be led up the grassy slopes of the Coolins to see Eigg far off, where our mother was born', recalled Frances Tolmie, who was taught the many lullabies and dandling tunes her mother remembered from Eigg.[2] Little of Mary MacAskill's poetry has survived, unfortunately, save a few songs handed down in the island tradition, like the one she improvised on the surprise visit of her beloved brother, the young heir of Coll whose tragic death by drowning in the sound of Ulva in 1775 was mourned in a touching elegy.

One particular song in the Eigg tradition is attached to the story of her thwarted romance with a MacLeod of Dunvegan, the dashing gentleman who had been her suitor before she married Maighstir Calum, who was considerably older than she. The tale was that he had become master of a ship up north and she hoped that soon he would sail near Eigg and come ashore to see her. Every day she walked from the Braes of Kildonnan halfway up to Struidh and waited there at the edge of the cliff to see if his boat would not sail through the Sound of Eigg. One day, at long last, the ship appeared but careered past Eigg in full sail, without so much as a lowering of the sail. The minister's wife was heart-broken:

> Though I saw the ship go sailing past
> I was looking for the boat being lowered
> O hoirionnan e ho ro
> O hoirionn o, I am so far from home,
> O hoirionnan e ho ro

She wished that she had a boat herself, and some strong lads with her to row so that she could have gone to meet the ship, for she would rather have

> Maighstir Calum dead under boards
> And MacLeod and I in the Isle of Man
> O hoirionnan e ho ro
> O hoirionn o, I am far from home,
> O hoirionnan e ho ro[3]

But she was a proud woman, and to see that MacLeod had forsaken her made her forget about him. She seemed to have settled in her marriage with Maighstir Calum, for she was to bear him ten children, seven of whom survived infancy. Her three boys were famed in the island for their uncommon strength and their role in island affairs, and many stories were told about them.

In the MacAskills' day as well as today, physical strength was a much-admired quality in the islands, and there were numerous occasions for contest and trials of strength. Tradition tells of a virility test which every young man had to undertake. It consisted of walking the narrow sheep track which skirts the edge of Bidein Boidheach – the beautiful pinnacle – at the back of Beannan Breaca which is the highest cliff on the island. A more common test was lifting and throwing weights: people would gather on Sunday afternoons in a field reserved for games and sport and they would be 'putting the stone'. Ewan, the youngest of the three brothers, was said to have thrown the *Clach Neart*, the stone of strength, a great big boulder of white granite weighing 25 lb if not more, a distance of 30 or 40 ft. The stone is said to be still lying where it landed, in a field called A' Leanag Fhliuch, on the far side of Cathalaidh na Marbh. Hugh MacKinnon, the last sennachie of Eigg, remembered well how he and his friends used to try and lift that boulder on their way to school: the boys could hardly lift the stone then. They used to try again as grown men, but none of them could even throw it their own length!

Another of Ewan's feats was to have jumped a distance of 33 ft in a contest in a field below the manse called Feithe na Bramanach, the bog of the awkward fellow. Pegs were placed there to mark the island record. Yet another exploit of his was to lay a barrel on its side on the top of the slight slope running from the graveyard to the flat land before Kildonnan House, and let it run down the slope. He would jump on top of it and dance all the way down with the barrel spinning under him until it reached the level ground. There was not much difference between Ewan and his two older brothers, Donald and Allan: 'One day, the three young men went to Rum with their father for a service. When they set foot on the pier, they saw these barrels of tar, and they said to each other: "He'd be a pretty good man, who could lift one of these barrels up above his head!" And one of them lifted the barrel from the ground high above his head and then he let it down his back till it rested between his shoulders. Then he lifted it up again above his head and lowered it gently to the ground. The second did the same as the first, but the last, that was Donald the eldest, he injured his nose as he was bringing the barrel down, having slipped a little. A stream of blood came pouring on his chest, and when they saw that, none of them would go to the service that day.'[4]

Like many of their contemporaries, the two youngest brothers went to sea to seek their fortune. Allan, the second oldest, became captain of his ship and amassed a considerable wealth before retiring on Mull where he bought the estate of Calgary. He generously bequeathed a sum of money for paupers on Eigg, and the islanders told for years to come the story of his adventures on the other side of the world.

Ewan, or Eóghain Mór, as he was known on Eigg, met with a crueller fate, despite or because of his great strength. Going ashore in Liverpool one day, he decided to take on a notorious prize-fighter. 'Hundreds of people gathered to watch the fight,' tells Hugh MacKinnon, 'and within one minute . . . Eóghain Mór gave the bully one blow and split his head open. And the crowd, this great gathering of people that had come to the place to see the fight, they were so angry that the fight had not gone on . . . that this sturdy lad who had laid out the bully, instead of congratulating him, didn't they go and turn on him? They were throwing everything they could lay their hands on and he was just catching it with his hands and keeping it off . . . In the last resort, when they found they couldn't get at him that way, someone went up some stairs and came to a window above the place where Eóghain Mór was standing, and what did he throw down but a spade. The edge of the spade pierced the top of his head. But anyway he dragged himself to the pier, and aboard the ship and oh, he hardly ever put a foot on the ground again as long as he lived.' Ewan was brought home to Eigg and the story is that 'he was lying in a bed in a room over there at Kildonnan, and one night that there was company in the house . . . they were drinking drams and they had pewter flagons on the table . . . and Eóghain Mór heard them saying to each other: "He'd be quite a man who could crush a pewter flagon together." . . . Eóghain Mór heard them, and said to his mother: "You can tell them that one came from your own body that could do it. You bring me the flagon here." . . . She took one of the flagons to him and he crushed it together like you might do to a bit of paper He didn't live very long after that. He died. He was still a young man.'[5]

His older brother Donald was to call his son after him. Donald studied medicine and was the first doctor in Fort-William, before taking on Kildonnan farm after his marriage, building there a substantial new house with a garden, keeping the place 'as a gentleman's residence should be'. He introduced small pox vaccination in the Small Isles, where the disease had previously decimated the islands every twenty years and his medical skills were in great demand from Arisaig to Barra and Uist. As Clanranald's baillie, he made a few changes on the island, notably moving the Glebe which was in the middle of his land to Sandaveg, giving it a generous mile-long tack which made it the largest in Scotland. All that was now required on it was a Manse, a proposal approved by the Presbytery of Skye, giving up plans of rebuilding the old church at Kildonnan. Costs for the new building, the largest on the island, two storeys high, with a slated roof and the prerogative of a walled garden, were spread between the heritors and tacksmen of the parish. This occasioned not a few complaints from some of them, like the Presbyterian Colin MacDonald of Boisdale who held the tack of Sandavore at the time. But Maighstir Calum did not live to see the splendid Manse completed in 1790, and it was occupied by Revd Donald MacLean, the new incumbent who succeeded him in 1788.

THE GREAT PIPER OF EIGG

Mary MacAskill's home was certainly not the only house on Eigg where there was music and songs. According to tradition, the best piper in the whole of the Clanranald lands, Ranald

MacDonald, or Ragnhall Mac Ailein Óg as he was called in Gaelic, was the island baillie at the time. A brother of Allan V of Morar, he held the tack of Cross in Arisaig, but his office allowed him frequent visits to Eigg. Ranald, who also played the harp and the violin, had found a gifted pupil in Donald MacQuarrie, the grandson of a tenant of Rum who had sought shelter from religious persecution in Grulin. Donald, or Domhnall Mac Dhomhnall 'ic Lachlainn, as tradition remembers him, was so good that in no time at all Ranald was able to teach him the tune of the Finger Lock, the very intricate pipe tune for which he was justly famous. He decided then to send his pupil to Skye to see if he could learn some more about piping from the MacCrimmons, the celebrated pipers of Dunvegan, who had established their own piping school. On his arrival at the school, the first tune that Donald played was the Finger Lock, and he had hardly finished when the MacCrimmons told him he need not have come. 'Why has Raghnall Mac Ailein sent you to mock us?' the pipers asked as they dismissed him, for it was obvious from his playing that he knew more about the art of piping than they could teach him! This was as much a compliment to Donald as a homage to his tutor, and on his return Donald became known on Eigg as *am Piobair Mór*, the great piper.

Donald remained in Grulin, marrying Catriona, a girl from Muck. But his wife longed for her old home which she could see quite well from her new abode. She was forever wanting to visit her family, and when her longing proved too much for her she would light a bonfire on top of a certain hillock, whereupon her brothers would row over to Grulin to fetch her. As to her husband, he had taken to playing a special tune every time she was away which is called to this day *am Port 'am Phiobaire Mór*. But in the end, Catriona's visits home grew so lengthy and so frequent that her husband resolved to find a way to keep his wife at home: he enlisted the services of an old veteran from the wars who succeeded so well in scaring away Catriona's brothers that they never came back for her again.

It seems as though the great piper of Eigg eventually found solace from conjugal strife in the bottle, for he is remembered in the island tradition as being very fond of a dram. His drinking companion was said to have been Ranald, the son of Raghnall Mac Ailein Óg and a piper himself who held the tenancy of Sandavore as an inn at that time.[6] But the great piper of Eigg was spending so much time at the inn that his two sisters decided to put an end to his drinking for his health's sake by frightening him into staying at home: one dark night, they dressed in white, covering their heads and their bodies in old sheets and awaited his return, posted on either side of the burn running past Galmisdale. As Donald arrived near them, 'tacking from side to side of the road', they remained still. Taken in by their ruse, he paused for a while, then he went on cautiously, thinking that maybe he was imagining things. They followed him. He hastened his step, they hastened theirs. The poor man started to run for his life, convinced that the ghosts were after him. Alas, he did not run long before he fell, utterly exhausted, so that his sisters ended up having to carry him home. Their ruse succeeded only too well: the great piper took to his bed from shock and died.[7]

A funeral of appropriate importance was arranged for him, with his drinking friend Ranald coming from Arisaig to pay his last respects. Donald's coffin was carried all the way from Grulin to the burial ground at Kildonnan. The pall-bearers rested only once on the way, stopping as they were reaching the boundary between Grulin and Galmisdale. As was customary, a cairn was built at that resting place to commemorate the great piper, each mourner contributing a stone. While they rested, the approach of Ranald's boat was signalled, and the mourners set off again.

The funeral cortège arrived in view of the burial ground just as the boat landed at Poll nam Partan. Playing his pipes, Ranald ascended towards the chapel and, meeting the mourners as they were coming down, led them around the church sunwise as was the custom and then to the grave. The great piper of Eigg was buried inside the roofless chapel like his music tutor Raghnall Mac Ailein Óg who, according to tradition, is buried in the recessed tomb bearing the armorial shield of the MacDonalds of Morar. To this day, the Great Piper's cairn still stands by the road below the Sgurr towards Grulin. It narrowly escaped destruction when that road was built, the island's tradition-bearers making a timely intervention to stop the road-workers from using its stones. Anyone who passes it by and knows of the great piper of Eigg is commanded by tradition to add a stone to it, as has been done ever since.

PIRATES AND POETS

Another Ranald earned himself fame in the island tradition but for much less glorious reasons. Ranald MacDonald, a tacksman from Knoydart where great upheavals were experienced due to the rack-renting of the Glengarry chiefs, had taken over the tack of Five Pennies above the Singing Sands in 1765. One of three pirate tacksmen in Clanranald's lands, Raghnall Óg was not above luring a cutter onto the reefs at the Singing Sands or Talm to get its cargo. He made his living smuggling whisky, an activity made very profitable by the government's ban on distilling since 1714. He was relentlessly pursued by the excisemen but he was never caught, as he had cleverly painted his boat black on one side and white on the other so that it appeared to be a different boat every time it turned about. His son carried on the smuggling trade from the mainland and was no less fierce: 'Being once hotly pursued while engaged in one of his illegal expeditions, he was boarded in a calm off Arisaig coast by a party of revenue men. He instead of surrendering fought them fiercely and gaining the upper hand, deprived them of their arms which he threw in the sea. He then unceremoniously tumbled his adversaries into their own boat, assuring them mockingly that "the government would comfort them and like a tender mother, pour oil over their wounds".'[8] Raghnall Óg's foul temper was legendary on the island and he is said to have thrown a galley boy overboard in one of his outbursts of anger, the boy being retrieved safely none the less. He never stopped quarrelling with his neighbour in Hulin over the boundary of their lands in Talm, so much so that he was taken to court in Inverness.

Lachlan MacKinnon was an altogether different character. This tacksman from Skye, who had moved to Hulin from Cleadale in 1770, was the first to try sheep farming on the island. Profits from sheep and kelp allowed him to build the first house of 'lime and glass' on the island. Until then, tacksmen's houses had differed little from ordinary clansmen's dwellings apart from their length, servants and masters sharing the same space in successive apartments. But Lachlan's new house was two storeys high, with a vast kitchen on the ground floor and bedrooms upstairs. On the other side of the kitchen, separated by a stone wall, the byre occupied one end, with a hay loft above it, sharing the same slate roof, the most modern house on the island apart from the manse. It also had a walled garden and the only orchard on Eigg. Its apple trees were to last only about sixty years or so in the harsh salt wind, but the sycamores which were said to have been planted at the same time are still standing.

Laig was the next house to be modernised, although this happened quite a bit later, probably when Angus succeeded his father Ranald Dubh MacDonald who took over the tack in 1770.

'Raghnall Dubh', as Ranald is known in Gaelic, was the son of Alasdair Mac Mhaighstir Alaisdair, the famous Moidart poet. He had been a schoolmaster of Eigg for two years before taking on the tack of the change-house of Arisaig and finally moving on to Laig. With him resumed the tradition of having at Laig a tacksman closely connected with the chief's family. Ranald Dubh had received a sound Gaelic education from his father, whom he would often replace as a teacher when Alasdair went on one of his Jacobite missions. It was on Eigg that he embarked on the task his father had been unable to complete, that of editing his extensive manuscript collection into a compilation of poems by various Gaelic authors, 'all set to music and composed in the last 200 years'. This task took two years to complete, Ranald bestowing on it 'much labour and expense' as he pointed out in the preface of his compilation entitled *Comh-chruinneachaidh Orannaigh Gaidhealach* published in 1776. It comprised work by his father, some MacMhuirich elegies, and numerous poems by Ian Lom and Ian MacCodrum the Uist bards; Mary MacLeod; Eachen Mac Gillean, the Muck Bard; and Iain Dubh Mac Iain 'ic Ailein, the Eigg poet. Ranald's stated aim was to help preserve his mother tongue, and he intended to publish a second volume devoted to older Gaelic poetry, going back three or four hundred years.

One of the most famous subscribers to this compilation was James Boswell, who met Ranald in Edinburgh, two years after his visit to the Western Isles with Dr Johnson. Boswell was so delighted to discover some Gaelic in print that he bought three copies and, after being shown some of the original manuscripts by a grateful Ranald Dubh, wrote the news of his discovery to Dr Johnson, insisting that some of them seemed to have 'all the duskiness of antiquity'. One of the aims of their journey in the islands had been indeed to discover evidence in support of MacPherson's claims that his *Ossian*, which had taken Europe by storm, was based on ancient Gaelic manuscripts, a claim difficult to substantiate since he had used mostly oral sources. They had been unable to find any and Dr Johnson remained unimpressed by Boswell's find, and wrote back that Gaelic was only 'the rude speech of a barbarous people who had but few thoughts to express'. He had made up his mind once and for all that 'Erse' poetry was nothing but a translation of old English epics and he was not prepared to change his mind in the face of any evidence.[9] His prejudice was not only his loss but Ranald's as well, for lack of encouragement prevented him from gathering the necessary subscriptions and the book failed to meet the interest it deserved. Discouraged by his lack of success, Ranald Dubh abandoned the idea of a second volume and in the course of time, he allowed some of his collection to be dispersed and destroyed. During a visit to Laig, Maighstir MacEachen, a priest connected to the family, was 'mortified' to see the precious papers used for various purposes throughout the house. Indeed according to tradition, 'little worth were the things in the book compared to the things that were not in it at all . . . Never was his kist of meal so full as the one in which he kept the bits of paper and the old skins brimful of writing'.[10] Luckily, enough of these manuscripts survived to form the Eigg Collection, now lodged in the National Library of Scotland, but it is possible that the famous missing Clanranald manuscripts could have been amongst those which were destroyed.

Johnson and Boswell had actually intended to visit Eigg, recommended to them as a 'popish island' like Canna where they would be able to find the 'antiquated beliefs' which the visitors were so eager to discover,[11] the Gaelic way of life 'full of savage virtues and barbarous grandeur' appearing as removed from the Age of Reason as could possibly be. They even found a guide in the person of Donald MacLean of Coll, the brother of Mary MacAskill, the wife of the Small Isles minister. If it had not been for bad weather, which prevented them from landing on the island, the two travellers may have at last satisfied their quest for genuine Gaelic manuscripts. They would have found at Laig ample evidence that Gaels, ancient or modern, not only knew the art of writing but excelled at it.

After Ranald Dubh's death, the manuscripts remained at Laig and his son Angus was able to show them to another illustrious traveller, the Swiss geographer Necker de Saussure, during his visit to the island in 1807. With a party which included the chief of Clanranald's brother, he had been detained at Laig for dinner and Angus had plied them all with drams before, during and after the meal. After greatly praising his chief and equally denigrating the Campbells, Angus diverted his guests by singing them some of the Gaelic songs composed by his grandfather with a few *port-a-beul* and pibrochs, 'pleasantly imitating the sound of bagpipes with his voice'. The evening ended with this 'charming old man with delightful manners belonging to another age' offering his departing guests a memorable *deoch an dorus*, the traditional farewell dram, drinking to their health before pouring out a bumper to each guest in succession. In the course of the evening, Angus had shown Necker de Saussure his manuscript collection and the traveller, observing that they were written in a distinct script 'rounded in shape and resembling ancient Saxon', concluded that they offered, to him at least, the proof that MacPherson's sources were authentic after all.[12] The manuscripts were all written in the old 'Hiberno-Saxon' script which had once been the calligraphy in use in Britain as well as Ireland from the days of monastic scholarship in Iona, Lindisfarne or Kells. It had been preserved longest of all in the west of Scotland by the learned men of Gaeldom like the MacMhuirichs of South Uist, formerly hereditary poets to the Clanranald chiefs, who taught Alasdair Mac Mhaighstir Alasdair. Indeed, with Old Clanranald of the '45, he was among the last people who could read and write that script, unlike most Gaelic poets of the seventeenth and eighteenth century who, sadly, were unable to write their own language, a fact that Dr Johnson, to his credit, had not failed to deplore.

RITUALS, PRAYERS AND PREMONITIONS

During their Hebridean journey, Johnson and Boswell had been particularly curious about beliefs in the supernatural. Dr Johnson naturally wanted to investigate the question of second sight in the light of his eighteenth-century rationalism, but he found people politely evasive on the subject, since admitting to such beliefs meant incurring the wrath of a clergy bent on stamping them out. But as Pennant observed in his *Travels in the Hebrides* of 1772, even the Protestants in the isles observed Yule and Pasch, Christmas and Easter, which among Presbyterians was esteemed 'a horrid superstition'. The islanders also observed the feasts of *Samhain*, All Saints' Day, on 1 November, the beginning of the winter season; St Brigid's day on 1 February which was the start of the spring; *Beltaine* on 1 May when the cattle moved to the hills for the summer; and *Lugnasadh*, Lammas, on 1 August when the cattle were brought back to the township. The shieling months were a time of courtship for the island youth. The lads would come and visit the girls in their turf and stone bothies. The accommodation was spartan, a fire at one end of the building, a bed of dry straw at the other, 'spread on the floor from wall to wall and fenced off at the foot by a line of stones, the middle [being] occupied by the utensils and products of the dairy – flat wooden vessels, a butter churn and a tub half-filled with milk, whilst a few cheeses soft from the press lay on the shelf above',[13] but the islanders looked on that time as the best of the year. Michaelmas signalled the beginning of the harvest and was marked by a horse cavalcade throughout the island. 'Every man in the island mounts his horse unfurnished with a saddle and takes behind him either some young girl or his neighbour's wife, and then rides backwards and forwards from the village to a certain cross,' observed Pennant on Canna. 'After the procession is over, they alight at the public house where strange to say, the females treat the companions of their ride. When they retire to their houses an entertainment is prepared with primaeval simplicity; the chief part consists of a great oat-cake called *Struan Micheil*, or St Michael's cake, composed of two pecks of meal, and formed like the quadrant of a circle: it is daubed over with milk and eggs and then placed to harden before the fire.'[14] Wild carrots were dug and offered by each girl to her sweetheart. It was another time of revelry and merriment before the dark winter nights.

Like calendar feasts, old supernatural beliefs and rituals inherited from a pre-Christian past were also preserved, integrated into the islanders' faith, for these formed an integral part of people's experience of life and death. In the harsh environment of the Hebrides, people considered that rituals to preserve luck were essential to keep misfortune at bay. Life amidst dangerous seas, at the mercy of storms and natural calamities which often brought famine, often took a fatalistic outlook. It was believed that everyone was born with his share of luck, depending on the state of the tide. There were those who, like St Columba, were born with the good luck of the flood – *rath na fionaid*, and those who came to the world with the bad luck of the ebb – *rosad an traghaidh*. The fate of a child could also be read in the number of rivulets running from Columba's well when its water was fetched to baptise a newborn baby: 'if there were nine, the child was as strong as the ninth wave on Laig strand or the nine rays of the sun, if there were seven, he was to be a rover seeing through the wonders of the seven elements and the seven days, if there were three, he would look towards the Triune and acquire knowledge of the three kingdoms, earth, sea and sky', recorded Kenneth MacLeod.[15] Nevertheless, even if a person's fate was predetermined in this way, the important thing was to keep one's share of luck from running out. Since days were divided between lucky and unlucky ones, people were careful not to start any work of importance on Fridays or Wednesdays, the day of crucifixion and the day 'when judgement went forth against the Lord'. Thursday, on the contrary, was an auspicious day for it was Columba's birthday. Bad luck surrounded the first day of each quarter year, and it was customary for the first person to be up that day to thrust a hen or a cat outside to cheat the bad luck which inevitably befell the first creature out of the door. At harvest time, each farmer hurried as much as possible to avoid the dumping of the *cailleach* on his field which would mean bad luck until next autumn. The *cailleach*, a sheaf of corn which represented all the corn reaped on the farm and was made in the likeness of a woman, the old wife of harvest, represented the spirit of hunger. The last farmer to finish the harvest became its keeper and thus responsible for *gort a' bhaile*, any dearth that might befall the township. It was feared and resented so much that the dumping of the *cailleach* could lead to violent incidents: the story was that the tacksman of Kildonnan once sent the *cailleach* to his neighbour in Laig. Riding a swift black mare, his servant placed the sheaf on a wall near the victim's house. The angry tacksman of Laig came in pursuit and fired several shots, in vain for the man escaped unharmed.[16] Great care was also taken whilst at sea to use special words to describe things that related to the land. Failing to call Eigg by its sea-kenning of Eilean nam Ban Mora – the Island of the Big Women – was to bring ill-luck and could prevent a safe return. In the same way, Rum was referred to as Rioghachd na Forraidhe

Fiadhaich – the Kingdom of the Wild Forests – in view of its past as a deerhunting forest for the Lords of the Isles. Muck was Tir Chrainne – the Land of the Sow – and Canna, An t-Eilean Tarsainn – the Island Lying Across. It was equally unlucky for sailors or fishermen to wear anything that was dyed with crotal as it was believed that the lichen would be attracted to the coastal rocks on which it grew.

In spite of all precautions, one could still come to harm through the evil intentions of people whose jealousy and envy brought ill luck. Care was taken not to praise cattle or children too much in case they fell prey to the evil eye and inexplicable diseases befell them which had to be cured by silvered water. If butter refused to churn, if milk curdled or became less abundant, it was believed to be the work of witches who could take the profit of the milk to them by magical means. To counter evil influence, rowan trees were planted near houses and byres, and charms were hung around children's necks to protect them. *Cno Moire*, Mary's nut, the smooth round Molucca bean brought to Hebridean shores by the Gulf Stream, was greatly sought after as a good-luck charm for infants and pregnant women.

The protective web of prayers inherited from Celtic Christianity was considered the best protection against harm. Nothing was ever done without asking for the blessing of God, Christ and the Gaelic pantheon of saints: Columba, protector of flocks and herds; Michael, the warrior and horseman, and Bride, the foster-mother of Christ whose help was invoked by women in childbearing, and who like Mary had taken over the attributes of the ancient Mother goddess of former times. The day started and ended with an invocation to Mary or Bride, whose protection was called over the household when the fire was brought to life in the morning or smoored at night so that, carefully covered with ashes, it would last from one ritual kindling to another.

Each work had its appropriate prayer, for going to sea, for milking cattle, for meeting a stranger. Even the stars and the moon had special prayers dedicated to them in those days when a glowing peat was the only light available to walk across the island in the dark. All Hebridean people held the moon in great respect and always hailed the appearance of a new moon in the following manner: the women curtseyed gracefully and the men bowed low, raising their bonnet reverently, bending their left knee with the right drawn forward towards the middle of the left leg. On Eigg, people had a slightly different ritual: on seeing the new moon, a man would put his right hand round the left leg and, in the name of the Trinity, make the cross of Christ on his palm with the spittle of his mouth.[17] Both men and women would then murmur the appropriate prayer:

> Hail to thee, thou new lit moon,
> I bend the knee, thou queen so fair
> Through the dark clouds thine the way be,
> Thine who leadest all the stars
> Put thy flow-tide on the flood,
> Send thy flow-tide on the flood.[18]

The power of the spoken word was great, as attested by the vast numbers of healing charms and incantations recorded in the islands. It could work for the good but also for the bad: amongst the many stories of curses which had been brought to pass was the story of Kate Frazer, the daughter of the Grulin tacksman, who wanted her beautiful daughter to make a good match by marrying a respectable islander by the name of Raghnall Mac Iain Bhan instead of her poor suitor from Canna. But whilst the wedding preparations were being made the lovers secretly arranged to meet one evening at the cattle fold after the milking, and eloped to Cleadale where the priest married them. They were walking back home together with the best man and the bridesmaid, when Kate Frazer met them and realised what had happened. In the heat of her anger she took off her boots and threw them at the two couples, cursing them that they may never have children. They never did and a song was composed about the sad plight of Nighean Bhan Ghrulin, the fair Grulin girl.[19]

In spite of all the precautions taken by people to safeguard themselves from ill luck, it was thought ultimately impossible to escape one's fate. This was not so much an expression of defeat as a belief in a certain amount of predestination, inherited from a Celtic past, as was taught in the stories of heroes who always unwittingly broke the prohibitions laid on them and fell victim to the very circumstances they were meant to avoid. Some individuals were credited with the power to see through that veil of circumstances and perceive the underlying patterns of fate, but ordinary people too could also experience premonitory warnings. There were indeed several instances of *manadh* (portents) and apparitions of *tabhasg* (ghosts of living beings) at critical times in the island history. But it was generally a death which was announced by strange lights and noises or the experience of meeting with a phantom funeral before the real one passed on the road. It was a common belief on Eigg that animals and especially birds, those images of the soul in both Christian and Celtic traditions, could sense things that humans would not perceive. A cockerel crowing in the middle of the day always foretold a death in the household and was immediately dispatched in order to avert it. The owl was a most potent omen: called *eun ban nam corp*, the white bird of the corpse, it brought warning of an impending death if it was seen flying to the ground and resting on the roof of a house. Tradition tells the story of a young lad who saw the bird flying to the ground near Cathalaidh na Marbh, the gateway of the dead, the site of a burn which formed a boundary between the two parts of the island, just as he was fetching the *bean tuirim*, the woman who dressed the body of the deceased, from Cleadale for someone who was dying in Grulin. Another story told of a woman who met with a violent death after the owl had flown into her. Hearing 'an Wick' was another significant omen which was held to have foretold the death of a minister and several other people. It was the mysterious call of 'a bird which was never seen but heard sometimes as if it came from the air above, sometimes as if it sprang from the ground at the very feet of the listener'.[20] The description fits the eerie sound of the snipe in its mating flight, but some people swear that the sound they heard was much more intense, like some weird echo from the cliffs. The apparition of a big grey hunting dog, the ghost of a bitch which had unwittingly caused the death of her master, the tacksman of Meoble near Arisaig, was also said to announce the death of anyone connected with that branch of the Morar MacDonalds. Yet if death itself was an occasion for sorrow, tradition held that mourning had to be kept within reasonable limits otherwise the dead would suffer even more. The noise of the sand at Traigh na Bigil – the strand of the whispering, as the famous Singing Sands of Eigg are called in Gaelic – was thought to be the voice of those who had died by drowning. They asked for their womenfolk to stop crying ceaselessly over them, since they were in *Tir fo Fhuinn*, the land under the waves, in the company of the best heroes of Lochlann. Every tear shed after the prescribed period of mourning became a drop of blood and they would drown a second time if their folks did not stop their weeping.[21]

Supernatural creatures could also announce an imminent death, like the *bean nighidh*, the washer woman, who was said to haunt the burn at Cathalaidh na Marbh. If she was seen kneeling in the water, it was the shroud of the onlooker that she was washing. She belonged to the people of the *Sidhe*, the fairy people, to whom the islanders attributed the prehistoric arrowheads which turned up in their ploughed fields. In their eyes, these arrowheads were none other than the magic weapons of the *Sluagh*, the fairy host, and great care was taken at night not to leave open any west-facing window, for fear that one of these fairy bolts would harm human or cattle. On the other hand, such arrows were also an efficient talisman against the power of these temperamental creatures inherited from the cosmology of their ancestors. Associated in the past with the cult of the dead, the *Sidheanan* were then believed to be that legion of angels who, thrown out of Heaven with Lucifer, were not wicked enough to end up in Hell but lived in a kind of intermediate state. Inhabiting an underground world parallel to the human world, these creatures were capable of assuming human shape and intruding at will in people's affairs, especially in those 'in-between days' marking the transition between each quarter-year and particularly at *Beltaine* or *Samhain*. Crafty and unpredictable, these creatures could be mild and even beneficial if shown deference: those who had a great gift for poetry and music were thought to have derived their power from their association with the fairy people. On Eigg, all the young people used to gather on the summer's moonlit nights on one particular fairy mound, Cnoc na Piobaraichd (the knoll of piping), in the hope of hearing the reels that would make the 'merry dancers' themselves go faster, and laments that would draw 'tears from the eyes of a corpse', such was the skill of the musicians of the *Sidhe*. But if the *Sidheanan* were ignored or offended, they could exact cruel revenge. It was only on Fridays, the day of the Lord's crucifixion, that it was safe to speak of them, and at any other time people took care to be on their guard. If a child was born with any deformity, it was the *Sidheanan* who had stolen it and replaced it with one of their own. And the perfect human baby would come to harm as it was given back again. Such was the story told on Eigg of a poor child left unattended in a field in Hulin near the well of Cuidh Chapuil (the mare's paddock) whilst the mother was working at the harvest, who was stolen and given back with a broken back.

The *Sidheanan* were not the only supernatural creatures feared by the islanders. On dark nights there was always the possibility of an encounter with the *bocan* (the bogeys) who haunted the hills or the shore. But bogeys, fairies, the devil and his envoys all saw their power disappear by daylight. The *each uisge* (water horse) was not so easily beaten. Adept at shape-shifting, the water horse would appear to men as a huge black hairy monster with a nightmarish snort and gnash. But to women he would present himself as a handsome stranger at first, as a Grulin girl found out to her mortal peril. 'She was a young maiden looking after her father's cattle in the hills below the Sgurr where the Grulin people had their shielings in the summer time. Shieling time was courting time, so that when she met that handsome stranger, she was well pleased with him and they spent much time together. One day, the sunshine was stronger than his wooing and he fell fast asleep with his head in the girl's lap. As she stroked his head, she found to her horror that some leaves like those of the water plants grew in his hair, and when she looked at his feet, she suddenly realised that they were both hoofed! Quick-thinking, she cut out the piece of her dress where his head lay and she fled home as fast as she could. The water horse woke up too late to catch up with her, but as she reached the township, she heard him shout that he would come back for her. And he did too, one day when she was sitting outside with a company of other young people one late afternoon. He snatched her away and took her back with him into the loch, her friends following in hot pursuit behind them. Alas, they arrived too late and all they found was her bloody heart and lungs floating on the surface of the water. And so the loch was named after the girl, Loch Nighean Dhugaill – the loch of Dugald's daughter.'[22] Nestling deep under the steep slopes of the Corravein where slim basalt columns fan out like frozen spray, Loch Nighean Dhugaill looks forbidding indeed, even under the most brilliant sunshine.

Not all supernatural creatures were bad. The *gruagach mhara*, as the mermaid is called in Gaelic, was an altogether nicer creature: she could sometimes be seen sitting on some distant reefs with a grey robe for clothing, but as soon as she was discovered she would raise her head and plunge into the deep. Mermaids were believed to be seal women reverting to their human shape: on Eigg, the legend was that a mermaid, once caught by the tide, left the imprint of her shape on the ceiling of a cave which was named after her, like a tune which is still played on Eigg.[23] Another *gruagach* was believed to a dwell in Lon nan Gruagaich, a pool below the Cleadale cliffs, and that name was also applied to another creature, thought to inhabit the hillock of Cnoc Oilteag, a shy, hairy being which gave its protection to cattle if it was treated with respect and given regular offerings of milk. This was by no means a belief unique to Eigg, and Martin Martin reported the 'universal custom of pouring cow's milk upon a little hill or a big stone where the spirit call'd browny was believed to lodge [and that] this spirit always appeared in the shape of a tall man having very long brown hair'.[24] Offerings were also made to the sea: the island boys used to go down to the shore and crush whelks and limpets in the natural cups in the rocks which were called 'the Mermaid's quaich'. This would lure the fish to the shore, but to ensure a good fishing they would not forget to pour three palmfuls of salt water into the rock cup and call out loudly: 'May the fish of the sea follow the water of the sea to the rock of the shore'.[25] In the same way, the limpet-gatherer in the islands would always throw his limpet-hammer into the sea after each day's gathering with the words *air sealbh bhairneach* (for abundance of limpets) to ensure a good supply for the next tide.

Thus, in the harsh natural environment which was theirs, the people found comfort in legends and beliefs which helped them to endure hardship with stoicism and conciliate unseen powers when life was precarious. These were an integral part of their culture, like the poetry and music which were valued means of expression and practised by all, from the highest to the humblest.

Chapter 5

DISPERSAL

THE ISLAND'S FIRST EVICTIONS

Angus MacDonald of Laig was described by Necker de Saussure as a charming old man with the delightful manners of another age. Yet this most generous host, who had entertained the travellers with songs, music and drams, was responsible for the first clearances on the island.

It was for his sister's sake that he cleared the land, not for his own profit, for he was living comfortably at Laig with his wife, a daughter of Maighstir Calum, and their four children. She had married a Knoydart gentleman, who had fallen on hard times as rents were increased and farms taken away from tenants to turn them into sheep farms on the Glengarry estates. Angus thought it a good idea to bring the couple to Eigg where his brother-in-law could farm the neighbouring tack of Cleadale, and to that end he issued notices to quit to the small tenants who held that farm in joint-tenancy. He was Clanranald's baillie, and, as it was to him that they paid their rent, whether they stayed on the land or not was entirely at his discretion. 'There was great sorrow and lamentation in the place when they left and it was over at Rubha Phuirt Bhain in Kildonnan, it was there', recalled Hugh MacKinnon, 'that they were put on board the ship and it was said that the women were weeping and wailing and tearing their hair and calling down a thousand curses on Angus of Laig.'

Having got rid of the people, Angus built a fine house for his sister and her husband. It was a two-storey building, just like Lachlan MacKinnon's house in Hulin, standing alone overlooking the bay where a whole clachan had stood, built in all probability with the stones from the cleared dwellings. But Angus's efforts were to be in vain, for 'when this MacDonald of Knoydart came to Cleadale and saw what had been done on his behalf, he was a man of compassion and humility, and he would not stay,' told Hugh MacKinnon: 'though his brother-in-law had gone the length of such destruction, driving the people away to make room for him, he went back to Knoydart'.[1]

Angus ended up offering the big house to a renowned fiddler from the neighbouring island of Muck, for he now fancied having his own musician at hand. A herdsman for MacLean of Muck,

Neil MacKay – whose father Calum was the first MacKay to settle on Eigg – possessed a beautiful instrument with a rare red patina, which had come all the way from Italy. It had cost him a cow to buy the *Fidheall Ruadh* (the red fiddle) from MacLean of Coll, who had himself bought it from a passing sailor. Neil was pleased with Angus's offer and moved to Eigg in no time at all, where he established himself as a weaver. It is said that when Neil played his fiddle in the evening outside Cleadale House, he could be heard at the far end of the township; but after a while, he found it hard to feel at ease in such a big house, having no use for a byre and a hayloft. On the other hand, the parish priest who resided at Sandavore at the time was complaining that his accommodation was too small and that he had no room to conduct services. They exchanged houses to their mutual satisfaction and from then on Cleadale House was used as the priest's residence, some of the land in the farm being set aside so that he could cultivate it to supplement his income. A room upstairs was reserved for church services but, as it was situated directly above the byre, many were the clerics who were to complain of the disturbance to their preaching caused by the noise of the cattle and hens.[2]

Tragic events were to happen to the Laig family, and it was always said on Eigg that they were a consequence of the curses laid on Angus by the people who had been driven out of their land. The first was the death of Angus's brother-in-law who was accidentally poisoned by his wife not long after their return to Knoydart. She had mistakenly given him some dye instead of his medicine one night.[3] After this unfortunate event, Mary, his widow, came to live on Eigg in her brother's house, keeping him company as he was alone with his children, his wife having died quite young. Some years passed until another tragedy occurred when Angus's children left the house one evening to attend a gathering on the other side of the island. 'When they returned in the night, or as the day was dawning, they found no one at home, and no one knew where on earth the old folk had got to, and there was nothing for it but to turn out and look for them all over the place. The alarm was raised among the neighbours and some of the people turned out and he was found dead about a hundred yards from the house, the old man Angus of Laig, with his musket lying beside him. He had shot himself and they found him dead at the place called Na Sidheanan. They kept on looking for the old woman and they went down by the shore of Laig and they went past Poll Creadhach and Clach Alasdair till they came to a place called Clach an t-Sionnaich, and it was in the cleft of the rock there that they found her, and she was half-naked, wearing nothing but her night clothes . . . and, so it was said, she had gone out of her mind.'[4]

Angus's suicide also vindicated in many eyes the prophecy made about him by the parish priest. 'There had been a funeral on the island and Angus and everyone in the place were gathered down at the Mill at Kildonnan afterwards. The parish priest was there too, Fr Anthony MacDonald, a Uist man, and the drams were flowing. And the priest and Angus of Laig had a difference of opinion on a thing they were discussing down there. And Angus of Laig – descended as he was from the line of Clanranald, and the blood running so proud and hot in his veins . . . he would not tolerate a rebuke from any man, even a man of the cloth. And the argument became so heated between them that he struck the priest: he raised his hand and he struck the priest. And the priest turned round to face the people who were standing about and he said to them: "Mark my words," said he. "It is the hand that struck me today that will part the soul from his body." '[5]

EIGG AND THE FISHERIES SOCIETY

Angus of Laig had lived in relative comfort, but the situation was not the same for other islanders. The 1794 *Statistical Account* compiled for the parish of the Small Isles by its new minister, Donald MacLean, did not present a picture of prosperity for Eigg or the rest of the parish: crops seldom afforded the inhabitants a competent subsistence, and great oats had been tried but had rotted because of the rain. Cattle prices were generally good but the tenants were at the mercy of mainland cattle dealers who did not always give them a fair price. The universal complaint was that of high rents, shortage of land, want of schools and an absurdly complicated salt law. The tenants' greatest luxuries were a dram of whisky and all the tea and coffee they could barter from the foreign fishermen who were fishing in island waters.

Foreign travellers like Necker de Saussure observed that, with some encouragement, Hebridean people could have easily competed with English and Dutch fishermen in supplying the continental markets with herring, cod and ling. But, as deplored earlier by Martin Martin, the government had been too preoccupied with protecting English fishing to follow up earlier efforts to encourage West Highland fisheries under Charles II. As it was, islanders were too poorly equipped even to think of competing with other fisheries. Although they spent their summer nights fishing for the pot, they simply did not have enough hooks, nets or lines, nor even enough boats to venture far from their shores. Nor did they have the funds to buy the necessary equipment: there were only fifteen fishing boats amongst the four islands of the Small Isles in 1794, and ten passenger boats. Only a few could make the trip to the Clyde markets where their catch would fetch a good price, although it was not without hazard: four boats out of five which made the trip in 1790 were lost at sea.

Yet, in spite of their lack of equipment, islanders were resourceful. Saithe for instance was so plentiful that it could be caught by simply lowering a basket into the sea or using white feathers as bait. Fish were also caught in *caraidh*, stone enclosures which trapped the fish at low tide. Convenient pools in Kildonnan, at Poll nam Partan (Crab Bay), would have bait placed at the bottom which lured fish in and left them stranded when the tide receded. The fish which could not be eaten straight away was thrown on the manure heap, such as saithe which was mostly used for its liver, which provided the oil burnt in the *cruisgean*, the little iron lamps fashioned by the island's smiths. Otherwise it was dried in the sun and wind, since the islanders could not salt their fish for sale or for winter use, because of the restrictive laws enacted by the British government in order to protect the English fisheries.

If the islanders wanted any salt at all for household use as well as for curing fish or meat, they had to go to the nearest custom house, which happened to be in Tobermory on Mull, grant bonds of security for any salt they could obtain there and promise to use it for nothing else apart from curing fish. Then they had to return to the custom house and show their barrels of saltfish and bring back any left-over salt – which they badly needed for all sorts of use – under threat of severe penalty if any salt was found in their homes for unauthorised use. The islanders complained bitterly about this unnecessary hardship, which obliged them to use seaweed ashes to preserve their cheese for winter and deprived them of curing fish as a reliable source of food in the winter months. It was hardly any wonder that illicit trading was popular in the islands.

One product at least which did not require salt was the oil extracted from the liver of the sun-fish, the basking shark, which the islanders used to hunt from May onwards, as soon as the shark appeared in their waters. This valuable oil, like the oil extracted from the blubber of young seals, was sold at a good price in the Clyde market. So were otter pelts and sealskins, which were also exported as well as crotal, a lichen which was scraped from the rocks and used for dyeing wool.

The Eigg fishing banks were not as good as those on Canna or Muck, but its position half-way between Tobermory and Skye could make it a convenient stop for the herring boats which came in ever-increasing numbers, provided it had a proper harbour. Canna was an even better location in the opinion of the newly formed British Fisheries Society, which was particularly concerned with the development of fishing in Scotland. Thus in 1788, the society approached John, the 19th chief of Clanranald who had recently succeeded his father, with a view to purchasing land in Canna and Eigg. Galmisdale, it was thought, would provide an excellent site for a fishing community. But Clanranald, who was spending more time in Geneva than in Scotland, let alone on his west-coast estate, wanted far more money than the Society was prepared to spend.[6] The scheme fell through, to the equal disappointment of the islanders and the British Fisheries Society. Clanranald's encouragement of the industry was limited to the building of a pier on Eigg by Statute labour in 1790. The islanders, labouring unpaid, built it on a ridge of pitchstone lava in the natural shelter offered by the sandy cove in Galmisdale, its entrance protected by a barrier of reefs opposite Castle Island. Unfortunately, Clanranald pier, as it is now known, could only accommodate fairly small vessels, under 70 tons, and was only accessible at high tide.

GLAD TO EMBARK FOR CANADA

Meanwhile, the end of the American War of Independence had signalled the start of a renewed bout of emigration in the area. Knoydart, for instance, was seized by 'a ferment of emigration' when tenants there found themselves confronted with rent rises which they could not meet and threatened with eviction to make room for sheep farms. They reacted by 'subscribing articles of mutual engagement to one another for the purpose of associating for emigration' in 1785. The leaders of the community made provision to charter a ship, and in the following year 520 people from Knoydart and North Morar left in close-knit family groups to find a better life in Upper Canada.[7]

Across the water on Eigg, the islanders had suffered the same hardships, surviving mostly on potato and herrings, for the two consecutive years of 1782 and 1783 had seen such a complete failure of crops on account of terrible weather induced by a volcanic eruption in Iceland that all the seed corn was given to the cattle in order to prevent them from starving. Some islanders resorted to the time-honoured custom of thigging, relying on clan hospitality and solidarity: J. L. Buchanan, a missionary in the Outer Isles, complained in 1793 that 'swarms of women from Uist and the Small Isles came in the summer to sponge off people in Harris and Lewis'. According to the minister of the Small Isles, the situation was aggravated by overpopulation: there were 399 people on Eigg, although the register of births was neglected because people could not afford to pay the registration fee. In his opinion, the problem was due to early marriages which caused land to be divided to accommodate young families, reducing father and son to poverty as more and more people tried to derive a living from the land. The fact was that the Highlands and Islands had experienced a sharp growth in population within the last thirty years. A major cause was the relative prosperity brought about by the sales of cattle combined with the now widespread cultivation of the potato which offered a hedge against hunger and fed almost twice as many people as cereal crops for the same amount of land. People were therefore more resistant to the ravages of frequent diseases which the minister listed as fevers, catarrh, diarrhoea, erysipelas, dropsy, jaundice and measles. Croup, pleurisy and whooping cough were all too often fatal – around 1790, an epidemic of croup had swept away a great number of children on Eigg – and smallpox had decimated the island every twenty years until Dr MacAskill carried out vaccinations. In any case the longevity of Hebridean people was far superior to the British average, and whilst three score and ten was still considered the normal life-span, there were five octogenarians and one centenarian in the Small Isles at the time of the 1794 census.[8]

The minister was 'no Ennemy to a well regulated Emigration of the Poor and dispossessed Population', but he regretted that those who went were 'the more wealthy and substantial who want not the Necessaries of Life and might raise comfort by the same measure of Industries which they must exert in a distant land'.[9] There was little other option open to tacksmen's sons who could not obtain farms for themselves. The son of the change-house keeper on Eigg went to try his luck in Jamaica. In Laig, Angus MacDonald's cadet sons went to Australia, New Zealand and India. It was always the better-off amongst the tenants who provided the bulk of emigrants because they were those who could afford to go. Despite the wishes of the minister, the landless people who made up half the population of the parish were simply too poor to leave. The cottars lived on the land farmed by the tacksmen and tenants, and worked it in exchange for a small plot of land, on which they grazed one or two cows, and a share of the harvest: a quarter of the crop made with the plough (cereals), and a third of the crop worked with the *cas chrom*, generally potatoes. Craftsmen were in a better position to emigrate. There were quite a few trades in the parish: masons, carpenters, shoemakers as well as five boatbuilders and two smiths, one residing on Eigg, five tailors and fourteen weavers. Yet, population pressure had sent a good number amongst the poorer islanders to seek a better future in the Lowland cities where the developing textile industry was now offering employment. Many young people in the four islands had also taken to hiring themselves for seasonal work in Lowland farms. Girls especially went away in great numbers for the harvest and were away from Whitsunday to Martinmas. They brought back little more than new clothes, to the great annoyance of Rev. MacLean, who would rather have seen them hired as maids or employed at home in flax or woollen manufacture.

The minister was even more annoyed to see that the emigration fever spread without check, so much so that a dance had even been invented which mirrored the effect of the contagion. It was a reel called *America*, which began with just one couple and ended with the entire floor whirling and spinning together! As news of those who had emigrated earlier was good, their letters urging friends and relatives to come and join them, the emigration agents now scouring the Highlands and Islands for people to join the colonies of Upper Canada had no trouble finding willing recruits. Rev. Donald MacLean raged against those people, calling them 'the enemies of their Country', attracted only by 'the love of Lucre and other selfish views'. Their emissaries, he warned, were sent out among the people with the intention of raising everywhere 'the Spirit of Discontent and Dissatisfaction with their present situation which they infamously brand with the disgusting name of Slavery, and to invite them to a land of Freedom and Happiness . . . The people are led to believe that in America, they would find Perfect Equality, Liberty without control, no Lords, no Masters . . . that all who settle in His Majesty's colonies will have out of His Majesty's stores provisions for 12 months after landing as well as land rent-free for ever.'[10]

A son of Spanish John, Miles MacDonell – who had emigrated in 1770 – was one of these recruiters. He had returned to Scotland to recruit more people for Glengarry in Ontario where his kinsmen of the 1786 Knoydart emigration had settled. By March 1790, eighty-eight islanders had responded to the subscription he opened on Eigg. The tacksman of Laig was likewise busy organising for people to go to Nova Scotia and St John where his own kinsman Fr Angus MacEachen was preparing to go and serve the emigrants' spiritual needs in the New World. All the would-be emigrants being Catholics, there was some alarm in the Catholic hierarchy at losing so many in their Highland parishes. The Small Isles parish priest, Fr James MacDonald, explained how his islanders 'were glad to embark for Canada . . . It was not that they wanted to leave their native country for which they have – especially the commonality – a blind attachment but they were overjoyed at the thought that providence would procure for them in another corner of the world that relief and help that was refused to them in their own country.'[11]

The islanders made their preparations for departure, selling their cattle, disposing of their land and belongings. The cost of the passage was still within reach of most; £2, the price of a cow, taking one person across the Atlantic and £10 a family. The hardships of the past few winters would have decided many to sell up and go. On top of the bad harvest, it had been so miserably wet that no peat could be cut or dried and many had been reduced to burning straw and heather as well as furniture and house timber! From the 182 people who left the island between 1788 and 1790, twenty-eight left for St John on the *Lucy* and the *Jane* which left Druimindarroch near Arisaig on 12 July 1790.[12]

Amongst the total of 328 Clanranald tenants who emigrated and ultimately prospered in areas like Pictou, Antigonish and Judique in Nova Scotia was John MacDonald, his wife Effie and their four grown-up children, his two brothers, his sister and her husband, John Ban MacDougall. Generations later, the descendants of John MacDonald, one of the Laig MacDonalds, who had earned his land in Nova Scotia in the king's service, were still known by their nickname of Bogainn MacDonalds, from *Bog an Lochainn*, the name of a bird on Eigg, the water-ouzel, which can still be seen fishing in the Laig burn. The MacDonalds' reputation for going out fishing in all kinds of weather, already well established before they left Eigg, had become as proverbial in their new home as the behaviour of a little bird which spends half its life under water in their country of origin![13]

Meanwhile on Eigg, alarming rumours reached the island as the people who had subscribed to leave for Upper Canada prepared to follow. Fr James MacDonald reported that 'at the information of some malicious people, a King's Ship was ordered to the Coast at the time of Emigration to impress everyone fit for service. This frightened the emigrants so much that few of them went off. . . [because they] were afraid of being obliged to part with their families. So that after losing the half of their freight and some of them more, they remained in the Country without Lands, Cattle, Crop, houses, firing or even work.'[14]

As a result only fifteen adults and thirteen children from Eigg embarked on the *British Queen* which left Arisaig for Quebec on 16 August 1790. (The rest of its eighty-seven passengers came from Morar, Uist, Arisaig, Ardgour, Moidart and Knoydart. Amongst the Eigg crowd, Peggy MacDougall, Allan MacDonald, Donald MacDonald, John MacKinnon and Lachlan Campbell, most of them tenant farmers, all left with their families for a fresh start in the New World, but with very little money between them.[15]) Their late departure meant that the *British Queen* only reached Quebec in mid-October, at the beginning of the winter season. As soon as they arrived,

Miles MacDonell, the emigrant leader, was forced to address an emergency petition to the governor of Quebec on behalf of the Eigg emigrants, describing the oppression which had driven them to Canada. 'They must inevitably Starve this Winter unless some Provision shall be made for them. They wish to go up above Montreal where many of their Countrymen, who arrived here as Passengers four years ago, are already settled.' Concerned that the emigrants might become a public burden, the Colonial authorities provided them with transport to Montreal. There the emigrants were reduced to throwing themselves on the charity of the public. The Montreal merchants responded generously and the Eigg emigrants managed to survive that first winter, settling in that part of Glengarry county which came to be called Eigg Road.[16]

THE PRESS-GANG COMES TO EIGG

The fear of the press-gangs which had prevented some islanders from boarding the emigrant ships in 1790 proved only too justified a few years later. Some recruiting for the British army had been carried out in the Small Isles by the minister in his capacity as a Deputy Lieutenant for the county of Inverness, but the steady flow of emigration made it difficult: 'we shall be deprived in future Emergencies of their invaluable Services towards keeping at a distance the inveterate Enemies of all we hold dear and towards checking a spurt of Licentiousness at home', he declared in an anti-emigration tract.[17] The fact was that no Eigg men, nor any from the Clanranald estates, would contemplate enlisting in a Campbell regiment although a few had taken commissions in the Frazer regiment, and the Clanranald chiefs had not taken part in the raising of the dozen Highland regiments which had occurred since 1757.

However, when Alexander MacDonald of Sleat was told that his credit in London would be greatly enhanced if he could raise a regiment in his name, he effectively combined offers of enlisting bounty and threats of eviction to raise a thousand men in seven weeks. But with the start of the Peninsular Wars in 1793, the chief found numbers on his land much reduced by eviction and emigration and took to recruiting on Eigg and Canna by force. Away in Geneva, John of Clanranald did not care much and neither did the board of Edinburgh trustees who acted as tutors for his son Reginald-George after his premature death in 1794.

Tradition recalls how the Sleat press-gang had already taken away many islanders when Donald Gorm (on Eigg every chief of Sleat was called Donald Gorm) came to the island of Eigg one more time. The press-gang took with them the last son of a poor widow who had already lost three sons to the war. She pleaded all she could but her tears would not move Donald Gorm. When the widow saw that, she broke into a fury and lashed bitter curses at him. Going to Kildonnan Point to see her son for the last time, she gave vent to her feelings in an improvised lament as she stood watching the press-gang ship disappear from sight:

> And hiuraibh o, I am suffering
> Alack I am in misery
> Since the day at the point of the White Port.

> And hiuraibh o, I am suffering
> And Donald Gorm though you have wronged me
> For you I am only one of many.

And hiuraibh o, I am suffering
Though you have taken the three from me,
With their father mouldering in the earth.

And hiuraibh o, I am suffering
And you got John and you got Donald,
And young Alasdair of the fair hair.

And hiuraibh o, I am suffering,
But if you had just left me Hector,
I would not mourn the others
And hiuraibh o, I am suffering.

The widow's curses were not to be in vain. 'One fine day in Spain, just before the battle, as the two armies were drawn face to face in battle order, Donald Gorm was riding up and down in front of his company. He was feeling in tremendous form, feeling just as strong and healthy as a deer in the hill as he sat in the saddle, and he glanced over his shoulder at the young men drawn up in ranks, and with a slap on his thigh, he said this: "Ha, what good luck the widow's curses are bringing me!" Hardly had he let the words out of his mouth than a single shot came from a great gun in the French battery over against them, and struck Donald Gorm just like that and his carcase fell in pieces into the dust at the feet of the young men he had commanded . . . That was the end Donald Gorm came to. He left his dust in Spain where there fell many a better man than he,' told Hugh MacKinnon.[18]

Another, darker story of jealousy and revenge recalls how one man in the township of Braigh above Kildonnan had used the arrival of the press-gang as an opportunity to get rid of his stepson. Knowing that his wife was hiding her son in a barn, he denounced him to the press-gang. But the young man, requesting permission at the last minute to bid farewell to his family, took that opportunity to plunge a dirk into his stepfather's heart.[19]

As the Peninsular Wars went on, it was soon the Navy's turn to send their press-gang around the island to find more recruits. The Navy ships took great glee in practising their firing on targets such as the rocks below the Sgurr in Grulin or the cross of St Columba in Canna, which had one of its arms broken in this way, and several cannonballs retrieved on the island bear testimony to their efforts. As often as not, these shots served as a warning for all the island men of recruiting age to run and hide. Unfortunately, sometimes they did not have so much warning and they had to resort to other tactics to evade them. The name of a rock near Laig Point recalls the trick used by an islander caught unawares in Hulin. He ran all the way to the point thinking that he could safely hide from the press-gang in the Pigeon's Cave, just past the point. But his pursuers were hot on his heels and, in desperation, he suddenly jumped into the sea and swam towards the half-submerged rocks by the point. The press-gang men were unable to make out his head among the rocks in the turbulent sea and he managed to escape out of sight. The rock behind which he disappeared is still called Clach an t-Sionnaich (the Fox's rock) in memory of the ruse which had outfoxed the Navy.

Other islanders were not to be so lucky. The press-gang recruiters managed to catch a young man who lived in Grulin with his old widowed mother. The poor woman was in despair to see her only child go, and he was in despair to leave her in the knowledge that his departure would make her destitute, depending on the charity of her neighbours. Seeing this, one of her neighbours offered to take her son's place. He was Finlay MacCormick, Hugh MacKinnon's relative. He went and nothing more was heard of him, many years passing without anyone knowing whether he was dead or alive, until a party of islanders went one day to fetch some stores in Sleat on the isle of Skye. There they met a veteran of the Spanish campaigns and they enquired about Finlay. It turned out that Finlay and the veteran had fought alongside each other in the Pyrenees. Finlay had been badly wounded and, with the help of his friend, he sought the shelter of a shepherd's bothy for the night. Unfortunately when the army marched on, the man had been forced to leave Finlay behind and he was sorry to say that he had most certainly died there.

A small relic of the Peninsular Wars was found on Eigg by Neil MacDonald, the Barra shepherd who lived on the island for thirty years until his death in 1986. In the deer grass cladding the hills near the Sgurr, he found a tiny little silver coin, the size of a 5p coin. It was French, dated from Year 3 of the new Republic, 1792, and bore the effigy of Bonaparte as its first consul.

GOLD FROM THE SEA

The Peninsular Wars had a tremendous effect on the islanders' life, as the islands and coastal regions now saw their economy shaped by events happening thousands of miles away. The demand for Hebridean kelp started to rise when the war with France cut off the main source of cheap alkali, barilla from Spain. As the islanders were turning into full-time kelpers, it no longer mattered how many people crowded onto the land: more and more hands were needed as the demand for kelp developed into a real boom.

By 1798, Cleadale was producing half a ton of kelp a year whilst Hulin, Laig, Kildonnan, Galmisdale and Grulin sent away a ton a year each.[20] The best kelp was made in Castle Island, which was no longer a quiet place for summer shielings but the scene of frenzied kelping activity. From April to August men, women and children were employed in harvesting the seaweed from which kelp was manufactured. They gathered the bladder-wrack and sea-tangle which was cast up by the sea in great abundance after the spring storms. They also cut the seaweed off the rocks at low tide, harvesting one section of the shore at a time in a three-year rotation, since it took that time for sea-tangle to grow back again. No offshore reef was too far to be harvested, and boats laden with the heavy weed were brought ashore at each landing place. The seaweed was then taken off by the creel-load by women and ponies and carried high up on the grass to dry. Once it was completely dried, it was finally put to burn slowly between two layers of peat in the kelp kilns, long trenches dug into the ground in the foreshore. An even temperature had to be maintained throughout the burning, and this last operation required a good deal of patience and skill. It took quite a long while for the seaweed to produce a slimy liquid which accumulated at the bottom of the kilns and hardened into the brittle substance which was the precious kelp.

It took 20 tons of wet weed – about fifty cart-loads – to produce the valuable alkali which was then shipped away to Liverpool. As a source of potash, kelp was used for all sorts of things, from the bleaching of linen to the manufacture of soap, alum, glass and gunpowder, the last being produced in increasing quantities as the Wars wore on. Consequently every bit of seaweed was saved for making kelp. Kelp officers were appointed to inspect the kelp shores, weigh the seaweed and strictly apportion it for manure on the orders of the tutors of Clanranald. Any tangle or wrack which was washed up on the shore had to be equally shared and no one was allowed to help himself before the others on pain of eviction. Kelp came first and foremost and any trick was good enough to get more of it. When Angus MacDonald of Laig realised that seaweed tended to accumulate at the mouth of the burn next to his land, he promptly resorted to changing the course of the burn running through his land so that it ran directly into the sea and he could claim more of the seaweed coming ashore. As for those who harvested kelp in Talm at the north end of the island, they had to be on the look-out for the men of Sleat who used to sneak there on their boats to cut the tangle on Eilean Thuilm (Seal Island) which they claimed belonged to nobody.

When kelping first started in the 1760s, the tacksmen had pocketed the profits which amounted then to little more than two guineas a ton. Then Ranald, the 18th chief of Clanranald, moved in to take his cut: 10s per ton of kelp produced and another 10s per ton carriage on his vessels, thus reducing the tacksmen's profits by half. However, since the price of kelp kept rising steadily, the tacksmen's profits rose accordingly and toasts were drunk to a high price for kelp as well as cattle at every festive occasion. By the end of the 1790s, the price of kelp had risen so much that the tutors of Reginald-George were able to treble the rents throughout the Clanranald lands. They also agreed to prosecute anyone carrying seaweed for manure, to encourage the tenants best at producing kelp and to remove those who manufactured a low-quality product. Anyone who paid more than the price which was fixed by them would incur a fine. Money had to be made, for John the 19th chief had left debts in excess of £70,000 after his death.[21]

As landlords had now taken complete control of the kelp industry, the rising price of kelp was no longer an incentive for tenants to remain on the islands. On Eigg as everywhere else it only meant that the wages received from kelping had to go towards paying a higher rent for which the yearly sale of a stirk was no longer sufficient to pay. The price of a cow was now £2 8s, the average rent was around £5 a year, whilst the most a family could hope to derive from kelping was £2, or £6 at the very height of the kelp boom. Out of the money which was left after paying the rent, meal still had to be bought, and in ever greater quantity since the islanders were being forced into full-time kelping to the detriment of tillage. The summer months were spent at the shore instead of working the land to its maximum capacity, and the land itself deprived of a valuable source of manure started to produce less and less.

The overall result was that in 1801, emigration flared dramatically again, helped by the efforts of the recruiting agents. Fortunes were made by agents cramming people into holds that had carried slaves in better conditions. Ships like the *Sarah* and the *Dove* which numbered Eigg folk amongst their 700 passengers were notorious for the awful conditions experienced by their passengers. Not only were they subjected to outbreaks of diseases like smallpox and whooping cough, which killed the weakest, but they also had to endure the threat of Royal Navy press-gangs who boarded the emigrant ships in mid-ocean to wrench some of the fitter men from their families for the war! The ships were so unseaworthy that accidents happened frequently, as when a ship sank off Gourock with an Eigg emigrant on board, a great-great-grandfather of Hugh MacKinnon's who was also called Hugh. He and his family were amongst the few who were rescued, but as the sinking of the ship left them bereft of their meagre possessions, it took ten years for the 'Black MacKinnons' (they were all dark-haired) to work their way back to their native island again! In spite of these dreadful conditions, the flow of emigrants from Eigg to Nova

Scotia and Cape Breton was to remain constant until the end of the century, so much so that the hilly district at the back of Antigonish came to be known as Eigg Mountain from that time onwards.[22]

Hebridean landlords were now greatly alarmed by this loss of their potential workforce. The trustees of Clanranald, who by then derived more income from kelp than from land-rents, were told that kelping would cease altogether if the present rate of population leaving the country continued.[23] Consequently, the kelping landlords immediately started lobbying Parliament to change the emigration laws in their favour and prevent the stream of emigrants from leaving the country continued. Their demands were promptly answered by the Passenger Act of 1803. With the price of passage to North America rising above what the average tenant could afford, emigration soon ground to a halt.

In the meantime, the price of kelp had soared from £10 in 1801 to £20 a ton in 1811. Clanranald – who had come to his majority in 1810 – and his fellow island proprietors became possessed by a real kelping fever. Having stopped the flow of emigration, they next sought to increase their workforce in order to tap this seemingly inexhaustible source of wealth, a wealth which Reginald-George would quickly dissipate at the gaming tables in Brighton. The general opinion was that 'immense sums could be drawn from the ocean and its rocky shores equal at least to the produce of the soil' and that 'the greater the number employed the better' since 'so much more would arise from the produce of their labour'.[24] And immense these sums were indeed: Clanranald derived £42,000 from all the kelp harvested in his estates between 1808 and 1810 alone. His bills for wages and shipping did not exceed a quarter of the price he received for each ton of kelp sold. As sole buyer of the crop, he had his workforce under total control, like all other Hebridean proprietors, and nothing prevented him from paying them the pittance which they received in compensation for their arduous labour. A traveller to the Hebrides at that time actually compared the kelpers' condition to a state worse than slavery: 'for hours together, wet to the knees and elbows with nothing more to eat than oatmeal and water and occasionally fish, limpets and crabs, sleeping on the damp floor of a wretched hut'.[25] The prosperity brought by kelp certainly did not filter further down than the tacksmen. And whilst Angus MacDonald praised his chief in Laig, his banker cousin, MacDonald of Dalilea, accused him of romantic naivety, for Reginald-George was more concerned with his rights as an absentee landlord than with the necessary duties of a chief, which had been quickly forgotten in the course of an education in Edinburgh and Eton. He was not concerned that the fertility of his estates was going to decline dramatically as the islanders turned into full-time kelpers with no time to work the land and no right to manure it with seaweed.

THE ISLAND'S FIRST CROFTS

Whilst the landowners were now writing the price of kelp in their leases, they also reserved their right to employ 'others not holding land' to compete with the existing tenants for the raw weed. Indeed, for each islander who had gone away to the colonies, there had been a number of people applying for the vacated land. It soon appeared that the best way to accommodate as many people as possible on the land was to replace the last of the joint-farms with single holdings held by individual tenants. Such tenants would therefore be more sensitive to rent increases and, in consequence, work all the harder at the kelping. This had the added advantage of doing away with the runrig system which had long been criticised as a lazy, uncompetitive way of farming.

The 20th chief put this theory into practice first of all on Muck, which had exported 20 tons of kelp every third year since the 1780s. His father had acquired the island in 1799 in payment of debts owed to him by its absentee owner, Lachlan MacLean, VI of Muck, governor of the Tower of London. Although Muck exported barley and oats in a good quantity, kelp was more valuable, and in 1809 the island's twenty-four tacks were soon divided into forty-seven plots for kelping families. A year later, Dr MacAskill was entrusted by Reginald-George with the task of dividing Cleadale at the north end of the island into similar plots. These were to be the island's first crofts, by definition individual holdings of enclosed land, with a share in a common grazing, of an acreage small enough to oblige their occupants to engage in kelping or any other form of money-making activity ultimately benefiting the landlord.

It could not have been an easy task for Dr MacAskill to apportion what had been one tack and a joint-farm cultivated under the runrig system into strips of equivalent value, enough land being taken out of Hulin farm to make three extra crofts. The strength of the old system had been to take into account the unequal value of the soil: the joint-farm of Cleadale and the tack of Knockeiltach were a patchwork of boggy meadows, grassy hillocks and fertile hollows stretching from the basalt cliffs to the edge of the sea. The ground which had been occupied by no more than a dozen tenants fifty years earlier was now shared out between twenty-seven families plus the Catholic priest, 150 people altogether. The twenty-eight crofts ranged from £3 to £14 in value, at a rate of about £1 per acre with nine plots under 5 acres and six over 10 acres.[26] This did not include the hill grazing which was added on top of that in a communal form, for it would have been too difficult to apportion it amongst so many people. Grazing was actually where the crofters were at a marked disadvantage compared with the island farms. The farms' proportion of grazing to arable was at least double what the crofters had now at their disposal: only 199 acres of grazing for 191 acres of arable. Four years earlier Cleadale had comprised 194 acres of arable, 209 acres of pastures and 397 acres of moor on Beinn Bhuidhe. The crofters had thus lost all the moor grazing to the adjacent farms, Hulin and Kildonnan. They also lost the ground for their summer shielings in Struidh, and the practice of yearly emigration to the hills was abandoned as all hands were needed for the kelp. The result was that they found it increasingly harder to derive their sustenance from the land.

The new division of land had the effect of completely changing the landscape of that part of the island. Where there had been two clachans of ten or eleven buildings fairly close together, one in Cleadale and the other in Knockeiltach, surrounded by enclosed infields of various shapes and sizes which followed the nature of the ground, there was now a grid of narrow parallel strips. The stone walls which neatly separated them from each other stretched across bogs and hillocks right from the base of the Cleadale cliffs. Each strip had a house built on it, standing in isolation from its neighbour, such a completely alien way of building that the three neighbours near Cnoc an Sitheanan managed in the end to build their houses close enough to reproduce the old clachan structure where neighbourliness had been so important. The common grazing was established on Druim na Chroise, just before the farm of Five Pennies, where ponies could now graze. Tradition reports that Dr MacAskill gave the best croft to Neil MacQuarrie because he was married to his daughter Margaret. In fact this former Lieutenant in the Militia had actually wedded a daughter of the Minginish MacAskills brought over from Skye by Revd MacAskill to work his Glebe. Neil's croft certainly included a good part of the best land that side of the island, the former tack of Knockeiltach. With a rent of £12 a year, it was also among the biggest crofts and could support four or five ponies and as many cows with their followers, whilst the smallest crofts could only support two ponies and two cows. The division into crofts was also carried out in Galmisdale and Grulin, but without the re-arranging of land into strips which had occurred on the North end of the island. Whatever the circumstances, Dr MacAskill had no part in it, for he was to perish in October 1817.

The story was that Dr MacAskill had gone to attend the autumn cattle fair in Arisaig, but that instead of returning with his nephew Allan, the tacksman of Laig, he chose to come back on the *Dubh Ghleannag*, MacDonald of Glenaladale's famous boat. But that night, the *Dubh Ghleannag* was hit by a sudden squall as she rounded Kildonnan Point. She was taken aback, the sail went and struck the mast, and she turned over, going down in no time at all. Everyone on board was drowned, except for Angus Òg, Hugh MacKinnon's great-grandfather, and a tailor from Arisaig who grabbed the tail of a cow which had been brought back from the fair, and floated after her when she made for the shore. The poor doctor was found the next day on the beach. He had died of a heart attack after trying to swim ashore in his heavy blue cloak.[27]

A REDUNDANT POPULATION

In spite of their efforts and hopes, the Hebridean proprietors were unable to make the kelp boom last after the end of the Peninsular Wars. By 1815, imports of cheap alkali were resumed to the benefit of the English market, and the price of kelp went down to £10 a ton. When a method for producing an even cheaper alkali from salt was discovered, it plummeted to £4 and even £3 a ton. Eigg was still producing 17 tons of kelp a year at £4 a ton, but by 1822 Clanranald found himself obliged to provide supplies of meal and tobacco to his half of his Cleadale kelpers in order for production to continue.[28]

Of all the people involved in the production of kelp, crofter-kelpers naturally found themselves the worst affected by the fall in the price of kelp. They were already treading dangerously close to the brink of destitution, for, as Clanranald's factor had already noted in 1813, 'if the kelp is to be given up, the small tenants cannot continue to pay the present rents, because the work they got enabled them to pay for portions of ground so small that they could pay nothing from the produce'.[29] The disastrous fall in cattle prices in the years following the Peninsular Wars contributed to worsening the situation. It became so difficult to meet the rent that many started to accumulate arrears beyond any hope of ever paying them back. Throughout the Clanranald estates, factors reported that those who found themselves in such a desperate situation slumped into a state of depression so deep that they ceased to make any effort towards their rent. The Cleadale kelpers in particular were in a terrible state of poverty: the kelp which they were making only paid part of their rents and they were deep in arrears.

Meanwhile, Hebridean landlords were trying to explore new sources of revenue. Some thought about manufacturing an alkali out of coal, salt and sulphuric acid in an attempt to rival cheap Spanish kelp. This was perhaps what the Clanranald trustees had in mind when they reserved for themselves the power to search for coal, freestone, lime and any other mineral when a lease was drawn in 1819 for the new tenant who replaced Dr MacAskill at Kildonnan. Sheep farming soon became the most obvious choice to bring in revenue. Everywhere else in the Highlands the blackface sheep had given the owners of the cleared lands a handsome source of profit, and the kelping landlords decided to follow suit. By now the 20th chief of Clanranald was depending more than ever on a high income, becoming a Member of Parliament for the rotten borough of Plympton, Devonshire, in 1812 after marrying the daughter of the Earl of Mount-Edgcumbe. He derived a considerable income from his estates, in the region of £20,000 a year,[30] but to be included in the Prince Regent's circle required even more. Spending at the gaming tables in Brighton was proving very costly indeed for his entourage. Reginald-George, who had hitherto left the management of his Hebridean estates to his board of trustees, took the decision to sell after acquiring the superiority of his lands back from the Duke of Argyll in 1805. That same year, William Bald, a talented young mapmaker, was instructed to produce detailed maps of Eigg and Canna in view of an extensive survey of the Clanranald lands prior to a sale. As land was parcelled up and sold, island by island, former tacks became new estates. Eigg was advertised for sale in 1824 as a perfect pasture for 'fine woollen sheep' with good arable land for turnip husbandry. The following year, the advertisement was less succinct and waxed lyrical on the suitability of the island for sheep farming. 'There was no spot in the west better adapted to the rearing of stock. Black cattle and sheep might be reared under peculiar advantages, and by the introduction of Cheviot sheep and some consequent slight alternations in the management of the farms on Eigg, the value of the land might be greatly increased. The pasture of the island is of the best quality while the arable land is not only of an extent sufficient to support the inhabitants of the island, but well adapted for the produce of turnip crops for the feeding of stock. Part of the island is upon a limestone bottom of superior quality and the grouse shooting upon the moorish part of the island is of the best kind . . . A good deal of Kelp is manufactured on the island of Eigg and Canna and is of very superior quality and there is good reason to suppose that the quality might be considerably increased, and in the last place, it may be observed that the occupiers of the land have had such employment and considerable profits from the herring and other fishing and which consequently may be assumed as a local advantage adding considerably to the value of the farm.'[31]

This was an optimistic survey: two of the island farmers, Allan MacDonald of Laig and Lachlan MacKinnon in Hulin, owed more than a year in rent arrears. Allan was pretty reckless with money, living in great style, but according to tradition much above his means. Lachlan MacKinnon had embarked on sheep farming without previous experience and was losing more than he was making with the sale of his sheep. The self-sufficient population was experiencing a lot of difficulty in supporting itself, the Cleadale kelpers in particular were in a terrible state of poverty: the kelp which they were making only paid part of their rents and they were deep in arrears. In all likelihood, the 'slight alterations' suggested by the sale advertisement were of the kind mentioned by Duncan Shaw, the estate factor, in a letter to the Clanranald trustees in 1826. He recommended the clearance of 150 people in Cleadale to make way for pasture land along with the disposal of 200 more in Sanday, Canna, who were equally wretched, as well as the 2,000 people in South Uist and Benbecula, all 'swarms of idle tenants'. This represented almost half the population of the four islands mentioned! Since the Clanranald funds were unable to pay for this wholesale deportation to Cape Breton, government assistance was sought at the rate of £2 per person.[32] Such a demand represented a total reversal of attitude from Clanranald's earlier stand at the height of the kelp boom. Predictably enough, the government refused its help, but continual pressure finally resulted in the removal in 1827 of any restriction imposed on emigration by the Passenger Act.

Rather than wait, some proprietors preferred to pay their tenants' passage themselves. On Rum, 300 inhabitants – described only a decade earlier as 'the happiest people on earth' by the famous geologist George MacCullough – were cleared to Cape Breton in 1826 to make room for 8,000 sheep. More humane than most, MacLean of Coll had allotted a seven-week supply of food per person. The last of the Rumach – only one family was to be left on the island – sought to leave a mark on the land of their ancestors from which they parted with so much grief. In one last symbolic gesture they rolled an enormous boulder – probably the *Clach Cuid Fir*, the manhood stone – to a prominent place not far from Kilmory where it still stands near the road, although few know of its origin today.[33] MacLean of Coll gaining a profit of £500 a year, the operation was repeated on Muck, which was leased to the famous Lochaber drover, Corriechoille. One hundred and fifty people were offered assistance to emigrate, but many of Muck's former kelpers preferred to build themselves huts in the village of Kiel near the harbour, where they managed to stave off emigration for a while longer. It is said that there were no fewer than thirty pipers in that crowded little village.

The 200 miserable crofters of Sanday in Canna were next to be shipped away by their new proprietor, Donald Mac Neil, who forbade more than one family in each house and any subdivision of crofts to the rest of the population, which meant that many more were obliged to leave. Within the parish of the Small Isles, the Cleadale crofters were to be the only people to obtain a reprieve from the threat of eviction, for the island was sold before Duncan Shaw's eviction measures had time to be implemented.

Eigg was bought for £15,000 in 1827 by Hugh MacPherson, Sub-Principal of King's College, Aberdeen University, where he held the chairs of Hebrew and Greek. He was not wealthy, with a large family of 12 children, but he was well connected, having married a MacLeod of Talisker, whilst his uncle and benefactor, Sir John MacPherson, had earned a knigthhood and a large fortune in India at the service of the Nawab of Carnatie, some of which may have helped in the purchase of an island which Hugh had admired as a youngster when living in Sleat on Skye. He was only to pay a few visits to his new estate, yet he made a point of visiting the islanders and speaking in Gaelic with them. Ironically, the sale of Eigg to Dr MacPherson was to settle an old score between his family and the Clanranalds, for the new owner came from a famous clerical family descended from a renowned Sleat warrior who fought for the MacLeods, Ian Ban MacPherson. His great-great-grandfather had been the Rev. Martin MacPherson, an outspoken minister in South Uist who had criticised the chief in his sermons. He woke up one morning to find his cattle and possessions gone. Eighty cows, eighty-eight sheep and lambs, and thirteen horses had been stolen together with utensils, corn and teinds to the value of 1,017 merks by John of Moidart in retaliation for the minister's criticism. The irate cleric left South Uist to seek the protection of MacLeod of Dunvegan, and presented a petition to the sheriff of the Western Isles, even to Parliament – but to no avail, for he never obtained redress. But as 400 years of Clanranald ownership ended, the wheel of fortune turned in favour of his descendants. The prophecy had indeed come to pass which an old seer in Uist had made at the time of the 1715 rebellion and for which he had been put to death. Reading a sheep's shoulder blade, he had predicted that the time would come when Clanranald's property would break into many little fragments. Of the ancestral lands Reginald-George had inherited from his forebears, nothing was now left apart from the ruins of Castle Tioram, and even these were to be sold later on.

Chapter 6

REVIVAL AND FAMINE

The sale of the island did not affect its inhabitants much at first. Dr MacPherson's lawyer had found the island better for cattle than sheep but in sore need of draining and improving. He established a rent of 12s 6d per arable acre, recommended fewer and larger farms and instructed the tenants to destroy hooded crows, ravens and eagles to promote game on the island. On the whole, the islanders, whose 'entire lack of agricultural knowledge' he deplored, were left alone. But all was not well: the tenants of Laig and Hulin who were £366 in arrears were unwilling to continue occupation of the land if they were not given a considerable reduction in rent. Dr MacPherson conceded the reduction but the two tenants were still persecuted for their arrears by Duncan Shaw, Clanranald's factor, even though Lachlan MacKinnon was claiming for 'meliorations to the ground', such as the building of his fine house in Hulin, against his arrears.[1] This refusal on the part of proprietors to consider improvements undertaken by tenants was a common source of dispute, so that many tenants did not bother improving houses or land in the knowledge that they would receive little or no compensation for their efforts. The outcome of the dispute was that Lachlan MacKinnon was forced to give up Hulin and died in poverty a few years later. The farm was then added to Kildonnan which was leased to John MacDonald of Balranald, the South Uist tacksman who had succeeded Dr MacAskill. The Rev. Neil MacLean was now at the manse, farming Sandavore with Castle Island as an added pasture.

Penning the *New Statistical Account* in 1831, the minister recorded few improvements in the parish: still no road, no village, no inn, except one on Eigg at Galmisdale, no churches, no post, no regular means of communication with the mainland. Most of the 1,015 inhabitants of the parish 'subsisted' on 240 to 320 bushels of potatoes a year, drawing their living from the annual sale of 300–400 head of cattle.[2] On Eigg, however, there were signs of improvement. Road-making had started on Eigg, employing all those who were in arrears of rent and no longer worked at the kelping. The parochial school was also renovated and extended. Classes had hitherto been conducted in an ordinary blackhouse in Sandaveg on what had been church land since the appointment of a parochial schoolmaster in 1792. The one-bedroom dwelling shared by the schoolmaster and his family was extended and an entire new wing was built to house the school in 1829, paid for by Dr MacPherson who contributed slates and windows for the entire building. The new proprietor was proving more conscientious in his duties than his predecessor since the erection of schools was by law the responsibility of the heritors of the land who had to share the costs with the principal tenants. The school was thus made very comfortable, reported the minister with a twinge of envy. Rev. MacLean took an even more jaundiced view of the rise in the schoolmaster's salary which went up to £30 in the course of a year. By comparison, he considered his annual stipend of £68 16s 11d 'a small living' in view of his expenses and the trouble he had of going from one island to another all year round. At least on Eigg he could now hold his services in the school, whereas on the other islands he was sometimes reduced to conducting them in the open air! The minister pointed out that the present schoolmaster was not conspicuous 'for his attention towards his scholars or his diligence in the discharge of his duty'. Parents often withheld their children from school in the knowledge that they made no progress under him, so that he seldom had more than twenty or thirty scholars. Some children remained at school until they were 15, but most left when they were 12, whilst girls often went into service as young as 11 years old.[3] Half the parish (600 people) still could not read or write. It was a situation which the Gaelic School Society, whose patron was none other than Reginald-George, the 20th chief of Clanranald, was keen to remedy, and from 1812 it had sent teachers throughout the Highlands and Islands with the express purpose of teaching reading and writing in Gaelic. Ninety-two Gaelic bibles and 105 Gaelic New Testaments had been sent to the Small Isles, a gesture much approved by the parish priest who noted that, 'whereas the islanders had formerly devoted the Sabbath entirely to idle conversation and frivolous amusements, they now regularly read the Scriptures, the parents being instructed by the children in many instances'.[4]

A new steading with byre and hayloft above it had also been built for the manse in 1830, financed by the Presbytery of Skye out of contributions levied from the heritors of the parish. This building with its graceful Georgian proportions and skilful stone masonry was better built than any of the surrounding blackhouses, but still the minister was not satisfied with his lot: because of its exposed situation, the manse needed more repairs than he could afford, and he much envied the only 'mansion house' in the parish, Donald MacNeil's new house on Canna, which featured a garden stocked with ornamental and fruit trees, the only trees growing on that island! By contrast, Eigg's new proprietor had been content with the conversion of a pair of cottages into a holiday lodge for his large family at Nead na Feannaig (the crow's nest), a place which commanded a good view of Galmisdale Point.

The island 'big houses' the minister described as tolerable, but even they suffered from the overcrowding which affected rich and poor alike. Kildonnan House offered a typical example of a traditional tacksman's household. Married with six children, John MacDonald of Balranald also had under his roof his mother, an old aunt, two granddaughters and an orphan boy from Sleat. He employed and housed a teacher from Luing; two local nurses; two house servants, one from Eigg, the other from Muck; a cook and a poultry woman from South Uist; a spinner, two herds, a dairy maid and a farm servant, all belonging to Eigg. On top of that, there was also the odd lodger! On the 143-acre farm, John MacDonald employed at least another dozen people, all residing in Braigh, the clachan above Kildonnan – five agricultural labourers, one herdsman and five of their older children who worked as farm servants. (One of these farmworkers was none other than Hugh MacKinnon's ancestor – also named Hugh MacKinnon – who had been rescued from his sinking emigrant ship and had found his way into John MacDonald's employment and had followed him all the way from South Uist when he took over the tack of Kildonnan, returning at last to Eigg after ten years.) By comparison, Laig Farm employed a modest nine house and farm servants, with two ploughmen and one herdsman on its 114 acres! At the other end of the scale, crofters had to make do with the one or two rooms of their blackhouses to house one or two elderly relatives, and sometimes a grown-up daughter or son with spouse and children as well as a servant or two with the nuclear family, which comprised four children on average, although six or seven children were common.[5] Three or four wooden box beds provided the necessary sleeping quarters in the tacksman's house as well as in the blackhouse, supplemented by more bedding in the barn if need be. In farmhouses, the kitchen was always big enough to house family and servants. In blackhouses, what room existed was found around the fire; they were certainly not crowded with unnecessary objects. Everything in them was strictly functional: a few stools and a bench, a couple of kists, a table to prepare rather than eat the food, the three-legged cast-iron pot and the griddle, a few creels to be mended and serving as seats, dairy implements, fishing gear and the spinning wheel. The main requirements of such living quarters were warmth and nightly shelter for people who spent their time largely out of doors. The only people who lived on their own were old cottars. Without any relatives, they depended on the charity of their neighbours as they could no longer cultivate what land they had, like 96-year-old Lachlan MacKay in Hulin. The parish minister, Rev. MacLean, counted ten paupers like him in the whole parish – five on Eigg – who lived in their hut or stayed with relatives. Listed on the Parochial Poor Roll, they received alms from a fund of 30s bequeathed by Allan MacAskill who had retired from the sea to Calgary on Mull, supplemented by the small proceeds of church fines collected throughout the parish.

Overcrowding was certainly becoming more and more of a problem on the island. Ten years after the *New Statistical Account*, the 1841 census recorded the highest population ever: 546 inhabitants, a little more than half the population of the four islands altogether, Eigg being the only island in the parish to have escaped clearances. Cleadale was still the most populated area on the island with eighteen crofts and a total of twenty-four households. Even though they produced excellent crops of potatoes, bere and barley, many crofters found it hard to pay their rent and fell into arrears.

This was not a situation which the new factor appointed for the island would tolerate. Duncan MacPherson, who came from the district of Tormore in Skye, was, like the notorious MacDonald of Tormore to whom he was related by marriage, an advocate of eviction as a method of land management. Tradition reports how his stock answer to anyone who found it difficult to pay their rent was 'whether they wanted to see the other side of Ardnamurchan Point'. The *croman* (the hunchback) – as MacPherson was called because of his stoop – came to be unanimously feared and detested on the island. He never let slip an opportunity to extract money from the crofters: the story was that, one day, he heard that John MacLeod (Iain Mac Dhonnachaidh), a crofter who was in arrears, had sold some stirks to Ewan MacAskill, the doctor's son who often came from Talisker in Skye where he had settled, to buy his cattle on Eigg. He gave John a good price and was about to leave when the *croman* appeared,

71

demanding his money. But Ewan was as tough and strong as his father and his uncles before him and he grabbed the factor's wrist as he was taking the money from the sale and he shook it so that all the coins went spilling onto the floor. The factor was then forced to kneel down, pick up every single coin and hand them back to John MacLeod, who was left in peace after this![6]

AN ILLICIT STILL ON THE ISLAND

The island craftsmen always fared somewhat better than crofters. The blacksmith, for example, lived in Cleadale (his descendants carried on with the trade until the Second World War). John Campbell could do all the work required by the crofters and farmers, making irons for the foot-plough and the peat-cutters, the chains to hang the pots above the fire, the cruisies and the rat-traps as well as shoeing horses and undertaking various repairs. All this was done in exchange for a yearly due from each of his customers, including the people of Muck. The crofters also had to supply the fuel in the form of peat which was turned into charcoal by slow combustion inside a closed chamber. The miller had a croft at Kildonnan. His mill was used by folk in Arisaig and Skye as well as the other islands. As often as not, he was paid in kind, keeping a tenth of the corn brought to be milled, since his customers seldom had money in their hands to pay him. One miller on Eigg – originally from Mull – also doubled up as joiner, making box beds, tables and chairs as well as being the local cartwright. However, most people on the island were adept at making their own furniture out of driftwood from the beach which they would turn into long lengths of planking in a saw pit which was installed on the shore in Cleadale.

A more widespread occupation was that of shoemaker. There were two in Cleadale, and another in Grulin. Visiting the island in 1845, Hugh Miller remarked how the shoes he saw being made on Eigg were shaped like little boats. They consisted of a sole of single leather stitched to the upper part with a thong of the same leather or, even better, of sealskin. Seeing his interest, the islanders set about making him a pair, accepting no payment: 'No, not from the Witness, there are not many who take our part, and the Witness does', they told him, as they all knew of his writing in support of the crofters. Enquiring about their deep madder colour, Miller was told that this was the result of tanning the leather with a brew of tormentil roots, which had to be changed three times.[7] The same tanning recipe was applied to fishing nets to prevent them from rotting. The whole process was very time-consuming, as a whole day was needed to collect enough roots for one brew. Fortunately, the plant grew everywhere – as it still does today – and the work was done as a communal activity. The hides, from Martinmas cattle killed for the winter, were supplied in turn by each household. Two pairs of shoes would last the year, since people walked barefoot a great deal of the time.

There were also weavers, one in Galmisdale and two in Cleadale. They were all women, weaving being considered more of a woman's trade. Weavers worked at home, although they would sometimes set their looms in the tacksman's house for the work needed. In the olden days, even the linen for women's mutches and shirts was spun and woven at home, but it was now imported since the collapse of the Scottish linen industry. Spinning, carding, teasing, dyeing and all wool work was definitely women's work and was undertaken during the long winter nights. Since the olden days, the few sheep which were kept on the land had always been the woman's property, as she was the one who disposed of their wool. In contrast, tailoring was a male trade.

One tailor in Cleadale, Eochain Caimbeul – Hector Campbell – was to be famous for wearing the kilt although he sewed mostly trousers!

Two merchants were recorded, one in Cleadale and the other in Galmisdale, both women who would have most certainly been selling whisky, a way to earn a living for widows. By 1841, however, Allan MacLeod had added a shop to his inn in Galmisdale and supplied essential goods like meal, tea, sugar and tobacco. He did not have far to go to get drink for the inn, for it was produced in an illicit still on the other side of the island. Such stills flourished in the Highlands and Islands at a time when whisky consumption averaged a pint a week for every person above 14 years of age in Scotland. There were two stills in the Small Isles alone, one on Muck and one on Eigg. The one on Eigg was owned by Neil MacQuarrie, who held one of the biggest crofts in Cleadale and on whose fertile ground barley would have grown very well. Tradition has it that Neil brought back his black pot from Inverness, which he went to fetch with his friend John Campbell the blacksmith. To be safe from the law, the maker of the black pot had to go several miles out of town before assembling all the parts which made up the still, and John the blacksmith would have been a great help.

Neil made his whisky in a little cave in the cliff below his croft to which he had conveniently diverted a burn. The cave is still called Uamh a' Bhriuthais – the cave of the distilling. However, all those who made or sold illicit whisky had to be on the look-out for the long arm of the law, and they had to be wary of the excisemen, the gaugers who prowled through the Highlands and Islands in the hope of catching them.

'The gauger used to come to the island from time to time, and he had some sort of suspicion that Neil was making whisky for himself, a thing that was certainly not allowed by the Law, but he had never caught him. It was said – I used to hear them speaking about it, my mother and my mother's brother, they were his grandchildren anyway', told Hugh MacKinnon. 'This time the gauger came ashore on the other side of the island but before the gauger got across, a message had reached Neil that he was on the island. And at that very time, Neil's wife was in bed after bringing a child into the world two days before. And Neil, the decent man, he had a cask of whisky full to the brim in the house at that very moment. And he had not the faintest idea where he was going to hide the cask from the gauger, but he decided what he would do. He got the cask of whisky and rolled it under the bed where his wife was lying. The gauger came to the house and they gave each other a sincere, friendly greeting, and says he: "well, Neil, have you anything just now?"

– "Oh no, I haven't a thing!" said Neil. "You needn't come here looking for whisky today, but anyway, come in for a while."

And he brought the gauger into the very room where his wife was lying in bed. And they sat down to talk and he turned to the gauger and said: "oh here's my wife, she has just brought a child into the world the day before yesterday".

– "Oh good God!" said the gauger. "I'm not going to stay there, bothering a poor woman who has just brought a child into the world two days ago." And out he went without the least suspicion that the cask of whisky was under the bed the woman was lying in.'[8]

According to Hugh MacKinnon, his great-grandfather Neil had been fond of a dram himself. 'Of all the pleasures the best, horo for the barley bree which sets my head on the spree', went Alasdair Mac Mhaighstir Alasdair's famous 'Song to the Dram'. It was a song that Neil made his very own. Many a man would have had a taste of 'the rich result of the distilling' because of Neil's fondness for the barley bree, remarked Hugh. John the blacksmith, with whom he often did the distilling, was his faithful drinking companion. One night after a session in Neil's house, the blacksmith was a little unsteady on his feet and Neil decided to take him home but, lo and behold, it was then Neil's turn to feel a little faint and the blacksmith felt he had to help him home in his turn. And so they ended up conveying each other home all night long. Neil's whisky had the reputation of being very good and it was in great demand for weddings and funerals, even as far as the east coast and certainly in the Small Isles. Indeed it happened that one day a Canna man came to see Neil about some whisky for his wedding on the island. But when Eochainn Mór (Hector MacKinnon) saw Neil's daughter Christina, he changed his mind about his wedding on Canna and decided to marry her instead! Neil MacQuarrie's black pot is now said to be buried under the earthen floor of a Cuagach blackhouse.

Neil was by no means the only man to be fond of his dram on Eigg. Allan MacDonald in Laig and Donald MacLean, the Small Isles minister, patronised the island inn, 'a ruinous two-gabled house' in Galmisdale. Whenever the islanders saw Allan's horse tethered outside, they knew that the minister was there too, 'imbibing peat-reek and whisky'. Allan of Laig was prodigiously strong, like his MacAskill uncles, and he had had a few fights in his time. One story was that, 'meeting with another Highland gentleman in Edinburgh, he overheard some sneering remarks passed by a party of young bears at Celts in general and the barbarity of their language in particular . . . A rough scrimmage followed, during which the waiters fled from the room, leaving the combatants to themselves. The civilians got their heads broken and had to retreat, but the damage to the crystal and furniture was much greater, everything in the room being a complete wreck . . . The landlord then appeared who, after grimly surveying the desolation among his household goods, advanced towards Allan and his friend, but instead of storming at them or suggesting compensation for his loss, cheerfully congratulated them on the excellent lesson bestowed on their adversaries, [being] a Highlander himself.'[9] Allan was certainly wild 'and cross-grained too', tells Hugh MacKinnon: 'There was one night when he was coming home from the other side of the island, from Galmisdale . . . and he was drunk. And he was going down by [the Laig short cut], coming to a place which we called Bealach Airigh Leir, and his own cattle were round about him there. The night was dark and he was stone blind drunk and he stumbled across this thing and a fight started and he did not know what on earth [his opponent could be] . . . He thought it was the devil he had run into. But the end of the matter was that he pushed this awful thing that was fighting with him, he pushed him over the cliff at a place we call Sloc Huilimgearraidh. And he went home and he told them there about the terrible thing that had met him up at the mouth of the Bealach. But the next morning when the household got up and went outside, the cowherd went up to look – there was no sign of the bull. And they looked everywhere for the bull, dead or alive, but at last they went up that way and it was found dead at the bottom of the gorge in Sloc Huilimgearraidh. It was the bull he had been fighting with in the night and he had thrown the bull over the cliff . . . He did that, sure enough!'[10]

Allan's strength and drinking habits were eventually to cause his demise. Hearing that his sister Mary was unhappy with the Englishman she had married, Allan set off at once to fetch her back before she left with him for India. From Arisaig to Leith, a journey of 140 miles, he never left the saddle once, stopping to jump from one horse to another in the change-houses along the way. Alas, he finally reached the port of Leith to see the ship leaving just as he arrived. There was nothing he could do but turn back and return to Eigg, where news eventually came that Mary had been taken ill during the journey and died, her body being buried at sea. Allan, who had come back with a very sore backside indeed, fell ill in his turn when his sores became infected. He was told that his injuries would never heal unless he gave up the dram, but that he could not do, 'fierce and wild as he was' and that was the end of him.[11]

THE FREE CHURCH ON EIGG

An islander walking back from the harbour one evening suddenly heard a galloping noise as he passed the manse. He stopped and saw a fearful vision: three black horses crossed the road in front of him making for the minister's steadings. They were ridden by three black headless riders, their bodies facing the wrong way. Two events happened on the island soon afterwards which were deemed to have been heralded by this strange vision. The first event was the trial of the Small Isles minister, for 'adultery, cursing, making use of irreverent oaths and drunkenness'. Donald MacLean's reputation as a heavy drinker and rumours about his patent neglect of duty had finally reached the Presbytery of Glenelg so that in 1833 a trial was arranged in the schoolhouse. In spite of unequivocal evidence the case dragged on until 1838 when he was finally deposed after committing the fatal mistake of appearing senselessly drunk in front of the General Assembly of the church in Edinburgh for one of his numerous appeals.

Five years later, the Rev. Swanson, the new minister presented to the Small Isles by Queen Victoria, left the Established Church to join other Evangelical ministers in the formation of the Free Church of Scotland. The Disruption of 1843 led to a new interpretation on the island of the vision of the three headless riders as its portent, unbeknown to the minister who had prided himself on having 'dispelled the islanders' dark superstitions'.

Until Swanson's arrival, the relationship between Catholics and Protestants on Eigg had been as cordial as the friendship between the Rev. MacLean and Allan MacDonald of Laig. The Catholics would jokingly urge Protestants to come over to them and 'have some religion, since it was palpable that they had none', and marriages occurred frequently between the two denominations. Fr Anthony MacDonald encouraged his congregation on the other islands to attend the minister's services. Loved and esteemed by all, the priest served the parish for forty-three years, and it was to honour his memory that the resting place of his funeral party was marked with a stone pillar on the road from Cleadale to Kildonnan.

From 1838, things took a different turn and sectarianism was brought into the island life. Fuelled by the minister's zealous anti-Catholicism, an unhealthy animosity grew between the two religious communities on Eigg. Belonging to the Evangelical movement which was now sweeping the Highlands and Islands, Swanson had indeed undertaken to 'import the animated life of the Reformation to Protestantism in his parish'. This meant fighting 'Popery' since 'its grand aim was to keep people in the grossest darkness' and bringing the Bible to the people in their own language.[12] To this end, the minister had a stone-and-turf bothy built at his expense in Sandaveg to serve as an alternative to the parochial school. The new school was welcomed enthusiastically and patronised by adults as well as children. Under the teaching of Donald MacKinnon, Eigg's first Gaelic schoolteacher and a native of Skye – where the Evangelical revival was particularly intense – more crofters found themselves able to learn to read and write than at any other times. As they now read the Bible in their own language, they came to realise that much in it was relevant to their situation of landless or oppressed tenants. This brought new converts to Swanson who like other Evangelists held decidedly anti-landlord views, a quasi-revolutionary attitude in the effervescent social climate of the Highlands and Islands where there was a mounting tension between the owners of the land and those who inhabited it without any right to it. Rev. Swanson could thus quote in one of his tracts the edifying example of one old Eiggach, who was won away from the Catholic Church. The other Catholics thought him mad when they saw him reading the Gaelic Bible and various Protestant tracts while tending his cattle, one or two cows only, crouching against a dyke or on top of a sunny hillock depending on the weather. The man died a Protestant, but his relatives made sure he was given a Catholic burial inside the ruined church at Kildonnan, placing a rude wooden cross on his grave for fear that his unanointed body might be taken away by evil spirits!

Swanson was certainly well loved by his parishioners for his unending dedication to the poorest among them. He visited them frequently, deploring how little the owner of the island was doing for them. As the only man in the Small Isles with medical knowledge, he attended to all. His sympathy also extended to social outcasts like a 'freebooter', once convicted for sheep stealing, who had arrived on Eigg one winter. Roderick MacKay had first been evicted from Muck where the factor had given him a boll of meal to get rid of him quietly, pulling down his house to prevent his return. The man then tried unsuccessfully to beg a living on the mainland with his two young boys before arriving at Kildonnan where his oldest son was the island miller. But Alexander MacKay did not want to hear of his father's plea for help, and in the end, Roderick built himself a flimsy shelter on the beach with two oars and a piece of sail, in full view of his son's house. The miller tried his best to shun him along with the rest of the community in the hope that he would eventually go away. The poor man was almost dying when the minister finally rescued him after a fearful storm and gave him leave to build himself a turf hut at the foot of the Kildonnan cliffs adjacent to the glebe. This was much against the son's wishes and the minister had to stop him more than once from pulling down the wall. In the end, the miller gave up this attempt to evict his own father and decided to emigrate instead.

As a result of the minister's dedication, the 200-strong Protestant congregation on Eigg wholeheartedly embraced the Evangelical Revival like many other Highlands communities in those times of hardship and social upheaval. Now that the 'earthly father figure' of the clan chief had vanished for good, the idea of 'a Heavenly Father whose properties were unchanging and who was merciful to the weak but implacably vengeful to the oppressor' was singularly comforting.[13] And when the minister joined the Free Church, the whole congregation joined with him apart from three people who chose to remain in the Established Church. But joining the Free Church meant that Swanson was no longer allowed to reside at the manse, where a minister of the Established Church was immediately appointed to replace him. Twice the Eigg people petitioned their landlord for him to be allowed some ground to build himself a house amongst them, only to be told that he did not wish a third place of worship on the island. Undeterred, Swanson bought a small sailboat – the *Betsey* – and turning it into a floating manse, cruised around the island, preaching to the people who had remained faithful to him. His friend, the geologist and writer Hugh Miller, described the arrival of the *Betsey* on Eigg, eagerly awaited by the parishioners who sent their minister eggs, milk and cream as soon as the boat was sighted in the bay as a token of their affection. He conducted the service in 'a low dingy cottage of turf and stone', the former Gaelic school, at little distance from the minister's former residence. 'It had an earthen floor and was lit by two windows streaming with water when it rained, scantily furnished with a rude pulpit and a few seats. . . . Old and young had walked from all corners of the island to meet their minister in spite of the wind and rain, gathering around him to shake his hand, like carder bees from their nest of dried grass and moss. There could be no possibility of mistake respecting the feelings with which they regarded their minister.'[14]

A DESTITUTE COUNTRY

By the 1840s, the island's crofting tenantry had practically doubled to forty-one crofting households in the space of two generations. The most populated townships after Cleadale were now Upper and Lower Grulin, with nine crofts each. Galmisdale was next, with seven crofts of varying sizes; Allan MacLeod, the innkeeper, held the largest with 14 acres. There were also twenty-eight landless families – farm labourers and herdsmen, who worked in Laig, Hulin, Kildonnan and Sandaveg which the factor held as his own farm. These landless cottars occupied the large clachans of Braigh near Kildonnan and Hulin at the north end of the island and a smaller one in Cuagach, that part of Laig which skirts the basalt cliffs near the steep pass which marks the entrance to the northern part of the island.

All these people had become increasingly dependent on the potato because it was the crop which produced the biggest return for the small amounts of land they held. Every inch of ground was cultivated, even amongst the boulders where only the *cas chrom* could reach, as the ribbed pattern of lazy-beds on every slope attest to this day. Now that the seaweed was no longer used for kelp it was spread on the ground to force a crop out of the most exhausted soil. The gathering of seaweed was just as strictly regulated as before, but this time everyone had their fair share of it. 'Whenever there was a large bulk of it washed ashore, every effort was made to salvage as much of it as possible. If anyone was to start bringing in the seaweed without informing the rest, they would descend on him and he would only get what was considered his fair share.'[15]

However, the uncertain climate of the west coast made it dangerous for people to depend on one single crop for their subsistence. If the crops were planted too early, excessive rain threatened them; if they were planted too late, they might not ripen and when the weather was bad all year round, the whole crop was endangered. This happened in two successive years when one bad harvest followed another in 1835 and 1836. Distress in the Highlands became so widespread, aggravated by cholera epidemics, that a report was commissioned in 1841 to investigate its causes. Its conclusion was that, 'In the opinion of the most intelligent landlords, there was no point in improving the land since it was cheaper to import meal from Glasgow than produce it and therefore the land was best left for grazing.' There was no point in developing the fisheries either as they did not bring enough revenue to be of consideration. The blame was put squarely on the crofting system which, according to the Duke of Argyll, had only been introduced out of 'motives of kindness and humanity to the people'. Distress would not disappear unless that system was put to an end by emigration, and the future of the region could only be ensured by the removal of 'the redundant unemployed population and of the squatters who had no land and paid no rent'.[16]

Even though people were no longer so eager to leave, the demographic pressure was so acute on Eigg that 140 people decided to leave in 1843 and take their chance in Canada, leaving their elderly relatives behind as they could not afford to take them with them. But conditions in Cape

Breton were not so favourable now that grants of land had ceased and the flow of emigrants had increased, so that the letters which they sent back were far from encouraging. Few decided to follow them, most preferring the misery they knew to one they did not. And misery there was aplenty, as witnessed by Hugh Miller, who found in Galmisdale one of the most miserable hovels he had ever seen in his travels throughout Scotland. 'It was hardly larger than the cabin of the *Betsey* and a thousand times less comfortable. The walls and roof formed of damp grass-grown turf, with a few layers of unconnected stones in the basement tier, seemed to constitute one continuous hillock, sloping upwards from foundation to ridge . . . The low chunky door opened directly into the one wretched apartment of the hovel, which we found chiefly lighted by holes in the roof. The back of the sick woman's bed – this woman had lived there bed-ridden for ten years – was so placed over the edge of the opening, that it had formed at one time a sort of partition to the portion of apartment some 5 or 6 feet square which contained the fireplace. The window, a hole in the turf wall, was opened this time, whereas it was usually stuffed with rags. The light of the opening fell on the corpse-like features of the woman, sallow, sharp, bearing at once the stamp of disease and famine . . . I learned that not during the 10 years in which she had been bed-ridden, had she received a single farthing from the proprietor, nor indeed had any of the poor of this island, and that the parish had no session funds. I saw her husband a few days later, a worn-out old man, with famine written legibly on his hollow cheek and eye and on the shrivelled frame that seemed lost in the tattered dress . . . They had no means of living, he said, save through the charity of their poor neighbours, who had so little to spare, for the parish or the proprietor had never given them anything. He had once, he added, two fine boys both sailors, who had helped them. But the one had perished in a storm off the Mull of Cantyre, and the other had died of a fever when on a West India voyager and though their poor girl was very dutiful and stayed in their crazy hut to take care of them in their helpless old age, what other could she do in a place like Eigg than just share with them their sufferings.'[17]

In answer to the pauperisation of the Highlands and Islands, the government amended the Poor Law in 1846 by making it compulsory for the owners and occupiers of the land to contribute something towards a poor rate. About one and a half shillings in the pound were to be collected by an Inspector of the Poor and redistributed through Parochial Boards which were to be established in each parish in Scotland. The new amendment immediately proved unpopular with landowners, who accused it of ruining them. Little was done to implement the Act and as a result, Eigg, like many other places, remained unassessed for years without any alleviation being made to the condition of the wretched people such as those Hugh Miller had encountered. The other problem was that the Act completely overlooked the plight of the impoverished crofters and cottars. It only made provisions for the old, the sick and the disabled, the widows with children, those who fitted in the pauper category. Relief for the able-bodied unemployed who swelled the number of destitutes everywhere in the Highlands and Islands was unthinkable. It would have been seen as a premium on indolence in the world of Victorian capitalism. Only as 'Occasional Poor' could destitute people be relieved out of the funds raised by assessments of the parish. Already flawed in its conception, the system of poor relief was totally inadequate to cope with the disaster that struck only one year after it was passed by Parliament.[18]

THE YEAR OF THE BLIGHT

In 1846, the unknown disease which had destroyed the entire potato harvest in Ireland and caused a terrible famine spread to the west coast of Scotland. After a year of particularly good crops, a few weeks of warm wet weather at the end of July provided ideal conditions for the blight fungus to develop and spread. By the end of August, the whole potato harvest had withered, blackened and rotted. By October, people with little or no land and no money to buy meal were trying to survive on shellfish, seaweed and anything edible they could find. Faced with destitution on such a large scale, the government had no choice but to extend to Scotland the help given to Ireland.

Famine relief operations started in winter 1846, entrusted to the man who had already succeeded in helping to relieve famine in Ireland, Sir Edmund Coffin. Preliminary investigation showed him that no help would be forthcoming from the landlords to the extent needed to alleviate destitution. Two meal depots were thus established, one in Mull and one in Skye, with two naval frigates fitted as depot ships to take the meal to the islands. There was no question of distributing the meal freely or even cheaply as an exceptional measure. Landowners were expected to buy the meal, borrowing money from the government under the Drainage Act, as had been done in Ireland. Then they could pay their starving tenants for effecting this useful drainage of their land.

The problem in Scotland was that few landlords bothered to respond to the scheme. They expected far more help than the government was prepared to give. For one MacLeod of Dunvegan who was doing all he could to help his tenantry, there were too many who did not feel at all concerned by the plight of people who paid little or no rent. As for Dr MacPherson, illness had prevented visits to Eigg for the past seven years, but his initial reaction had been prompt and compassionate. As he heard about the failure of the entire potato crop on Eigg, he instructed his factor to bring in supplies of meal to be sold on credit at cost price, and gave him instruction to leave the November half-rent in the hands of the smaller tenants. At the same time, the Free Church, which had immediately started collecting relief funds throughout the country, distributed free supplies on the island as well as everywhere else, helping to prevent the worst.

In spite of these immediate measures, alarming reports about Eigg, and especially Arisaig where the situation was really disperate, reached Coffin in early January 1847. A few days later, a Captain Baynton was dispatched to Eigg to ascertain the islanders' condition. Visiting the tacksman of Laig, the minister and the schoolmaster, he learned that all the food which had been sent was now finished, including MacDonald of Laig's own supplies which he had ordered from Glasgow and distributed among his own people. Only two sacks of meal were left out of the 80 bolls brought by the factor, who was expected from Skye with some more. 'Were he not to arrive soon,' the tacksman of Laig told the Captain, 'actual want would take place. Many of the small tenants had already nothing left to eat and had started on their seed corn. Only a few islanders had managed to catch some herring but they were unable to sell it. In any case, they were so under equipped that they did not even have the longlines necessary at the beginning of the fishing season.'[19]

Out of forty-one crofting families, sixteen were now completely destitute, with an additional twenty paupers whom no Inspector of the Poor had yet seen. The proprietor's son had been on Eigg in the autumn but had offered nothing. Captain Baynton concluded that severe distress would take place if some employment was not provided soon by the proprietor or his tenants for those islanders who had no means of purchasing food but were anxious to work. So far only the minister had already started to hire people to drain his land and considered giving them permanent employment. He felt that a lot more drainage could be done on the island and had advised Angus MacDonald that if he could start draining his land, he would be able to raise the necessary funds and obtain meal for cash in Tobermory for his tenants. The young man, who had inherited a great burden of debt from his father, had replied dispiritedly that he might do so if he remained on the island. His other suggestions were that the proprietor could offer work for the completion of the unfinished road and the building of a small pier between Castle Island and Galmisdale Point which would encourage fishing.

Sir Edmund, whose policy it was to try and awaken the landowners to their responsibilities towards their tenantry, wrote to Dr MacPherson demanding a justification of his apparent inaction. This prompted an angry letter from Mr Gordon, his Edinburgh lawyer, stating that the proprietor had done enough since he had already spent £100 on meal, given an additional £50 for further supplies and given up the November half-rent of the smaller tenants. 'The moral obligation of a landowner in such case must have a limit,' felt the lawyer, 'a proprietor cannot be required to supply subsistence to a redundant population who remain at home and sit idle rather than migrate where they can earn a fair day's wage for a fair day's work.' Not even the farmers were spared: the lawyer's excuse for not starting any drainage operation was that the land was occupied by farmer-tenants who had 'hitherto resisted all proposals for the adoption of an improved system of husbandry'.[20] The lawyer's reaction was certainly not untypical. The Highland tenantry was held in contempt for living in the past, and crofters were simply accused of laziness if they did not avail themselves of the opportunity of a free passage to Greenock where provisions and necessary assistance were provided by the Highland Destitution Fund for those who looked for work in the south. It did not matter that what work could be had was already taken by the Irish famine victims who had flooded the Lowlands in search of subsistence, as the islanders had already found out for themselves.

AN UNEASY RECOVERY

By the end of January 1847, the islanders were still waiting for the meal promised to them by the proprietor. The factor had not yet come back from Sleat where his son's illness detained him. Luckily those on the brink of starvation were relieved by the arrival of fresh supplies from Glasgow distributed by the Free Church, which was doing a great job of alleviating suffering in Catholic and Protestant districts indiscriminately, ensuring its unconditional support on Eigg for many years to come. Meanwhile the government was passing the responsibility for famine relief to charitable committees within the Central Board of Management for the Relief of Destitute Inhabitants of the Highlands. The deputy for its Edinburgh section, Sheriff Frazer from Fort William, came to inspect Eigg, Arisaig and Knoydart, the worst areas on the coast of Lochaber. On Eigg, Dr MacPherson was coming round to the idea of drainage, but complained about costs, and nothing was being done at all. The islanders had barely enough subsistence for a few days and suffered from dysentery and jaundice from eating too much shellfish. Sheriff Frazer came back with eight sacks of barley meal and eight sacks of Indian corn meal, recommending to the islanders that they apply to the Fishing Board for longlines.

Fishing could at least bring some source of food immediately, if not of revenue in the long run.

Another report on the state of the Small Isles was compiled the following April. There was no mention yet of drainage started on Eigg, nor of an Inspector of the Poor nominated, but there were two stores of meal on the island. One was given by MacLean of Coll for the minister to dole it out to those Muck paupers who had settled on the glebe whilst the others had to travel to the island once a fortnight to receive their share. Another three indigent widows lived on the glebe, whom the minister allowed 'the privilege of taking from his sea-ware to manure their ground for potatoes'. The other store was kept by the factor. The islanders in distress – including the nine regular paupers – were now receiving a stone of meal every fortnight, on the basis of one-and-a-half pounds of meal per man per day, three-quarters of a pound for a woman and half a pound for children under twelve. The factor allocated it more than grudgingly. According to tradition the *croman* would keep back as much meal as he could for himself. Duncan MacKay remembers the story of that poor widow's son who was sent to fetch his mother's free meal. 'Well,' MacPherson said to the boy, 'go and get that whip in the stable first.' Then he told the lad to lift his kilt and he gave him a good few lashes on the backside. 'That's all you are getting today,' he said before turning him out. 'Well, there was nothing they could do,' added Duncan, 'nothing at all or they would be asked if they wanted to see the other side of the Ardnamurchan Point. That's what MacPherson used to say to the poor crofters!'

Relief had to be made necessarily unpalatable, stressed the official relief policy, and the factor was doing his best to ensure it was. The only vent people had left to express their feelings was for them to demonstrate their loyalty to the Free Church, to which the factor did not belong, being a pillar of the Established Church. It was certainly felt that divine retribution had struck when the *croman* became blind in his old age. Many were the curses which had been muttered against him by crofters denied any recourse against his arbitrariness. The *croman* died a miser and not even his children managed to get their hands on his pot of gold! The story was that one day, a ship laden with meal had arrived on the island, but that his son did not have enough money to buy any. The old man slipped outside, calling on one of his grandchildren to follow him and guide him to the boundary wall that separated Galmisdale from Grulin. But when they reached the wall, he told the boy to sit down and wait for him. Intrigued by the old man's behaviour, the boy decided to follow him at a distance. He saw the old man search alongside the dyke until he found a hole, and out of that hole he took a jar, and out of that jar he took a few gold coins before he replaced it in the hole. Then the old man called the boy and together they returned to the house where the *croman* gave the coins to his son and told him to run down to the ship and buy as much meal as he could. There was much rejoicing that night in the house and for many nights afterwards everybody had a full belly. But the old man died suddenly without revealing the location of his secret treasure, and searching high and low as they did, no one was ever able to find it again![21]

Emergency relief, however, was meant to cease as soon as the harvest of 1847 enabled people to secure their own supply of food. This wildly over-optimistic expectation was ruined by rains, gales and a renewed outbreak of blight. Many in any case had nothing left to sow, having eaten their seed potatoes out of desperation since they could only receive assistance when they could show that their means were absolutely exhausted: this meant no seed potato and no livestock left. By 1848, nine such 'occasional Poor' were given assistance over and above the twenty-one paupers registered in the parish. Two years later, the number of these 'occasional Poor' had mounted to fourteen, with seventeen applications turned down. With £65 per year allocated to their relief from Central Board funds, a Parochial Board was finally established and provisions were made for a poor's-house to be built on each of the four islands of the parish.

Most importantly, money was allocated for medical care: in the aftermath of the famine, typhoid had struck repeatedly and tuberculosis had become endemic in the insanitary and cramped conditions endured by the great majority of people, preying on the weakened population. On Eigg whole families were decimated, infants, children and elderly the first victims. Angus MacKinnon recalls how, for instance, only two survived from the Grulin MacCormicks he counts amongst his forebears. In 1850, four orphans were added to the Poor Roll who had lost all relatives capable of sheltering them, which says something about the ravages of the disease on an island where most families were related.

Those crofters fortunate enough to have retained some livestock – or rather not destitute enough – were at last given some employment as drainage started on Eigg. Road-building was also resumed. As work on the 'cattle road' from Cleadale to the other side of the island progressed, a new road linking Galmisdale to Clanranald Pier was started. The Grulin, Kildonnan and Laig roads followed, providing work for the next two decades. Work was also offered on Rum where the new owner, the Marquis of Salisbury, now intended to build a pier, roads and a dam to develop the island into a sporting estate. His total workforce amounted to 300 people drawn from the surrounding famine-stricken districts. Like everywhere else, the half-starved tenantry received the lowest wages ever paid at the time – relief having to be necessarily unpalatable – one and a half pennies for a day's wages for a man, a penny for a woman, 5 pennies for an average family if everyone worked. Since a boll of meal cost between 22 and 23 shillings, it therefore cost four weeks' work for a family to feed itself.

Unfortunately, land was allowed to lie fallow whilst people were working for their meagre subsistence. This was a problem which Sir MacNeil, who supervised the system of poor relief, was well aware of: he had suggested that those who did not have any food should be helped in cultivating and improving their land instead of 'having to throw themselves on drainage and road-building' which ultimately benefited their landlords. 'If arrangements could be made', reasoned Sir MacNeil, 'by which the crofters could secure their land for a number of years in the benefit of the improvements made to it, instead of depending on yearly leases', such security of tenure would prove advantageous to both crofters and landlords in the end. Unfortunately such an idea was far too revolutionary for the times. Government officials maintained that land improvement was the sole responsibility of the landowners, and that no outside pressure could be applied to influence their policy without creating 'an irreparable damage to the fabric of social order'.[22] But as blight kept recurring, ill-fed crofters and cottars started to sink into a state of apathetic desperation, which led officials to declare that the situation failed to improve because of the population's chronic laziness. By 1851, the universal conclusion was that the only long-term solution for the Highland crisis was the removal of its pauperised population. Emigration now appeared as 'a necessary improvement of the land' on a par with ditching and draining. Landowners also supported emigration as the solution for their problems, but for quite different reasons. Since the price of wool was soaring again, they thought it timely to dispose 'at once and forever of their burdensome dependants' for whom they would now have to pay a high rate of relief under the Poor Law. Assisted emigration would allow them to make room for more sheep farms, denounced Hugh Miller in his newspaper, the *Witness*. But public opinion was so overwhelmingly in favour of emigration as a solution for all the ills in the country that a new Emigration Act was passed in 1851. A year later, the Highlands and Islands Emigration Society was founded to encourage its implementation, especially now that Australia and New Zealand were advertising for emigrants. Feelings of dejection were running so high that many came to accept emigration as a preferable alternative to starvation. Like the two cottar's daughters from Galmisdale who took their unmarried sister with them, many young islanders opted to leave for Australia.

THE COMING OF THE BLACKFACE SHEEP

With emigration becoming government policy, the islanders found the ring of clearances closing upon them. In the space of a few years, ships filled with people from all the surrounding islands: Skye, South Uist, Barra, Coll, Tiree. In Benbecula the barbarity of the clearances reached new heights as its Aberdeenshire owner, Gordon of Cluny, hunted down with dogs the tenants unwilling to board the ships. Moidart, then Knoydart, were next to be brutally cleared, although a handful of people in Knoydart managed to squat in their roofless cabins, in the shelter of makeshift covers made out of old sails.

As this news reached them, the inhabitants of Eigg felt increasingly despondent. Rumours that Angus Òg at Laig was now contemplating emigration brought the threat of evictions uncomfortably close, when a strange incident happened which was taken as an omen of things to come. 'Two Laig herdsmen were working in the hills one day when the figure of a man appeared suddenly to one of them. He could see him perfectly well, but his companion could not see anybody there at all. The herdsman soon realised that he could only see the stranger if he stood still in the same position, otherwise the figure would vanish if he moved or if he sat down at all. Then he saw something else behind the man, a flock of sheep coming down from the hills. He knew then for certain that the apparition was the *tabhaisg* [the ghostly double] of someone who would appear for real one day.'[23] Shortly afterwards Angus Òg announced his decision to give up the tack of Laig. The famine had aggravated his already precarious financial situation and, being only twenty-four years old, he hoped for a better future in the American army. Obtaining a commission in the 11th regiment of Wisconsin, he moved there with his mother, sister and cousin, but, fighting bravely in the Civil War, he died of his wounds a few years later. Ending the unbroken succession of Clanranald tacksmen at Laig, the departure of Angus Òg severed what was left of that sense of kinship between tenants and their traditional leaders.

Before long, Laig and the two Grulin townships which were included in the tack were advertised for rent. A Borders farmer made an offer for it, but, like all graziers, he did not care much for 'swarms of poor crofters unable to pay their rents' since he wanted the land for sheep. He consequently offered to pay a much higher rent if the population of Grulin was cleared. Predictably enough, his offer was accepted and the fourteen families of Upper and Lower Grulin were given notices to quit at Martinmas 1852 for the following Whitsun. 'Our proprietor was like plenty of proprietors in the Highlands at the time', told Hugh MacKinnon. 'And this did not trouble his conscience very greatly. It was just a case of telling the poor crofters who were in Grulin that they would have to clear out, and there was nothing else for it: they just had to turn out at Whitsun in the year 1853 and take themselves off to America.'[24] In June 1853, all but three families left to embark for Nova Scotia, joining the ranks of Highland destitutes whom the

Canadian authorities had to feed and clothe as they arrived, close to starvation and dressed in rags. Nothing was ever heard of them.

Alistair MacKinnon and his two sisters were among the three families that were able to stay behind, and they moved to a cottage close to the shore in Galmisdale. One of the sisters never recovered from the evictions and threw herself in the sea from the cliffs of Castle Island. The other two families found shelter in Cleadale where they had relatives, the MacLellans and the MacCormicks. Finlay MacCormick's wife was Mòr MacQuarrie, daughter of Neil MacQuarrie the famous whisky distiller of Eigg. Hugh MacKinnon, their descendant, tells the story of their moving to Cleadale. 'This is how my grandfather was able to stay behind and not go with the others: his own father-in-law, Neil Mac Quarry, Niall mac Lachlain as they called him, he had a croft and a house in Cleadale, and rather than see his daughter, who was married to my grandfather – her name was Mòr – rather than see her going to America, he said to my grandfather that he had another croft in Cleadale, besides the one he was working himself and that he was very welcome to take it. My grandfather came into that croft in 1853 down from Grulin, and I am on the very same site to the present day.'[25] According to tradition, the Grulin cattle found it harder to get used to their new environment. They found their way back to their old pasture at the first opportunity and it was a while before they were persuaded to return.

When the new tenant of Laig arrived on the island, it was realised that Stephen Stewart was the very man whose ghostly double had been seen by Angus Òg's herdsman. The vision had been vindicated for with him came the sheep, bringing Stewart a handsome profit. The land which had been so carefully tilled by the Grulin crofters was revealed to be such rich pasture that for the first two years all his ewes had twin lambs. In the first year alone 500 lambs were marked. Meanwhile, houses in Grulin were plundered of their stones to build a wall for the sheep farm until all but one remained intact, kept for the shepherd, one solitary house in a ghost village.

The following years were to see the disappearance of another three townships on the island as more and more islanders decided to leave. Hector MacQuarrie, Mòr's brother, worked as a shepherd for Stewart for a couple of years but he missed the cattle and he preferred to try his luck with his kinsmen in Nova Scotia, followed by John Mackenzie, whose wife Sarah, the daughter of the innkeeper, also had relatives there.[26] By the 1860s, the townships of Sandavore and Sandaveg had lost so much of their population that the two were amalgamated in one township. With only eight out of sixteen houses remaining inhabited, Sandavore now comprised the factor's 60-acre farm, the glebe with its four cottars and paupers, and the schoolhouse. There was only one croft, held by the island smith, John Campbell. An Gobha Mòr, as he is known in the island tradition, moved there from Cleadale in search of a better water supply and was now close to a burn deemed never to run dry.

A comparable decrease in population occurred at Kildonnan after MacDonald of Balranald left over a dispute with the factor who wanted to use one of his fields for his own cattle. No sooner had he gone than John MacLean moved in and turned Kildonnan over to sheep. A Moidart grazier, he was notorious for his clearance of the township of Keill in Canna, paying the famished islanders who remained one-and-a-half stones of meal a week out of the Relief Fund to build walls to separate arable and pasture for sheep. His first gesture as tenant was to get rid of the labourers and herdsmen in Braigh and use the stones from their blackhouses to build a sheep-fank – *faing ruadh* – and a boundary wall, no doubt using Relief Funds once again to finance the work. Then he went on to clear Hulin which had been included in the tack of Kildonnan since

Lachlan MacKinnon's return to Skye. The clachan had seen its population decline steadily through the last decades, cottars descending into poverty as they aged. Two houses remained inhabited, occupied by an 83-year-old pauper from Muck and a family of cottars. The stones from the other five houses were used to build a sheepfank now that the big house housed MacLean's shepherd, a Moidart man like himself. Ten years later, in 1871, he was the only one to remain in Hulin. Cleadale and Galmisdale were now firmly established as the two crofters' strongholds, separated by the large tracts of land which were given over to sheep in Laig, Grulin, Hulin and Kildonnan. With eighteen crofting families, Cleadale now housed the bulk of the island's population. Galmisdale had fewer inhabitants, the innkeeper and his 30-acre croft, nine crofter families with far smaller plots of land and two landless households, a family of cottars and an elderly widow. Thus, in the space of twenty years the island population had fallen to just over 300 people. Five townships had disappeared, changing radically the physical and human landscape of the island.

The same process of depopulation was happening in the rest of the Small Isles. The Muck grazings were let to a Border farmer for his Cheviots. In Canna, evictions continued until the population dwindled to forty-one people in 1871. In Rum, forty people remained alongside 10,000 sheep. Among those whose passage was 'assisted' were the last of the native islanders, one of whom came back after a few years. He sought in vain to get 'the site of his two soles of a bothy and the breadth of his two shoulders of a grave in the land of his heredity and the land of his fathers'.[27] Only one indigenous islander was left on the island, the sole custodian of unwritten traditions soon to be lost forever. Under the intensive grazing of sheep brought in such numbers to the four islands of the parish, their ecological degradation started. As the sheep ate only the finer sort of grass, coarser species multiplied until land which was once luscious and green became covered with heather and bracken.

Chapter 7

THE CROFTERS FIGHT BACK

VICTORIAN EIGG

When Dr MacPherson died in 1854, the island was left to his four unmarried daughters. Isabella, the eldest, had taken up semi-permanent residence at Nead Na Feannaig, where her numerous relatives came to stay every summer or on leave from India, where they served in the army, the medical or the civil service. Some sixty years later, Hector MacQuarrie's sister could still remember the time when Samuel, the eldest of the family, came back from India where he served in the Indian Army: 'They took peats up to the top of Scuir and made a bonfire. Samuel was given a grand reception and there was a ball. It was Arthur [a younger brother who ended up as High Court judge in Calcutta] I danced with, and I was not twenty then, I think he was about the same age.' Isabella was described as a most capable woman, 'tall and stately, with wavy brown hair with hardly any grey in it to the end of her life. She was full of interest and kindly and shrewd in conversation, [who] knew all on the island and was kind to all.' Local elders much approved of such proprietors, 'who for many years supported the interests of the Church by their invariable presence here at the Lord's table and their exemplary and devout attendance on the means of Grace and their liberal contributions to every charitable cause among the people.' Isabella's kindness and dignity was never forgotten by the crofters. 'Whatever was done on the island, it was she or the professor that did it.' The professor was her brother Norman, a lawyer who from 1865 held the highly regarded chair of Scots Law at Edinburgh University and held office as Sheriff of Dumfries and Galloway.

Norman MacPherson took some interest in the progress of farming on the island but he left it firmly in the hands of his factor. Embracing the Victorian passion for bloodsports which had become the hallmark of the landed classes, he was much more interested in developing the island shooting, which had been so promisingly advertised when Eigg was sold to his father. Rabbits were certainly plentiful and offered an easy shoot. In the absence of predators, apart from birds of prey which were themselves hunted down, they had become a real pest since their introduction to the Hebrides from England as a new source of food by the young heir of Coll – Maighstir Calum's brother-in-law. Crofters of course were not allowed to hunt them, and woe to the poachers who did not carefully dispose of their remains, for that would be enough for the factor to evict them. Grouse shooting was actually quite poor on the island, and an attempt was made to introduce grey partridge. When this species failed to thrive, it was decided to embark on pheasant breeding. To encourage them, trees were planted all around the MacPhersons' house, giving rise to dark mutterings on the part of the Galmisdale crofters, for that land around Nead na Feannaig was deemed to be some of the best arable ground on the island.

Not all the MacPhersons were keen on shooting. Norman's sister Christina and her husband, Michael Packenham Edgeworth, retired from the Indian Civil Service, came every summer with their daughter Harriett, and favoured more gentle occupations like walking, sketching and investigating the island's complex geology, a description of which had just been published by the Scottish geologist George MacCullough. The diaries kept by Edgeworth from 1858 to 1881 draw a picture of long holidays punctuated by Sunday church services and excursions to Grulin or the Singing Sands when the factor would lend them his pony and trap, or along the coast in the minister's boat to the caves, Castle Island or Port Skitaig in Grulin. The weekly routine was to go down the new road to Clanranald pier and wait for the mail to arrive, Edgeworth finding it hard sometimes to endure 'this entire silence from the rest of the world' and looking forward to his copy of *The Times* or *The Spectator*. Since 1863, Eigg had been included in the Oban–Gairloch steamer route, and postal deliveries were less hazardous than before, when the mailcoach from Fort William took ages to reach Arisaig where a smack would take the mail to Eigg once a week, weather and inclination permitting. Letters for Eigg could now come via the steamer, addressed to 'the Clerk of the Clansman Steam Packet c/o Custom House, Greenock, for Post-Master Arisaig', and would arrive twice a week, on Tuesdays and Fridays when the *Clansman* – from the Hutchison MacBrayne company – flew her flag at half-mast to summon the island ferry for mail or passengers before calling on Arisaig and Skye.

The first Eiggaich to work as ferrymen were two Galmisdale men, Roderick Campbell (Ruairidh Ruadh) and Alasdair MacKinnon, who manned the MacPhersons' boat, the *Isabella*. As the steamer could come at any time between ten in the morning and seven in the evening or even later, depending on the cargo it had to unload on the way, once Ruairidh Ruadh and Alasdair were on duty, they had to wait all night if need be until the steamer arrived. Their families were quite used to it and they did not worry if they were late. 'What happened one day', tells Dougald MacKinnon, who was to work on the island ferry all his life, 'was that after meeting the steamer, when the ferrymen tried to come back ashore fully laden, they just found themselves unable to steer the boat against the wind and the tide. They tried everything they could, they even threw the cargo overboard, all of it, apart from the mail-bags, they still couldn't make it to the shore. So what could they do but drift away with the waves and manage the best way they could. They were lucky to land where they did, not far from Rhu Arisaig which was the steamer's calling port, so that they were alright in the end. And who was surprised but Ruairidh Ruadh's wife when she got a telegram telling her that they were safe and sound? She thought they were on Eigg all the time!'

Like many of their contemporaries, the Edgeworths were keen on botany: they identified and collected various species of ferns, starry saxifrage on the Sgurr, moss campion on Sgriubh path, melancholy thistle near the manse and honeysuckle and wild strawberry on the 'great road' across the island which was finally completed in 1881. Experimental planting of ferns at St Donnan's Well and Rum water-lilies in Struidh were attempted, mushrooms 8 inches across were picked in August, and an aquarium with sea anemones was admired at the manse. During these walks across the island, glimpses of islanders working on their everyday tasks were recorded: men and women with their peat-laden ponies met on the moss road near the Sgurr, a crowd of islanders shearing in Grulin or disappearing to catch a good tide for gurnard, fishermen seen landing their catch at the Cleadale landing place 'between two strange reefs made of large flat stones, very commodious but on a rough day I should think very dangerous'.[1]

Fishing on Eigg was lagging well behind Muck where the new owner, Captain Swinburne, had established a salt depot and equipped the islanders with smacks capable of fishing Rockall, but it was catching up, especially since the arrival of Rev. Grant and his son to the parish in 1848. Grant added to his income by catching basking sharks, and island tradition recalls how in the summer months, the minister's smack would often be seen to divert its course in pursuit of a shark whilst on its way to a church service in the other islands! George Grant, the minister's eldest son, who had retired to Eigg from the Indian Medical Service, was now employing a crew of islanders to catch herring and gurnard on long lines. Fish were so plentiful that in one afternoon George Grant and two others managed to catch 494 gurnards with only three hooks! Fishing boats came back with creels brimming with fish, but it was not until 1865 when the iniquitous law which made it illegal to fish for herring in the Hebrides during the summer months was repealed, that fishing took off as a commercial activity on the island, enough to keep a boatbuilder in year-round employment in Cleadale. The development of Mallaig on the mainland as a thriving fishing port and curing station also offered new opportunities: squads of island girls would go away to work at the herring during the season. The men went away too, to join the herring fishing in Antrim. It enabled emigration to slow down a little after the numerous departures which had followed the famine.

The Edgeworth diaries made much of the polite social intercourse between the MacPhersons and their tenant farmers: the MacLeans in Kiell, as Kildonnan was called then, the Stewarts at Laig, the minister and his family. The schoolmaster and the priest were also guests at Nead na Feannaig where 'reeling in the parlour' provided an agreeable distraction from reading novels and studying botany, when the young Grants occasionally dropped in with a fiddler. Visits to the farms, to see the progress of march dykes and fanks or haymaking at Kiell and crops at Laig, invariably ended with an offer of dinner or tea: 'capital lamb and carragheen pudding with the richest cream at Kiell, scones and oatcakes, butter and milk cheese at Laig', where the guests witnessed the chopped curd being put under press, and the rows of 40 lb cheeses ripening in the dairy. Good harvests of oats, turnips, barley and potatoes were reported at Laig, farmed 'admirably' by Stewart on the 30 acres of marshland he had reclaimed by drainage, although a July gale in 1862 blew kales off the ground. Great improvements were noticed on the glebe: 'capital oats in the morass Revd Grant had been draining, and all the ground up to it also except the rocks beautifully cultivated', 'fine oats near St Donnan's well'.[2]

From time to time, visitors who came from the other islands or the Sunday service were entertained: the Thorburns and Captain Swinburne from Muck, or the MacNeills from Canna whose children spoke only Gaelic. Church services were held in the schoolhouse, the English service following after the Gaelic one before the start of Sunday school in the afternoon, Edgeworth marvelling how the minister could bear three hours of preaching at a time. Mention was made of visiting clerics from Skye, Ayrshire or London but none of the good number of islanders who remained faithful to the Free Church, whose missionary now resided in Cleadale. From 1862, services were held in the new church built out of local freestone and described as 'exceedingly nice in every way, simple and neat', with its high windows and wood-panelling adorned with quotations from the Scriptures in Gaelic and English in Celtic interlacing, and a new set of communion dishes provided by Norman MacPherson.

Having set up a school trust, the MacPherson family also took a great interest in the island school, monitoring the children's progress in learning English, which they viewed as a help to social betterment. The number of children on the school-roll was still surprisingly small, about twenty for a population of 300 islanders, but it was not until 1872 that school attendance was made compulsory. Such progress as they made was quite irregular, as no English was spoken at home: the pupils could read and spell fairly well, but only a few could 'satisfactorily translate English into Gaelic'. Isabella and Christina made a point of witnessing the yearly examinations which took place on the last day of the summer term. A little celebration was organised afterwards with the girls dancing and the boys throwing weights and jumping. Tea and coffee were then served with enough currant loaves handed around for each child to bring at least two or three home afterwards.

This picture of rural contentment under this regime of benign paternalism represented the typical viewpoint of the Victorian middle-class city-dwellers who had started holidaying in the Highlands. The tears shed by young Harriett as she left her beloved holiday island were undoubtedly sincere: islands such as Eigg offered a wonderful experience of nature and its beauties to a romantic city girl. But the fact remained that for the MacPhersons' relatives the picturesque scenery of Eigg was almost entirely devoid of island people. They were small figures in the background, speaking a quaint language for which an interpreter like the factor or the minister was needed. The island poor are mentioned in passing, visited by Isabella and Christina, 'laden with packets of tea', and only for the picturesque detail, like an old cottar whose pig slept in front of the fire with a cat sleeping on top of it as if on a cushion. One islander only was singled out in the Edgeworth diaries, not a crofter of course, but 'a wonderfully lady-like old person' who collected eggs, the unmarried daughter of Lachlan MacKinnon, 'whose father and brother were tenants of a large farm, but broke down and died'.[3] In a society now composed of a few sheep farmers and a large number of crofters who were beyond the pale of social respectability, this left the factor as the only intermediary between absentee proprietors and their tenantry. The factor came to wield so much power and influence that he was quite unchallengeable.[4] It was as unthinkable to complain about the exactions of the *croman* to the MacPhersons as it was impossible to communicate with them. It was no wonder that, on Eigg like everywhere else, the factor was both hated and feared.

Little attention was given to the islanders' lives or their traditions; on the contrary, they were encouraged to learn the language of what was still to them an alien culture. The distant past was held to be far more interesting than recent history. It was particularly significant that when the spate of road-building in the 1860s led to the discovery of ancient burial mounds, it aroused in the proprietor of Eigg that other Victorian passion, the collecting of antiquities. Bringing with him an antiquarian friend, Norman MacPherson eagerly supervised the opening of a cairn at

Kildonnan and speculated whether objects found in the churchyard offered a clue to the burial place of St Donnan. The various finds were listed in the report he made to the Society of Antiquaries in 1878 and presented to the Museum of Antiquities in Edinburgh where they are to this day. In that same report mention is made of 'a blind old man chanting Ossianic tradition' on the island.[5] Norman MacPherson perhaps deemed it worth mentioning but it was undoubtedly less important to him than the discovery of a Viking sword at Kildonnan. Soon it would be realised – only too timely – that the songs which that old blind islander chanted were as much of a treasure as a Viking sword.

A SONG IS BETTER THAN A GOLD COIN

In the 1880s 'chanting Ossianic tradition' on Eigg, like everywhere else in the Hebrides, was the natural accompaniment of work or recreation. 'Whatever people might be doing or whatever they were engaged in, there would be a tune of music in their mouth', recalled Frances Tolmie, Mary MacAskill's granddaughter and one of the pioneering musicologists of her time. 'There would always be heard a man here and a woman there, a lad yonder or a maiden at hand, with a cheerful strain of music in the mouth of each. It might be that no person could be seen, but then voices would be heard up and down here and throughout the townland.'[6]

It was natural for island folks, as in all other traditional communities, to set all aspects of their life to music. That there was an appropriate song for each activity was in itself a ritual reassurance against an uncertain outcome, and the protection of the saints and the Holy Trinity was always called for. It was also that rhythm and rhyme greatly lightened the drudgery of repetitive work, bringing to it the pleasure of ear and hand in harmony. Much entertainment was provided by those singers quick at inserting an improvised reference to a topic of actuality within the songs. And there were enough tunes to put new words to them whenever those who had a mind for composition fancied a try. David MacKay, for example, who was related to Neil the fiddler, was one of the island's wits, and there was much merriment whenever he was back in Cuagach, visiting his cottar mother. According to the islanders, one of his songs was included in J. Mackenzie's *Sar Obair nam Bard*, the Gaelic anthology of songs and poems, although it was attributed to another.

One activity in particular where singing took pride of place was the waulking of home-spun cloth. Such cloth, the dark blue striped *iomairt* reserved for women's skirts or the tweed for men's clothes, was generally woven up to 33 yards long and would be shrunk to 30 yards during the fulling that took place at the waulking. As the cloth was often steeped in fish oil and tallow to waterproof it, it was also cleansed at the same time. Whenever a waulking was called for, the woman of the house assembled a company of girls with a few experienced matrons alongside a wooden board, the *cleith*, 12 to 20 feet long and 2 feet wide with a groove in its middle. The waulking women worked in pairs across the board, having first measured their arms against each other so that they would be evenly matched for the long and energetic task to follow. At the foot of the board sat the woman whose role it was to fold up the cloth which had been unrolled and laid across the board. She also had to keep it wet after its initial soaking in urine and warm water for a thorough cleansing. At the head of the board presided the most experienced woman of the company, the lead singer. Her role was to measure the cloth for shrinkage and to judge how many songs were needed for the complete fulling. Passing the cloth sunwise down the board, she started the songs, singing one verse at a time for the women to repeat it after her and adding the chorus after each line. Thus the thumping of the women on the board was kept regular by the repetition of the melody, its rhythm increasing as the women warmed up to the singing and the fulling. Several songs could be needed for a full waulking but none could ever be sung twice. Their themes could be love or war or praise of a chief unless one of the old heroic ballads was used, adapted for the purpose. Any song could be used as long as the verse was sufficiently short and the chorus sufficiently long. There was a progression in the rhythms starting with the slower 'heating songs' to get into the swing of work, followed by the livelier 'tightening songs' to 'break the back of the work'. Then came the 'frolic songs' – which were very much enjoyed by the onlookers gathered for the occasion: this was the time for improvisation, and the name of each girl in the company was coupled to that of her sweetheart to whom some slighting allusion was invariably made. The witty banter carried on as the girl was expected in her reply to resent this and praise the slighted one to the skies. If she chose not to praise or sing him, the result could be civil war in the township, and the breaking of hearts if not of heads! When the lead singer judged the cloth to be finished, then came the stretching and clapping songs, the women slapping the cloth with outstretched hands, using all their might to smooth out every crease. This again was an occasion for merriment as the girls coupled in the songs the names of real or imagined sweethearts. By contrast there was a moment of great solemnity when the cloth was finally folded. First the cloth was slowly turned sunwise along the board and at each turn of the cloth, each member of the household was mentioned for whom the cloth was intended. Then it was spat upon and slowly reversed end by end in the name of the Holy Trinity until it stood again at the centre of the board, and this was the end of the waulking.

Janet MacLeod in the schoolhouse, the island sewing mistress, was one of those experienced lead singers of waulking songs. She belonged to Snizort in Skye, coming to Eigg in the 1870s with her brother, the new schoolmaster, helping him to raise his children as he was a widower. Descended as she was from a long line of famous Snizort tradition-bearers, it was not surprising that her nephew Kenneth MacLeod became the well-known folklore collector and author of the song and book *The Road to the Isles*. It was thanks to him that when she was 80 years of age, Janet was able to give Alexander Carmichael the best version he was ever to record of what she called 'the choice of waulking songs', 'Seathan, the son of the King of Ireland'. Janet was justifiably proud of her reputation for improvisation at the waulking. 'It is not through vainglory I say it, but though many a lad was matched with me, I never left one of them unsung. Indeed I would consider it no small disgrace that a poor lad should be matched with me and that I would not raise him above the rest in the fore-front of a verse.' But most of all she was proud of her inheritance: her father's people were famous for their old songs and 'was it not about them it was said that they never forgot any poetry or lore but were constantly adding to the cairn?' When her father himself came from MacLeod's country to Snizort, she explained, 'he brought with him enough poetry and lore to fill the world'. To her that was the best legacy imaginable, for as she quoted an old Gaelic proverb, 'a gold coin does not go far in company, but a good song will suffice for a whole world of people'. 'Seathan, the son of the King of Ireland' was such a song, and she had heard it and sung it many a time. It was a lament composed by Seathan's wife, explained Janet. 'But he was not as good as the song makes him out to be . . . The man he would not kill in the north he would kill in the south, and the rapine he would not commit in the west, he would commit that and more in the east. At last every town and village was on his track in pursuit of him and he was three years an outlaw, and three years in sanctuary in Cill Chumha, and three years among his kin. His wife had him hidden and not even the tiny mouse knew where he was. But he was caught at last by his own clumsiness and the snares of women.' By itself, the song was sufficient to complete a whole waulking, however tough the cloth, and the version she sang to Carmichael comprised no less than 194 verses. 'I myself remember but little of it today,' she regretted, 'compared with what I knew when no waulking was complete without me.'[7]

Seathan, the son of the King of Ireland

Woe to him who heard of it and did not tell it,
Huru na hur i bhi o
Woe to him that heard of it and did not tell it,
Na bhi hao bho bao bhi o an o

That my darling was in Minginish;
If you were, my love, you had returned long since:
I would send a great ship to seek him there
With a famed crew, fresh and bright and expert
Young men and lads would be there . . .

He would visit here when he returned,
I would spend a festival day dallying with him,
I would sit on a knoll and engage in sweet converse,
I would curl thy hair as I did often times,
I would lie in thy arms and keep the dew from thee,
I would wash a fine-spun shirt full white for thee
So long as any water remained in the pool,
And I would dry it on a moorland branch . . .

But Seathan tonight is a corpse,
A sad tale to the men of Scotland,
A grievous tale to his followers,
A joyous tale to his pursuers,
To the son of the Hag of the Three Thorns . . .

When I thought you were giving chase,
You were dead in the conflict,
Borne on the shoulders of young men,
And about to be being buried.

When I thought you were in Galway,
You were dead without breath,
Borne on the shoulders of scornful men,
And as cold as the mountain snow.[8]

A GAELIC REVIVAL

Tales and songs like 'Seathan, the son of the king of Ireland' remained the traditional entertainment at fireside ceilidhs throughout the Gaelic-speaking counties. Meanwhile, in Scottish and English cities, people's imagination was fired anew by MacPherson's *Ossian* and its imagery of passion and freedom in the midst of a wild and untamed nature. Offering a stark contrast to the materialism of a scientific age, *Ossian* was as popular as ever, re-edited eighty-eight times and translated into eleven languages 100 years after its first publication! Queen Victoria herself subscribed to this fashion for the Highlands, and her aristocracy became fond of posing as wilderness-taming heroes, dressing up in the trappings of a romanticised Highland garb to enjoy the thrill of deer and grouse shooting in the grandiose settings of moors and mountains – now empty of people. Consequently, owning a shooting estate soon became the latest status symbol for the Victorian *nouveaux riches* and more crofters were cleared as sheep farms were turned into deer parks throughout the Highlands, as in Rum which had finally reverted to deer since shooting was now more profitable than sheep farming.

The Ossianic fad had also reached intellectual circles. Influenced by the 'Celtic Twilight' movement which looked back to Ossian's original sources, the Gaelic myths themselves, folklore studies led to a reappraisal of the Gaelic way of life. Hitherto condemned as economically unviable, plagued with endemic poverty, it now appeared to preserve as valuable a treasure of folklore as Lapland or Hungary. Andrew Laing, the famous Scottish folklorist, looked into Gaelic culture to investigate what he called 'the elemental and spiritual' roots of humanity, such 'archaic' values, emotions and artistry as were thought to belong to a pre-scientific age. For scholars like J. F. Campbell of Islay, who recorded traditional tales in Argyll, these were perhaps the only 'redeeming features' in a society which otherwise he thought 'may perish without disadvantage',[9] imbued as he was with the traditional prejudices of the landed gentry against crofting. The result of that surge of interest for ancient Celtic society was that when the Scottish historian W. F. Skene published his *Celtic Scotland* in 1883, a new and influential view of ancient Highland society, it was widely read and acclaimed throughout Britain. Gaelic societies sprang up in all large Scottish cities, publishing learned papers on the culture of the 'fine people of the Highlands and Islands'. Proud of this sudden interest in their heritage, those sons and grandsons of crofters who were now city-dwellers joined up enthusiastically. As the crofters' plight was now attracting the support of a growing number of Scottish liberals, the time was ripe for public opinion to turn in the crofters' favour.[10]

People like Alexander Carmichael were largely instrumental in bringing about public awareness of the insecurity and poverty besetting crofters. As an exciseman, Carmichael had spent his life travelling the islands, collecting the songs, prayers and beliefs of a people whose confidence he had managed to win in spite of his chosen profession. Painstakingly taking down the rhythms and rituals of life in Hebridean townships, he was thus able to draw the picture of a communal and pastoral way of life eminently suited to the land. Seeing for himself how it was hindered by exactions and taxes and nearly destroyed by the landowners' appropriation of the land for sheep farms and deer parks, he became a staunch supporter of the crofters' cause. At a time when the powers that be could neither understand nor accept that people in the Highlands and Islands should prefer to remain where they were, 'dividing and subdividing among themselves their narrow crofts of unrewarding land in a dismal climate . . . instead of gravitating towards employment opportunity or hope offered to some by the Lowlands and to all by the outside world',[11] his work went a long way to justify this attachment of the Gaelic people to their native soil, whose possession was worth more in their eyes than the pursuit of a better income away from it. The five volumes of his *Carmina Gadelica* showed a way of life which, like so many threatened rural societies of its time, was not so much 'archaic' as steeped in and directed by tradition, a tradition which was still stronger than the dictates of market forces.

When the crofters came at last to express their grievances, they found themselves in a climate of sympathy for their cause generated by the Gaelic revival. It was eventually to lead to the recognition by politicians of 'the historical differences between the way Gaelic people in Scotland and Ireland perceived the land and that common to the rest of the United Kingdom'.[12] The old concept of *duthchas* – the kindness to the land – so doggedly defended by the inhabitants of the Highlands and Islands was at last about to be formally acknowledged.

CROFTERS' FIGHTS AND CROFTERS' RIGHTS

By the 1880s, the climate of relative contentment in the islands had given way to smouldering resentment as people experienced new hardships after a succession of poor harvests and fishing seasons combined with a slump in wool prices and industrial depression. Eigg at least was spared the renewed outbreak of potato blight. On the contrary, MacFarlane, the new tenant in Kildonnan, made a handsome profit selling his potatoes at the time. He had the considerable stretch of arable land between Kildonnan and the Bealach Clithe under plough – using tram horses especially imported from Glasgow, building his own little pier at Rubha na Crannaig to load his smack for export to the mainland, according to Duncan MacKay. At Laig, another tenant – Peter Cameron – had brought cattle from his native Ayrshire and was now busy producing butter and cheese in such quantities that he was able to build new steadings for the farm out of the profits.

Meanwhile, in Skye and the Outer Isles especially, those islanders who had been driven out of their fertile straths and glens to scrape a living by the sea had seen sheep grow fat on their former pastures. Now that wool prices were falling, they witnessed even more land being taken away and turned into deer forests whilst more evicted people came to join already overcrowded districts. Halved again and again, crofts became so small that crop rotation was no longer possible and harvest returns became lower than the amount of seed put into the exhausted ground. Unsurprisingly, crofters and cottars – the latter growing to be as numerous as the former – blamed their economical difficulties on the shortage of a land they still considered to be theirs. But if they cowered in silence before the factors for fear of losing the little they had, they were now being taught in their Free Church assemblies that this state of affairs was not right. The message was that according to the Bible, it was every man's right to have a decent portion of land to cultivate and landlords had no rights to keep the land away from people. This went a long way towards giving people confidence that their grievances were justified, and the Free Church was fast becoming the major religious influence amongst them: by the 1890s on Eigg, there were only thirty Catholics left out of a population of 233 people. Another important factor in the changing of attitudes was the influence of radical newspapers like the Inverness *Highlander* founded in 1873, which helped break the feeling of isolation in the townships and develop a political consciousness of a type never seen before in the Highlands.[13]

94

As the *Highlander* broadcast the progress of the Irish Land League's campaign for an improvement in the conditions of the Irish tenantry, the news also reached the islands by word of mouth. Many crofters and cottars from Skye to Kintyre, including Eigg, went to the Irish fishing and heard at first hand of the three Fs demanded by the Irish Land League: fixity of tenure, fair rents and freedom to inherit a holding. When this active campaign of landlord intimidation, rent-strikes and mass demonstrations was followed in 1881 by the passing of the Irish Land Act, there were quite a few in the Hebrides who declared 'that they had a mind to turn rebels themselves'.[14] Duncan MacKay recalled for example how his father, who was at sea with an Irish skipper, was assured that he would come with his crew and his guns to give a hand to the Eigg crofters if need be!

And turn rebels the Scottish crofters did, starting with rent-strikes in Skye. In November 1881, the people of Braes fought their epic battle with the forces of the law which brought the weight of public opinion on the side of the crofters. Trouble spread rapidly throughout Skye and reached the other islands, Bernera, Lewis and Tiree. The crofting community's grievances which had never attracted much public interest outside the Highlands suddenly forced the politicians' attention. By the end of 1882, a pro-crofters coalition emerged on the political scene, headed by 'Celtic intellectuals' such as Charles Fraser-MacIntosh, the Liberal MP for Inverness. The next year saw the creation of the Highland Land League Reform Association (HLLRA). Two thousand crofters, gathered at Fraserburgh for the fishing season, met to discuss the land question and resolved to set up HLLRA branches in their parishes. The spreading of rent-strikes and boycotting of seasonal work for sheep farmers advocated by the HLLRA began seriously to affect the landowners. By 1883, the government was forced to appoint a Royal Commission of Enquiry into the Conditions of Crofters and Cottars in the Highlands and Islands, the Napier Commission. Encouraged by the presence in the commission of Fraser-MacIntosh and Professor Donald MacKinnon, Edinburgh's professor of Celtic, both fluent Gaelic-speakers, the crofters made their message clear, once they were able to receive assurance that their testimony would not prejudice them in the eyes of their landlords or their factors. There was too little land and precious little security for it, and too many people on what land there was, but if the land which had been taken from them was returned to the people, hardship would disappear.[15]

THE PASSING OF THE CROFTERS' ACT

No testimony was actually taken down on Eigg by the Royal Commission of Enquiry, perhaps because Charles Fraser-MacIntosh's frequent visits to the island had enabled him to present a summary of the islanders' situation, and because the pressure to get land on Eigg was not as acute as on other islands. The report nevertheless recorded twenty-eight crofts on the island, shared between the two townships of Cleadale and Galmisdale.[16] By that time, Laig, Sandavore and Sandaveg were no longer listed as townships, reduced as they were to a farmhouse and a couple of surrounding blackhouses: the last two decades had seen a steady drop in numbers, from 282 in 1871 to 233 in 1891. Fraser-MacIntosh had calculated that, on average, a croft comprising 3.7 acres of arable ground with enough grazing to feed one cow and its followers had to support a family of four. What little grazing there was also supported three sheep, two swine and one horse.[17] The shortage of grazing was such that the Cleadale crofters had to keep their horses on top of Beinn Bhuidhe: it is remembered what an exacting task it was to go up the steep zig-zag path early in the morning before taking them halfway across the island to the peat banks under the Sgurr. However, the acreage of arable could be as low as 1.3 acres for the poorest crofters, most crofters in Cleadale making do with 2.2 acres and the better-off with 6 acres, the average rent including the grazings being £5 9s 1d. The Liberal politician made no mention of the island cottars, elderly people on the Poor Roll, too old to harbour any grievances about land. The fact was that, as everywhere in the Hebrides, the crofters had set up their own system of assistance to such elderly members of the community: in Cleadale, they had obtained leave from the farmer at Laig to cultivate the slopes of the Laig burn, taking turns in planting, hoeing and harvesting potatoes for the old cottars who lived at the Cuagach end of the farm. Nor did he mention the squatters: Duncan Campbell (Donnachadh Gobha) the blacksmith's son, whose cabin was built on the Cleadale common grazings, ploughed a little bit of ground on Crown land near the Singing Sands. John MacKinnon (Iain Mhuilleach), the fisherman from Mull, had been given leave to build his hut above the tide line at Poll nam Partan by the minister in exchange for ferrying him wherever his duties called him. His single-room house, which sheltered at one time no fewer than nine people, was so close to the shore that on the day of the famous Tay Bridge Disaster, his daughters had been obliged to pile all their scant furniture against the door to prevent the huge tide from breaking in! Both Iain Mhuilleach and Donnachadh Gobha derived their subsistence from the sea and it was said that there was not a lobster hole that they did not know about in their respective patches of coast.

If the land hunger on Eigg did not compare with other places – there were 1,200 cottars in Tiree alone – there was certainly a need for more land to be made available, especially for the younger islanders who were often left with no other choice than to go away to earn a living, relying on the death or the departure of a relative to obtain some land for themselves. The census of 1881 showed that hardly anyone under the age of forty was in possession of a croft. A lot of young men went away to work in Lowland or east-coast farms for the best part of the year, coming back in time to lend a hand with the harvest or peat-cutting. Others went to sea until their fathers could no longer manage the crofts, like Dougald MacKinnon's father who went twice round the world in one of the last great East Indiamen. But too many were the young who took the steamer to Oban and boarded the Glasgow train to join the increasing number of migrants who went south to find jobs in domestic service or industry. On the outskirts of Glasgow, villages like Clydebank near the Clyde shipyards were now becoming fast-growing 'Highland towns'. The problem was the same in Canna and Muck, where the now landless MacKay, MacLean and MacKinnon descendants of former tacksmen would have gladly recovered some of the land leased to the Thorburn brothers.

The conclusions of the Napier Commission were geared less towards a reclamation of the lost land, as crofters had hoped it would be, than towards a recreation of the old joint-farm as a kind of *paysan commune* with jointly owned arable and pasture, and a collective responsibility for taxes and rent at the township level where a constable would be elected annually as an executive officer for the smooth working of the system. This was by and large influenced by the historical scholarship of the Gaelic Revival provided by Skene and Carmichael. It went towards the crofters' wishes in that it suggested giving the townships the right of compulsory purchase over adjacent privately owned land, but it only recommended security of tenure for the largest crofters on the grounds that the townships were hopelessly congested. The problems of the smaller holders and landless people were still not addressed.[18]

This proved totally unacceptable to the HLLRA, and as the Third Reform Act was at last extending the right to vote to small landholders and tenants such as crofters – landless people and those on the Poor Roll were excluded – the Crofters' Party was founded to represent their views. Fraser-MacIntosh, who was instrumental in the creation of the party with a few other like-minded liberals, was one of the candidates campaigning under the crofters' banner. He conducted his West Highland campaign in a thoroughly original manner: on board the *Carlotta*, a steam yacht which took him from Lochinver to Tobermory during the month of September 1885. This had the great advantage of taking him to the remotest parishes and he was met with great enthusiasm whenever he went. On Eigg, 'the leader of the people was Thomas MacDonald, an intelligent young man and one who has already made a prominent figure in the Highland Land Law Reform movement. The priest of the island, Father MacLellan, and the Free Church minister, Mr MacKenzie, [were] both in perfect sympathy with the people and with each other upon the land question.'[19] The outcome of the meeting on Eigg was that the islanders, who in their vast majority intended to vote for Fraser-MacIntosh, hired a sloop to take them to the polling place at Arisaig. They offered a passage to the five or six in the island who intended to vote for the Conservative candidate but their offer was declined as a yacht belonging to the owner of Raasay was to take them to Arisaig. Owing to the severity of the weather, the latter never turned up and the Conservative supporters lost the chance of recording their vote whilst the occupants of the sloop arrived safely in Arisaig and voted en masse for the people's candidate! Fraser-MacIntosh was elected in 1885, with a considerable majority as one of the four candidates elected to Parliament under the Crofter's banner, ousting such prominent anti-crofter members as the Duke of Argyll.

The following year, Gladstone's government brought in an Act which virtually conferred on the Highlands and Islands the three Fs it had granted Ireland a few years earlier: fixity of tenure, fair rent and freedom to inherit. The 1886 Crofters' Act gave security of tenure to all crofters, compensation for improvements and some facilities for enlargement of holdings. Security was perpetual and could be passed on by the crofter within his family – though he could renounce it after a year's notice – upon statutory conditions: payment of rent, fair maintenance of the holding and respect of agreement with the proprietor. The Act also provided for official revision of rents by an independent body, the Crofters' Commission, establishing a 'fair rent' proportionate to the produce of the croft and the value of improvements carried out. It effectively ushered in a system of 'dual ownership' where the tenant now had the possibility of owning the buildings on his croft, and saw his rights increase and his position secure, but where the landowner still held considerable power over the land, which could not be disposed of without his consent.

However, 'by the standard of an age accustomed to regard landed property and private contracts between landlords and tenants as inviolable, even sacrosanct, the Crofters' Act was a measure so radical as to be little short of revolutionary'.[20] It was a historical watershed in that at last the threat of evictions was lifted: crofters could now call their own the houses they lived in as well as their portions of land, along with any improvement they made. No more shifting from pillar to post according to the family's fortune, the factor's whim or the landlord's dictate, leaving for someone else the benefit of years of intensive labour on the land without hope of compensation. But the problem was that the Act still did not answer the plight of landless people, modelled as it was on the Irish system of land tenure which was based on arable rather than pastoral land, unlike the Highlands and Islands. The Liberal government was aware of the differences but felt that direct intervention on its part to buy the land and redistribute it since the people were too poor to buy it themselves was unlikely to be accepted by the Commons. Only where land was available for enlargement on land adjacent to the crofts, and when the proprietor was unwilling to let it on reasonable terms, could the crofters – any five of them – apply for it. This measure quelled for a while the land hunger, returning about 72,000 acres to crofting. On Eigg, applications for enlargement of holdings at the expense of Hulin – that part of Kildonnan Farm adjacent to the crofters' land – were received by the commission. As a result two crofts were established for the two landless families living near Hulin. When the common-grazing squatter, Donnachadh Gobha, moved into the Cleadale croft vacated by his relative, the tailor Hugh MacLeod, there was no more landlessness on Eigg. But there was still not enough land to make a decent living.

The measure proved inadequate to solve the land hunger throughout the area. In over-crowded areas where scarlet fever appeared yearly owing to unsanitary living conditions, crofters reasoned that security of tenure and fair rents were worthless without the proper means to get their livelihood from the land. Land-raiding resumed, and the unrest reached such proportions that in 1893 a new Royal Commission of Enquiry was sent to the islands to investigate the people's needs. Two years later, its published conclusions were overwhelmingly in favour of the land-raiders, recommending an extensive reversion of land from deer forests and sheep grazings for the crofters' and cottars' use. From its visit to the Small Isles, the commission reported Grulin, Struidh and Hulin on Eigg as suitable for division into crofts, as well as that part of Galmisdale which was used for grazing by the MacPhersons' new factor and which was named after him, Scott's Park.[21] The scene was set for conditions on Eigg to change, but that hope was soon to be quashed. By 1895, Norman MacPherson had become deaf and increasingly blind, his sisters were now too old and feeble to visit Eigg, and the island was put up for sale.

Chapter 8

A TIME OF TRANSITION

THE THOMSON YEARS

Lawrence Thomson MacEwen, or Robert Lawrie Thomson as he preferred to call himself, bought the Isle of Eigg in 1896, along with Muck and the estate of Strathaird in Skye. Well-off, but not hugely wealthy, Eigg's new owner was a retired armaments dealer, who, from humbler beginnings as ironmaster, had led an adventurous career taking him to Chile, then to Japan and China where he was for a while foreign correspondent for *The Times*. The new Laird's arrival on Diamond Jubilee Day – 22 June 1997 – was meant to be celebrated by a huge bonfire on the Sgurr. Old boats were broken up and carried to the top of the Sgurr in a gigantic pile, but as the proprietor stepped ashore, mist and rain spoiled the effect: no one could see anything. Thomson had more success with a fire lit on the Sgurr to celebrate Japan's victory over Russia in 1904.[1] Very fond of Japan, the new owner had brought enough mementoes of the Far East to fill a whole 'curio room' in his new home in the Macphersons' lodge, where his housekeeper was Annabel Campbell from Cleadale, a formidable character.

A new factor was appointed, MacDonald of Tormore. A Skye man notorious for his opposition to the Land League and his high-handedness with the tenantry, he was unlikely to support any of the Royal Commission's recommendations about extending croftland on Muck and Eigg. In fact, since Thomson's main interest in Eigg was its potential as a shooting estate, the shifting of the entire population of Eigg to Muck, kept as a sheep and dairy farm, was considered at first, so that Eigg could be turned into a deer farm.[2] However, now that crofters could no longer be shifted at will, Thomson settled instead for a concentration of all crofting to the north end of the island, 'where he could not see the poor people', wryly explained one islander. In compensation, the Galmisdale crofters were offered larger holdings than their existing ones, in Cuagach, that part of Laig Farm which extended from below the Bealach Clithe to the start of the Cleadale cliffs, hitherto inhabited by a handful of cottars. This offer was hardly an incentive for the innkeeper and postmaster, the enterprising Duncan MacLeod who did well out of the burgeoning tourist trade with his Scoor Hotel, and held an amount of land five times as large as the other crofts. At least he could now claim compensation for improvements under the 1886 Act when giving up his tenancy. Opting for emigration, MacLeod joined his relatives who had prospered in Nova Scotia.

Whatever misgivings the five crofters left in Galmisdale had about leaving their ancestral patches under the Sgurr hills were finally assuaged by Thomson's offer of a brand new house for each family. Roofed with Ballachulish slates brought by puffer to Laig beach, these five identical houses represented the height of modernity and an undeniable improvement in living conditions with their two upstairs bedrooms, parlour, kitchen and boxroom downstairs, wooden panelling and cast-iron range. Cuagach, or more properly *A' Chuagach*, the twisting place, became a new crofting township with its own common grazing at the top of the Bealach Clithe. From the base of the cliffs to the sandy dunes of Laig bay, the land was divided in five portions of unequal shapes but of equal surface. It included much of the land reclaimed by drainage in the 1850s, which was now good and dry instead of the boggy meadow covered with rushes which had preceded the draining (and to which the ground is now reverting).

The crofters had mixed feelings about the move. Some, like Neil MacDonald, were looking forward to a larger and better piece of ground where a horse or two could be kept. Others like Ruairidh Ruadh, the ferryman, were sad to move away from their relatives at nearby Craigard. His house at the foot of the Sgurr also offered him a convenient view of the steamer rounding Ardnamurchan Point. Instead of a short walk down to the shore, he would now have a long trek across the island without the means of knowing whether the ferry had arrived or not. He was not long in acquiring a bicycle which he shared with his two neighbours when the three of them set off for a fishing expedition in his boat, each of them getting to pedal a third of the way! The crofters' dwellings in Galmisdale were pulled down and their stones dragged away on sledges to build a new wall running from Galmisdale to Sandavore. Only one building remained standing, Ruairidh Ruadh's house, which was to be turned into a gamekeeper's cottage although Donald MacLeod, the crofter who had been appointed to the job, preferred to remain in Cleadale. Nearby, the Scoor Hotel was turned into a hunting lodge and entirely refurbished with hot water, wood-panelling, shining brasses and bells in the kitchen. Thomson liked to stay there himself, for he enjoyed the view better than from his own house.

The factor's brief was also to reorganise the farms: Galmisdale was amalgamated with Sandavore. Laig and Kildonnan were taken back as 'home farms' under a grieve appointed locally, and shepherds were employed to work Grulin and Hulin. Meanwhile, in Cleadale, the crofters had not forgotten that there was still a chance for them to enlarge their holdings by applying to the Congested Districts Board, created in 1898 by the newly elected Conservative government to solve the problem of land hunger. Donald MacKay, the township clerk for Cleadale, had been assured by the Land Court in Inverness that the farm of Hulin would be allocated to them provided that a minimum of five crofters applied for it. The land available extended all the way to Ceann-na-Ghàraidh, the old boundary between Talamh and Struidh, and included land that was once part of Cleadale Farm. This large amount of land, argued the township clerk, would offer the crofters enough grazing land to expand on their livestock and start a joint sheep farm as was now done in Skye and the Outer Isles. The proposal undoubtedly generated much debate on that particular hill next to Tigh na Sidheanan where the Cleadale men used to meet for a talk and a smoke of their pipes. This meeting place was called 'the smack' as it dominated the surrounding hillocks like a ship on the crest of a wave: old Duncan MacLellan would often be seen sitting there, smoking his pipe on his rocky throne. The result was that the crofters started to build a wall for their future livestock at the north end of the Cleadale cliffs. It was never finished, for the land in question was part of the shepherd's hirsel in Hulin and both he and the factor combined to undermine the crofters' resolve. The shepherd, who stood to lose his job, pointed out that the crofters, who knew little about sheep farming on that scale, might find the venture too costly for them. If it failed it might even prove ruinous, as had happened to Lachlan MacKinnon. It was unfortunately not in the powers of the Congested Districts Board to assist crofters in stocking the land it encouraged crofters to reclaim, although it provided help with fencing and construction of new outbuildings. The expense of buying the necessary stock did appear quite daunting and the Cleadale crofters were forced to admit that it was for them an adventure into the unknown, one in which they could little afford to fail. Against this uncertainty, they weighed the offer of seasonal work on the estate farms which the new factor made to those willing to abandon the scheme. They were told that it would still leave them enough time to cultivate their crofts and give them a reliable income. The offer compared only too favourably with the joint sheep-farm scheme, and land-reclaiming was abandoned. The crofters all got their jobs on the estate apart from Donald MacKay, branded the Cleadale hot-head, who was black-listed for quite a while until he was eventually given a job as rabbit trapper.[3]

Rabbits proliferated to such an extent that every year, the estate had to employ two trappers from the mainland to help the four crofters employed from October to March in order to keep numbers down in those myxomatosis-free days. Like shepherds on their hirsels, each trapper worked on his own patch, using snares as well as gin-traps. Trapping went on well into the 1930s, and in his first winter Dougald MacKinnon remembers how he managed to catch as many as 2,000 pairs in Talamh, at sixpence a pair! The rabbits were hung on wire lines, so many lines for each trapper, protected by metal squares from predatory rats, in a purpose-built shed at the pier, ready for inspection by the gamekeeper each week, who would also count the guts which had to be brought back as well, the factor had ruled, to prevent cheating. The rabbits were then sent to Glasgow in great wicker hampers. At a profit of one shilling per pair, they actually represented the estate's main source of revenue at the turn of the century! However, rabbits had little value as game, and mountain hares were introduced without any more success than black grouse or grey partridge. In the last resort, an extensive tree-planting programme was started to provide the necessary cover to encourage pheasants to breed. Four head foresters were recruited amongst the islanders, with some more men under their orders. A tree nursery was established and much fencing carried out.

Thomson, who owned his own steam yacht, the *Scoura*, also wanted to improve access to the island. Since the Congested Districts Board was offering help to those landowners willing to improve the infrastructure on their property, Thomson availed himself of that opportunity to have a pier built at Galmisdale point, in the shelter of Castle Island. It was close to a deep-water channel, where the motor boat he had brought in to meet the steamer could be moored. Crofters were employed to build the pier, using their horses and carts to transport the stones. It was hard work for the poor animals, and Donald MacQuarrie soon devised a double-bottom for his cart, a stratagem speedily adopted by the rest of the crofters!

Apart from forestry and labouring, seasonal work was plentiful on the estate, especially at haymaking time. There was much shifting of workers between Eigg and Muck. 'As many as 18

Cleadale men would be scything from dawn to sundown, a long day in the summer. It was even longer when they went to Muck! There was no question of counting the time it took for them to walk over to the pier, cross over to Muck, and do the same in reverse in the evening. There was no question of overtime in those days', told Duncan MacKay. The islanders were also employed in cutting bracken every spring in both islands. They were even sent one year to Argyll where Thomson rented an estate with a fine castle near Loch Awe. But what money they earned after a whole day on the hill was still not enough for them to spend it lightly on a glass of beer. The story was that one evening, 'the Eigg men walked all the way to the inn, it was the only place for miles in that bit of the country. They were joking about it, saying it was like the bright lights of New York, but when they came in and asked how much it was for a pint, they thought it was not worth it, they couldn't spend all that money on a drink and they turned straight back. That's how much they were getting paid in those days!' told Dodie Campbell whose father had been among the squad of bracken cutters.

Even if it was not much, the islanders were only too grateful for this opportunity to earn a bit more than what the sale of a few beasts brought them at the annual sale below Sandavore. Working for Thomson also brought other perks: he allowed those who worked for him very long loans without interest, repayable twice a year at rent times from what they earned on the farm, and people started to renovate their houses. Dry-stone walls were plastered inside and outside, wooden floors were put in with a linoleum covering, an extra bedroom fitted under the roof. Thatch was replaced with tarred felt and corrugated iron. Roofs had been thatched with a great variety of material in the past, the islanders using whatever was available: barley straw, marram grass, yellow iris and bracken even, but mostly heather and rushes, bound into place with heather ropes hung into place with stones. But it was a time-consuming job, the houses requiring a new cover every other year at least to be really watertight, and it was hardly surprising that the islanders chose to give it up at the first opportunity. However, tin roofs were expensive, so that byres and sheds kept on being thatched for a good while longer.

Not everyone was dependent on Thomson's help: Tearlach MacKinnon's good fortune had been that his brother, luckier than most, had struck it rich in the Klondyke Gold Rush and sent enough money home for an entirely new house to be built in 1896. The old house was turned into a byre and Bayview, the most modern house in Cleadale, was the first crofthouse to take in visitors. 'My uncle did very well in Canada afterwards and I believe there is still a block of flats named after him in Vancouver!' tells Dougald MacKinnon, who remembers seeing his uncle once in his childhood. 'He was wearing a fur-coat, right down to his ankles, we'd never seen anything like it!' Secure employment allowed the crofters to have more money to spend than they had ever had, so that Donald MacKay was able to start a shop at one end of his house. At first he only sold the basic supplies of tea, sugar, meal and tobacco in great twists of bogey roll, the *tombaca dubh* as the islanders called it. The sugar was kept in great big sacks and Duncan MacKay remembers how he would surreptitiously plunge his fingers in the sacks and lick them clean, for the jars of boiled sweets and sugar almonds were neatly lined on a shelf tantalisingly out of his reach. The stock soon increased to include the hardware needed by the crofting community, from nails and sawblades to scythes, tackets and leather for the islanders' home-made boots. Then Donald MacKay started to sell tea and currant buns on Saturday afternoons. Enough tea was consumed for him to receive a barometer as a gift from his suppliers, the very first in the possession of a crofter! Tea was good but beer was even more popular, even though MacKay had no licence and had to keep the bottles in a shed at the back: Dougald recalls how he and the other boys in the township would be scoffing buns and keeping an eye on their fathers to help them home if need be! They also helped collecting the empty bottles which were sent back in great big hampers. The beer trade must have been profitable enough for another shop to open soon afterwards, one house down from the MacKays, selling beer, tobacco and whisky. Old Mrs MacLellan's ability to measure exactly the right amount of bogey roll on her index finger was much admired: 'she never needed to add any shavings on the scale to make up the weight', recalls Duncan MacKay. As cash was always in scarce supply on the island and eggs always plentiful, the islanders soon came to use them as currency, exchanging them for groceries. Telling the shopkeepers that 'the hen was on the nest' was a way of asking for credit. Children were encouraged to keep their own hens and vied with each other as to who would produce the most eggs and buy more sweeties. The island boys found it a good idea once for a prank to raid the shopkeeper's own henhouse and sell him his own eggs back! As to the old people who now received the pensions introduced at that time by Lloyd George, they too enjoyed the advantages of having a shop: Angus MacKinnon recalls how each week his own grandmother, old Katie Bheag, was able to buy a pot of the strawberry jam she was so fond of. As to Morag Campbell's mother, she was so thankful that she never failed to include the Prime Minister in her evening prayers.

Thomson was also instrumental in bringing the telegraph to the island as he needed to be able to contact the outside world more rapidly than by post, notoriously slow in that part of the world. In 1899, a telegraph cable was laid from Skye to Canna, Rum and Eigg, where it ended in Laig Bay: a little wooden hut was erected at the terminal and was staffed by the postmistress who sat there for hours on end, the post office being moved to Laig Farm when the Scoor Hotel was closed. But it was too far for Thomson and both post office and telegraph were relocated in a more central position in a corrugated extension built on the former mission house for the Free Church. It was very near the school, and the schoolchildren soon earned themselves some pocket money by delivering telegrams all over the island: 6d to Cleadale, 9d to Laig or Kildonnan and 1s to Grulin!

By the eve of the First World War, Thomson's seventeen-year tenure of the island drew to a close. Suffering from diabetes, he found solace in solitary night walks until his health required him to spend his last days with his relatives on Muck. It is said that, fearful of delays occasioned by the weather, he had ordered his coffin and kept it in the Lodge, and that he watched his own grave being dug on the highest point on Castle Island. He was buried there on Christmas Eve 1913, his body laid according to his instructions, his head towards Strathaird, his feet pointing to Muck, and Eigg at his side.[4] He had proved a conscientious landlord in the end, taking the well-being of the islanders to heart, and his tenantry mourned him sincerely. His last gesture to the islanders was to present the brand new Catholic Church, built in 1910 on the site of the old tacksman's house in Cleadale, with a pair of antique silver candlesticks and a valuable painting depicting the descent of the Cross, attributed to the school of Zurbaran, the famous Spanish artist. Yet, it could be said of him that he had ushered in an era of unprecedented landlord control over the land, a situation which would contribute to the loss of the island's agricultural potential in the following decades and an unhealthy situation of dependency on the estate for work.

EDWARDIAN VISITORS

It was during the Thomson years that tourists started to come to Eigg, contributing to the modest prosperity enjoyed by the islanders at the time. Eigg could be admired on the train journey to Mallaig which had become a must-do on the Highland tour or during the week-long tour of the west coast, following the route of the royal yacht advertised by David MacBrayne's company. No fewer than ten paddle-steamers did the tour every week during the height of the season, and as they progressed along the coast, tourists would admire the Sgurr, one of the much-vaunted views described in their guide books. Eigg had little in the way of amenities compared to Kyle or Glenelg but it was the only island in the Small Isles which could be visited: Muck was not even on the ferry route and permission had to be requested from the factor to land on Rum. Those few tourists who ventured onto Eigg did so out of a real sense of adventure, before the trend of looking for wild lands took off in the 1930s. Modest lodgings could be found in Cleadale and Cuagach, and Laig Farm now doubled up as a Temperance hotel. Described as one of the oddest pieces of construction imaginable, owing to the succession of outbuildings adjacent to it, it had cramped quarters and poor lighting but the warm hospitality of the manageress amply made up for it, felt M. E. M. Donaldson, one of the people who had 'discovered' the island and kept coming back to it. Her description of the steamer voyage to Eigg shows that things have not changed a great deal in island travel: 'It is always amusing', she noted, 'to watch the attitude of the conventional tourists taking the regulation trip between Mallaig and Oban, when the steamer slows down at Eigg and prepares to receive the ferry boat. Women, fashionably clad in garments quite unsuited to the Highlands, and some of the men no less absurdly dressed cluster behind the rails and wonder who can possibly be going to land in such rough fashion at such an unheard of place? The sailors throw our luggage into the boat as if it was rubbish of which the steamer was well to get rid of . . . We tumble on top of our belongings and push off from the steamer under the pitying glance of the passengers, who are obviously thanking their stars that they are at least bound for a place mentioned in every guide book. When the tide is low, there is an element of excitement in the landing, which can only be effected by a process of slipping and sliding aided by dexterous balancing efforts on sea-covered boulders, prior to a sheer clamber up on the stone landing stage. There, we are met by an old ramshackle pony-trap to convey both ourselves and our luggage over to the "hotel". The marvel it was, to see the same antiquated machine turn up unfailingly every year, for one supposed it could not survive another journey of jolting up stiff hills over ill-made roads, culminating in a voyage over a rough field.'[5] Pony and traps had been for hire in Cleadale since the days of the Scoor Hotel, and a tour of the island in this fashion was popular with visitors.

Miss Donaldson was a keen photographer, amateur botanist and travel writer. Other photographers, like Murray of Hawick or the laird of Gargunnock in Stirlingshire, left stunningly detailed views of the island, but she was a lot more adventurous, thinking nothing of traipsing through hills and bogs from the Sgurr to the Singing Sands in search of a picturesque shot, with her 'green Maria' loaded with the glass plates which she would develop herself. She also liked to photograph the islanders. They submitted willingly to her camera, unlike others in more remote parts who were inclined to think of her apparatus as a peculiar version of the evil eye. Young Katie-Ann MacKay was portrayed at St Columba's Well, dressed very properly for the occasion in her Sunday best, whilst her neighbour wears less self-consciously her everyday clothes and tackety boots to draw water for the family. Other pictures show crofters standing on the pier, sitting outside their house, or bringing the peats home, offering an interesting contrast to the formal wedding photographs duly framed and hung on the wall of the best room which showed solemn faces, men with beards or moustaches, women matronly in their long dresses and best aprons, taken by the schoolmaster on Muck who had his own darkroom at Pier House. She was also very prone to the flowery romanticism inspired by the Gaelic Revival. To her, the experience of watching 'the illumination of Rum by the hand of the master painter' was to witness 'Ossian's address to the setting sun' come to life in front of her very eyes.[6]

Like many of her contemporaries, Miss Donaldson had been introduced to the Gaelic Revival by the work of Kenneth MacLeod, the famous 'Celtic Twilight' songwriter, folklorist and minister, who was born and brought up on Eigg. His widely read poetry and lyrics drew their inspiration from his childhood experiences on Eigg and held an instant appeal for city-dwellers with romantic ideas. A brilliant Gaelic scholar, MacLeod, who published his first folklore collection at the age of 16, started to evolve his own blend of Celtic mysticism, aware of the combination of pagan and Christian elements in Hebridean beliefs. Such views were certainly in sharp contrast to his fellow ministers who all too often followed the rigid God-fearing teachings of the Free Church in condemning music and dance throughout the Highlands and Islands. On Eigg, for instance, a minister had refused permission to marry the daughter in the MacKay household unless they disposed of their grandfather's fiddle! The family resolved to destroy an old fiddle and keep the beautiful *Fidheall Ruadh* which had cost MacLean of Coll the price of a cow. (They eventually sold it for 11 shillings to a travelling dance-master who then sold it for a fortune to the Museum of Antiquities in Edinburgh when it was found out to have been made in Cremona by a contemporary of Stradivarius!)

Adopting the Celtic vision of Heaven and Hell and bringing *Tir nan Òg* – the land of youth – into his preaching did not further MacLeod's advancement in the church but appealed to the coterie of enthusiastic Gaels led by Alexander Carmichael in Edinburgh, where he met Marjorie Kennedy-Fraser, a professional musician who had already successfully included in her recitals some of the Gaelic songs she had 'discovered' during a tour of the west. It took a good while before Marjorie Kennedy-Fraser managed to persuade Kenneth MacLeod to accompany her to Eigg to help her do some recordings for the second edition of her *Songs of the Hebrides*. He finally agreed, a little apprehensive that the island would not live up to his memories, and they set off for the island in 1913. He should not have worried, for the old people gladly gave him what they could recall, and, spurred by what he remembered himself, they told tales and songs which they had not thought of for years! They found a lot to record on the wax cylinders of Mrs Kennedy-Fraser's phonograph, the clumsy and primitive recording machine of the time, from tales of Cuchulain to the songs and stories of St Donnan and St Bride, from working songs and milking croons to peat-smooring prayers, lullabies and love songs. A lively *iorram* (a rowing song) was recorded from 90-year-old Widow MacDonald in Cleadale, who astonished her audience with the vigour of her singing. Marion MacLeod and Ishbel MacLeod gave them some fine *port-a-beul*, the Hebridean mouth-music which supplied the islanders with dancing tunes without the need for any musical instrument apart from the singer's voice. For Marjorie Kennedy-Fraser, Ishbel was 'one of the gayest singers [they] had ever met in the isles. It was a pleasure to see her beaming in the doorway as we scrambled up from the shore to greet her. To an uncommonly strong voice, she added a good repertoire of songs . . . She also danced and sang to us an exhilarating *Port-a-Beul* used for foot-waulking in the days when blankets were shrunk by dancing on them.'[7] Hearing one of these recordings on the radio, Ishbel's great-niece, Chrissie MacLean, recalled with peals of laughter how her aunt had said at the end of the song that she would have sung better if it had not been for the baby: she was the baby her aunt had held in her arms whilst being recorded! Chrissie remembered her great-aunt well: 'she was never away from the spinning wheel. She was at it all through the day, especially if it was a wet day and nobody was out, and we used to help with the carding, and she used to sing all the time.' The fourth singer from whom they collected was Kirsty MacKinnon, who provided with her brother Angus MacCormick most of the material they were able to record. Kirsty had 'a voice of peculiar charm and a rare memory for the old tunes'. Her brother had an equally good memory and 'carried himself with the unconscious rhythmic bearing and far-away look of one of the heroes of his ancient tales'.[8] Marybel MacDonald remembered what a 'real old gentleman' he was, with a long white beard reaching to the middle of his chest, 'who often came to visit her great-aunt Ishbel for a wee crack'. Aonghas Fhionlaigh, as Angus was known in the island, and his sister were two of the great tradition-bearers of their generation. There was also Duncan MacLellan – Donnachadh Mór – who was renowned for his wit and humour, from whom Duncan Ferguson was to learn so much of the island lore. But Aonghas Fhionlaigh had no equal when it came to genealogies, especially the history of the tacksmen of the Morar family and the MacAskills. Before their marriage, both his parents had been in the service of the MacDonalds of Laig as a farm servant and a table maid, and 'there was not much to be told about the MacDonalds that they did not know', recalled his nephew Hugh MacKinnon.[9] Hugh and his brother Angus were the two young men whom Marjorie Kennedy-Fraser had noticed at Kirsty MacKinnon's house, eagerly listening to the impromptu ceilidh. She had hoped that one day they would carry on in their uncle's footsteps, and that they certainly did!

One of Marjorie Kennedy-Fraser's aims as she collected these songs and tales was to help rescue what she called rather patronisingly the 'floating fragments of a fast disappearing tradition'. In fact she was very much like those nineteenth-century antiquarians who opened grave-mounds and took away anything they found interesting, leaving the rest to be destroyed. Comparing her work to the art of the jeweller, 'setting the airs in a harmonic and rhythmic framework of piano-forte wrought metal as one would do a beautiful gem, a cairngorm or the likes', she actually processed everything she recorded for her public in the UK and abroad, in many cases changing tunes and words round to suit her taste, and getting Kenneth MacLeod to compose new words if needed be. Quite often, MacLeod resorted to giving approximate renditions of Gaelic sounds in English, the result being known to cause Gaelic speakers much hilarity, but he generally applied all his poetic talent to preserve a 'good sound-colour as well as rhythm-clang and emotional content',[10] as in this *port-a-beul* originally recorded from Marion MacLeod.

> Dance to your shadow when it's good to be living, lad,
> Dance to your shadow when there is nothing better near you,
> Dance to your shadow when it's fine to be living, lad,
> Dance to your shadow when there is nothing better.

> Ho ro haradal, Hind ye haradal, Ho ro haradal, Hind ye handan.

Dance to your shadow when it's hard to be living, lad,
Dance to your shadow when it's sore to be living, lad,
Dance to your shadow and let Fate to her fiddle, lad,
Dance to your shadow for it's fine to be living, lad.

Ho ro haradal, Hind ye haradal, Ho ro haradal, Hind ye handan.[11]

Although Mrs Kennedy-Fraser and Kenneth MacLeod tended to present Gaelic culture as a fossilised heirloom rather than a living culture, they did a lot to popularise a more positive view of Gaeldom and boost the self-confidence of a people who had been taught for generations that their culture was worthless. Few were the households on Eigg who did not have a copy of Kenneth MacLeod's book, *The Road to the Isles*, which included so many of his recollections from the island.

LEARNING IN ENGLISH, NOT IN GAELIC

In spite of Kenneth MacLeod's misgivings, life on the island was still very much led according to tradition in the first decades of the twentieth century, each crofter content to follow in the steps of his forefathers. However, the progress of mechanisation was ushering in different ways of doing things. The work songs started to disappear little by little from the fields. There was no need for cloth to be fulled since wool was sent to the north-coast mills where it was spun, woven and returned as blankets or cloth ready to sew. Waulking songs were now heard in the context of the ceilidh, the island women miming the work of fulling the cloth with a handkerchief. Spinning was perhaps the only traditional activity still carried out, but only by the older women who produced all the fine yarn needed for producing socks and underwear for the whole family. Islanders growing up during the First World War remembered only too well the itchy woollen combinations, drawers and long johns which their mothers and aunts kept knitting whenever there was a spare moment. The wool which was used was still dyed in the traditional manner, iris roots for dark green, crotal for brown and peat soot which 'would give a good orange that did not run! They would use it, my mother and old Mrs MacKay next door, they did that!' remembers Morag Campbell in Cleadale. She could still picture the huge pot which was put to the boil near the burn behind the MacLeods' byre, where the women of the three neighbouring crofts came to do their dyeing.

Apart from the inevitable modernisation of life, the most important threat for the future of crofting life was the steady fall in the island's population (233 islanders in 1891, 211 in 1901, 160 in 1911), as each departure severed a link in the chain of tradition. There was no longer a question of extending croftland on Eigg although the land war still raged on in the Outer Isles. The existing crofts could only support so many, and if work was not to be had on the estate, the young islanders had to leave the island as soon as they finished school. As always, a certain number joined the Merchant Navy until their parents retired from the croft. But more and more youngsters joined the swelling Gaelic communities of Clydebank where work was on offer at the Singer factory, the shipyards or the Glasgow Tramway Company. Soon there was at least one son or daughter in each island family who had moved to or married in Clydebank.

Because of all these departures, there were fewer youngsters at the ceilidhs and fewer to learn the island traditions and pass them on; for the ceilidh was the cinema, the music-hall and the university of the community. At one time, remembered Kenneth MacLeod, tales and ballads were so plentiful 'that a man could live his full four score years on Eigg and yet hear something new at the ceilidh every night of his life'.[12] This was in his youth in the 1870s when there were still people who could boast that their parents were taught a little reading and much poetry by Ranald Dubh of Laig. Some of these tales were now forgotten, but the island's rich inheritance still nurtured and moulded the islanders' minds. The tradition of song-making was alive and well, especially the ancient tradition of bardic satire. Verses were still composed to satirise rats into leaving the houses they plagued, like *Aoir do Rodan*, the song which Donald MacLellan made at the request of Domhnall Gobha, the shoemaker. But any topic was good enough to make a verse or two to the tune of a well-known melody, making fun of an unpopular factor, or praising a girl, a rare catch of fish or the quality of a good bottle. The ceilidh was still the best place for native talent to emerge, and amongst their peers, Hugh MacKinnon and his brother Angus were widely acknowledged for their wit and their song-making. They were also amongst the few islanders who could read and write their own language – being taught at home by their uncle Angus MacCormick. It often fell on them to write down the words of a song composed by someone who was not able to write in Gaelic.

The problem was that even though Gaelic was the life-blood of the community, education authorities still considered it a language best to be forgotten, or confined to Sunday school. Gaelic was thought to be a hindrance to social advancement and only an education in English could 'add rungs to the ladder of opportunities, opening the possibility of becoming at best a minister or a teacher, or at least giving the ambition to break away from crofting'.[13] This was very much the view of the factors, ministers and farmers who had dominated the parish school boards since their creation in 1872.

The Small Isles parish school board was unusual in that it included a crofter, Angus MacCormick, the highly respected ground officer, alongside Thomson's factor, the proprietor of Canna, the Rum factor, plus the minister and the priest for a balance in religious views to which Angus, as a Catholic, was very much attached. Yet this did not prevent the board from supporting the official policy of preventing children from using their own language as soon as they entered the classroom and punishing them if they used it, even in the playground. The board's role was confined to fixing the dates of school holidays, seven weeks in the summer, one week in autumn for the potato harvest, a week between Christmas and New Year, and one at Easter, and paying out all the expenses relating to the school as well as teachers' salaries.[14] The money collected from the local rate was supplemented by a grant allocated by the government after inspection of the schools. This depended on the standard of achievement reached by the pupils during a yearly assessment. Great importance was attached to their mastery of English, as well as domestic skills for the girls and navigation for the boys as they were expected to find employment in service or in the Merchant Navy. Those who displayed academic abilities were encouraged to prepare for the grammar-school examination which could lead to Inverness Academy and to further education depending on the bursaries they received.

The biggest problem encountered by the Small Isles school board was attracting teachers to Eigg. Most found the salary of £70 per annum poor, in spite of 'the partially furnished house and good garden'. Some were such bad teachers that they were dismissed at the parents' request: schooling was considered too expensive to be wasted in such a way. At any rate, not one of the teachers appointed by the board managed to leave fond memories behind, in spite of any academic achievements that may have been attained. The fact was that, in accordance with the educational methods of the time, they made an all-too-frequent use of the strap and the pointer – so much so that one day, Dougald MacKinnon hit on the great idea of stealing the strap and disposing of it in a rabbit hole, only to discover that the teacher had a spare one!

Whiteford, who was appointed on the eve of the First World War, was chiefly remembered for his habit of sitting in the sun at playtime, ready to hammer anyone who forgot they were not supposed to speak Gaelic in the playground. He also had to rely on his pupils to supply him with water by carrying it 'for a considerable distance, uphill all the way', so that after much deliberation the school board finally agreed to provide him with a decent water supply instead of a rain barrel. As for Johnson, who had terrorised the Rum children before he was appointed to Eigg, he was so obnoxious that the children could not wait to see the back of him: 'If you saw him coming with his slippers in the morning, you thought "that's it, he'll no be going out today", but if you saw him coming in with his boots on, all polished up, it was fishing day and he would be away in the hills, and we'd feel great', recalled Chrissie MacLean. Johnson's only redeeming feature was that he taught Gaelic at night classes so that islanders like Duncan Ferguson or young Donald MacKay were able to learn to read and write in their own language. MacKinnon, the most brutal of them all, was actually certifiable and ended up in the asylum. 'I remember being hit on the head with two thick books as he passed through the rows, and that was when I was in the infant class', recalls one islander. 'If you laughed you had a slap across the face and the ear that sent you reeling across the floor. One of us, Barbara MacKay, she was a shy and nervous girl and she could not stop fidgeting in her seat. Well, that man, he caught her by the hair and he lowered her from her seat to the floor three times! The poor girl, she made straight for the door but he caught her by her hair and he pulled her back to her seat. Well, as soon as we were out of the door for playtime, she bolted through the heather and she ran straight home and she never came back to school until the teacher was fired through her father's complaint. And that was a good thing too.'

The 1918 Education Act allowed a better class of teacher to be appointed by the Inverness County Education Authority which replaced the parish school board. Two teachers were needed for the forty island children who attended school from the war years onwards. There was one of each denomination and the islanders remember how they were separated into two groups every morning for religious education. Some of them were fondly remembered, like Miss MacLennan from Benbecula who taught her pupils the rudiments of Gaelic. Others, like one teacher from Harris, unfortunately brought their sectarian prejudices with them.

If the islanders had few good memories of their time on the school benches, they remembered with pleasure the games they played outside. Boys and girls played 'chuckie' with stones or whelk shells. The girls practised the intricate Scottish country dance steps to perfection. The boys played shinty with their home-made camans, but as football grew increasingly popular, they finally put thruppence each towards the cost of a ball. And if the ball was damaged, woe to the one who had done it! He was barred from playing and 'for two weeks he'd sit in that window sill till he'd bring the money for his share. Well,' exclaimed Chrissie Maclean, 'there was not the money like now that you could say – here you are, here's the money!' All children liked playing rounders and a cops-and-robbers game called *Seonnachan*, where the one who was caught had to stand in the place where iris grew until he was freed. But this did not mean that boys and girls played together in the playground. They hardly mixed at all when they were young. 'Oh no,' explained Marybel MacDonald, 'the boys did not want to have anything at all to do with us. They were horrible to us, always playing tricks on us or throwing stones. They'd wait for us at the top of the Bealach Clithe ready to shower us with stones as we came home, so that we had to go through the hills and come back down at the other end of Cuagach.' On warm summer days, however, it was equally difficult for girls and boys to resist the temptation to stray on the way to school. The Creagard children for instance would set out in an orderly file for the mile-long trek to school in the morning, each child holding the other's hand, but by the time they were out of sight of their parents, Lachie Campbell would disappear as often as he could: he would rather spend his time day-dreaming in the hills. In Cleadale, one of the girls always dreamt up new games on the way to school: 'she used to boss us around, making us take off our coats and spread them on the fence to jump over it – let's play kangaroo, she'd say – and we would get late and get the strap', laughed Marybel MacDonald.

School attendance was very strictly monitored, the attendance cards being filled twice a day, morning and afternoon. Anyone who was late for school would be punished with the strap and those who were present every day were allowed out half an hour earlier on Fridays. Many children took their attendance records very seriously: as late as the 1950s, Dr MacLean was obliged to ask the school to close for the day since the poor girl he had diagnosed with a bad case of fever was adamant that she would still go to school. She had a perfect attendance record and did not want to spoil it! The only concession to bad weather conditions, in those days when the children had to walk to school whether it was pouring with rain or blowing a gale, was to start school at 10 in the morning during the winter. One bad winter's morning, one of the girls who had been given a brand new cape – a police cape sent in a parcel of clothes by a relative in the Glasgow Police – had a lucky escape when the wind got hold of her past the post-box: she went flying up the hill and landed down in a field well below the road! Winter was tackety boots time: the crofters used to put new soles and new tackets in the children's shoes at the beginning of winter. Big skins of leather for re-soling the boots were bought at the island shop, soles were cut out and soaked in water before they were nailed into place, shaped with the iron boot shapes that every crofter possessed, and then tackets were put on them. 'It was like walking on nails at first before you got accustomed to them and they wore out a little!' The children could not wait for the moment where they could leave their tackety boots at home, and from May to October they always went about barefoot. The introduction of plimsolls later on was hailed as a great thing by the girls, who always managed to injure their big toes on the stones in the days before the road was metalled and tarred.

Winter and summer, the island children took their lunch with them to school, their 'pieces' consisting of a scone with marmalade and jam and a bottle of milk. 'Sometimes you would eat your piece at playtime or on the way over or the schoolmaster's dog would get at the milk, and that was you for the day.' The provision of a school meal had been rejected as too expensive by the parish school board and the children had to content themselves with the dry sailor's biscuit and the cup of cocoa provided for them in the winter months out of a fund created by Thomson for that purpose.

RIDING BAREBACK ON THE BEACH

The island children earned what few pennies they had by their own labour. They could earn money by delivering telegrams for the Post Office. This was by far the best job, but it was by nature irregular. They relied otherwise on selling eggs from their own hens. Sometimes there would be odd jobs like catching young trout for the gamekeeper to restock the lochs. Duncan MacKay and his friends caught a good number in the Laig burn by damming it with heather. They had been supplying the gamekeeper for a while when they noticed that the exact number of fish was never checked. Overconfident, they started to cheat on how many exactly they provided, until the day they were found out! All hell let loose and the poor boys never got a penny for their efforts. Combing the beach could always be relied on for some rewarding finds such as rubber, which was paid at a given rate by the Receiver of Wrecks.

However, it was only after they had done their share of work on the croft that the children had free time on their hands. They were expected to help at the potato planting and harvesting as well as at haymaking and corn harvesting. In the spring, from May onwards, they had to help with the peat. Even though Thomson had introduced coal to the island, supplying it cheaply to his employees, peat was still cut on the island until well into the 1930s. It was not so efficient in the new cast-iron ranges, but it was fine in the open grates of the wall fires. Marybel recalled how she would be given a live peat as a torch to come back from their neighbours on dark nights when there was no moon. Securing the yearly supply of peat was a gruelling job and the children would have to go to the hills above Laig straight after school to join in the peat stacking. 'First of all, you had to put a big peat with two slanting against it to dry them well. Then you had to make little stooks and you stacked it all before you brought them back with the ponies. At the house, you started to build a big stack by the side of it and when it was finished you brought the ponies back to the Horses' Park. And all you got for that was a scone and jam', recalled Chrissie MacLean. 'But that was the best job, taking the horses there or back to the croft! The further they were away, the best it was, because you had the longest ride! We used to ride bareback, just hanging to the mane. And the horses weren't trotting, they used to gallop and you weren't stopping at a fence, you jumped over it! When I think of it now, we could have all been killed, but you never thought of the danger then. I remember when Duncan Campbell fell, right enough: he fell over the horse's neck and went right under it. That was at the wall this side of the Singing Sands . . . Well, it was a miracle he wasn't hurt.'

Everyday chores were divided between girls and boys. Washing was for girls; they had to tramp on the blankets to clean them on washing day, when mothers lit a little fire outside and put a great big pot of water on to boil for the tub. Milking was also a girl's chore. 'Anything to do with the milking, that was a girl's job,' recalls Angus MacKinnon, 'but I had to do it sometimes if my mother was busy, and I had to make butter too! You had to put the fresh milk in shallow basins, and after two days, you skimmed the cream off the top and you put it in an earthenware crock and you left it for three days – no more – otherwise it would not churn. And we used to churn away at it, with the plunger churn or the circular one. That was my biggest chore of all! There was always something wrong. If the weather was warm, it wouldn't set. It was the curse of my life to try and make it set. I tried everything, putting a little cold water helped sometimes, well, it could take half an hour or it could take two hours . . . But you got to drink the froth when you did the milking and that was good. We used to make "*fuaran*" with cream and oatmeal, and that was nice too.'

It was more of a boy's job to help with the cattle and the horses and cart. 'It was so much part of your life to help your parents that you never thought much of it and you loved it. You see, I was told how to harness a horse and how to take it off when I was really young. But things had to be done properly and without flagging, otherwise that wasn't too good for you', explains Angus. 'I remember one particular instance, I was about 10 years old. This day, it was in the springtime, and my father – oh he was quiet, hard as nails, you know – my father and I we were going to the pier. He used to cart things up for the shop. Well, that day, I heard him going up the stairs: the tackety boots. And he says to me: "Where did you put the halter?" "Oh I don't know where it is," I said and I felt terrible, because I knew he hated having to say anything to me. "Go and get it, get it done, laddie." That's all he said, no shouting at all. And that was worse than shouting. It was all to do with respect. I only had to look at him and I knew. And ever since then, I made sure everything was where it should be.'

After work came freedom to do as they pleased. Each gang of children had its own patch and, although they stayed within their territory, they all competed to carve their initials on the most inaccessible rock, or on that particular boulder, up from the Singing Sands, where it was customary for each generation to leave its mark. 'Oh, we used to live on the shore', told Marybel and Chrissie, laughing as they reminisced together. 'We made tunnels and canals in the sand and we played boats. I can still picture the day we took our brother Ian to sea in our washing tub. It was big, a great big barrel cut into two, we took it down to the beach from our house at the top of the cliff. We dragged it down the path and we let it sail with Ian in it, never thinking he was just a wee boy, and of course we forgot him. Well, I can still remember the water lifting me up when I went to catch him, I must have been in quite deep. In one dive I got hold of the rope – I couldn't swim. I could only snatch at the rope – and I pulled him in. Well, our mother must have seen us, for she came down with the axe and she split that tub into smithereens!'

Duncan MacKay used to play with his neighbours, the MacDonald boys, on a little lochan behind their houses at the foot of the cliff which has now disappeared. They built a proper raft with a sail on it and they would play on it for hours on end. When winter came the water would freeze solid and they would go skating there. 'It used to be really cold in the winter, we would be stuck inside for days because of the snow', recalls Dougald MacKinnon. 'There's no snow like that nowadays, and no summers like we used to have, real summers, running around in our bare feet, picking wild strawberries, munching watercress stalks . . . I mind we used to find honey sometimes in the hayfields, wild honey, oh, that was good. You wouldn't find any today!' There were no sophisticated toys for the crofters' children but they improvised with what they had on hand. Iris leaves made wee boats which were raced down the burns. A piece of driftwood with four matches stuck in it and a potato balanced at one end became a rocking horse. There was no time to get bored, there was too much to do and plenty to keep busy when the chores were over.

Each season brought its own excitement. Seagull's eggs were collected in the spring and hard-boiled eggs were rolled down the hills at Easter, Grulin being a favourite place for that. The Cleadale folks would walk there to the shepherd's cottage as he would invite everyone to a great spread at that time of the year. 'It was terrible,' recalled Marybel, 'he used to put everything in brine, mutton, birds, anything, and he would cook it all and we had to pretend to eat it not to offend him.' In the summer, fishing was a favourite occupation. The Campbell boys at the pier were always rowing to Grulin to cast their longlines. There was also the shearwater hunt in late July or early August, a tradition which endured until the 1930s. During his visit to the island in 1926, the naturalist Charles Connel had been able to record that 'there was an unwritten law which forbade the islanders to approach the nests of the Manx shearwaters, nesting then on the cliff tops and accessible gullies of Beinn Bhuidhe, as well as the sides where they nest today, until an appointed day. Then, the whole island, young and old, set to work to scour the dizzy and treacherous cliffs, and in a single day, they cleared the accessible portions of their living food store.'[15] According to Dodie Campbell, who went hunting for shearwaters with his own father, the oily *fachach* – the young shearwater – was so fat that 'you could just squeeze it and the oil would pour out of its beak. It was great for waterproofing your shoes', he added with a satisfied grin at the horrified gasp which generally greeted that anecdote.

As autumn came, Hallowe'en was a treat all the children looked forward to. They went round from house to house in disguise, taking particular care to hide their faces so that the grown-ups would have great difficulty in identifying them. They would sing a song, tell a rhyme or sometimes they mimed little satirical scenes involving the minister or the factor and they would earn themselves a treacle scone or a sweet in each household for their trouble. That night, all kinds of pranks were allowed and the older children would spend a lot of time lugging the carts about the township. The owners would wake up in the morning to find a different cart in their shed if it had not disappeared altogether.

Midwinter brought the thrills of Yuletide. Christmas was not much of a celebration, especially in the Protestant households where work carried on as normal that day. But it was still the only time of year when fresh fruit would be seen in the shop, and it was a great treat to be given a few oranges and apples. Christmas parties were introduced on the island by Sir William Petersen, the next owner of Eigg, but it was not until the 1940s that they became a yearly occurrence in the school calendar. Hogmanay was much more of an event, with houses full of people and music as everyone went first footing from house to house. Bagpipes and fiddles were brought out and there was a fair bit of dancing. For the children, however, this paled in comparison with the shinty match which followed on New Year's Day, when the whole island would gather on Laig beach by midday, when everyone had done the rounds. 'I have seen the beach black with the number of people that used to come, women, children, old people!' recalled Marybel MacDonald. 'I remember my old father going on his two crutches.' The under-14s, the schoolchildren, were not allowed to play, as it was considered too dangerous with the hard wooden ball that was used for the game. They had their own game at the end of the beach. 'They would not get a shot of the ball anyway if they were amongst grown men', explained Hugh MacKinnon. The fun was to see the teams being chosen and the best players do their star turns. 'Oh, there were some good players. I remember Gillesbuig, son of John son of Angus, he was about 80 years of age, he did not have a stitch on but his trousers and his shirt – it was a particularly fine New Year's Day. He saw the ball coming from the other side, it was rising too high, so that the only thing he could do was to stick his chest out and stop it that way.'[16]

At one time, the shinty season had started on All Saints' Day and continued through Christmas, New Year and the feast of the three Kings. 'Epiphany was the last day they had of the shinty, the generation before me and other generations before that,' recalled Hugh MacKinnon, 'and if the tide allowed them, they would stay until night had fallen and the stars were in the sky before they came home. And they would be so tired that they couldn't sup milk from a spoon by the time they came home!' In Hugh's days and the days before him, the islanders would have had to make their own gear. The ball was made out of a lump of hazel root. 'They'd whittle at it with a knife first of all and then they'd rub at it and make it smooth with a rasp and a file. And to make it tougher so that it wouldn't split apart, they would boil it in a pot of water over the fire, that is what I used to hear, yes, they did that and I can assure you, if you were hit by those balls, you would feel it!'[17] The camans were made out of willow or hazel especially if the hazel trunk had a natural bend on it. It was quite a craft to produce a good caman, involving a lot of work and care. The shape was whittled away first, then the wood would be put in a clamp to bend it at the desirable angle. 'You would get a *lorg* – that's what they called the piece of wood – a straight "lorg", maybe about four feet long or so. And you would put the heavy end of it in the fire, about a foot or so up from the lower end of it with the embers and little bits of burning peat around it. But you had to be careful not to burn the wood. The bark would obviously be pretty burnt away, but you had to be careful, it was very liable to happen that you would burn the wood itself! And when you put it in the clamp, it would split, you know. But the ones that were good at making camans and that, they would put it in the clamp and they would bend it as nicely as you would ever see. Now, if you got the heat right in the burning, you left it, oh, perhaps three days or so in the clamp and you took it out and it would keep that shape. They didn't have a special piece of equipment for the clamp at all. But if you had a ladder or something like that, you fixed another bit of timber across and you could make the spaces between the rungs narrow, perhaps three inches or so, and you put it there, and you bent it and tied it with ropes . . . And when it was done, you cut the lower end – the *bois*, the palm of the caman, you cut it to make it triangular.'[18]

Caman-making was a typical example of the ingenuity displayed by islanders in their everyday life, in their use of whatever resources they had at hand. But as the popularity of football grew after the First World War, and the schoolchildren abandoned shinty on the playground to adopt football as their favourite game, the art of caman-making was no longer passed on. Yet another island tradition was given up. There were still some pretty good games of shinty after the war. But one New Year's Day – 1925 or 1926 – Hugh MacKinnon witnessed the final demise of an old island game: 'the shinty sticks were laid aside and the football brought out. That's what the young ones wanted.'

Chapter 9

THE AGE OF THE MAGNATES

EIGG AND THE GREAT WAR

The Small Isles contributed a contingent of twenty-two men to fight for their country in the First World War. They were dispersed to the distant battlefields of Flanders, northern France, Greece and Turkey, in the Cameron Highlanders, the Lovat Scouts or the Highland Light Infantry regiments. Twenty of these men were from Eigg, and, by a peculiar coincidence, they were all Catholics. The parish priest was said to have preached sermons full of patriotic fervour which drove many of his parishioners to volunteer at the beginning of the war. There was to be only one roll-call of honour, for the rest of the eligible islanders were exempted when conscription started in the second year of the war. They were all employed on the estate which contributed to the war effort by raising extra crops of oats on land set aside especially for that purpose in Hulin and by keeping herds of pigs which ploughed the hill black on the southern slopes of Beinn Bhuidhe.

News of the troops' movement and progress was followed anxiously by each household. Every mail day, newspaper cuttings were pasted in the Post Office window, which the schoolchildren read on their way back from school and related to their families. The reality of war manifested itself by the amount of wreckage which came ashore from torpedoed ships. Kegs of butter or dried fruits, sacks of flour and meal were found and were instantly divided amongst the islanders. These helped make up for the shortage of supplies now that the two shops found themselves obliged to close, owing to a sudden increase in freight charges and a growing scarcity of money on the island. The islanders were now dependent for essentials on orders taken by travelling salesmen from big companies in Glasgow which would send oatmeal, flour, tea and sugar by monthly cargo. For the rest, they bartered baskets of eggs for supplies from MacDougalls' in Arisaig. It was a lean time for sweeties as far as the island children were concerned. Duncan MacDonald remembers how they had sucked with delight a tube of minty toothpaste left by visiting relatives: to them it tasted like the best humbug!

115

In this time of dearth, the island children turned into assiduous beachcombers, the adults keeping an eye on them to decide if it was worth going down to the beach. As German submarines started to wage war in Hebridean waters, beachcombers had to be wary of the occasional mine washed up on the shore. Mary MacQuarrie earned herself a pound for the torpedo she found at the Singing Sands and reported to the Receiver of Wrecks. The minister's son was lucky to escape with his life when he started to throw stones at a large round mine in Grulin which exploded right away. Submarines did not hesitate to threaten civilian vessels and in the summer of 1918, the crew of MacBrayne's steamer was lucky to escape unharmed, firing back at the Germans, whilst the captain and his mate had taken to the lifeboat!

It was towards the end of the war that the terrible outbreak of Asian flu which had swept the country reached the Small Isles. The death toll was particularly high on Eigg amongst the old and the very young. Dougald MacKinnon remembers how everyone in his household had been confined to bed for days, unable to move with the flu. He considered his family lucky not to have suffered any casualties, unlike most households on the island. The whole community was in mourning, for the flu epidemic coincided with the news that only ten of the twenty island conscripts were to return. At Tigh na Sitheanan, the loss was particularly tragic: three brothers – Angus, Archibald and Donald MacLellan were killed in Flanders, Donald earning the Military Medal for his bravery. Only Neil, the fourth and youngest brother, came back. But like John MacLellan, his friend in the next croft, he was badly affected by gas poisoning in the trenches. 'It was so cruel . . . they suffered agonies with it': all too often the soldiers' only defence had been a urine-soaked kilt. Both died within a few years of their return. Neil was buried in Rome, where he had gone to study for the priesthood.

Among the veterans who made it back safely were Hugh and Angus MacKinnon, who returned to the croft tended by their mother and their uncle in spite of their age. Hugh had witnessed tragic events in Greece where he spent most of the war, but to find himself in the land of Homer, in the setting of the classics he had learnt in his youth, had been a moving experience for a man of his poetic temperament. Many years later, he would recall the experience to his friend, Fr Ross, as they watched the sun setting over Rum: 'I have never seen a more beautiful evening unless it was one night when I stood upon the plains of Greece and watched the sun go down behind Olympus. You will have read the Iliad, of course, Maighstir Antony?'[1] On his return to Eigg, it was a very different feeling which now inspired his poetry. Words of grief and sorrow kept welling up in him, following the rhythms of familiar tunes as he resumed work on the croft, for he sorely missed the men who had not returned from the war. They ought to have been there with him, ploughing, fishing, ceilidhing. They ought to have been there to ease the burden off ageing shoulders and give new strength to the community, but they were not. In the elegies he composed for them, Hugh sang the grief of an island depleted of much of its hope for the future. He sang the lasting damage which the Great War had wrought on the fabric of the community, as in so many other parts of Europe.

> Oh, I am deep in gloom today
> It's not my good spirits that drive me on
> Oh, I am deep in gloom today. (refrain)

I took a turn down to the shore
To try and pass some hours away.
The wind was tearing from the West
And the sea swelling in the green glens.

Passing by Camus Sgiotaig
I was moving as in a dream.
It had affected my thoughts
To be alone on that walk.

Where we used to gather in a band
When we were young without a care,
Full of life, full of joy,
Full of fun, guileless and innocent.

Where we ran and jumped and wrestled.
Where we lay around the banks,
The putting stone so often handled
Overgrown with grey lichen amongst the rushes.

It has fallen asleep among the rank grass
Since no hand comes near it to move it,
And if it had the power of speech
It would complete the burden of my song.

And it would tell of valiant lads
Who would poise it on their shoulders.
It would be no disgrace to go and listen to the tale it has to tell
How they went away wearing tartan

When the Kaiser struck his blow.
And how they went away and did not come back
The cause of my sadness at this time:
That's what has left me alone here today
That's what has left me feeling deserted.[2]

SHOOTING AND SHOUTING: A NEW PROPRIETOR

As they returned home, the veterans found the island had acquired a new proprietor during the war. John MacEwen, Thomson's nephew, had decided to keep Muck as a sheep farm and sell Eigg in 1916 to the rich London shipowner who had rented the island shootings since Thomson's death. The rumour was that Sir William Petersen bought the island quite cheaply on account of a mysterious fire which had destroyed Thomson's house.

Petersen's first gesture as proprietor was to order a platform to be erected near to the school from which to address his tenantry. On the appointed day, the islanders dutifully gathered to hear him list the many wonderful improvements he had in store for them. But returning soldiers like Angus MacKinnon or Archie MacLeod were sceptical, having seen too much in the last few years to be easily taken in. They lost no time in composing some satirical verses which were promptly circulated around the island. 'When we heard him we thought our troubles would be over, that we would be secure for ever . . . it was something like that, in Gaelic of course', recalls Dougald MacKinnon. The rosy picture painted to the islanders seemed hardly convincing after witnessing the shambolic ceremony orchestrated by Petersen for his arrival.

On the big day, everything had gone wrong. The tide was not right when Sir William made his arrival on his splendid yacht and he was unable to set foot on the pier in the dignified manner he had anticipated. Told by Big Lachie Campbell, the boatman, that if he had waited, he could have been rowed ashore in the proper boat, the new landlord let it be known that 'if' was not a word he tolerated. The island children had been made to signal 'welcome, Sir William' with semaphore flags, but as they got all muddled up, they too incurred his displeasure. Everyone was made to feel the brunt of his temper and unfortunately, his temper was in proportion to his size. He was a huge bear of a man and boasted about it as a sign of his Viking ancestry. Acts of generosity were offset by arbitrariness and excessive control. Petersen offered the island children the first Christmas party they had ever experienced, importing a huge fir tree from Norway to display the presents that he distributed himself, dressed up as Santa. The rest of the time, he insisted on children showing him proper respect by lining up on either side of the road, girls on one side, boys on the other, as soon as they heard his motor car – the first ever brought on the island. The estate employees, who were at the receiving end of his frequent bouts of anger, were hired and fired in such quick succession that there was hardly a day's security. Crofters could go to work in the morning and return in the evening without a job. Factors were no more immune than them and Petersen went through five of them – including the parish priest – during the nine years of his ownership. 'One of my uncles was working his notice,' tells Iain Campbell, 'when the factor who fired them told him he was safe, he was the one that was going!'

The fact was that Sir William had little genuine interest in his island estate. A Scottish shooting estate was simply the indispensable status symbol any newly titled business tycoon required to be part of the landed elite. It was a bit more conspicuous than the luxury steam yacht – also part of the necessary trappings – which Petersen already had. What the new proprietor needed to complete the image was a new lodge. It was finally built in 1920, a huge but flimsy timber-framed construction reinforced with steel, the walls made out of chicken wire and plaster, with a matching cottage for the island factor nearby, that the islanders lost no time in renaming 'cardboard cottage'. Set in the midst of the mature plantation dating back to the MacPhersons, the Petersen mansion, with its crenellations and central tower, was of a style more suited to southern resorts than a Hebridean location. It was the appropriate setting for the lavish entertainment which Sir William liked to provide for the large shooting parties he brought with him during his short visits to the island. These gatherings of glittering socialites and prominent members of the Establishment were the pretext for much extravagant spending. On one occasion, a guest was led to confide to another that, should their host become bankrupt, which seemed likely to him in such circumstances, he would be more than happy to acquire the island.[3]

Whereas Petersen rarely visited except in the shooting season, his daughters, Lady Wilson and Mrs Bullteel, took up residence on the island, moving to Laig when the tenant's lease expired in 1922. Katie MacKinnon's father, John MacKinnon, was appointed to manage the farm and produce milk and cheese for the estate. The ladies had their own cook and servants and used a glass verandah overlooking the sea as their parlour. They were just as profligate as their father but were well liked on the island, employing girls from crofting families in their service – Flora and Eilidh Campbell – and standing as godmothers for the MacQuarrie girls at their confirmation. They were especially popular with telegram boys and girls as they were generous with their tips. Little did they guess that they had a distant kin on Eigg in Donald MacKay, as their mother descended from a cousin MacKay branch who had emigrated from Muck to Dundee where they had done well in the jute trade.

Having brought their racehorses to the island, the sisters spent much time riding them on the hard sand of Laig beach at low tide or jumping them over the sand dunes. One of the horses – a Derby winner – was a stallion and he became notorious for fighting with the crofters' ponies, killing the MacKinnons' grey pony, Charlie. Dougald still remembers to this day how his sisters had cried their eyes out over him. Another of their pastimes was taking a cruise on their father's yacht, the *White Eagle*, which was moored in the deep channel under the cliffs of Laig Bay. 'That steam yacht was real luxury,' recalls Pat MacArthur from Rhu Arisaig, where it used to anchor when sailing to the mainland. 'Sir William used to send his crewmen to our well for fresh water, yet my father, who used to take day-trippers to Eigg on his fishing boat, was not allowed to set foot on the pier. No, he had to take his visitors to the old Clanranald pier and half the time the tide was too low for that, so he had to stop bringing them in the end.'

However, the halcyon days for Petersen and his family were to be short-lived. In neighbouring Rum, the deepening economic crisis caused the great heated glasshouses to be abandoned and the castle's vintage champagne bottles to be shipped away for auction in London. On Eigg, the Petersen reign which had started with a fire ended with a fire. Five years after its completion, the Lodge tower started to buckle and bend and one day the whole building was destroyed in a blaze so high that flames could be seen across on the mainland. When the fire finally subsided after three days, the islanders were summoned to look at the charred ruins. A few months later, they were gathered again at Kildonnan, this time for the burial of Sir William Petersen who had died in Canada but wished to be interred next to his wife and daughter. As the schoolchildren paid their respects to the dead man, they peered at him through the glass lid of a coffin so heavy it had to be winched into the grave. The sight of Sir William's embalmed body, dressed in black with the gold chain of his pocket watch shining brightly against the dark suit, was to eclipse their remembrance of him as Father Christmas and became one of their most enduring childhood memories. Some of them also remember how they 'made a bomb', bringing to his daughters at Laig the condolence telegrams which poured in from all over the world. But it was not long until the ladies departed from the island. Inheriting too many debts from their father, they found it expedient to part with the island at the bargain price of £15,000. It went to one of their father's creditors, the very same person who had expressed an interest in Eigg whilst visiting the island as their father's guest. He was another shipping magnate, Sir Walter Runciman, Baronet, owner of the Moor Line and government minister.

THE UNSTEADY TWENTIES

From the crofters' point of view, the Petersen ownership had been in sharp contrast with the stability they had enjoyed under Thomson. Not even the one significant improvement of the decade – a final land gain for the crofters – managed to stem the steady decline in numbers experienced by the community.

The islanders benefited from the post-war land reform ushered in by a successful campaign of land-raids and rent-strikes in the Outer Isles. The Board of Agriculture (replacing the Congested Districts Board in 1912) had been given powers and funds to compensate landowners and provide more land, but the process had been so slow that little had been achieved. With land hunger so acute in the Outer Isles, it took radical action from the returning war veterans for them to finally obtain some of that 'land fit for heroes' Lloyd George had promised them through the Land Settlement Bill of 1919.[4] The Eigg crofters were not slow in taking advantage of the new bill. As early as Martinmas 1919, applications were lodged for more grazing land in Cuagach and Cleadale. By the summer of 1922, Petersen finally agreed to take 103 acres of moorland plateau stretching from Cam Lon to Bealach Clithe out of Kildonnan farm. They were added to the 45 acres of Cuagach grazing. In Cleadale, the crofters gained the 50 acres of Hulin farmland which had been put under the plough during the war. Situated above the Singing Sands next to the horses' park, it doubled their existing grazing.

This increase in acreage was supposed to enable crofters to keep more cattle and improve their position, but fell short of its aim as stock prices collapsed after the war. Crofts on Eigg were still too small. All crofters now relied on extra income to keep their families, which was generally provided by the estate. 'Whether you were poor or a little less poor depended on the number of children in your family. I was lucky, I was an only child', Dodie Campbell reflected wryly. Large families did struggle, resorting to bartering eggs for groceries from the shop in Arisaig. The 10 shillings a week as a farm worker on the estate made quite a difference, and for that reason the uncertainty of employment under Petersen was a constant source of worry. The only other alternative was seasonal work on the glebe, intensively farmed by Rev. McWhirter, the Irishman with a penchant for cider who was the new minister for the Small Isles; or on the Isle of Muck, now farmed by Thomson's nephew, Commander MacEwen. The Sgitheanach Roddy MacRae also needed a hand with his 500 sheep in Kildonnan. Two young islanders were employed full-time to look after his cattle and horses. But they were lucky to have found employment after leaving school at 14. The youngsters who did not had to earn their keep by helping on the croft and at the fishing as well as trapping rabbits in the winter. Crofts were not big enough to support grown-up sons and daughters, and a few more islanders left for Glasgow where their relatives had done well on the trams or in the Clydebank shipyards.

But the Depression meant that job opportunities were no longer so plentiful on the mainland. By 1922, the government was reduced to passing a bill encouraging a move to the colonies, and advertised job prospects in Canada. There, the provincial government of Ontario was actively seeking farm workers to replace its agricultural workforce depleted by a mass exodus to the Detroit car factories. The Board of Agriculture consequently advertised emigration as the one chance of a bright future for landless people and struggling crofters: the following year nearly 2,000 people left for Canada from Lewis and Glasgow. On board the *Marloch*, which sailed from Glasgow in 1923, were the MacDonalds and the MacQuarries from Eigg, eleven people in total.

55. *Top*. Mairi Kirk, shopkeeper and post-mistress, *c.*1980.

56. *Left*. Unloading the flit-boat, 1990s.

57. *Below left*. Mary Campbell, retired QA nurse, and Glasgow "Green Lady" serving in the shop, 1980s.

58. *Below right*. Marie Carr with her three children and brother DJ at Sandavore, 1982.

59. *Top.* Eigg public holiday: goodbye to Schellenberg, 1995.

60. *Middle.* The Isle of Eigg Trust is handed over to the islanders: Barry William, Tom Forsyth, Fiona Cherry, Duncan Ferguson, Alastair McIntosh, Peggy Kirk, Dr Tiarks, Katie MacKinnon.

61. *Bottom.* "Let's crack it! Back the Eigg appeal." Launch of the buy-out campaign: islanders and friends, 26 August 1996.

62. *Top left.* Working it all out: Davie Robertson, Angus MacKinnon and Karen Helliwell.

63. *Top right.* Nick Reiter, Colin Carr and Simon Fraser celebrating the transfer of ownership to the Isle of Eigg Heritage Trust.

64. *Above left.* Dougald MacKinnon and Dolly Ferguson unveil the commemorative plaque on 12 June 1997, with Marc Cherry, IERA chairman looking on.

65. *Above right.* Angus MacKinnon and Katie MacKinnon opening the Pier Centre, 12 June 1998.

66. *Below left.* Last of the Eigg ferrymen: John Cormack and Donald MacFadyen.

67. *Below right.* Pulling together: Eigg lads at the Small Isles games' tug of war
(Alistair Kirk, Birgg Lancaster, George Carr, Joe Cormack, Greg Carr and Neil Robertson).

68. *Top left*. Pier session: Moidart fiddler Ian MacFarlane and Eddie Scott.

69. *Top right*. Donna the piper.

70. *Above left*. Opening the new Pier: Eigg school children with Transport minister Nicol Steven and local MP Charles Kennedy, 31 September 2004.

71. *Above right*. Four generations of MacKinnon women: Katie with her daughter Catriona, grand-daughter Kathleen and great-grand-daughters Catriona and Breagha.

72. *Right*. Bob and Nora Wallace and the Earth Connections Centre.

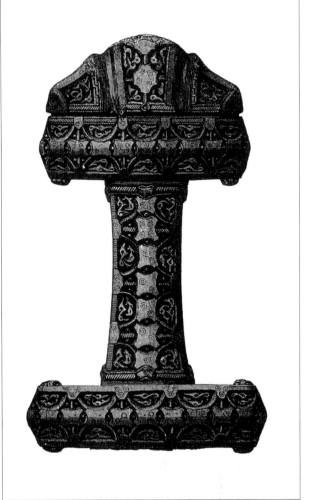

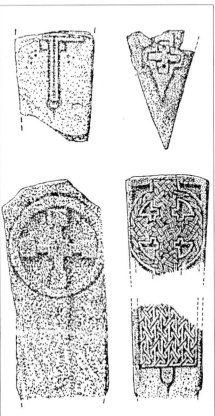

1. *Top left*. Medieval carving of the Sheela-na-gig, one aspect of the Celtic mother goddess, Kildonnan church.

2. *Left*. Early Christian cross-slabs, 7th-9th century. The cross potent on the bottom left may have been at the centre of St Donnan's monastery. The ringed cross with key patterns on the right shows influences from Eastern Pictland.

3. *Above*. Richly decorated bronze sword-hilt found at Kildonnan, early Viking period (8th-9th century).

4. *Right.* Tobar Caluim Cille, Columba's well, Cleadale: Joanne MacLellan and Katie-Ann MacKay fetching water *c.*1920.

5. *Below.* Entrance to Uamh Fhraing, Eigg's Massacre Cave.

6. *Bottom.* Roofless post-medieval church at Kildonnan, with St Donnan's pillow stone in the foreground.

7. *Top.* Laig farm and steading.

8. *Below.* Galmisdale: farmhouse and crofts *c.*1890.

9. *Bottom.* Cuagach cottars, c.1890.

10. *Top.* Cleadale township *c.*1890 with Bidein na Tighearna (the Pinnacle of the Lord) and the Cleadale cliffs in the background.

11. *Above.* The MacLellan family, Cleadale crofters, *c.*1903.

12. *Top left.* Lobster fishermen, Alexander MacDonald and Lachlan MacQuarrie, Cleadale *c.*1890.

13. *Top right.* Ishbel MacLeod bringing peat home with one of the MacKinnon lads (possibly Dougald).

14. *Left.* Shearing sheep at the fank, *c.*1900. The estate factor is sitting on the wall behind.

15. *Bottom.* Gamekeeper Donald MacLeod (second from the left) with a shooting party in front of Thomson's Lodge.

16. *Top.* The new croft houses built by Thomson in Cuagach.

17. *Above left.* Donald MacLeod, MM and Angus MacDonald, Queen's Own Cameron Highlanders. Both served in France, where Angus was killed in action.

18. *Above right.* Duncan MacLellan, who lost all four sons in the Great War, and stepson Duncan Ferguson. Both were outstanding tradition-bearers.

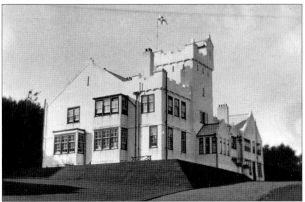

19. *Top*. School children, 1923.

20. *Above left and right*. Petersen's Lodge and yatch – "a self-made man's status symbol".

21. *Left*. Sir William Petersen and grandchild.

22. *Left*. Marybel MacQuarrie (centre) and family, with Aunt Ishbel Macleod on the right.

23. *Below*. An Lossit, the MacQuarrie's home and last thatched house in Cleadale, *c*.1925.

24. *Bottom left*. Three generations of tradition bearers: Mary and Hugh MacKinnon with their baby Peggy and Hugh's uncle Angus MacCormick.

25. *Bottom right*. Roderick Campbell, (Ruairidh Ruadh) Eigg's first ferryman.

26. *Above*. Puffer at Eigg pier and Donald MacQuarrie with his horse and cart.

27. *Left*. The Runcimans' modernist lodge built by Robert Mauchlin, with its semi-tropical garden.

28. *Below left*. Lord and Lady Runciman and family.

29. *Below right*. Hector MacAskill and Lachlan Campbell, the island blacksmith.

30. *Top*. Duncan Mackay and estate ploughing team, home farm, *c.*1938.

31 and 32. *Middle*. Dougald MacKinnon sharpening his scythe, his wife Katie and daughter Flora.

33. *Right*. Forestry team (Jimmy Greig, 3rd from right, and Duncan MacDonald, 4th from right).

34. *Left.* Tea-break for the MacKinnon family and friends.

35. *Middle.* Mary MacKinnon and Kirsty MacLeod planting potatoes, 1949.

36. *Below left.* On Laig beach after Sunday service at St Donnan Church (Peggy, Chrissie and Angus MacKinnon on the left).

37. *Below right.* Duncan Ferguson bringing in the hay harvest.

38. *Top.* Washing day in Cleadale.

39. *Above.* Family fun for the Cleadale women at Glasgow Fair time.

40. *Right.* Lads paddling on Cleadale Lochan.

41. *Top left.* Duncan Campbell, who joined the Arctic Convoys, and his father JD.

42. *Top right.* Morag MacKinnon, Capt., Queen Alexandra's Royal Army Nursing Corps. Morag served in Africa and Italy.

43. *Right.* Roddy Campbell, conscripted in the Royal Navy, and his sister Catriona, ATS.

44. *Bottom.* Dougald MacKinnon's taxi service, late 1950s.

45. *Top left*. Dougald MacKinnon guising on Oidhche
Samhain (Hallowe'en).

46. *Top right*. Eigg primary school children, *c*.1960.

47. *Above left*. House ceilidh at Laig with Peggy and
Donnie Kirk, Donald MacKinnon and Duncan Ferguson.

48. *Above right*. Eigg ferrymen Roddy Campbell and Dougald
MacKinnon with Angus Kirk and postman Dottie Campbell.

49. *Top*. Peggy and Donnie Kirk with their children Marie and Angus bringing in the hay at Laig, late 1950s.

50. *Above*. Dr MacLean piping the bride; Marie Kirk's wedding, 1976. The Glasgow cab was the Laig taxi at the time.

51. *Right*. Dottie Campbell about to fire a good luck shot for the bride and groom, 1986.

52. *Above*. Maggie Fyffe at Cuagach Crafts,
the little tea-shop set up in her home, *c*.1980.

53. *Right*. Eigg Primary school, 1984.

54. *Below*. The Isle of Eigg Ceilidh band, 1986.

These two large families had found it difficult to make ends meet on their Cuagach crofts and it was the parish priest, Fr MacIntyre, who had strongly encouraged them to avail themselves of the opportunity. It was not difficult for Neil MacDonald to part with his croft, known locally as the 'killer-croft': it was so boggy that it needed constant drainage and very hard work for very little return. The day of their departure was marked by much sadness on Eigg. As the schoolchildren stood silent in the playground when the carts laden with luggage passed the school, Duncan MacKay decided he could not bear the thought of returning to the classroom without saying goodbye to his best friend. He slipped to the back of the school and ran all the way to the pier. He said his farewell, both he and his friend standing awkwardly on the rocks, promising to write to each other, a big lump in their throats but feeling that they were too old to cry.

The Eigg families headed for Ontario where men and women would work as farm labourers and domestic servants for a year to pay back their share of the passage. The scheme was that after that they would be able to acquire a farm of their own. Reality proved quite different as many emigrants found it difficult to adapt to the changes they encountered. Older folks found it especially harder – Neil MacDonald was in his sixties when he left – and many did not thrive. Younger folks had more of a chance of success. Charlie MacKinnon, Dougald's eldest brother, who went on the *Metagama*'s second and last voyage from Lewis in 1924, fared much better. Taking night classes during his year on the farm. Charlie soon moved to Toronto where he found work in an ice-cream factory, working his way up the ladder and ending as manager.

With all these departures, the island population fell from 150 in the census of 1921 to 138 in the census of 1931. It would probably have gone on falling if it had not been for the change of ownership. The arrival of the Runcimans on Eigg ushered in an era of unprecedented prosperity on the island, and this was to halt the population decline for some time at least.

THE GOLDEN AGE OF EIGG

The great advantage that Walter Runciman had over other island proprietors was that he was very wealthy. His father, a Borders man, had built the family fortune estimated at £3m, starting as a cabin boy at 15 and ending as owner of the Moor Line and Member of Parliament. Adding insurance to shipping, Walter Runciman followed his father into politics and became one of the first cabinet ministers to be drawn from business rather than aristocratic ranks under Asquith in 1908.

Runciman, unlike Petersen, did not look to his island estate as a status symbol to flaunt his wealth but as recreation from his ministerial responsibilities. He was keen on shooting but also on birdwatching – ironically enough – and fond of watercolour painting. His wife, one of the first women MPs, was quite a personality, proud of her Scottish ancestry and sensible upbringing: she used to tell her grandchildren that all her family could knit a sock, row a boat and milk a cow by the time they were seven. Her particular interest in farming made her granddaughter describe her 'as someone whom nowadays we would think of as rather "green" and ecologically minded and she cared very much about good husbandry and community'.[5]

Lord and Lady Runciman shared the ambition of making the island self-supporting, and as they had the resources to do so, it was done without stinting. A capable farm manager was appointed, David Donald from Tomintoul. 'He was a great man for draining', remembers

Duncan MacKay. And draining he did, in Castle Island, Kildonnan and that part of the glebe which the estate acquired at that time. New fencing was carried out, including the area of common grazing which should have been done under Petersen. The fencing material was entirely produced on the island under the direction of the new Head Forester, Jimmy Greig, who was brought in to deal with the neglected woodland. The islanders recall how the fence posts and stobs were left to cure for months in a huge creosote container. They are still standing today whereas more recent fencing has lasted less than a decade.

Farming was reorganised again, with a ten-year lease for Laig given to a Dundee farmer by the name of Goodenough. Sandavore become the home farm, to which Lady Runciman devoted quite a lot of thought and interest. John MacKinnon was moved from Laig to Sandavore and was able to put his experience of dairy farming to good use with the brand new dairy installed there. Derelict buildings were entirely renovated, running water put in and electricity supplied from the new state-of-the-art hydro-electric system which powered all estate properties nearby. The dairy now housed six milch cows and their followers. 'It was kept so nice and clean that you could have eaten off the floor', recalls John's daughter, Katie MacKinnon. 'You can hardly believe it when you see it today, it's heart-breaking.' Lady Runciman would come to inspect the dairy as soon as she set foot on the island: she insisted that every employee in the dairy wore a white blouse and followed strict rules of hygiene. The home farm also produced poultry in vast quantities, with three flocks of hens of different breed and two flocks of geese. The existing nondescript herd of cattle was replaced by a herd of seventy-five hill cows, Galloway crossed with Aberdeen Angus. Potatoes were produced in vast quantities, the estate workers being allowed their own rigs, and the farm produced all its own hay. Bracken was controlled by crushing it at the growing stage with horse-drawn rollers with spikes. The place had become a model farm and the islanders, particularly those who were employed on the estate, took great pride in those improvements. It was the Golden Age of Eigg.

Measures were taken to improve the shooting on the estate. For a start the lochs below the Sgurr of Eigg were restocked with trout. Pat MacArthur remembers how these baby trout were brought to Rhu from a hatchery in Bonnybridge in four huge galvanised tanks which were shipped to Eigg, two men taking turns in changing the water every two hours until the trout were brought to the lochs. Unsuccessful attempts were made to establish a colony of wild goats and reintroduce the grey partridge in 1928. The birds died out three years later and the goats had disappeared by the late 1930s. Pheasants, on the other hand, prospered after their reintroduction in large numbers during 1933 and 1934. From then on, Lachie Campbell and his brothers would have the task of rearing dozens of pheasant chicks every season, hand-feeding them in their cages in a large field below Galmisdale farmhouse. The crofters' hens were commandeered to help with the hatching. Although it provided their owners with a few shillings, the women used to complain that their poor hens came back thoroughly exhausted. When the pheasant season opened after New Year, young islanders would earn some extra money – about 9 shillings – as beaters for the Runcimans and their guests. There was plenty of game on the island to satisfy the keenest gun, with snipe and woodcock in great quantity and the occasional grouse and mallard. Woodcock wintered on Eigg in large numbers, favouring the manse wood in particular, and, according to the Runcimans' shooting diary, a phenomenal total of 611 birds were shot one year, with 131 birds shot at Grulin alone over six days!

Lord Runciman was regarded as a great sportsman by the islanders and he got on very well with his gamekeeper, Donald Archie MacLeod, who had been in the job since Thomson's time, replacing his father who had been gamekeeper before him. The only problem for Donald Archie was that Runciman was a teetotaller whereas he regarded the occasional dram as one of the perks of the job. The story was that when Runciman asked his gamekeeper to check the barometer, to see whether the glass was high or low, Donald Archie would reply pointedly, 'Very empty, sir.' His hints were ignored, his employer considering that whisky should only be used as medicine, and he surreptitiously started to help himself from the silver flask which he always carried for Runciman on their outings. Knowing it was never touched he would just top it up with water every time. Inevitably, it happened that at the end of a particularly tiring day on the hills, Runciman felt so tired and cold that he asked for his flask. Donald Archie was taken aback but he had no other choice than to hand him the watered-down whisky. Runciman took one mouthful and turned to look at his gamekeeper. Without a word, he handed the flask back to him and carried on walking. That look was enough to cure Donald Archie from further temptation and he never tampered with the flask again. It was this kind of attitude which earned Runciman the respect of his employees. He was strict and a stickler for punctuality – he demanded that his employees were dead on time, not one minute late, nor a minute early – but he was fair. He was considered a real gentleman and he was respected as such.

Donald Archie was much appreciated by the children and grandchildren of the family. 'The arrangement was that Donald Archie would call at the Lodge at nine in the morning to accompany whoever was staying out fishing in the lochs, or shooting, or just walking. 'When it was just me,' recalls Lord Runciman's granddaughter, 'he would come a little earlier and take me fishing for little trout in the burns. He would thread the worms on the hook and we would very quietly make our way up the burns through the hazel bushes looking for the dark pools where the trout could be found. If we were in luck, there would be trout for breakfast!'[6] The gamekeeper would also walk the children on their long pony treks all over the island, looking for the golden eagles which could be seen flying near the Sgurr or Beinn Bhuidhe. There was no motor car, just ponies and a pony and trap. These were sufficient for the family expeditions which took them to Grulin or Kildonnan or occasionally to the beaches on the crofters' side of the island, which the children very much perceived as a separate part of the island, and all the more exciting because of this. If the weather was suitable, they would also be taken out mackerel fishing by the estate boatmen, which they considered a great treat.

Archie MacDonald and Lachie Campbell, the estate boatmen, were in their glory under the new regime. They were fitted out with good-quality suits which were made to measure, and all their oilskins and sou'westers came from the famous Barbour clothing firm so that they all looked extremely smart. They had to man two boats, the *Dido* and the *Elissa*. The *Elissa* was a converted lifeboat with a double-skinned hull and was beautifully refitted. It could go in all kinds of weather and was placed at the doctor's disposal for his visits to the islands. The islanders were welcome to use it in cases of emergency. The *Dido* was reserved for the proprietor's use and for estate business. It sailed over to Rhu Arisaig to fetch Lord and Lady Runciman when they arrived for the summer, driven all the way in their Rolls-Royce. The Rhu road was not very good and Pat MacArthur remembers helping to push the Rolls out of the mud, earning himself 5s each time for his trouble. The two boats were given a thorough overhaul twice a year by engineers who came especially for that. Anchors and chains were checked to ensure that the boats would not drag their moorings like Petersen's boat, the *Foch*, which ended up sold as firewood after being washed up in Morar after one particularly nasty winter gale. The ferry boat was checked at the same time, Runciman saying that he could not afford to have his mail undelivered.

Improvements took place at the pier where new store sheds were built with a waiting room for locals and guests. Their flat roofs and fancy crenellations were rather odd in the rugged setting of the pier, a little too reminiscent of estate gatehouses, but that was after all what they were meant to be. The new Lodge, built where Petersen's flimsy mansion had stood, was more stylish. Completed in 1927, the Lodge was designed by architects Mauchlin and Weightman, who were instructed to place the dining room in such a way that Lord Runciman could enjoy the view of the Sgurr from his dining table. With its flat roof, balcony and front terrace in Italianate style, the Lodge completed the Mediterranean illusion suggested by the palm trees lining the drive. Coal-fired central heating, en-suite bathrooms and electricity from the dam nearby provided ample comfort in wet weather. After her daily swim on the beach which is now called after her, Lady Runciman could sit at her grand piano in her drawing room and enjoy the display of colours across the lawn, where rhododendrons combined with fuchsias and hydrangeas to hide the kitchen garden from sight. This garden was again a special interest of hers. It was developed to produce all sorts of vegetables as well as luscious fruit which her grandchildren delighted to plunder on their annual visits. Around the house, a Chilean flame tree, magnolias, strawberry trees, New Zealand daisies and other exotic species gave way to copper beeches, horse chestnut and eucalyptus trees. The warming influence of the Gulf Stream had allowed Sir Steven, her son, to choose a wealth of exotic species, taking his inspiration from the wonderful garden created at Inverewe by Osgood MacKenzie, trying out any plant he had seen and liked. The whole effect was stunning: such a wealth of colours in sharp contrast with the stark moorland at little distance from the Lodge. A manicured lawn lined the drive, backed by an assortment of conifers which gave shelter to a rose garden, a tennis court and an apple orchard near the gates. Drifts of daffodils and narcissi grew to profusion in the spring, so many in fact that they were exported to the Glasgow flower market. The son of the estate boatman and blacksmith, Gordon Campbell remembers how magnificent the Lodge garden had looked to him as a child, his nostalgia including the memory of the wonderful plum tree he had secretly visited! He had sneaked in many a time even though the estate factor did not allow him or any of his brothers and sisters to take the short cut through the Lodge garden on their way to school. Seventy years on, however, the garden is still an amazing sight with the conifers grown to a majestic size, the roses rambling around the terrace. The difference is that the island children play hide and seek amongst the exotic bushes or tumble across the deserted lawn when they come to the nearby hall after school.

A FEELING OF CONTENTMENT

At a time when the country was recovering from the Depression, the islanders felt that they had never had it so good. Each estate worker received free milk, fifteen hundredweight of potatoes and four tons of coal a year on top of his wages. This represented a considerable saving for each family, and allowed them to save some money to take advantage of the house improvement grants available at the time. The estate had actually taken the lead with house improvements by starting to renovate its cottages one by one. Another great novelty was holiday pay and a half-day on

Saturday: 'at first, when one of the foresters told us everyone had their half-day on Saturday on the mainland, no-one believed him,' recalls Duncan MacKay, 'then we thought, perhaps it does happen on the mainland, but we don't deserve it here on the island. We got it in the end all the same, save when it was hay-making time, then we stayed in the fields until there was no more daylight and there was no overtime either. And another thing we never had before, that was going home an hour early on Christmas Eve!'

With work so plentiful on the farm and in forestry, Eigg experienced at least a temporary reprieve from emigration during the pre-war years. Duncan MacDonald, as a school-leaver, started in the forestry at 5s a week and was earning £5 a week by the time war broke out. Duncan Ferguson, taken on as a cattleman, was sent on a course in dairy farming. Duncan MacKay followed his brother Neil on the farm: 'I started on the estate at 15 and I retired at 67 years of age', tells Duncan, sucking on his pipe. 'I started in the bothy at Kildonnan, when MacRae had it. He had been to Montana when he was young and he used to tell us all about it, cowboys and all that, you know. Then he left after five years and it was Katie's father, John MacKinnon, the grieve, who was put in charge of the farm until he retired in 1935. I mind Katie's mother, she used to bang a stick on the floor to wake us up in the bothy below, Duncan Ferguson and me. He was the cattleman and I was ploughman-shepherd. My first job when I got up at 5 o'clock was to feed the horses, then it was up to the hills to feed the cows, and my last job at night was to take the horses down to the shore to put their feet in the tide. That's what I had to do, seven days a week!' As for Dougald MacKinnon, when he came back to Eigg in 1938 after his years of 'tramping in the west' to look after his widowed mother, he had no difficulty getting a job at Sandavore farm. 'I had to look after the geese, fatten them up for Christmas, you see, well . . . I was young and not very patient so when the time came to kill them and they still didn't look fat enough, well, I just filled them up with water to make them look really plump and that did the trick, the cook never knew any better.'

The situation was not quite the same for girls. Whatever employment could be had at the Lodge was only seasonal and it was more difficult for them to stay on the island after school. 'Oh you couldn't stay on the island, you couldn't, you had to work, as soon as you left school!' exclaims Morag Campbell, who was not to return to Eigg before she reached retirement age. 'I was sad to leave when I was young but now I'm glad I went away and saw a bit of the world!' Cooking and cleaning at the Lodge provided them with a good start, then some would move on to Muck, where the MacEwens needed help in the kitchen and the nursery, before spreading their wings further afield. 'How we scrubbed and polished that hall!' sighed Marybel MacDonald. Like Morag, she started in service at the Lodge after school, 'If Lady Runciman found the tiniest little spot, she would make us do it again. Oh, she was a real tartar!' Nursing was an alternative to working as a maid or a cook which was actively encouraged by the island's doctor, Dr Josephine Shephard. Compared with teaching, another favourite profession for girls with academic abilities, nursing was better because student nurses did not require financial help from their families, so that a number of island girls left as soon as they were 17 to train in Glasgow, Edinburgh and even London. 'There was eight of us altogether although we didn't all go away at the same time. And you had no grant at that time, you had a little pittance of a pay but you got your food and lodgings in the hospital, so that was convenient for us, we were so young', recalls Janet MacDonald, who was to retire a matron. This pattern of female emigration was fairly typical of its time. It raised the age of marriage higher than it had ever been before, a factor which was to contribute to the fall in population. However, it was still expected that at one time or another the girls would return for good, especially if their parents' health was failing. They generally enjoyed their time away but returned home as often as possible, life on Eigg being still a desirable goal for most island girls. But some of them really wanted to leave, like Barbara MacKay, whose older sister Katie-Ann had an enviable position as a housekeeper in Helensburgh's famous Hill House. 'I was so desperate to leave the island that I lied about my age – I should have been fifteen – to get a job at the Marine Hotel. Then I went to Arisaig House. That was really hard work, they were so strict in there but I didn't mind, I was away on the mainland.' Unlike her, her brother Duncan was content with the life he led on the island: 'We used to do our own cooking in the bothy, Duncan Ferguson and I. We only went home once every two weeks, one week, it was him, the other week, it was me and we'd walk all the way, there was no motor car on the island till after the war. In the evening I used to make harnesses, bridles, saddles even. I learned how to work with leather when my father had the shop and he used to get big thick skins. We'd cut them out to re-sole our tackety boots: you soaked them first, then the sole was nailed and shaped and the tackets were put in. Everybody used to do that! Another thing I used to do was training. I had that book by Charles Atlas, Mr Universe, and I completed the course. Then after seven or eight years, Duncan Ferguson left to work on his croft and I did not like it on my own in the bothy, so I went back to live at home. We were building the house at the time and I used to go to the shore and pick the stones after I finished work, and my brother Neil would take them out in his cart. When our house was finished in 1938, we were the first house on Eigg to have the wireless after the minister! We got it with the cigarette coupons. They offered money back for a thousand coupons, we collected so many, my brothers and I, and we saved for a radio.'

Improvements to the MacKay house were made possible by the new bill passed in the early 1930s for roof and house improvement grants. Houses in the crofting counties were still characterised by overcrowding, with too many dwellings where animals lodged under the same roof. On Eigg, there was only one house left where hens perched for the night in the rafters and the cow lived on the other side of a wooden partition, Old Neil Robertson's in Hulin. But families had to make do with one room as sleeping quarters, fitted with several box beds. The daughters would share one, the sons another, with the parents and the youngest child in a third one. Hugh MacKinnon, then Donald MacKay, were the first crofters to avail themselves of the new grant, replacing earthen floors with concrete, cementing the dry stone walls, installing wooden panelling inside and adding a second storey with gabled windows. The only modern convenience introduced at that time was the dry toilet built in a lean-to shed at the back of the house, the *taigh beag* – the little house. It was another twenty years before proper sewerage was installed.

Two-thirds of a total housing stock of thirty-five were still relying on water from the well for all domestic use. The problem was that the water supply tended to be erratic in warm weather. Lack of sewerage combined with wandering cattle meant that it easily became contaminated and bouts of dysentery occurred frequently especially in periods of drought, although islanders used to claim a special immunity denied to visitors. But one particular well in Cleadale was famed for its qualities: St Columba's Well did not run dry and its water was kept clean by a resident trout. The children who fetched water from the well were forbidden to disturb it in any way, recalls Morag Campbell. Duncan MacKay, her neighbour, could still picture his father having a wash at the well, stripped to the waist, whether it rained or not, when he was well into his eighties!

Improved living conditions finally helped eradicate tuberculosis. The disease was now on the wane after preying so heavily on that malnourished generation who had grown up in the aftermath of the famine. It had been brought back by islanders returning from a spell in Glasgow where it was rife. Contamination had been inevitable in the old crowded blackhouses, although, once it was diagnosed, people went to great lengths to avoid spreading the disease. Those who suffered from it were cared for by their relatives but kept in isolation, like Iain MacLellan who had caught it during the war. He moved to a little hut which was built for him at the back of his parents' house. His relatives brought him his meals and came to see him any time he signalled for help by pulling a string which linked the hut to the house. He remained there until his death, a few years after his return. Hugh MacKinnon's own father had died of TB in 1908 at the age of forty-six. To avoid passing it on to his wife and two young boys, he had gone back to live with his old mother, Katie Bheag. His brother died of it too, a few years later, and it was a testimony to family loyalty that, when he asked his sister-in-law to take in his mother after his death so that the old woman would be spared the poor's-house, she did not hesitate to do so.

TB was feared for a long time afterwards. When parcels of clothing came from city relatives, cautious enquiries were made to ascertain whether the wearer had been free from TB, otherwise they were burnt straight away. The islanders remembered only too well when scarlet fever had been brought to the island, killing two children, through a parcel of clothes sent to one family by their Glasgow aunt. The whole household had been struck with scarlet fever, even the mother, so that neighbours had had to bring daily baskets of food to the door without daring to go in for fear of contagion. Children were always told to change out of wet garments and stay out of draughts, such was the fear of any chest infections. They had to submit to the daily ritual of taking cod-liver oil. Even the animals were treated in this way. Seal oil was generally used for them but Marybel MacDonald remembered how her father and the other crofters had made oil from the blubber of a whale washed up on the beach in 1919. For general ailments, islanders relied on favourite patent medicines, camphorated lotions, Cascara syrup or Castor oil which was used for the purge deemed necessary to help in any circumstances. Whisky of course was considered an all-round cure, and was especially used for toothache, but it was in short supply during the 1920s and 1930s. Eigg was known as a 'dry place' at that time.

In cases of emergency, the islanders now benefited from the presence of a resident doctor on Eigg whereas before they had needed to fetch one from Arisaig or Tobermory. The Small Isles Parish Council for the Poor Law had finally appointed a Medical Officer in 1897, who was paid a yearly salary out of the rates collected in the four islands. He was required to visit the other islands on a regular basis, which was understood to mean 'at least three or four times a year', apart from emergencies, when he could be summoned by telegraph. Medical attention was now within the means of ordinary folks and was free for the parish poor. Yet the parish school board had deemed the yearly inspection and vaccination of schoolchildren too expensive at first. After the 1908 diphtheria epidemic, funds were found to inoculate the parish against it as well as smallpox, although measles, croup and whooping cough still took their toll.[7] Acute conditions presented the gravest danger in such isolated conditions. In the early 1920s, Dr MacDonald had managed an emergency trepanation on a kitchen table on Rum, saving the girl's life, but any child sent away for an operation such as appendicitis at that time stood a 50 per cent chance of coming back in a little white coffin.[8] The nearest hospitals were in Glasgow, a ten-hour train journey away from Mallaig, with much delay with ferries or boats before that. For that reason, there was always a bed reserved for emergencies from Eigg and the Small Isles at the Glasgow Royal Infirmary, and islanders used to organise a yearly dance to contribute to its upkeep. Dougald MacKinnon certainly used that bed more than most as he had to undergo a series of operations for his cleft palate as a young child. He used to be left on his own, looked after by his brother Charlie, who was a tram driver in the city. He is fond of telling how he had woken up from one operation feeling ravenously hungry. Seeing the food trolley wheeled past him, he got out of bed, grabbed a plate of fish and mashed potatoes, and wolfed it down, ignoring the nurses' warnings which he could not understand, having little English at the time. The result was burst stitches and a frantic phone-call to his brother at 5 o'clock in the morning when everyone thought he was going to die. This was counting without Dougald's remarkable stamina. Joking about being the family weakling who survived all his siblings, Dougald recently celebrated his golden wedding anniversary, surrounded by his numerous grandchildren and friends.

The island was assured of a permanent medical service in 1925 with the creation of the much-acclaimed Highlands and Islands Medical Service. This followed the success of a campaign to guarantee a minimum income for doctors working in isolated conditions, when it was finally recognised that adequate medical provisions would greatly improve living conditions in the region. Dr Martha Devon, appointed to Eigg in 1928, caused quite a stir by landing a plane on Laig Sands as part of the Service's campaign to establish a Hebridean Air Ambulance. She did not mind lodging with crofters in Cuagach and holding her surgery at Bayview in Cleadale, as it proved difficult at first to find accommodation for a doctor on Eigg, Petersen ignoring the Small Isles Parish Council's polite requests. The islanders remember how she had praised the virtues of porridge cooked in old-fashioned pots for extra iron and encouraged them to eat vegetables by setting a prize for best garden produce. From then on, parsnips, kale, cabbage and rhubarb became a greater part of the islanders' diet, and to this day currant bushes grow by each cottage on the island. Her successor, Dr Josephine Shephard, was eventually provided with a brand new house, built in 1938. The doctor's house was one of the many benefits the community was to incur under the ownership of the Runciman family.

Another improvement was the building of a dance-hall for the islanders, built out of wood and situated at the entrance to the Lodge gardens. With their customary practicality, the Runcimans made it double up as a place where their laundry could be dried on rainy days. Until then dances had been held in the school, or in the barn at Laig or at Kildonnan. The young folks on Eigg still relied on live music for their entertainment. Duncan Ferguson was an excellent fiddler. The minister had taught him to read music at night school when he was 14, but he had taught himself to play. He used to play a lot, often accompanied by Jimmy Greig the Head Forester. Donald MacKay played the pipes, like the parish priest who had a home-made set consisting of a sheep-skin body and bought drones and chanter. 'Dances started at 8 o'clock on the dot. If you were late, you couldn't get in. The last dance was at 2 o'clock and everyone had to walk back, and there was many a tumble in the heather on the way home, I can tell you', recalls Duncan MacDonald with heartfelt nostalgia. Marybel MacDonald used to go to the dances with her best friend, Mary MacLean: 'once we came back so late that Mary's mother said to her: "don't bother going to bed since it's already daylight. Keep your clothes on and light the fire!" Another time, Dougie locked us up in the byre on the way back. I can still picture Mary's legs as she climbed up to bang on the window. It wasn't until Big Neil Mór passed by, hours later, that we were let out!

There were so many of us about at that time, we had great fun. You would go out at night, and there were a dozen people on the road, there used to be a string of people going up the Bealach Clithe. Now, you only see a car or two and that's all.' It was particularly busy when all those who were away to work came back for a holiday, generally at the time of Glasgow Fair in mid-July. 'I remember Kirsty MacDonald next door, shaking out the bag of flour at the end of the Glasgow Fair holiday', said Duncan MacKay. 'She would have fed up to sixteen people in her house, her own family and all those who came to visit, and a boll of flour, that's 140 pounds, lasted her only ten days!'

The Muck people often came to the dances on Eigg, and there was much competition on the dance-floor to see which island had the best dancers. Dougald MacKinnon could remember one occasion at Kildonnan when the Muck folks won, but only because it was a wedding and the Eigg dancers had overindulged themselves, taking full advantage of a rare supply of whisky! Visits to the mainland were other occasions for a few drams, as when the estate boys took the cattle off for the sales, especially if they got stormbound as happened from time to time. The Eigg football team once lost 12–nil to Arisaig after making the fatal mistake of stopping in the pub before the game.

Eigg's links with Muck were quite strong at that time, the Muck men regularly coming to Eigg for the mail. They also came to the smithy which was conveniently situated on the hill above the pier. Descending from the long line of island blacksmiths which originated in Lageorna, Lachlan Campbell was very skilled at his craft. 'He could do anything from shoeing horses to repairing and making farm implements or rabbit traps. He was famed for his hammer-welding which was so good you could never see where the two parts were joined', recalls Angus MacKinnon. 'As for tempering metal, he had no equal. He would wait for the metal in the forge to get to the right colour, and you could give him a hand with the bellows, but when it came to the crucial moment, he would shoo you out. He didn't like anyone watching him doing it, he didn't want to give away any of his secrets!' His son Gordon didn't like to go near the old smithy, for he could still picture his father working there. But his father was taken ill prematurely and it was his mother who was left to bring up her large family of eleven children. A tough little woman who could carry a boll of meal on her back from the pier to their house at Creagard, Rita Campbell was a real character, who came to Eigg without a word of Gaelic and learned to speak it as well as any islander. Brimming with energy, she was always on the go, cleaning the Lodge, taking in washing for the MacEwens on Muck, picking whelks on the shore, or filling the cupboard with pots of jam and jelly. She was forever knitting, even on her way to the shore, and when she sat down it was to make or repair guernseys and socks for her brood. 'You got new clothes, once a year, from J. D. Williams catalogue, it was a suit – short-legged trousers and a jacket – and that was your best', explains her son Bobby, smiling at the recollection. 'The rest of the time you went about in an old suit handed down from your brother with the guernseys our mother knitted and you had on multi-coloured socks after she had repaired them a few times. She used to unravel wool from the stuff we could not wear any more!'

One of the improvements which made life easier for the islanders, especially the women, was the new Co-op shop and Post Office situated in the middle of the island. It was close enough to the school for children to nip in and bring groceries back for their parents. The Co-op started on the initiative of a missionary from Tiree where the crofting community had been particularly strong and well organised since its victory in the Land War. Neil MacLean had encouraged everyone to join the Co-op. As in many other isolated places, it had been a real success, every member earning 2s and 6d for every pound spent in the shop. The crofters saved £40 for a new township bull and were so pleased with the scheme that Hugh MacKinnon composed a song in praise of the missionary.

Independent at first, then taken over by the Scottish Wholesale Co-operative Society, the Eigg Co-op was the smallest in the country but supplied the rest of the Small Isles. It was run by Hugh MacKinnon's twin sisters-in-law, Bella dealing with the Post Office at one end of the building, Katie-Ann with the shop at the other. 'It was very well stocked: there were groceries, feeding stuff, paraffin, all sorts of things. There were barrels of herrings, big rounds of cheese, oh they were enormous, a lovely rolled bacon which was sliced on the machine, and bread which came straight from Glasgow by train in big hampers. I mind Ian, Dougie's brother, hiding from us in one of them, we were talking away sitting on the hamper, and he was listening to us all the time! Oh, they had a lovely gingerbread in that shop, it was so very gingery with a shiny crust on it, it was beautiful, well, you could buy a piece of that gingerbread, a great big slab, for 6d. And it was a penny for a packet of caramel! If you tidied up the playground next to the shop, you'd get 6d and you could get six packets of caramels! It was great. One thing which used to amuse us a lot as children was the toilet rolls that Katie-Ann displayed in her window. She had a little display just like a shop on the mainland, and she'd have a card with lovely hairslides, and on that card there was a picture of a really elegant lady, and we used to look at it and look at it and wonder how long it would be before the slides were all sold and we could get the picture to put it on the wall in our bedroom!' recall the island women with much merriment.

There was always a great deal of bustle on boat days, with Hugh MacKinnon bringing supplies from the pier in his horse and cart. Children who were hanging about were given the job of unravelling all the string from the parcels that came and rolling it into a big ball in exchange for a sweet or two. The mail would be sorted out behind closed doors and the postman's haversack would be weighed before he would start on his round. 'Letter service', as it used to be called in those days, was quite an exacting job. The postman, Angus MacLellan, had to do all his deliveries on foot from one end of the island to the other. When he had to go and deliver a letter to Grulin, on the far side of the Sgurr where one lonely shepherd used to live, his round came to a good twelve miles. Whenever officials came to inspect him, Angus used to take them for an especially long run. 'He used to say in Gaelic behind the inspector's back: "Ah, he'll not be so clean by the time I'll have finished with him!" And he would take him through every bog on the glebe, telling him "yes, yes, it's the right way". He would finish with Laig, saying to the inspector, "There's a short cut through the Sgurr if you prefer to take it, otherwise, it'll have to be the long way by the road." The poor man would always choose the road of course!' laughs Duncan MacDonald.

Chapter 10

THE END OF AN OLD SONG

EIGG ENTERS THE SECOND WORLD WAR

When Mary Campbell and Morag MacKinnon left the island to start their training as nurses, London and Edinburgh seemed as far from Eigg as they would ever be likely to go. Yet only a few years later, they were amongst the first islanders to be sent to the four corners of the globe when the Second World War broke out. Reading the weekly paper, even if it came late, and listening to the radio, the islanders were aware of mounting international tension. They heard that their proprietor, now President of the Board of Trade in the Chamberlain government, was given the delicate but ultimately futile task of mediator in the Sudetenland Crisis of 1938. Sir Walter Runciman was said to have undertaken this last mission reluctantly, only after a personal intervention from George VI, before his failing health caused him to retire from politics.[1]

Memories of the First World War were very much in the minds of the older islanders when it became obvious that war was inevitable. Considering the slaughter of the previous war, they urged the young islanders to join the Merchant Navy before it was too late, reckoning that there were better chances of survival at sea than on land. Events proved them wrong: the Merchant Navy sustained terrible losses in the Battle of the Atlantic. Once again, it was Eigg which contributed the largest contingent in the Small Isles, with eleven men in the Merchant Navy and four conscripted into the army, the navy or the military police. Unlike in the Great War, islanders were no longer drafted into the same regiments and went very much their separate ways as their military papers arrived. Donald MacDonald, for instance, saw the war in the Scots Fusiliers from the D-Day landing to the final advance on Germany; but, drafted into the military police, John Angus MacDonald never left Britain. Donald Campbell went from Malta to Singapore via Egypt and Ceylon in the Royal Marines whilst Roddy Campbell was moved to a Navy patrol on the south coast of Britain.

The island girls responded swiftly to the news of their brothers' and friends' conscription by enlisting too. Catriona Campbell volunteered to join the ATS: 'I went to a training camp near

Edinburgh to learn how to prepare food in a field kitchen. It was really cold there, we had to get up early in the morning and take our mess kit to the canteen for our breakfast before exercise and training. It was quite difficult to cook something nice for the officers with all the rationing, I can tell you!' Ishbel Campbell went into the WAAFS where she became one of the first female balloon operators, whilst her sister Catriona volunteered as a VAD nursing auxiliary. Morag MacKinnon and Mary Campbell both joined the Queen Alexandra Royal Army Nursing Service. The QA, as it was known, had a reputation for courage and excellence which the Eigg nurses were soon to deserve. They both earned medals for their bravery, Morag in North Africa and Italy, Mary in India and then Burma, pulling wounded soldiers onto evacuating ships under Japanese bombs during the siege of Singapore.

Back on Eigg, Sir Walter's factor had managed to claim exemption for those who worked on the estate farm or the ferry. The island lost its foresters to Raasay where wood was cut for the war effort. The gardeners were conscripted one after the other and it fell to the oldest of the remaining Campbell boys to take over the job. Gordon had just left school and could have easily obtained a scholarship to study in Inverness. But at 14 years of age, he was the only one left to ensure that the family would keep a roof over their head since theirs was a tied cottage. 'I didn't have much choice, we would have been out', said Gordon with a shrug. 'I didn't mind the work but I didn't like the way the factor used to blow his whistle when he wanted you. Wherever you were, whatever you were doing, you had to drop everything and rush to see what he wanted, just like a slave in the plantations! Campbell had started under Petersen as a gardener himself, and when he became Runciman's factor he really thought he was a cut above everyone else!' Campbell's attitude was typical of his job. His idea of fairness was in the strict application of rules. Four pints of milk from the estate dairy were allowed daily for the family of each estate worker and the surplus of milk had to be thrown away, even though, behind his back, the dairyman gave the children as much milk as they could take. It was the same for the coal allowance: he would not even contemplate the loan of few extra hundredweight for an elderly crofter one particularly cold winter, which the family offered to pay for in the spring. The only concession he allowed was the packets of tea and tobacco given to the crofters' wives when they came to pay the rent twice a year as their reward for paying on time.

General mobilisation throughout the country also meant that civilians had their role to play. As the west coast assumed great strategic importance, the island ferryman was drafted into the Coast Watch. Two special constables were appointed, one on the estate side, one in Cleadale to report anything suspicious to the Mallaig police. An identity pass carrying a photograph was required to travel anywhere beyond Fort William, and Angus MacKinnon, who travelled back and forth from college at Inverness, got into trouble when he forgot his. Security was particularly tight on the coast beyond Mallaig since Arisaig House was now the centre of a network of Special Operation Executive Paramilitary Schools, which were located in all the 'big houses' in the area. Agents belonging to resistance teams from all over occupied Europe came to train in all aspects of underground warfare, learning sabotage with people like the author Gavin Maxwell and Tex Geddis, his friend of the shark-fishing venture. This was all very exciting stuff for impressionable young Eiggaich like Dougald MacKinnon and Duncan MacKay, who always tried to gatecrash the Special Operation dances in Arisaig whenever they brought cattle to the mainland.

The whole rugged terrain from the rough bounds of Knoydart and Moidart to Fort William was used for the training of the hard-striking force raised after the Dunkirk disaster of 1940.

Subjected to a gruelling physical and mental regime, the men of those now legendary commandos were all hand-picked and the islanders derived quite a lot of pride from the fact that one of them, Donald MacKinnon, had volunteered and been accepted. The sound of explosions and depth charges from Ardtoe (one of the training beaches in Ardnamurchan) could often be heard from Creagard where Gordon Campbell could see flares and tracing bullets very clearly at night. Unlike Eigg folks, mainland people had grown used to men suddenly bursting out of cover with blood-chilling cries. It was therefore quite a shock for the inhabitants of Cleadale when, one fine morning in 1942, they were woken up by the sound of flares and gunfire coming from the sea. An almost full-scale assault-landing practice was taking place in Laig Bay, with about 700 soldiers scrambling in the water from their landing crafts towards the dunes. Snapping the crofters' fences, the soldiers made their way through the island to rendezvous with a 300-strong group which had landed at the north end of the island. Not only did they practise arrests on bewildered islanders, like Marybel MacDonald who was detained for ages before she could go home, but they also used them as targets! 'I was going to work as usual,' tells Dougald MacKinnon, 'walking up the Bealach Clithe, and I was just about to reach the top of the hill when I heard gunfire and I saw bullets whizzing in front of me. They were so close I could smell the gunpowder! Anyway, I carried on as if nothing had happened, but when I turned in the Sandavore road, this soldier popped out of the heather and stopped me at the letter-box in the corner there. Oh, he asked me all sorts of questions and I figured out from what he was asking that they must have been checking their radio-links . . . Well, with all that live ammunition, it was a wonder that there were so few casualties because they were at it all day and all night, just two stretcher-cases if I remember rightly. The next day, we saw them at the pier, waiting to be picked up, and some of them were so tired they were asleep on the rocks, on the grass, just where they were.' Commenting wryly that the landing had provided the island with the highest population it had ever known, Gordon Campbell, who collected a lot of empty cartridge shells and practice grenades afterwards, remembered 'flares going off and tracing bullets everywhere!' on his side of the island.

Another cause of excitement was the landing of a plane on Laig Sands when Lord Runciman's daughter Mrs Fairweather or her husband, who were both pilots in the ATA, called to visit those members of the Runciman family who had taken refuge on the island between flying missions. On another occasion, Mr Fairweather flew right over the Lodge on his way to a mission up north and dropped the mail which missed the lawn and got stranded in the trees! (Sadly, they both lost their lives in flying accidents before the war was over.)

Apart from episodes like these, the islanders were less directly affected by the war than most civilians. They did not suffer as many privations as city folks, since they relied as always on the produce of the land, their own eggs, milk, butter and potatoes, although they endured a shortage of tea, flour and sugar. The vast quantities of sugar given for jam-making in rural areas which Lady Runciman had distributed to all islanders at the beginning of the war had only lasted for so long. The islanders, worried above all about the safety of relatives and friends, listened avidly to news on the radio, catching Lord Haw-Haw's propaganda broadcasts too sometimes. 'What a horrid voice he had', remembers one islander. 'They used to broadcast the tonnage of shipping lost at the beginning of the war, but we didn't like it, we were glad when they stopped, it was better not to know when there were any losses with so many that were at sea from Eigg.' The islanders were reminded what fate could happen to their sons and brothers when the bodies of two British Navy sailors were washed up in 1942. Their vessel, HMS *Curaçao*, was escorting a convoy bound for America and was carrying out the necessary zig-zag manoeuvres to deter enemy submarines, when the very ship which they were escorting ran into her and cut her in two.

A FIERY CROSS IN THE SKY

'The men of lights', as the Northern Lights are called in Gaelic, were always considered a bad omen. When they appeared on the evening of 13 March 1941, the islanders felt distinctly uneasy. The lights that night were particularly impressive: the colourful beams which spanned the sky like searchlights gathered for a moment to form a huge shimmering red cross right above their heads. For the islanders, there was no longer any doubt: this fiery cross could only portend disaster in the present context of the war. When Hugh MacKinnon reported what happened later on that night, they braced themselves for the coming of very bad news.

That same night indeed, Hugh had woken up as the cockerel which roosted at the bottom of his garden started to crow. No sooner had it stopped than the hens perched in the tree cackled loudly, filling the household with apprehension, for this was another bad omen, one which generally foretold death. It was therefore no real surprise for anyone when, shortly afterwards, news came through of the Clydebank blitz. So many of their relatives lived there, including Hugh's own brother Angus. Considering the devastation wrought by the bombing, the official number of casualties was low, and fortunately no one with connections to Eigg was counted among the dead or injured.

Angus MacKinnon was amongst those whose home was destroyed. As bombing continued around Glasgow, he decided to send his family to Eigg, to the delight of his three children, who were ecstatic at the idea of going to school in the very place where they went on holiday each year. There were a few other evacuee children on Eigg, from London and Orkney, which increased the school roll to twenty-two, although nine-year-old Ann, Lord Runciman's granddaughter, did not attend the island school but took lessons with her cousin in Galmisdale. For Ann as for Angus's son Chick, this was a period of great happiness. He spent most of his time at the lochs with Donald Archie MacLeod, the gamekeeper, who taught him all there was to know about fly-fishing. The rest of the time, he was roaming the beach with the other children, looking for things to salvage like the great big bales of raw rubber which brought a bob or two from the Receiver of Wrecks. Donny Morrison, who grew up at Shore Cottage, can still picture the time in 1944 when the ferrymen found a heavy drum washed up on the sand near the pier. Archie MacDonald, his uncle, and Dougald MacKinnon approached it cautiously, in case it exploded like the mine which landed at Laig and went off in a huge blast whilst everyone was at mass. 'Oh, they circled it, and they poked it and prodded it,' recalls Donny, 'and then they finally rolled it ashore and Dougie pierced the lid of it and, oh, you ought to have seen their faces, when they found out that it contained 40 gallons of pure spirit!' The alcohol found on the beach was shared out between each household. Some of it was used neat in Tilley lamps instead of paraffin which was hard to come by, but most of it was saved with another purpose in mind. After a few experiments conducted by Dougald's mother, the conclusion was that a dilution of two-and-a-half to one, with the addition of a bit of treacle for colouring and taste, produced a very satisfying dram in these times of dearth. Dodie Campbell, who arrived on leave from the convoys just at that time, was offered a dram of that still very potent mixture in each household he visited, which gave him one of the most memorable hangovers of his life! The island had been 'dry' during all those war years, except for the time when bottles from the *Politician* found their way to Eigg, thanks to the gamekeeper whose wife was a native of Eriskay. Donald Archie told the factor that a new mare was urgently needed on the estate. He really couldn't do without one and, as it happened, he knew someone in Eriskay who had a mare for sale of a far superior breed to the Rum ponies which the estate usually bought. Needless to say, Donald Archie did not come back from Eriskay empty-handed.

The convoy lads certainly deserved a bit of cheering up when they came home, for Merchant Seamen had found themselves involved in the war right from the beginning, since it was absolutely essential that vital supply lines were kept open in spite of relentless attacks from German U-boats. Often bedevilled by bad weather, convoys were difficult to protect and received only distant cover from the home fleet, and the casualty rate in the Merchant Navy was the highest in all the forces. Incredibly, most of the Eigg lads escaped unharmed. Like Archie MacDonald, Iain MacQuarrie was torpedoed twice in the Atlantic and made his way to New York to look for another convoy. Penniless – owners stopped the pay of sailors forced to abandon ship – but resourceful, Iain managed to get suits for himself and his four companions and they had the time of their life at the Seaman's Mission in New York! As for Duncan Campbell (Cleadale), he held himself extremely lucky to have survived at all. Arctic convoys were the most dangerous of all, having to contend with ice, snow and thick freezing fog as well as the Germans, with no chance of survival if torpedoed. 'He did not like to talk about it, recalls Duncan MacKay, 'but he had a medal from the Russians for being in the Arctic convoys. They would have starved without the convoys. He did also get a medal from the British government, but that was a long time after the war. He got it for saving his ship. They were under heavy fire from the German Navy, when a phosphorus shell hit the deck and went right through to the magazine room. It was a matter of time until it exploded and the Captain asked for a volunteer to go down and defuse it. I suppose there was a good risk of being blown up during the operation, but on the other hand, if it did explode, that would have been the whole lot of them, gone. There was no chance of survival at sea and that would have been them, so that's why he volunteered. He did not really talk about the convoys much, except to say that folks up in Archangel or Murmansk, they were just like us in the Hebrides, and their vodka was good, when you could get hold of it.' Duncan Campbell (Tigh a' Muillear) was not so fortunate: serving as gunman on an ammunition ship, he was killed by a German shell during the assault on Crete. Donald MacKinnon was to die in a Naples hospital from wounds received in the Monte Cassino inferno, his last letter describing the terrible conditions of the siege, five days in a shell-hole without any water or food, hell let loose around him. As for Duncan MacIntyre, who lost his health in the desert campaign, he was to die on his return, fours years later.

None of the men was back home for VE Day, which was celebrated quietly on the island, although young Angus MacKinnon played the pipes on VJ Day, marching up and down Cleadale. It was a while before they returned, and for many of them this return would only be a brief visit to their families before going away again.

AN AGEING COMMUNITY

Although losses could not compare with the slaughter of half a generation during the Great War, the Second World War had just as profound an effect on the island population. With only two men out of the sixteen who went away to the war coming back to live on the island, Eigg was in danger of becoming an ageing community lacking in energy and strength. The fact was that in the immediate post-war years, there was hardly a crofter under 65 years of age on Eigg. At the north end of the crofting township, the 'Racket' in Hulin was tenanted by a sprightly octogenarian, Annie MacDonald, who lived to be 101. In the rest of the township, the crofts were all in the hands of elderly crofters whose children worked on the estate. Two houses were now actually vacant. It was no different at the other end of the township. 'Well, there were five cailleachs in Cuagach, and there was always one who had fallen out with the others! The three that were on their own, they would perhaps get someone to cut their hay in the summer, but they kept cattle on their croft the same as anybody else!'

The problem was not that the land lay fallow, because elderly or not, the crofters worked their land with love and dedication. 'Old Annie had two cows and she scythed her own hay and she carried it up the hill creel by creel on her back. She was always out, cutting any bracken that would dare show itself', recalled Dr MacLean. 'I can still hear her saying that as long as she had a breath of life in her body, you wouldn't see a blade of bracken or a leaf of ragwort on her croft!' As for Katie-Ruairi in Cuagach (she was quite a character, once a tram conductor in Glasgow, who always went out with her beret and an army coat tied at the waist with a piece of string), 'She was always out with her cow on the croft,' recalls Peggy Kirk, 'and my father-in-law, Papa Kirk, oh well, if he had a cow calving, there was nothing he wouldn't do for her. The old people, they treated cattle like family.'

The problem was that there were not enough young folks to take the land over from the older generations. The situation was the same everywhere throughout the Highlands and Islands. The Small Isles were just an extreme case, with numbers down to fifteen on Muck, forty on Canna, whilst the population on Rum consisted of a handful of servants and gamekeepers for the castle, nobody apart from the minister, the priest or the doctor being allowed to set foot on the island. There were certainly more people on Eigg but as more and more girls left for the mainland, it was becoming quite difficult to find a suitable marriage partner, one who was from the same religion or who was not too closely related, and the rate of unmarried people was getting far too high. It was a vicious circle: depopulation meant impoverishment in energy and ideas since the young folks were missing who would perhaps question the old ways of crofting and search for innovations, who would have the necessary enthusiasm to grab hold of the new grants and schemes which appeared after the war. Without them there was a real danger of stagnation which in effect drove even more young people away until communities finally reached a dead end.

As in other places, the war had propelled many islanders into the world outside Eigg and it was a world they eventually preferred. But the fact was that in most cases they really had no other choice. There was little prospect for them on an island where all the crofts were occupied and no more land was available. It was not that they did not want to come back, for a number of them, anxious to come home, had actually thought of going into tweed-weaving like others had done in the Outer Isles. But they were given so little encouragement and found themselves confronted with such a host of regulations on top of the initial financial outlay, without the possibility of a temporary exemption from Purchase Tax, that they abandoned the idea.[2] They went back to the Merchant Navy or to Glasgow. There were plenty of jobs elsewhere and, as Angus MacKinnon wryly put it, 'It didn't take them very long to work out they could make 5 bob a hell of a lot easier and faster on the mainland than on the island'.

However, the war had merely accelerated a process which had already been at work for a long time. To quote Angus again, 'it was a foregone conclusion that those who could would go away. If they wanted to get on, they had to get out', because further education for crofters' children had always meant a future away from the islands. Teachers had certainly fostered in pupils and parents the feeling that crofting was only second best and that more family pride would derive from the children who were away with their diplomas framed on the wall of the best room than in carrying on with crofting. Angus MacKinnon's experience of being sent to college in Inverness was typical of many: 'There were quite a lot of us at college in Inverness, all from the same crofting background. If you were found capable of studying, you were pushed: in my case, it was with the idea of serving the community, it was an ideal, and that's why I wanted to be a doctor.' But at the end of the war, there was a two-year waiting list to study medicine. Conscious of the burden this would impose on his parents, Angus went for engineering instead and ended up in the Royal Engineering Corps in Lockerbie: 'it was 1945, and I had spent all my free time training as a cadet in the Queen's Own Highlanders, so I decided to see a bit of action in my turn, and after six months' training I was away in Palestine. That's the other thing I really wanted, to be away! I spent two years near the Suez Canal doing patrols and reconnoitre work. Well, I came to have a deep understanding of the Arabs, with their oxen and their buffalos, working the land like we used to do. I used to join them sometimes when they were playing their flutes, I tried one once, funny things they were, not much more than a reed, but I managed to get a squeak out of it. They'd play their own tunes, and I'd play mine on the chanter, it was a great experience! But that was me afterwards, I went into engineering and I was away from Eigg for the best part of thirty years.'

Possibilities for a return home were not so easy when there were not enough well-paid jobs on offer. The conclusion of the 1936 Hileary Commission, appointed by an unusually sympathetic Scottish Office to investigate what was seen as the Highland problem, had been that only a programme of economic regeneration based on tourism, forestry and hydro-electric power would go towards redressing the balance of population and alleviate poverty. The war and its imperative requirements had put an end to implementing these ideas and the problem was still there in 1945. A new survey of all crofting areas was commissioned in order to identify a cure.[3]

Frank Fraser Darling's famous West Highland Survey was a pioneering work, providing the first extensive ecological survey of the area. His conclusion was unequivocal: devastated landscapes, a decline in tillage and land use, a bankrupt pastoralism. These were the consequences of a policy of land use which had started 200 years before with the introduction of large-scale sheep farming which had as devastating an effect on the region's natural history as it had on its social history. Only a truly well-thought-out conservation policy would, in his opinion, bring back the complex ecological balance which could make the Highlands once again a productive environment where people had their place, rather than a man-made wilderness for 'the jaded townsman'. The fact was that in an increasingly urbanised Britain, the Highlands, once the playground of the rich, were fast becoming a recreational park for the leisure of middle-class urban dwellers.

As far as the Small Isles were concerned, Fraser Darling felt that, compared to Canna and Muck where arable cultivation was of a high standard and the cattle–sheep ratio not too wide, Eigg had been 'allowed to go almost to dereliction' despite the high potential fertility of its basalt loam. 'Engulfing the sheep walks, forming jungles along the streams and creeping avariciously

137

towards the little crofts', bracken was all too prevalent on the island, colonising only too well the basalt slopes where the natural goodness of the ground allowed it the utmost luxuriance of growth, its rhizomes continuing to grow underground throughout the mild west-coast winters, deplored Fraser Darling. Its unimpeded growth was a direct consequence of intensive sheep farming, and despite the estate bracken-crushing machinery, without enough cattle to keep it in check, it was a losing battle.

Looking at the Small Isles population, he felt that Canna retained 'the firmest hold on a continued, dynamic, social and agricultural existence', whereas Muck would have difficulties retaining its population without its 'tenacious and benevolent ownership'. On Eigg, with so many of its crofters being elderly, he feared 'the future of the island as a crofting unit was precarious'. In his view, the lack of a proper harbour on either island impeded the possibility of further development, compared to islands like Eriskay which had a population of 300 people for less than half the size of Eigg and a much less fertile soil, but a safe anchorage and a thriving fishing community.[4]

Not only was he touching there on the problem of infrastructure but he also hinted at the crucial role played by proprietors in maintaining a stable population. Both Muck and Canna benefited from resident owners who managed their islands themselves with great sensitivity. Rum was a case on its own: it was gifted to the Nature Conservancy Council in 1950 and was run as a deer observation station. But farming on Eigg was now suffering from a lack of proper management, so that in the post-war drive to increase crop and cattle production, the estate was forced to embark on a re-stocking policy. The island was let in 1947 to Robin Gowans, a Black Isle farmer who brought in a stock of 120 Galloway cattle, reversing the trend of keeping too many sheep. Gowans also brought the first tractor to the island and was credited with introducing the first wellington boots ever seen on Eigg. (He kept two pairs, a large one and a small one, which were used in turn by his five farm workers!) But in spite of his success – good crops of oats at Kildonnan – his tenure was short-lived, for Viscount Leslie Runciman, and his brother Steven who inherited the island in 1949, did not renew Gowans' five-year lease, preferring to regain control of the island. In the stark economic reality of the post-war years, which saw a long-awaited increase in agricultural wages but a decrease in hill-farm prices, the farm had to pay its way: Leslie was said to be much less willing to spend large sums of money on the island than his parents. Eigg was mainly a secluded holiday retreat for the Runciman family and the islanders complained that they left its running to factors who knew little about farming. They felt that the success of the farm was in large part due to the estate boys – sixteen of them – who kept the place in good order, because they all knew what they had to do and they did it without needing to be told. However, in spite of their being absentee owners, the Runcimans made sure that whatever profits were made from the farm were ploughed back into it. Aware that the island population was dwindling, they also maintained employment at its highest level in an attempt to keep people on the island.

By contrast, events just across the water from Eigg were highlighting only too well what could happen when a landowner had no sense of responsibility to his tenantry. Lord Brocket, who owned the Knoydart estate, was an absentee landlord who had actually spent the war interned in Arran for his support of the British Fascist Party. He absolutely opposed the claim made by local people returning from the war, the seven men of Knoydart, for some of his land to be turned into crofts. The Knoydart men were forced to take their case to the Land Court where they were defeated, largely because of a lack of political will to support their cause, even though other returning soldiers had managed to reclaim some land up north. Knoydart lost the last of its indigenous population, but not without Lord Brocket being driven out in his turn. His exit followed a mysterious night explosion which destroyed the estate pier, aimed with such precision that the windows on the house nearby were not even shattered. His boat-shed went up in flames and as a final insult his pigs were let loose in the kitchen garden. The land question could not be ignored so easily.

WEDDING BELLS ARE RINGING IN CLEADALE

Happier times returned for Eigg towards the end of the war as wedding bells started to ring on the island. Dougald and Katie MacKinnon's wedding in November 1945 was the first to be celebrated. 'It was quite a good wedding,' recalls Katie, 'considering that there was rationing and that many of the young folks were still away. Duncan MacKay was the groomsman and one of my cousins from Skye was the bridesmaid. We had the ceilidh in the school and there was plenty of music and dancing and singing: Duncan Ferguson was on the fiddle and Hugh MacKinnon composed a song specially for our wedding, it was quite humorous. The priest was singing too, he was a Uist man and a good Gaelic singer. Well, that's what they said about our wedding: the minister was dancing and the priest was singing. Of course, some of the old ones, the Wee Frees, they thought it was the worst thing they had ever seen, the priest and the minister enjoying themselves, and in each other's company as well!' The poor minister was to confide some years later that this wedding had almost cost him his collar, as one of his parishioners had complained about his dancing and singing. The fact that it did not was at least an admission that attitudes in the Church were now more relaxed and this allowed sectarianism on the island to become less and less acute, even though it would take another decade for a Protestant islander to dare cross the religious divide and marry a Catholic.

With four more weddings, and the return in the early 1950s of the two Merchant Seamen to take over the croft from their elderly parents, there were just enough young people out of seventeen crofting households to ensure some continuity. The trouble was that crofting only offered part of the income needed to live on, let alone to raise a family. As Angus MacKinnon points out, the Eigg crofts with their three acres of arable had hardly kept a family a hundred years before, and it was no easier now. Opportunities for paid employment were grabbed fast, the younger islanders taking over the postman and ferryman jobs as people retired, or falling back on employment on the estate to ensure a regular income.

Those crofters who remained independent from the estate had to depend on their wits and enterprise to provide an extra income. Dougald MacKinnon had plenty of these. He was the first islander to own a car and the first crofter to own a tractor. That car, converted into a small van, was the first motor car on the island since Petersen's time. 'It was handy to get the stores from the pier', tells Dougald, and it was not long before he able to take over the haulage contract when Hugh MacKinnon retired. He soon managed to get a proper truck with a tarpaulin at the back. The truck – an ex-army Fordson V8 – was fairly temperamental and did not like cold mornings, and Dougald used to coax it into life by warming the engine up with a paraffin heater under it at the front. The big problem after the war was petrol which was still rationed. Always resourceful, he would use paraffin once the engine had warmed up and it would go quite well. The trouble was that when Dougald did away with the horse and cart, his wife Katie no longer had her messages carried to her door, for the old road did not reach beyond Cnoc an t-Sabhail, and she had to climb that hill with her shopping until the new road finally reached their house.

Eigg still had a dirt road, always muddy, built in the previous century. It was now in the remit of the local authority (the county of Inverness-shire which had replaced the old Parish Council in 1929) to surface it. The Highlands and Islands Counties' road policy certainly did much to provide employment throughout the area, and Eigg was no exception. 'Well, this surveyor from the Council, MacDonald was his name, he came to have a look at the road', tells Dougald, puffing on his pipe as he tells the story. 'It was just a cart track and after the Sgumban it was so boggy that many's the time my lorry would go in, right up to the axles! I supposed I knew the road like the back of my hand, and that's how I got the job as a foreman when they did the road. They left me in charge and I saved them a lot of money they would have had to spend on more surveys. But it was quite a responsibility, because I had five or six men under me. I had to write all the hours on a big ledger at the shop, and I had to write them down properly otherwise there would have been trouble. Well, it was quite a big job, you had to make a solid bed of rock before they could tar it, and they didn't do that until 1966. I remember when we started because it was at the time of the Korean War, so it must have been in 1951 or thereabouts. We used a lot of dynamite, you see, we had a lot of blasting to do and, oh, well, well, I mind some of the boys were really mischievous – Dodie and Angus – they were devils! Well, they were blasting at the corner of the Bealach Clithe, and old Feemie who lived down in the first Cuagach house, she used to come up to the well at the Bealach to get her water. Well, they used to time the blast for when they saw her coming . . . It was for sheer devilment but they were young . . . And the poor woman, she said, one time that there was a big shower of stones with the blasting, she said she might as well be in Korea!'

The road contract, the haulage and the ferry were only a few of the jobs that Dougald managed to undertake to maintain his family of five. A gifted mechanic, he was also entrusted with the repairs to the cranky telephone exchange which had been installed in 1938 and required quite a bit of attention. There were only twelve numbers in the exchange and when Dougald got the phone, his number being Eigg 12, he could hear the telephonist making wisecracks to her colleague: 'I've got a dozen eggs, have you got the bacon?' Then, when butane gas was introduced, he installed the gas piping for lights in each house on the island and became the local gas dealer. On top of all this he become the island taximan in the early 1950s and drove the children to and from school as well as taking the old cailleachs out to the shop every Friday afternoon.

A HARD BUT PRODUCTIVE LIFE

The standard of living was still fairly low on Eigg as in the rest of the Hebrides. There was so little cash around that Russell Kirk, an American who visited the island in 1950, remarked that 'the income of one of the poorest sharecroppers of Georgia would greatly exceed the currency the Eigg families see from one year's end to the next'.[5] It was a constant and strenuous struggle to keep just above poverty level as the type of farming crofters were engaged in was very labour-intensive for its return. It was still little more than subsistence farming, yet compared with the poverty experienced by their forebears a few generations before, their situation was one of great improvement. In today's terms, the islanders would be congratulated for having achieved an almost complete self-sufficiency.

Apart from the production of potatoes, all the agricultural activity revolved around cattle. It meant careful planning in the production of fodder, hay and turnip for the cattle, oats for horses. The type of cattle raised on the island was still determined by the choice of an Aberdeen Angus as the township bull, following the trend set by cattle dealers. Bred with an Ayrshire or Shorthorn cross it produced a good beef calf which was weaned at birth and sold at eighteen months. Blue-greys were also a popular breed for cows, but due to the predominance of the Aberdeen Angus strain, the cattle produced were not hardy enough to be outwintered in the hills. In the summer, the crofters kept the cattle on the outrun. From mid-October, cows and calves were brought in at night, unlike the horses which were left outside all the time. They were put out to water in the morning and left to forage on the croft all day although they were fed hay morning and night, with turnips and potatoes from time to time. Corn was given at calving times or during really bad weather when the cows were kept in all day except for watering. As it took about two tons of hay to feed a cow through the winter, it meant that each crofter had to produce between four and eight tons of hay each summer.

With calf production the mainstay of a crofting livelihood, calving was always an anxious moment for crofters who had to time it well so that it came at the best moment in the year. 'When Papa – my father-in-law – had a cow calving, he'd be skirling round her with a bucket of warm water and oatmeal in it, he would really pamper her! And he would not sleep at all, he'd be up there in the byre to see if she was alright!' recalls Peggy Kirk. 'Newborn calves were put into separate pens and taught to drink their mother's milk from a bucket. From that time on your first job in the morning was to do the milking,' explained Ann Campbell, 'then you'd turn the cows out, feed the calves – as they grew, you had to add calf meal to the milk, you could get that at the shop – then you would let them out in the field with their mother and deal with the rest of the milk. You would drink it of course, but you would also make your own butter and cream; everyone made their own in those days! It was all strained through muslin into a large round scalded basin, you took what was needed for the household and the rest, you left it to separate. Later on, you'd skim the cream with a clean scalded saucer. You'd do the night's milk and you would put the cream in a crock: when the crock was full you'd tip it in the churn and make butter. Well, making the butter was quite a long job, it could take ages in the churn, then you had to wash it three times in cold water to get rid of the buttermilk. You would use the buttermilk to bake scones and pancakes and also for drinking: it was good with a little oatmeal in it, quite a refreshing drink at haymaking time. Well, when you had dealt with the milk, you washed and scalded every utensil you used and you still had to go and muck the byre!' Needless to say, all the water needed for cleaning and washing had to be carried from the well or the tap outside. Carrying it and warming it up all day long to cope with all the various domestic chores was extremely time-consuming. Katie MacKinnon remembers the years when her children were young as a time of constant hard work. She had to get up at 6.30 in the morning, go to the byre in the winter and run up to the hills in the summer to find her three cows, milk them, feed the calves and bring back two pails of milk before getting the children ready for school. For her and all the other crofter wives, life on the island was 'thirled to the croft', yet the moments of relaxation spent in the company of other families on the customary Sunday afternoon visits or during the frequent and lively ceilidhs brought enough pleasure for the island women to consider themselves happy with their lot. 'You did not think about it, you got on with it', says Katie with a shrug.

Although each croft was properly fenced it was a full-time job to keep the cows in. 'If they strayed, it was in your best interest to get them back straight away or that would cause some strife! You would hear of it at the next crofters' meeting. Broken fences were repaired with anything that was on hand, with old iron bedsteads a great favourite.' It was hardly surprising that each crofter felt strongly about invasion by another's cattle since the production of fodder and grazing was so crucial to their economy, crofters still relying largely on meadow grass rather than sown mixture to make their hay. Haymaking started in late June and carried on through July and August, weather permitting. 'The midges could be really terrible, but our neighbour, old Lachie MacAskill, well, he was never bothered with the midges', recalls Mary-Ann Campbell. 'His neck would be black with them and he wouldn't feel a thing, he was really wonderful, the way he would scythe without stopping.' After cutting, the grass was allowed to dry in swathes; then it was turned the next day and worked with a fork whenever the weather was right. If rain threatened, the hay was forked into little quoils then it was spread out again. Then it was made into proper quoils, the hay being shaken by hand onto the quoil and the outside combed through the fingers so that it was watertight and would not blow over easily. A piece of sacking was put on top of the haycock and it was tied down with ropes. 'It was still hair ropes that they used, made out of plaited horse hair,' remembers Ann Campbell, 'and they were never knotted, just twisted with a handful of hay and then tucked inside the stack. You watched your rick and you waited until it was really dry before you would take it in, otherwise it could catch fire as happened to Dodie once! The hay was left to cure for a fortnight. Then, on a breezy day, it was spread again to dry some more before it was carted away in the hay shed or built into a stack in the yard behind the house.' Needless to say, the hay obtained in this time-consuming way was of excellent quality and the crofters were careful to preserve the fertility of their meadowland by applying a topdressing of seaweed in the winter. They also practised a good crop rotation: 'the land was worked in strips with corn being planted on newly ploughed land, then it was used for potatoes or turnips, then it was corn again with two or three years of hay after that', explains Angus MacKinnon.

The corn harvest started in September, which was generally a dry sunny month, with a full moon around Michaelmas which enabled the islanders to work late at night to finish the harvest. 'I have seen Katie and me up until two in the morning to finish cutting the corn', recalls Dougald. 'You had to, in case the weather changed. The whole field could be flattened and that was your harvest ruined.' Horse-drawn reapers were used to cut the sheaves with one or two people behind to make the sheaves into stooks, three or five together. Then, when the stooks were dry enough, the corn was taken in and the corn stack carefully built, sheaf by sheaf. 'You'd be careful to put the sheaf at an angle so that the rain would run on the outside and not go in the stack', explains Katie. 'When the stack was built, you could just take a handful of corn at a time to feed the horses or the hens. You had to winnow it first before you'd give it to the hens.' Dougald could picture it still: 'I mind Angus and his father going to the top of the quarry in Cleadale to winnow their corn, there was always a good breeze there'. 'In my mother's time they would have taken the corn to the mill at Kildonnan and they would have had their own oatmeal', recalls Katie.

The potato harvest followed after the corn, from late September through to October and November. They had been planted in the spring, straight on the dung from the midden which

142

was spread thickly in the drills, ploughing starting in February and going till May, depending on the weather. Manure was the only fertiliser used for potatoes, as seaweed was deemed to make the potatoes too 'wet'. Apart from maincrop varieties like Kerr's Pink or Golden Wonder, the islanders used to plant Edzell Blue, an almost black potato, or Midlothian, Landworthy, Arran Corracle and Arran Banner. Duncan Ferguson reckoned that they would get a return of nine hundredweight for each hundredweight of potato seed sown, a return which showed a land kept in good heart with a lot of manuring. The bulk of the crop was lifted and stored in a dry straw-lined area of the byre, the 'bullets' being kept aside for the hens and the seed potato saved for the following year. Potato planting and harvesting was a communal affair and therefore a very social time. Neighbours and family were drafted in and at the end of the day's work, everybody sat down to a feast of boiled tatties and corned beef. 'There would be a big pot of potatoes put on the boil and a great big pot of tea was brewed. Then the corned beef was opened – it was a huge long tin, you never see them nowadays – and we had a great time, everyone was in high spirit', recall Mary-Ann and Catriona Campbell.

With their hay, potatoes and corn safely stored, the crofters were more or less self-sufficient. They had hens and ducks which provided them with plenty of eggs, the surplus being preserved in waterglass for winter use. Katie even kept turkeys at one time. Some kept a few sheep – crofters were not supposed to keep them but the factor had allowed a few per family as a concession, provided that they were kept tethered – which were slaughtered for the winter. Every bit of the meat was used and preserved in brine if not eaten straight away. The wool was sent to the Brora spinning mills and came back as yarn ready to knit. They had their own milk, butter and crowdie and they had fish. In the summer, they'd have fresh fish of course. Of the nine boats which Marybel MacDonald remembers in her childhood, there were still five or six left, and if they had nothing else to do on the croft, the islanders would go out for a bit of fishing in the bay. The catch was always shared amongst the community, so that everyone had plenty of fish all summer. Lachie MacDonald, for one, used to dry and salt his saithe for winter use but others would order half a firkin of salt herring from the fish merchant and that would make two or three good meals a week. Rabbits of course were shot and eaten in vast quantities. Considering the post-war austerity which still gripped the country, crofters dined as well as anyone else in Britain and perhaps better, concluded Russell Kirk. He admired the islanders' thrift and frugality which allowed them to derive food and income from such a small amount of ground. The only money that was needed was for coal, gas and the shop and this was brought in by the sale of two or three stirks, for £150 to £200 each.

Yet in spite of all this hard work in a pretty adverse climate, Russell Kirk observed that crofting was perceived as inefficient in machine-age Britain, a way of life which was out of synch with the rest of the country. The American visitor would echo a lot of people's thoughts when he wrote that crofters would not last out the century if 'society continued to follow its present course'. To him, places like Eigg were 'the last of an old song', and although 'it seemed inevitable that the song would fade away' he felt that the world would be the poorer for it.[6]

THE LAST OF AN OLD SONG

Yet, at the very moment when some people condemned the crofting system as backward and not adapted to modern life, others were rediscovering the values which had made it survive for so long and finding them increasingly attractive. The war had induced a sense of malaise in civilisation and these people felt the need to go back to simpler values, to come closer to nature, and it appeared that the Highlands and Islands were the best place for this voyage of rediscovery. A sort of Highland Bloomsbury set had appeared, with George Orwell in Jura, Gavin Maxwell near Skye, Compton MacKenzie in Barra, John Lorne Campbell and Margaret Fay-Shaw in Canna and George MacDonald bringing Iona out of obscurity as a place of spiritual renewal. Moving to Eigg on John Lorne Campbell's recommendation, Edinburgh writer George Scott-Moncrieff joined the trend.

Recently widowed with three young children, he found on the island the kind of peace he was longing for. 'The mind is not so full of images, the soul is receptive therefore and quiet, the faculty of perceiving truth is not yet fully atrophied', he wrote in his island travel book. Island living amounted for him to a spiritual experience. Foremost in that experience were the people themselves: 'islefolks may not be a pack of saints, they share the universal ills, but remoteness and the inevitability of being often alone and quiet, do give them a chance, too rare in the predominantly urban population, to live with their eyes beyond the world. They may be seldom able to put words to what they see, but it is immanent in their capacity to act intuitively.'[7]

George Scott-Moncrieff was impressed by the deep religious feeling on the island. Prayer in Catholic households was not something out of the ordinary but a part of daily life. Church services were attended every Sunday, being held in English and in Gaelic in both Catholic and Protestant churches. The priest involved himself actively in the island life, encouraging the youngsters to play football and adults to take evening classes in all sorts of subjects, although it was not long before falls in numbers would no longer warrant a resident cleric. Missionaries – those lay preachers who replaced resident ministers when a similar decrease in numbers caused the parish to be amalgamated into Mallaig and then Arisaig – had good relationships with the priest, anticipating the ecumenism now firmly established on the island, although religious differences were still taken very seriously. Observance of the Sabbath was held as highly on Eigg as in other Hebridean communities. Sundays were spent reading the Bible. 'You could feed the cow and milk her, you could feed the hens but you could not collect the eggs. It was very strict: I never heard the end of it when I did a drawing of the cliff from the back bedroom one Sunday! I never did it again!' recalls Ann Campbell, whose mother-in-law had asked her if she had been 'saved' when she was first introduced to her.

Even though islanders, Protestants or Catholics, were very strict in their religious observance, they still retained a lot of their traditional beliefs. Omens and instances of second sight were talked about as a matter of fact, how flickers of lights were seen near an old byre before the clothes of the deceased had been burnt, or how Hugh MacKinnon had experienced an encounter with a phantom funeral when he was young: he was walking home past the lodge when he found himself forcibly pushed aside until he was almost in the ditch. A few days later someone died on the island, the funeral cortege passing by that very spot. Old customs were still observed, about the new moon or the cuckoo in the spring: it was unlucky to hear the cuckoo for the first time on an empty stomach, so it was wise to have a piece of bread or oatcake in one's pocket, and the island children would sleep with a piece under their pillow in case they heard the cuckoo in the morning! Neil Mór would turn back if he met a woman on his way to the shore to go fishing. Like George Scott-Moncrieff, his visitors – his relative Neil Usher, the American academic Russell Kirk or the poet Kathleen Raine – were fascinated by their discovery of this island lore which the islanders dispensed freely with their hospitality. The Hebridean social code meant that no one would pass a house without being invited to step in and given a *strupag*, the ritual cup of tea and piece of home baking. 'What is happening in the township today?' the host would ask, and the guest would tell his news. In return there would be the telling of some island tradition that related to the topic discussed. The Scott-Moncrieff children were always at their neighbour's house, where they were kept enthralled with stories of genealogies and place-names. Night visits were the pretext for more elaborate storytelling in these pre-television days. There were several 'ceilidh houses' on the island, Neil Mór being very popular for he liked playing whist and was renowned for his sense of humour. Duncan Ferguson's house was the one for a tune on the fiddle and Lachie MacDonald's the one for fairy stories: he came from a family renowned on Muck for their storytelling and his story of an encounter with the little people was famous.[8] As far as the history of Eigg was concerned Hugh MacKinnon's was the place to go to. He was considered locally the best historian in the Small Isles. 'One sits in Hugh MacKinnon's neat parlour, with its sturdy furniture, drinking milk from his cows and munching biscuits,' recalled Russell Kirk, 'and he summons one story after another from his memory; he would have ten times as many, twenty times, he declares, if he had paid attention to old folks in his parents' generation.'[9]

Not surprisingly, Hugh's stories soon attracted the attention of folklore collectors: Calum MacLean on his 1946 Scottish tour for the Irish Folklore Commission, then a few years later, Donald Archie MacDonald from the newly founded School of Scottish Studies in Edinburgh, who was able to record twelve hours of stories, songs and legends about the island. Hugh was, in his opinion, one of the best traditional historians he had ever recorded in all his career. 'He was a poet at heart and much more', wrote Fr Ross after Hugh's death in 1973. 'His mind moved freely in time in a way which was disconcerting at first to those who did not know him. It was as though he lived the whole tradition of the community as his immediate experience, referring to three hundred years ago as easily as to the events of the previous year, talking about people from the past with the warmth given to personal friends and acquaintances and often with well phrased humour. An evening at Hugh's was to witness an animated and informed discussion with his wife Mary and brother Angus as valuable foils and critics as well as supports, for they both shared his love of tradition. Hugh loved Eigg and its traditions passionately, but jealously guarded his community against the scorn or disrespect from the outside world. He had to be sure of those he was speaking to before opening the treasure house. Had he been sure of the survival of the community in the future, I doubt if he would have put as much on record as he eventually did', concluded Fr Ross. 'He accepted the tape-recorder only so that the tradition of the people of Eigg should not be utterly lost.'[10]

The passing-on of tradition was certainly a problem in an island depleted not only of its population but also of its youngsters. Whereas before, they had stayed at school on the island until the age of 14, they now had to go away at the age of 11 to continue their education in mainland schools. Not only did the youngsters miss out on the island social life which they would have normally shared but they also absorbed different values and looked for different means of entertainment. Hugh must have also become aware of the erosion of Gaelic as a language on the island. The newspapers, the wireless, all meant that English was used a lot more and that old words were being forgotten as modern English terms intruded in the islanders' speech, reflected the island missionary.[11] Yet Gaelic was still the language of the playground. Children were no longer punished but congratulated instead for the use of their native language by school inspectors. However, without an official policy to make Gaelic the teaching medium, it was difficult to keep the language up. Marie Carr for instance spoke only Gaelic when she started school in 1964. She can still recall what a shock it was to be thrown into the all-English environment of the classroom: 'I can remember feeling extremely frustrated because the teacher did not understand me. In fact she was not very sympathetic at all, and I remember thinking that she wasn't very nice. There were twelve children in the school and they had to translate to the teacher for me, so I managed to learn a few words that first day. I taught them to my brother as soon as I came home. I thought he'd better know something before he went to school! And that's how my parents stopped speaking Gaelic to us, because of that teacher.' Within a few years, as the factor's and the farm manager's children started to attend school, Gaelic was abandoned as the language of the playground. Children would speak in Gaelic to their parents but amongst themselves they would speak in English.

Language and oral tradition were not the only things on the wane. The efficient working of the family crofting unit had depended on all members of the family from grandparents to grandchildren. But intergenerational cooperation was no longer the same, due to the changes in schooling and the emigration of the young to work away from the island. With the introduction of modern technology the very tradition of sharing work was now becoming something of the past. As tractors gradually superseded horses and ploughs, crofters were not so dependent on one another for help, and although there were still many occasions where cooperation was required, the older element of communal interest in working the land together had disappeared. That decline in social intercourse of the type existing in the pre-war crofting township inevitably led to a certain decline in crofting practices. Yet elements of traditional cooperation were still alive, particularly at the fishing, as boats were too heavy to be put into the sea or taken out single-handed. The catch was still shared amongst the community. Unloading supplies at the pier on ferry days was also communal (and remains so to this day). When the yearly supply of coal arrived by puffer, for example, everyone mucked in for the three days it took to load the coal into bags and take it round the island. That social bond between people in the crofting township was certainly strong enough to be remarked upon by outsiders. For Scott-Moncrieff, it was one of the reasons why he had to defend crofters: 'if they are often miscalled lazy, it is because they are willing to stop for half an hour and talk, that is their distinction, and they will make up for it by working until sundown. They have work in a true proportion, it is not a slice cut out of their being, but as with everything they do, part of their being.'[12] For his friend Russell Kirk, it seemed that the very survival of crofters in the modern world was a criticism, however feeble, of centralised and industrialised society, and he suspected this was the reason why the modern state did not want such minorities to exist. He feared that if they were destroyed, something very precious, like St Kilda, might be lost which could not be retrieved again.[13]

Chapter 11

THE ERA OF UNCERTAINTY

Post-war legislation tried to address what was seen as the 'crofting problem' in the drive to make the country agriculturally self-sufficient. In 1954 the Taylor Commission had concluded that crofting, with diminutive holdings combined with growing absenteeism, was fighting a losing battle against the social and economic forces of the day. Advised that the future for the region lay in hill farming, the commission took the view that crofting had to become a full-time occupation to survive. The only way forward was to encourage amalgamation and create fewer and larger holdings helped by an assortment of subsidies.

However, the creation of economically viable holdings was difficult to achieve in the case of small crofting townships. Amalgamation was necessarily restricted to the amount of land available. On Eigg, Dougald MacKinnon already worked three crofts; his own, the one he had acquired by marriage and another his father had taken over when its tenant, old Robertson, became bedridden and unable to work it. Hugh MacKinnon worked two crofts. 'Six acres of arable, and it was not in one piece, it was all scratchy bits here and there, but it was ploughed, it certainly was, right to the house', recalls Angus MacKinnon, who regretted that the powers-that-be did not push for the creation of new crofts. 'They should have taken land from large estates and then you could have had really viable units. To support a family from crofting, you would have needed a holding big enough for twenty cows and a hundred sheep.' But this was one issue entirely avoided by the Taylor Commission, although one of its members did lay some of the blame for crofting problems on the present system of ownership.[1]

The creation of the Crofters' Commission by the Act of 1955 was meant to ease the gradual reallocation of the land from the less active to the more active members of the crofting community by controlling the letting of vacant crofts, and the transfer of crofts between tenants. But for all its good intentions, this amalgamation policy was soon perceived as a threat to the survival of the system as a whole. By 1961, a new bill made it possible for crofters to decide if and to whom to sublet their croft. The islanders took full advantage of that bill, and by the 1960s most crofters were able to work more than one croft, either by subletting or by amalgamation. In the space of a few years, from 1953 to 1959, the number of cattle tested by the visiting vet doubled to a total of forty-seven cows and fifty-five followers for the twelve crofters in the two townships of Cleadale and Cuagach.

The Crofting Counties Agricultural Grants, introduced in 1956, were specifically designed to bring the land back to full production and to foster better living conditions. 'You got so much money per acre – it was about £7 – that you put back into cultivation,' explains Dougald MacKinnon, 'so you went round your land, and every seven years you could reapply for the grant.' A whole variety of farming operations qualified for grants: fencing, draining, bracken clearing, reseeding of hill pastures. 'We started on the rye grass, you would sow it at the same time as the corn, just roll it a few weeks after the corn and the year after you could cut it for hay.' Shell sand and fertiliser were introduced to improve the ground as traditional manure was no longer available due to the change in cattle husbandry. Premiums for suckler cows now made it a better deal to outwinter cattle on the hill rather than keep them inside, especially as the replacement of horses by tractors had released more grazing for cattle. The Department of Agriculture now supplied the crofters with bulls of different breeds and a hardier cattle was being produced. Following Hugh MacKinnon's example, the crofters themselves started to acquire Highland cows at the Oban sales to contribute to the establishment of this hardier type of cattle.

It was becoming easier to improve houses, but only one or two crofters managed to take advantage of the grants. 'The Department of Agriculture supplied so much of the material and it would also advance the contractors so much and the crofter would pay the balance once the work was carried out', explained Angus MacKinnon, who installed a septic tank, built a generator shed out of railway sleepers he imported from the mainland, re-roofed the barn and installed a Nissen hut for his corn. However, scarcity of labour and materials was a drawback for many islanders and the missionary commented that more crofters would have been prepared to accept government aid 'if they themselves were not called upon to meet so high a proportion of the cost'. Water was brought to most houses after it was discovered that an English mail order firm was selling water pumps for £49 – a considerable sum at the time – Dougald MacKinnon initiating the change to water on tap in 1956. Septic tanks and inside toilets gradually followed and gas piping was installed for lights and cookers – Calor gas being used universally on the island by 1960. All these improvements made life much easier for the island women.

The new legislation brought about a modest increase in prosperity. The problem remained that not enough crofters were in the position to take advantage of these favourable conditions. Those who were employed by the estate followed the change in the cattle-rearing regime but they had little or no incentive to avail themselves of the full range of opportunities which were on offer. One of the problems neglected by the Taylor Commission was that crofting was never meant to rely solely on agricultural income. Little was done to encourage the growth of tourism or fishing. 'It was particularly difficult for us on Eigg', explains Angus MacKinnon. 'It was different in the other islands, like in Uist, where they had the machair, a far better land, and they had the county road, the rocket range and the seaweed factory. It was easier for them to make a living than for us.'

Tourism was nevertheless starting to take off as an alternative source of income. By the mid-1960s the number of houses for let almost equalled the number of inhabited houses in Cleadale, indicating the shrinking number of active crofters. Tourism still meant mostly family, as the islanders' relatives returned to see their family for a fortnight each summer. 'We always came at the time of the Glasgow fair,' says Mairi Kirk, 'and our cousins from London would come up the week after and we would all stay at Hulin. The weather was always wet and we would have red rims on our legs from welly-rub! We did try to go about in our bare feet like the island children but we were not used to it and it was sore . . . Our parents would go to the dances but we would not be allowed to go and it was our grandfather Angus who stayed in to look after us. He would tell us ghost stories all night and we would be petrified!'

Families brought friends and these became regular visitors, adding to the few tourists, who, having discovered the place, came back year after year. These were mostly people interested in wildlife and walking, following the growing trend in Britain for exploring the countryside. Dolly Ferguson's visitors' book also recorded quite a few visitors from Ireland interested in the island traditions and in its early Christian settlement. They enjoyed wonderful hospitality and fare, lobster from the pot, lamb from the farm, home-made butter which the island women made a point of serving pressed with traditional patterns. The estate too had started to rent out one or two houses to some of the regular visitors. And when Donnie Kirk, a young islander who had been away in Glasgow after a spell in the Clyde Coasters, was offered the tenancy of Laig after getting the house with a job on the farm in 1959, he was told that his wife would be able to contribute to their income by taking in visitors. 'Lord Runciman's factor told us: "We are going to let Laig because it is too far away from the rest of the estate, and we'll give you the first option" ', tells Peggy Kirk. 'Donnie asked: "What's the alternative?" "Galmisdale", he was told. Well, he was keen on Galmisdale but I was not, I preferred Laig. The rent was not that much but it was still high and that's how I really started with visitors.' Donnie still found himself obliged to go away and work on the Ballachulish ferry for three months of the year to make money for the farm. Peggy picked whelks to help out: 'You could get eleven bags in a tide in those days, you could just shovel them they were so plentiful! It was the same at the pier, and I would get there sometimes. We would wash them to get rid of the sand and we'd put them into bags and they would go on the estate boat, the *Dido* and they would be sent directly to Billingsgate in London and they would send you the money back. The price was quite good at the time.'

It was not quite so easy for other shellfish. Lobsters required more care and with transport from Mallaig to Billingsgate being so slow, the catch was often dead on arrival and fish merchants did not want to pay for them. These conditions drove Donnie Morrison to give up his hopes of earning a living from fishing after the war. He had been around boats since he could walk – his uncles being the estate boatmen – and spent his childhood rowing to Grulin and fishing from a long line, but he found himself obliged to leave when he would have liked nothing better than to stay on Eigg. It was not until Mallaig was developed in the early 1960s, with better railway links, that lobster fishing became viable. Donnie Kirk, who started with a small dinghy, then changed to an 18ft open boat, finally managed to buy a bigger boat in partnership with young Duncan Ferguson. 'With the *St Donnan* – 38ft long, capstan Hauler, toilet, galley – they were able to fish Eigg, Muck and Rum', recalls Fred Longrigg, who was Donnie's crew for a time. 'Donnie also did hires, for the fuel run, or to take the doctor, the missionary or the vet around the islands. He was a great character with tremendous energy. And a good musician as well! Many's the ceilidh they had at Laig with Young Duncan Ferguson on the button-key accordion and Old Duncan on the fiddle.'

Giving Donnie Kirk the tenancy of Laig was an example of the way the Runcimans tried to encourage islanders to stay on the island in order to maintain a healthy population level. They also made sure that retiring employees or elderly people living in estate houses were given the chance to stay on the island, like the Campbell sisters in Garden Cottage or Archie, the former boatman, at the pier. Mary Campbell, the former Queen Alexandra nurse who finished her working life as one of Glasgow's famous 'green ladies', was offered the cottage that she wanted to do up for her retirement rent-free for life. 'There was a good spirit of cooperation between the estate and the rest of the island in those days', remarked Angus MacKinnon. Rutherford, the capable engineer who was appointed factor in 1956, saw to that. He installed at the pier a saw mill and a lathe which enabled all the stobs and rails needed for fencing and repairs to be produced on the island, as well as an engineering workshop where he could turn or cast anything that was needed at all in the way of machine parts. In any case an agricultural engineer would come with a fitter once a year – in true Runciman style – to check all the machinery and would come back in case of emergencies. Like Rutherford, they would help the crofters with any repairs they needed. The Runcimans had taken advantage of the available farming grants to modernise the farm, ploughing any profits back into it. Binders, tractors and balers were brought in and even a hay-drying machine which was the most modern of its kind in the area.

The Runcimans still kept a close interest in the island's economy and population even though they saw it primarily as a holiday place for their family. Leslie came to the island every summer, bringing shooting parties with him until the gamekeeper's death, when his brother Steven, who disapproved of shooting, persuaded him to give it up. Sir Steven spent a lot of time at the Lodge which he considered his country home. A distinguished academic best known for his *History of the Crusades*, he found the peace and quiet ideal for writing. He arrived with a suitcase full of books and another full of groceries, and did his own cooking and shopping, walking to the shop with his basket under his arm. He even picked up a few words of Gaelic which he tried on the postman, and never forgot to throw a party for the island children every Easter. They all looked forward to the ceremonious opening of the great big globe – just like the one in the classroom – full of little presents for each of them. His favourite form of relaxation from writing was to play on his Bechstein grand piano and in the summer he would invite his friends to share the beauty of the island. They included diplomats, members of the Royal Family and musicians like the famous violinist Yehudi Menuhin, whom he took to the islanders' dances held in the hall built by his father, 'a handy man for a ceilidh' as Dougald MacKinnon put it. These dances were remembered as one of the big excitements of life on Eigg by the young people at the Lodge. 'Though I might get uncontrollable giggles at some of the ladies' solo songs, once the dancing started I was in seventh heaven, especially if one of the boatmen invited me to dance', recalls Sir Steven's niece. 'Once or twice late at night, when the men were well charged up with whisky – which they used to hide under the bushes outside the "hut" – the men would launch into the Eigg War Dance. This was something which people were very secretive about. I remember trying without much success to get some explanations out of Donald Archie. They certainly never danced it when my grandparents were around!' The Eigg War Dance was actually an old Highland circle dance – *An Dannsa Mór* – which the Elgol men had taught the men of Eigg when they found themselves working side by side in Rum where all the famine-stricken islanders had been drafted in to build the Bulloughs' extravagant castle in the 1880s. It involved a circle of men stomping on one foot, taking turns in engaging in mock fight, hurling rhymes at each other before resuming the circling and stomping, making it look like an American Indian dance, hence its name in English. The islanders thought it vastly entertaining and adopted it as their own. Another ceilidh party piece that was still performed in those days was *Marbhadh am Biasd Dubh* – killing the otter. Like the better-known *Cailleach an Dudain*, it was more acting than dancing, originating in a forgotten past and already rare when Alexander Carmichael recorded it in other places. It mostly involved looking for the otter behind or even between the women's legs. 'You made a laugh of it and you came in with the otter on your back and it was supposed to be alive and escape and disappear again and again', explained Dougald MacKinnon, who is the last islander to have performed it.

When Leslie's son Garry came to his majority, the islanders gathered in the hall to present him with a beautiful fishing rod. To them it seemed natural to think that Garry would follow in his father's and uncle's footsteps and that he would one day take over the estate and run it as smoothly as it had been run for the last forty years. Yet it soon became obvious that this was not the way it was to be. Garry's wife, a South African, disliked the August drizzle on Eigg and Garry himself showed little interest in the farming side of the island. At first the prospect of selling the island was brushed aside by Sir Steven but he finally resigned himself to the idea of finding a more accessible country retreat, and the island was put up for sale in 1966.

THE END OF STABILITY

'Eigg had provided us with a holiday home but there is no reason why it could not be made into a profitable thing. Somebody prepared to live here all the time could do probably quite all right,' declared the Runcimans when the island was advertised for sale. Two Scots who had close connections with the island were very interested in taking on that challenge: farmer Neil Usher, a relative of George Scott-Moncrieff, and hotelier Angus MacDonald who was related to a Cleadale family. With Hugh MacKinnon, the crofters' grazing clerk and old Duncan Ferguson, Usher had discussed in detail his plans to revitalise crofting by making land available for a sheep club as had been done in Skye and in the Outer Isles. On the estate side, he favoured a division into three farms with individual tenants: Kildonnan, Galmisdale and Laig where Donnie Kirk would be given back the original hill grazing. Angus MacDonald was to develop the Lodge into a small hotel and capitalise on the growing interest for tourism in the Highlands which the newly created Highlands and Islands Development Board (HIDB) was keen to encourage.[2] To their regret and that of Hugh MacKinnon, a Welsh farmer, Captain Robert Evans, beat them to it with a higher offer, buying Eigg for £66,000.

The Runcimans wanted someone who would work the island and would not treat it as a rich man's toy, a fate which they felt had beset too many small islands, and in that respect Evans seemed to them a worthy successor. To the islanders, he seemed the perfect gentleman, but too old a gentleman. No one was surprised that he did not come to live in the island. However, Graham Murray, the new factor, turned out to be easy to get on with and to work with. 'He knew his job and was not afraid to get his hands dirty', commented the islanders who worked under him. 'He had an interest in Gaelic, if he came in and we stopped speaking in Gaelic out of politeness, he would tell us to carry on because he wanted to learn it!' An energetic man from the Borders, Murray soon got things going in the community, starting badminton in the hall, a men's darts night, and introducing the yearly Burns Supper which everyone attended. On the farm, things started well with Evans bringing in a large number of Hereford cattle, increasing the herd

151

to about 120 beasts. Unfortunately the new cattle failed to thrive, unused to island conditions. Many died of red-water, a cattle disease brought about by bracken poisoning or damp conditions. Then came the problem of transporting cattle and sheep to mainland markets since the railways no longer offered stock transport facilities. Transport problems worsened when the estate boat hit a rock and was never repaired. It made the islanders sad to see the *Dido* left to rot by the shore – she had been such a great boat – and they wondered why Evans did nothing about it. It soon transpired that Evans, who had really bought the island on the strength of the profits shown by the books, was disappointed by the Hereford failure, even though Murray felt that, given time, the cattle could have acclimatised. He was not prepared to invest more on the island than he had already spent, and after five years, the island was put up for sale again.

When Neil Usher heard about the sale, he decided to have another try at buying Eigg. This time, his nephew Gavin Scott-Moncrieff – who was brought up on the island – was to front the bid. A development plan which included all the ideas expressed five years earlier was sent to the HIDB in the hope that the Board would be able to help finance the new bid, which had the backing of Dr MacLean, the Small Isles GP and former district councillor, and Fergus Gowans, the new Independent candidate for the Small Isles. There was little motivation in the crofting community to back the Usher plan for a sheep club. 'They had got too used to doing things on their own, they did not want any changes, what they had was enough for them', recalled Angus MacKinnon. 'There was little interest in a scheme involving sheep, crofters have never been keen on sheep here.' The fact was that the last time there had been sheep on the crofts, it had caused so much trouble over grazing amongst crofters that Runciman's factor had been called in to sort things out and had banned sheep altogether for the sake of peace. Conditions were obviously not ripe. A stock club would have demanded more cooperation and unity than actually existed at the time.

The problem was that the old traditions of cooperation had been badly affected by demographic changes and that their erosion had also been aggravated by the sectarianism introduced by outsiders like teachers or missionaries, which fostered an unhealthy atmosphere of rivalry between the two denominations in the crofting community. A typical example would be that at haymaking time, whilst Protestants had to observe the Sabbath, Catholics were allowed to work on Sunday after mass. As there was always a race to finish first amongst all the crofters, this was resented as taking an unfair advantage and led to petty revenge. Such feelings were preventing people from pulling together in the interest of all. 'I tried to get a machinery club started when I came back to help my father, there was money available for it, but no one was really interested apart from Donnie Kirk – he was an innovator. So we got a binder and other machinery and we worked together. It made sense, but it was as far as we got. It could have been otherwise', recalls Angus MacKinnon who had made his return to crofting at the time, turning his back on a lucrative engineering career. After forty years under the Runcimans, it was as if the island was suspended in time. The islanders were used to a certain way of doing things. They still went by the 1930s social code, where it was the proprietor who dictated what happened on the island. The idea that they could make a difference to the outcome of the sale or that they could even have a say in it was quite alien to them. Only the island doctor or Fergus Gowans, the councillor, who belonged to a very different social class with his Etonian background and private means, felt entitled to voice an opinion as to who should own the island.

The HIDB headquarters' answers to the Scott-Moncrieff development plans for Eigg were most evasive: 'the "sorry, we seem to have mislaid the document, do try again" type of thing'.[3] The official policy in the early 1970s was that the land issue was not a priority on the HIDB's agenda and that the Board was best to steer clear of assisting any purchase of land. This was best left to market forces, although financial aid would be given to development projects once the land was purchased.[4] With no help forthcoming from the Board, the Scott-Moncrieff bid was rejected in favour of an offer made by an English charity, the Anglyn Trust, which wanted to run the island as an adventure school for handicapped boys. Feeling that he was doing the island and the trust a favour, Evans sold the island for £110,000, justifying the substantial increase in price for the island by the amount of expenditure he had incurred to keep it going. Even with the rise in inflation, this nevertheless brought him a handsome profit.

Bernard Farnham-Smith, head of the Anglyn Trust, arrived on Eigg in 1971 with his family, one teacher-cum-administrator and a few boys who did not seem particularly handicapped in any way. They were 'difficult' children from wealthy families who had run into trouble at boarding school, the type of children on whom the trust had founded its reputation in Sussex, where it had assets in the form of two large farms, one of which was sold to finance the purchase of Eigg. The new owner was of a very different type from his predecessors: 'a Cockney who had come up in the world and an inventor who held patents for all sorts of things, a kind of Mr Fix-it'.[5] Introducing himself as 'Commander Farnham-Smith' and telling stories of his Navy days in China, he won people over by keeping an open door at the Lodge and generally appearing kind and good fun.

His first move was to appoint Angus MacKinnon as farm manager. 'Well, I devised a five-year plan for the estate farm and he agreed with it. So we started to buy cattle in, four or five at first, but when he realised the price of it all, he was not so keen. That was his problem, lack of cash', explains Angus MacKinnon. 'Too many ideas, not enough means.' There was talks of a tea-room, pony-trekking, a garage, even an abattoir. To achieve all this, Farnham-Smith wanted to attract people to the island. He did not offer paid jobs, but opportunities. 'It was quite clear when we came to Eigg to have a look at the place that he was encouraging young people to come and settle on the island', explained one candidate for island life. 'He said he could not employ me but that I could have any house I wanted. We thought that Galmisdale had potential for B&B, so he gave us a lease and we had a go at it and it went pretty well.'[6] People were also attracted to life on Eigg by the friendliness of the islanders. 'The islanders would not let you go until you had a *strupag* and drank a few cups. You had to give them a yarn, they were interested and they were interesting people in themselves, who always had something to tell you; they had the willingness to share any knowledge they had in history or natural history. They were very well mannered, very polite with strangers.'[7] Hospitable by nature, the islanders were actively welcoming to anyone who wanted to be part of their community, especially if the incomers had children. The islanders felt that they needed some new blood to keep the island going since the school roll had dwindled to one child in 1973.

But bringing a few people in to the island was not enough to remedy what soon appeared to be a chronic lack of means and direction. There seemed to be no coherent strategy for tourism or farming which could steer the island's economy away from stagnation. Farnham-Smith's ideas were too vague or ill-defined to get off the ground or attract the support of the HIDB. Repairs and general maintenance ground to a halt whilst questionable investments were made, like the

75ft Baltic schooner brought by Farnham-Smith to replace the *Dido*, in spite of islanders' warnings that no boat over 40ft would hold its mooring in a gale, let alone a three-masted sailing ship which was so big it completely dwarfed the pier.

It was not long until Farnham-Smith stopped free milk and coal, the perks which went with the estate jobs, which he thought were too highly paid at £14 a week. This caused considerable discontent, enough for one young family to leave and look for a better opportunity on Canna. He then decided to evict an estate worker and his wife to provide his elderly administrator with a home for her retirement. For Iain Campbell and his wife who were expecting their first child, it was a rude awakening to the power of landlords. Shore Cottage had been occupied by the Campbell family for generations, Iain succeeding his uncles as estate boatman. During all that time, there had never been any worry about security of tenure. Iain and his wife had just finished decorating the house when they were given notice to quit. 'We were given two weeks and that was it. In that time we were expected to make ready the old crofthouse Iain had inherited from his father. We could have been awkward about it but we felt that there was no point. There was not much we could do or anyone else. Everyone depended on the estate for wages', recalls Iain's wife. 'He was within his rights to get us out, even though I was pregnant and there was no water and no toilets in that house. Fergus Gowans had to give us some plastic sheets to put over the windows to keep the draughts out. It was terrible.' A veteran of the Normandy and Africa campaigns, Dr MacLean later described that period as 'living under enemy occupation, without the satisfaction of being able to shoot the bugger'. When journalists starting to look into the Anglyn Trust revealed that all the proprietor of Eigg had ever commanded was a fire brigade, what credibility he had left disappeared. Judging his position untenable, Farnham-Smith put the island on the market in late 1974, the third time in less than a decade. This time the asking price was around £200,000, twice the amount of money he had paid for it in 1971. But Highland estates were now highly attractive to large pension funds, pop stars and foreign investors, and Farnham-Smith was determined to cash in on the sale of this 'perfectly secluded island of the Old World, the very beautiful island of Eigg' as the Runcimans had called it.

THE SPIRIT OF FREE ENTERPRISE

This time, the Eigg goings-on attracted the HIDB's attention and the Board tentatively offered to buy it. However, the island had also come to the notice of Keith Schellenberg, a wealthy businessman and sports enthusiast based in Aberdeenshire, who had contemplated buying Gigha but was won over by the variety of scenery on Eigg. The story is that he almost missed this opportunity of showing the state what private enterprise was capable of. Finding himself locked in at his home of Udny Castle, Schellenberg resorted to abseiling down the walls along a fire-rope in order to beat the deadline and offer Farnham-Smith £274,000, £70,000 more than the HIDB were prepared to pay. Becoming the island's seventh owner on 1 April 1975, the ex-Olympic bobsleigher promptly electrified the island population when he flew in to pay his first visit as proprietor, leaving his plane in the care of a bewildered islander with instructions as to which button not to press. The button was pressed and the plane was a write-off. The new ownership had started with a bang.

Originally from Yorkshire, where his father had made a fortune in manufacturing gelatine, Schellenberg had diversified into a Ford dealership and various other enterprises in Whitby which involved boatbuilding, power-boat racing and a restaurant which his titled friends used as their headquarters. He now had an interest in farming connected with Udny estate which was owned by his second wife, a Scottish aristocrat. Acquiring Eigg – in joint ownership with his wife, with whom he entered into a limited partnership for the island – appeared to him to be the perfect challenge for his middle years.[8]

After the uncertainty of the past years, the initial reaction on the island was positive. The islanders did not much like the idea of a take-over by a government which had shown little sign of willing to help them in their problems with piers and freight. Renovation of the pier had been placed at the top of the list of regional priorities since the early 1950s but nothing had ever happened. John Campbell, the last resident missionary on Eigg – a Harris man – highlighted how freight charges were strangling the life out of the island, a problem that the government consistently failed to address throughout the Hebrides. Although the islanders had benefited from the HIDB – grants had allowed Peggy MacKinnon to re-open the shop and caravans to be bought to accommodate visitors – they favoured a private owner of substantial means who would perhaps bring back what was now seen as the golden age of the Runcimans. 'The crofters are delighted that after years of decline, capital is being pumped into their island by the new laird', announced the *Press and Journal* in August 1976.[9]

Angus MacKinnon hoped that the optimism generated by the new landlord's personality and plans would encourage young people to return to the island after their secondary education in Fort William. No community could thrive without income and young families, and the island population was at an all-time low of thirty-nine adults, with only two children at school. He wanted to see the farmland improved, stock increased and forestry expanded. Tourism was needed but a balance had to be struck, he did not want to see it overdone as on Skye. Like Angus, Dr MacLean, the missionary and Fergus Gowans felt that the island's future depended now on how much employment was available.

Schellenberg's goal to bring the island into self-sufficiency and develop tourism appealed to all, including the government agencies, which hailed tourism as the miracle industry which would solve the Highland problem. From 1969, the HIDB had embarked on a massive marketing and upgrading effort, and over £5 million of its budget had been earmarked for development, three-quarters of it in the form of grants at first, then loans as improvement progressed. By 1976 the level of help on offer amounted to 50 per cent of costs in loans and grants, but 70 per cent was quite common.[10] Schellenberg had also suggested that the Board should offer him a grant or an interest-free loan to bridge the difference between what he had paid and the original asking price, arguing that it had been raised because of their interest.[11] The Board refused as it was not in the business of helping in the purchase of land, but it was willing to help development with a substantial cash aid towards proposed improvements under its attractive package for tourism expansion.

Farming was to be the other mainstay of the estate. Those islanders who had been employed since the Runcimans were kept on, and four islanders were taken on, some of them school-leavers, under a new farm manager, Sandy Carr, from Stirling. The idea was that Eigg would act as an extension of Udny estate, with the island cattle taken there to be fattened before sale. The whole herd, which had gradually built up from the original stock introduced under Runciman and Evans, was sold off in 1975 and HIDB help was sought to replace it with cattle of breeds favoured by mainland buyers in Perth. The scheme also included a further 800 sheep to be

155

introduced to complete the change-over from blackface to Cheviot already initiated. Land reclamation was to be funded as well as fencing and road-building. All these plans generated an atmosphere of buoyant optimism. 'It was brilliant, something was happening at last on the island, it was like a breath of fresh air. There was plenty of new machinery, lots of work to do. You didn't care how many hours you worked, if it was overtime or not, you were giving it your best because you felt you were part of something new and exciting after all these years of inertia.'[12]

Apart from hiring out the odd rod for trout fishing in the lochs, Schellenberg never considered the sporting side of the estate as a means of income. A committed vegetarian, he could reconcile himself to the need for sheep and cattle farming on his estate, but like his wife on her Udny estate, he did not approve of shooting. He was certainly very unusual amongst Scottish landowners for his stand against bloodsports. In fact, his enthusiasm for wildlife and conservation made him an almost unique figure in landowning circles. Discovering on taking over the island that it had three areas – Cleadale, The Sgurr and Glen Caradal – designated as Sites of Special Scientific Interest (SSSIs) in 1964, he resolved to actively undertake their protection. Contact was made in June 1975 with the Scottish Wildlife Trust (SWT), a newly created charitable organisation for the protection and management of Scotland's ecological heritage. The SWT was delighted to be offered a chance of involvement, such a move on the part of a Scottish landowner being an all-too-rare occurrence. Work was started on the creation of three reserves which would overlap the SSSIs, an agreement which was finalised in September 1978.

Taking into consideration that numbers could affect the island wildlife and environment, Schellenberg believed in opening the island up to as large a public as possible. His feeling was that 'it is necessary for people working under oppressive urban conditions to have a place where they can restore their fundamental values'. Eigg was therefore marketed as 'the most enchanting British Isle', and every effort was made to attract visitors 'to come there rather than anywhere else in the world because of its different and special appeal'.[13] Indeed, apart from its scenic beauty and its wildlife, the island now possessed an attractive vitality which the new owner had helped to unleash. Whereas Farnham-Smith had kept the wooden hall under lock and key, using it as a storage place, Schellenberg's first move was to offer it back to the community for recreational purposes, kick-starting the island hall committee back into life. He could not have made a more popular move in the eyes of the islanders, the young especially, who immediately congregated for games of badminton in the winter and dances in the summer. 'We must have had 25 ceilidhs that first summer', recalls Marie Carr. 'I would phone Annabel and say to her: should we have a dance tonight? She'd say, "yes why not?" And we would have a great time.'

Social life on the island had also improved by the mere impact of all the people brought in to take part in the building of the island as a holiday business. A sort of Hebridean corps had been drafted in to tackle the renovation of buildings into holiday homes, the establishment of a craft centre and the running of the new estate boats: the *Golden Eye*, 'a sort of gin-palace type of fast motor-cruiser', and the *Sunart*, a luxury yacht operating from Glenuig as Schellenberg's private ferry. In the space of a few years, the population of the island jumped from thirty-nine to sixty people and the school roll rose from two to twelve.

For newcomers like the Fyffe family, Eigg had instantly felt like home. 'It's the first place I had ever known – and that includes my birthplace – which made me feel I belonged', said Wes Fyffe, who came from County Tyrone in Northern Ireland. 'People accepted you and made you feel welcome. They didn' t care what you looked like or sounded like, they took you on as a person.'

He and his wife Maggie, who was from Lancashire and had Irish and Scottish roots, had followed the hippie trail to Afghanistan. On their return they had settled on the east coast where Wes worked on a dairy farm with a sideline as blacksmith. It was through their craftwork connections that they came to Eigg in 1976 with their 4-year-old son as recruits for the farm and craft centre. John Cormack, a graduate from Dingwall, had come to Eigg as handyman after a job as summer warden on neighbouring Rum. He too liked the crack on Eigg and felt the island could easily become his home. Other employees answered ads in the Scottish press, like the Helliwells, a young couple from Suffolk, who were looking for a smallholding, a place where they could live and raise children. Jeweller Natalie Vardey was also recruited through an ad in the papers. 'I saw this ad in the *London Evening Standard*,' she explains, ' "Summer in the Hebrides: cook/housekeeper/person Friday/driver/business-minded craftspeople wanted." Well, I replied to it saying I could do all that, but I went to see him as a craftsperson. It was a bizarre experience: he was having his hair cut. The hairdresser and I did our best in difficult circumstances: no face-to-face discussion here; eye contact was difficult in lopsided reflections! Still talking, he nodded at his mirrored rear view, paid his bill and hailed a taxi. I just followed. We negotiated percentage marks round Hyde Park Corner and I was just beginning to find out about the power supply when he stopped the taxi, pointed to a green door across an elegant square and told me to go and introduce myself and have a cup of tea. I baled out and the taxi drove off, and I was left wondering to myself what was I letting myself in for. "Well," I thought, "I have nothing to lose, it'll be an experience".'

THE HOLIDAY BOOM

By the summer of 1979, the 'holiday side' was operating at full capacity. Kildonnan was turned into a guest house, the craft centre had been inaugurated in great pomp with the chairman of the HIDB and a ceilidh attended by a crowd of Schellenberg's friends. The tourist brochure offered a large variety of accommodation: from 'typical island cottages' to 'modern dwellings which blend subtly into the contours and outline of the farm buildings' – in other words, caravans. 'In the long term we would like to have only the traditional stone crofts which over the years we will rebuild from rubble remains', said the brochure. In the short term, the 'sensitive reconversion' of old buildings had already been undertaken.[14] In the 'old smithy' everything that remained from Lachie Campbell's work was disposed of, thrown outside to rust in the rain, apart from one or two horseshoes used as decorations. The bellows were salvaged, needed for the craft centre. The eighteenth-century 'old water mill' found itself converted too, concrete poured over the works, the grinding platform turned into a sleeping area, the remains of the drying shed, demolished under Evans, making way for a window. The visitors loved it.

Schellenberg's ambition was to provide them with a wider range of facilities than anywhere else in north-west Scotland, so that even his children were drafted in to help. It was all part of the 'team spirit'. In addition to the new tea-room, bike and moped hire, everything that could possibly be thought of was advertised: craft courses, day cruises, dinghy sailing, sea-angling, loch fishing, pony trekking. The tourist brochure invited visitors to take part in gathering or shearing the sheep, help at the haymaking and go lobster fishing.[15] The only trouble was that when the tourists arrived on the island, not all these activities were actually on offer, and some holiday-makers were not happy at all.[16]

157

Meanwhile, worrying trends had started to emerge in the proprietor's behaviour towards the people he had brought to the island to work for him, which resulted in an alarmingly high turnover of staff. The Devlins were amongst the people who came and went. Duncan Devlin gave up his job as an art teacher on the east coast to move to Eigg in 1975 with his family to run Kildonnan as an arts and crafts workshop and guest house, and be part of the 'team' Schellenberg needed to rebuild the island. Unfortunately, by the time they arrived, the funding package Schellenberg had hoped for to finance all this had not materialised. As time went on, no mention was made of any work starting on the house, which was so run-down that gales rattled around the living room where the Devlins had to use polythene for window panes. Without any funds, Duncan Devlin persevered, setting up evening classes in enamelling, stone polishing and painting which were attended by the islanders, and doing some rewarding work with the schoolchildren. Matters soon came to a head when the Devlins were served with an eviction notice. Thirteen months and three legal battles later – the first two for harassment, the third for breach of contract – the Devlins left, their rights vindicated. 'Maybe it is because I am a Glaswegian that I took a stand. The locals [were] used to generations of lairds . . . On an island of sixty people, passing someone on the road without them saying hello as if you were not there, it was horrible and tense . . . He was a great guy so you must be a rat to go against him. That was the poison put about.'[17]

But finding people to come and work on Eigg was certainly not a problem for Schellenberg. Time had proven that plenty of people wanted to come to work on Eigg for the experience alone, and a new squad of seasonal workers could be drafted each summer without any difficulty. The problem was that people wanted to stay. Karen and Simon Helliwell, for instance, had come on a trial basis on the understanding that if all went well they would get to buy some land, renovate a cottage and live off Simon's woodwork. Working an eighty-hour week with no overtime – the arrangement being that he would get time off in the winter to do his craftwork – Simon Helliwell spent months getting the *Sunart* ready as a charter boat. He then found himself having to use the luxury yacht as a passenger ferry doubling up as a cargo boat for cement, building material and fertiliser. 'That was not the way I saw my job as boatman and I resigned', recalls Simon. 'That's how I blotted my copy-book, I suppose.' After their first eighteen months on the island, there was still no sign of Schellenberg selling them any land. When it was suggested that they move into another derelict cottage, just after they had done one up, they thought it would be better to be independent. They moved to the crofting side of the island, renting an old crofthouse in the winter, living in a caravan in the summer when Dodie Campbell's visitors arrived.

Island managers enjoyed no stabler conditions. Ian Carlton was amongst the many who succeeded one another in the job. Carlton left within a few months, unhappy with the definition of his job as 'island manager' rather than 'factor', a job he understood to mean 'getting things done in the best interest of all'. 'We still had tenants who had rotten floors, no inside sanitation or adequate water supply', explained Ian Carlton. 'The Lodge with its almost cost-free hydro-electric system was in stark contrast to every other house on the island.'[18]

PLAY LIFE AS HARD AS YOU CAN

With its idyllic setting, the Lodge had become open house every August to Schellenberg's relatives, friends and guests whose names would be familiar to assiduous *Hello!* readers. From the days of his power-boat racing to those of his vintage car rallies and winter sports in St Moritz, Schellenberg had acquired a reputation as a great sportsman and genial host, a trifle eccentric. 'You must be able to guess, it's Mr Toad. First it's a canary-coloured caravan and then it's a motor car . . . poop, poop, poop and all that', remarked one of his friends. 'I mean, Keith actually wears those round goggles and he's always arriving in places with a lot of noise and clouds of dust.'[19] The 1920s were often a reference point when referring to the Lodge or its proprietor. 'We spent our days as if we were Somerset Maugham characters, sunbathing or playing croquet on the manicured lawn', recalled a Lodge guest. 'We piled onto the running board of the stately 1927 Rolls and made our way leisurely to jewelled beaches for long, lazy picnics or midnight games of moonlit hockey and football.'[20]

Not only friends and family were invited to share the proprietor's passion for games. Awed tourists often found themselves drawn into an impromptu game of football, cricket or hockey. In fact, dreaming of establishing his own Highland Games, Schellenberg had no sooner arrived on Eigg than he had invited the islanders of Muck to come over for some inter-island sports ending with an evening dance in the hall with the island musicians. Dougie and Roddy threw the hammer and the wellie, Angus tossed the caber and the rest of the islanders came to watch as estate workers ran hill races against the Lodge guests. It seemed as if Schellenberg had completed his 'Balmoralisation', recreating single-handedly that idyllic Victorian vision of the old society's harmony between chief and clansfolks.

It was not long, however, before the friendly inter-island joust became 'a very private bit of sporting fun' for the Schellenbergs and their guests.[21] The games had now become the highlight of the Eigg 'season' and had their place in *The Field*'s holiday diary: 'several teams compete over three days in a multifarious range of events often with more bravado than expertise: croquet, petanque, badminton, swimming, sailing and wind surfing, every form of running race including a marathon and finally a war game between the Hanoverians and the Jacobites, the latter team led by the Clanranalds mounting a come-back in their own traditional territory'.[22]

'All you can do in life is play as hard as you can. I am not worried if I don't win, I just don't want to lose', declared Schellenberg, for whom the sporting ethos seemed to have become an all-encompassing philosophy.[23] The only problem for the laird of Eigg was that he was now dangerously close to losing the challenge he had set himself for the island. In 1976, he had described the 'great leap in self-sufficiency' for the island which had come about through the wages he paid his workers, at a time when 'he could not see any kind of crofting system tackling the job'.[24] By the early 1980s, progress was stalling on the farm and tourist business. It had a lot to do with Schellenberg's separation from his second wife, the Honourable Margaret de Hauteville Udny-Hamilton, followed by their divorce two years later in 1980. In the terms of the divorce settlement, she remained joint-owner of the island as she had put half the money towards the purchase of Eigg. An agreement was reached whereby any dispute or disagreement with regard to expenditure and actions that adversely affected her investment in the island was to be arbitrated by the chairman of the HIDB, which had spent a considerable amount of money in development projects on the island.[25] The big difference was that the farm on Eigg now had to do without the support of the farm on his ex-wife's estate. Problems had started earlier when the original Eigg herd had been sold off at a loss to be replaced by expensive mainland breeds favoured by east-coast markets. The logistics of transporting cattle for fattening in Aberdeenshire before their sale had already proved costly and complicated. Without the back-up of the farm in

Udny, it became an impossible proposition. Difficulties were compounded by the fact that the HIDB wanted repayments on the loan given for the purchase of the new cattle. An adviser from Scottish Woodlands, which by now had a growing interest in the island as Schellenberg was contemplating afforestation, advised to sell at a loss. Without any cattle, and with a serious deficit owing to repayments due, the whole farm bill was too costly. After a blazing row which saw the farm manager quit in 1980, three farm employees were made redundant that same autumn. From now on the estate was run as a sheep farm, allowing the wages bill to be pared to the minimum. It was a shock, though not a surprise for the islanders. With so many comings and goings of employees in the past few years, the feeling had grown that the estate could no longer be depended on for secure work, not like in the Runciman era. In fact, Dougald MacKinnon's son Charlie had already given his notice as estate mechanic, unable to secure a house with the job for him and his wife.

Schellenberg's next move was to bring in forestry to the island in partnership with a London friend. The government was making extraordinarily generous tax concessions available to forestry investors in order to boost the country's timber output for little cost. In 1982 and 1983, grant aid was approved for 218.7 hectares of moorland below the Sgurr to be planted with conifers, mostly foreign softwood species like the fast-growing Sitka spruce, although a small proportion of broadleaf trees was included. The snag was that some of the tree planting had taken place in the area surrounding one of the designated SSSIs on the island. The SSSI protected the Blar Dubh bog above Laig, easily the richest area of bogland on Eigg for its plant and insect diversity. Within a few years, due to the effect of drainage and soil acidification, blanket conifer plantation led to its deterioration into ordinary wet moorland.

The estate was now run on a shoestring. Colin Carr – the previous farm manager's brother who had stayed on as shepherd – remembers that money was so tight at one time that none was found to supply enough diesel for the farm. 'I'd be in the middle of a feeding round and the tractor would run out of diesel. I'd have to walk back from Grulin, or wherever I was, to the pier, fill up a 5-gallon drum from the tanks in the estate boat and walk back all the way again because the estate manager would not allow me to buy any.' It was not an easy position for him and his family in a tied house at Sandavore, but one he was familiar with from his own upbringing. However, he considered himself lucky to be able to speak his mind to Schellenberg, feeling that because he was now responsible for the success of the farm, their relationship was based on mutual trust. Marie, his wife, was born and bred on the island, and had extended to Schellenberg the warm welcome she dispensed to all. She felt particularly indebted to him for the kindness he had shown the family when her father was dying. He in turn responded by sending the couple's oldest son to Aberlour and then to Gordonstoun, when they found themselves confronted with the dilemma of sending him away or moving to the mainland as he reached secondary school age.

The tightening of the belt on the estate had for effect a decline in the amount of funds spent on repairs to estate properties. Exposed to such a wet climate, the island houses required constant maintenance to counteract damp and wind damage. Empty holiday homes deteriorated faster and needed ever more work on them every spring. Tenants' homes were little better: in spite of their efforts to patch it up, the Carrs' leaky roof at Sandavore started to get worse and worse, but without a lease in the tied cottage, they could not access any improvement grants, and it was too big a job to take on without security of tenure. Meanwhile, the craft centre, opened with such flourish a few years before, was left empty to gather dust after the departure of its last occupant, a potter. In these conditions the tourist business started to suffer.

Yet it was vital for the island's economy that tourism should be well organised. It certainly was vital for the survival of the shop which Mairi Kirk had taken over from her aunt Peggy MacKinnon. She wanted to carry out some essential improvements like bringing in water and power. But the shop belonged to the estate and she required the proprietor's consent to carry out any alterations. 'Schellenberg had sent his valuators round the island to see if he could not get a bit more money here and there and anywhere and they had valued the shop rent at £2,000 a year', recalls Mairi. 'Angus had just been made redundant from the farm and there was no way we could afford that rent unless we priced the shop out of reach of everyone on the island. So we had to go round and see him, cap in hand, and explain what the situation was and how the whole island would suffer and we wouldn't be able to make it, so he agreed to bring the rent down to £200 a year. But I had to keep the shop as it was, with a counter in the middle. I was not allowed to modernise it because he liked that old-fashioned look and the personal touch it provided for his visitors. So, because of that I was obliged to pay someone to work with me in the shop. It was quite tiring too: I must have done a thousand miles in all the to-ing and fro-ing I had to do! When I explained that I wanted to improve the building, bring in water and toilets and a generator for lights and a fridge, and that I would have to get a grant because I couldn't afford to pay for it myself, and that I would need a lease, he nodded his head and he told me "to get in touch with my lawyer".' Mairi Kirk did get a lawyer. 'Four years after that meeting with Schellenberg, the lawyer eventually got back to me: "this was totally ridiculous", he said, "but try as he could, he had been unable to get any response from Schellenberg, and did I still want him to carry on?" I told him to forget it, I was not prepared to spend any more money on trying to get a lease.'

The fact was that in landownership circles, the received knowledge was that, under the existing tenancy laws, it was not in a proprietor's interest to give out too many leases or to have too many tied cottages. This could depreciate the market value of the property, an important asset in Schellenberg's case. Since his divorce, he had formed a family company – Cleveland and Island Holdings – registered in Middlesbrough, allegedly to protect his assets for his children, and of which he was managing director.[26] In the logic of a market-oriented economy, the higher the value of Eigg, the higher the proportion of freeholds on the estate.

This did not help much those people who were trying to stay and make a living on the island, hoping to fulfil their aspirations of self-sufficiency. There were few answers to the problem of accommodation: get a croft if one became available; approach the crofting community to rent a holiday house; purchase a building plot which entailed the decrofting of that plot, a lengthy procedure; or else ask permission to put a caravan on their land as a short-term solution. By the early 1980s, many of Schellenberg's former employees had resorted to one of these solutions. The Fyffes had bought a derelict crofthouse in Cuagach and were doing it up, fencing and working the land which went with it. The Helliwells were building a house on land generously decrofted and sold to them by a crofter. The Cormacks were living in a caravan on Laig beach. Not long before their wedding, which took place a year after their arrival on Eigg, Schellenberg had suggested that they would be better off pursuing their life on the mainland since he was worried about an increase in the 'hippie' population on the island. When they assured him that they preferred to stay and live on Eigg, he advised them to ask 'their crofter friends' for help. Enquiries to Angus, the crofters' grazing clerk, resulted in Dodie Campbell offering the young

161

couple a flat bit of ground at the edge of the beach. Crofters were sympathetic to the plight of the people who had come to join their island community. They did not want to see numbers go down again and did what they could to help. Unable to secure any other accommodation, another three former estate employees moved into caravans within the next few years.

The new Cleadale dwellers set out to survive independently from the estate, making woodwork, jewellery and other craftwork to sell in the summer, doing odd jobs and picking whelks to make ends meet, going on the dole when there was nothing else. There was little their ex-employer could do about what happened on the crofting side of the island, but he certainly did not like the presence on his island of people he branded as 'wandering itinerants who found the island a nice refuge but were not mentally strong enough to cope with the life and earn a living in the environment'.[27]

That these people could 'expect and get government hand-outs'[28] contributed to his 'disappointment' that even the Conservatives – with whom he associated for their 'encourage-ment of self-help and the rolling back of the State monopolies' – did not have the slightest effect on what he saw as the 'anti-enterprise environment which pervades the North-West High-lands'.[29] As Schellenberg struggled with the difficulties encountered by Eigg estate, his other often-reported complaint was that central government channelled back 'the substantial amount of taxes' he paid into what he considered to be 'white elephants' like the State-owned MacBrayne ferry service and 'examples of bureaucratic folly' like the new digital exchange and the recently built surgery on Eigg,[30] although it had taken Dr MacLean thirty years of lobbying to obtain it. By 1986, the proprietor of Eigg, whose plans for the island included 'a golf course, perhaps a tennis court', found that 'the pressures of maintaining a balance between conserving the wildlife, opening Eigg for the public and keeping a viable economy' were becoming 'depressing'.[31]

Chapter 12

THE RISE OF THE COMMUNITY

A SENSE OF COMMUNITY

By the mid-1980s, the community on Eigg had undergone a great many changes. The core of people who had moved to work on the island and had left the estate to live on the crofting side were now becoming established as permanent members of the community. This process was speeded up by the fact that the numbers of native islanders was still declining. Most had reached or were reaching retirement age. They were great characters but there were few younger people, apart from incomers, who could benefit from their wealth of experience. Donnie Kirk, who was such an innovator in his time and provided the link between the old and the young generations, had died in 1975 after a long illness. Two island couples had already gone in the late 1970s. The 1980s saw another three families leave to look for opportunities elsewhere. For those with children reaching secondary school age, it was a solution to the dilemma which faced every island family in turn when the time came to send children away for their education.

With all these departures, the crofting community lost another two young crofting households, the fourteen remaining crofts being in the hands of increasingly older tenants. Crofting as an activity on the island was not in a healthy state. Old Duncan Ferguson was pessimistic: he felt that the only way to survive on the croft was now 'a mixture of the dole and fishing'. Too much land was in the hands of absentee crofters who sublet it to their neighbours, but as these were getting on in years, it was no longer worked, just used for extra grazing. Haymaking was largely abandoned: there was little incentive in spending three days harvesting hay when the same amount could be bought with a few hours' earning at the fishing. To make ends meet and feed the family, priority had to be given to the activity which was most financially rewarding, like fishing, bed and breakfast, or running the shop and Post Office. Working the land came last on the list, and crofting production remained confined to cattle, with hay for those who had time to make it. The only crofter still attempting to produce anything in the way of vegetables was an incomer. Wes Fyffe was also raising pigs and goats and, like Katie MacKinnon and Peggy Kirk, supplying fresh milk to neighbours and visitors. 'It was all very idealistic in those days', recalls Wes. 'It was just so great to be independent of the estate, I wanted to have a go at being self-sufficient. I was quite impressed by the crofters' way of doing things: Dougie for example, he would cut his hay, do his school run, come back to cut some more, take a wee bit of time for a dram and a crack with his neighbour and do something else on the croft afterwards. He had it down to a fine art, balancing all these things he had to do in the day. It seemed to be a good way of working things out. But it is difficult to go beyond self-sufficiency. Apart from cattle production, there is not much in the way of income from the croft. Perhaps if there had been a few more young crofters, we could have got something worked out together . . . But there was very little in the way of crofting organisation at the time, apart from getting the cattle to the pier or gathering them for the vet's visit.'

In comparison with the decline of crofting, the social life on the island had never been better. In sharp contrast to the early 1960s, when Iain Campbell would complain that a gap of twenty years separated him from the next younger person on the island, and Donnie Morrison felt he had to move away if he ever wanted to get a girlfriend, there were plenty of people in their twenties and early thirties. There had been three weddings in 1980 alone and the atmosphere on the island was one of optimistic buoyancy. 'There was a kind of golden glow about the place,' recalls Mairi Kirk, 'well, we were all young and carefree, I suppose.'

For some of the incomers who had decided to remain on the island, the experience was often one of self-discovery. 'When I came here,' explains a former Lodge employee, 'it was to work and live on the island. When the job didn't work out, I carried on living here. It was my choice. I didn't see any reason to leave because I liked it on the island and I wanted to know if I could manage it on my own. That was seventeen years ago, and I am still here, I couldn't imagine living anywhere else. Although I now live in a house with my family, I never thought it a hardship living in a caravan; it was a good experience in survival. You learn your good points and you learn your weak points, you get to appreciate the little things in life, to take each day as it comes. I think everybody should have that chance to experience a bit of life in a place like this, to be away from materialism, from the hustle and bustle of life in the town.'

The sheer physical demands of island life ensured that only those who could put up or cope with it would stay. The business of keeping warm and dry, of producing electricity from cranky generators or doing without electricity at all, of securing food and fuel supplies, took a lot more time and energy than are taken for granted in urban conditions or even in the rural mainland. Being able to cope with isolation and remoteness brought in itself a new sense of identity, but long winters with constant rains and gales could also be exacting on mind and body and tax inner resources to the limit at times. That was where the 'ceilidh tradition' came into its own. The winter season, when the islanders had traditionally held their house-ceilidhs, became the time when close bonds were forged between the people who had come to live on the island and those who were born or brought up on it. The old croft house in Cuagach where Wes and Maggie Fyffe now lived became 'the' ceilidh house on the island, where each peripatetic party would end. So many tunes were played around their fire and so many discussions were held around their table and the two so often merged together that a fiddle tune was eventually composed in praise of 'Maggie's table'.

Compared to other parts of the Highlands and Islands, the arrival of strangers in their midst had caused surprisingly little resentment amongst the islanders. Older islanders were somewhat puzzled to see incomers willing to adopt a way of life which they had largely encouraged their children to move away from, but they were willing to help them settle in if that was what they wished to do. 'We saw that they were prepared to acquire our traditions and our way of life and we accepted them', explained Katie MacKinnon. The fact was that incomers in general were very much aware of their status and were mindful of how carefully they had to tread. It was not easy to gain acceptance from such formidable personalities as Angus MacKinnon, the Cleadale grazing clerk, or his sister Peggy who used to run the shop and Post Office. It was through working and socialising together, through helping each other in the hard business of island living that everyone ended up sharing a common sense of place, a common sense of belonging.

Raising children on the island was a further step in consolidating that sense of belonging. Another was taking on essential jobs or responsibilities held until then by indigenous islanders, whether it was postman or ferryman, coastguard, special constable or fireman. This went a long way towards helping integration, for without incomers to take on these jobs, the island would have effectively ceased to operate as a viable unit. There was also the Schellenberg factor, which undoubtedly played a part in their transformation into a stronger, more cohesive group.

GETTING INVOLVED

In a land tenure system where rural development still depended in large measure on the proprietor's attitude and interests, local landowners' opinions carried a lot more weight than would seem acceptable in an urban environment. Up to the creation of community councils in the late 1970s, there was very little community representation in the decision-making process. This became obvious when in 1975 the proposal was made to replace the Small Isles ferry by a medium-sized ship capable of carrying six cars, equivalent agricultural machinery or 100 sheep, with increased facilities for passengers. But Schellenberg, who had just bought the island, favoured instead a privatised scheme which would serve the Small Isles with 'a small fast motor boat, a landing craft and an 80 ft mailboat'. This plan, which involved a private operator being the main recipient of the ferry subsidy, had initially received HIDB backing. However, it was soon pointed out that a private ferry offered no guarantee of service for Rum or Canna, unlike Caledonian MacBrayne, a nationalised shipping company under government contract to serve all four islands in the Small Isles. Three years later, the newly elected Small Isles Community Council voted overwhelmingly in favour of Caledonian MacBrayne retaining the contract. By that time the rate of inflation caused the ferry which was eventually supplied to be considerably smaller, without facilities for handling stock or machinery, a problem still dogging the islands to this day.[1]

Established in 1977, the Small Isles Community Council was the first really representative body through which the islanders could express their grievances. However, it was mostly concerned with broader issues common to the four islands and met too infrequently because of the obvious travelling difficulties between the islands. Consequently, it was decided in 1983 to found a residents' association which would address issues specific to Eigg. The Isle of Eigg Residents Association (IERA) acquired charitable status three years later. The creation of the association, one of 2,000 voluntary bodies in existence in the Highlands and Islands, marked a turning point in island life which was a crucial step in the islanders' social development. It was very much a learning process, as Maggie Fyffe recalls. Before becoming the association's treasurer, she had been 'the token incomer' on the hall committee and her role had been mostly confined to making sandwiches for the ceilidh and organising who would make the tea. As visitors to the island had observed early on, there was little formal organisation on the island, and until the creation of the IERA no particular need was felt for any, other than the hall committee and the film club. It had always been the estate factor who dealt with officialdom regarding the pier, ferries or any other major development issue. There was also the feeling that word of mouth was enough to pass on any important information and that there was no need for formal discussion. The problem was that although gossip had a useful function in maintaining social cohesion in the community and controlling any intrusive influence, it also fostered a guarded watchfulness. It was traditional to hold back from expressing an opinion in public which might give rise to conflict. On the contrary, incomers were used to committees and were generally not so shy about expressing their opinions in public. It was also convenient to place them in a position of responsibility: it did not endanger the status quo and they were easier to blame if anything went wrong. It was uncharted territory but what mattered in the end to crofters and estate employees, old or new islanders, was to have their own representative body.

The inhabitants of Eigg, who had hitherto had little to do with decision-making at a local level, now found themselves in direct contact with their governing powers, Lochaber District Council and the Highland Region. One urgent problem was whether the Small Isles would be able to retain their existing medical service, as Dr MacLean, who had served the community since 1951, was due to retire. He had relentlessly fought to retain a good level of service for the islands ever since he had been in the post and he had been a founder member of the Inducement Practitioners Association in 1982, which defended the interests of isolated medical practices throughout the Highlands and Islands. He did not view the idea of supplying the four islands with a helicopter service based in Mallaig and Arisaig as either safe or cost-effective. The IERA's fight to retain a doctor for the Small Isles, conducted through an energetic campaign of letter-writing and petitioning, was the first battle won by the islanders. They were less successful in their struggle to resolve the issue of rubbish disposal, which was left to individual initiative. Rats had always been a big problem on the island, and the lack of a coherent waste-disposal policy on the estate encouraged their proliferation. Lengthy correspondence with the council only resulted in unacceptable proposals on the part of the proprietor: the only waste-disposal site he would allow was where the bulk of the population lived.

Shortage of adequate housing was now an acute problem. Families were raising children in caravans or houses which only had chemical toilets and the most rudimentary plumbing, gas lights still being the norm on the island. These were conditions which many elderly islanders found increasingly difficult, like Morag Campbell who had returned from a lifetime in service to struggle valiantly in the family's derelict crofthouse, fetching her water every day from the well. But it was when her sister Mary, a veteran QA nurse, became really frail, that the islanders started to voice their concerns about the elderly, pensioners now equalling the number of active people in the community. No matter how proud of their independence the pensioners had always been, it was now imperative to rely on a less informal system. Assistance for a 'soup-run' was sought and the Fort William branch of Shelter responded by sending someone to investigate the situation on the island. The outcome of that visit was that, in cooperation with the islanders, the Social Work Department in Fort William organised a weekly lunch club and set up a home-help service. Cooking facilities were installed in the hall and, on a volunteer basis, the island women took their turns to prepare lunch and drive the pensioners to the hall and the shop in the minibus donated by the social services.

The housing survey undertaken by Shelter was also a major step forward as it had made the local authorities aware that most houses on the island were still below tolerable standards. Eigg was declared a housing action area, and, in view of the low incomes on the island, the grant available for housing improvements was extended from the usual 70 per cent to an exceptional 90 per cent. The problem was that this offer was only available to those islanders who owned their homes or had a secure lease. This included the crofters but none of the people who lived in estate houses or in caravans, although the local housing association was willing to have a look at the possibility of building new houses to remedy the shortage of accommodation. Schellenberg's reaction to queries from the council on proposed improvements was not encouraging. Feeling that he was doing enough by 'allowing people to occupy some of his properties rent-free', he questioned the 'impact of renovation on an island landscape of great conservation value', and worried about 'an invasion of undesirable caravan dwellers to the island, all expecting government handouts'. His opinion was that his lawyer would need to look into it.[2] For authorities at district and regional level, some of whom had had to deal with other island proprietors, like Raasay's notorious 'Dr No' as the newspapers had called Dr Greene in the 1970s, the whole operation highlighted how easy it was for a landowner to question the provision of amenities taken for granted in other parts of the country.

Securing a lease for the hall had also been at the top of the IERA's agenda as the wooden hall built by the Runcimans was badly in need of repair. The islanders were more than happy to contribute to its upkeep, but, to raise funds for major repairs and a new generator, they needed a lease. The use of the hall where the community gathered for its social functions was still entirely at the proprietor's discretion since it was his property and was situated so near his house. The older islanders always insisted that the hall had been built for community use, but Farnham-Smith had included the hall in the island sale as a games hall, and Schellenberg's games hall it was going to remain. The community finally offered to build a new hall, a proposal which was initially greeted with enthusiasm and a donation by Schellenberg, who personally favoured a kind of big corrugated iron shed. The islanders had other ideas but they thanked him politely and embarked on their fund-raising effort. 'Few of us had a phone then and we must have written hundreds of letters', remembers Maggie Fyffe. 'Then we thought about having a raffle. We made the tickets ourselves, we did the perforations with sewing machines! It was amazing how everybody on the island responded to the requests for prizes. Katie MacKinnon made a black bun, Peggy Kirk made a dumpling, people knitted, sewed and painted: it was a great community effort. We found out the following Easter that we had made very nearly £2,000 when the most we'd ever had was a hundred pounds or so for the children's Christmas party and the New Year whisky, and this gave us all a tremendous feeling of achievement!'

THE FIRST CHALLENGE

As a community, the island had enough vitality to continue attracting newcomers. But they encountered exactly the same problems as the people who had arrived before. No one seemed to be getting anywhere in their dealings with the proprietor. The worst was the element of unpredictability: 'You never knew where you stood with him', recalls John Cormack, who was now the island postman and ferryman. 'The conclusion I came to was that he would be willing to part with something until he realised how much you really wanted it, and then he would retract his offer and he wouldn't let go.' The Cormacks had tried without success to buy or rent an old derelict house in Cleadale: 'We could have done the house up under the 90 per cent grant, it would have been an asset for the estate at no cost to himself. Nat could have had a decent workshop with electricity instead of working at her jewellery in a shed on the beach, in conditions which were positively medieval. He finally agreed to let us move in on a temporary basis. We did not have much choice. Life was becoming increasingly frustrating in the caravan with the lack of space as the boys were growing. We'd only been in the house a couple of years when he wrote us a letter, just before Christmas, to tell us it would be better if we looked for somewhere else to live as he needed the house for his estate workers. Well, we knew fine it was just a pretext and we pointed out all the problems we had that year. It had been a disaster for us, with Nat and the kids in hospital one after the other. He wrote back and told us that there was no hurry for us to get out. But that did not leave us with a great sense of security, to say the least.'

Amongst the newcomers who gave up their attempts to stay on the island was Ian MacKinnon, whose father was Angus MacKinnon's cousin. He had decided to leave Glasgow and try his luck at the fishing. But even after his wedding on the island – it had been quite a do, the weather blew the day before and the guests, family and priest had to be taken to Eigg by the Mallaig lifeboat – and despite the fact he had such strong connections with the island, his approaches to Schellenberg had been in vain. He had been unable to secure any other accommodation than the caravan he had put on his sister's croft. 'The happy crofter dream which I had since childhood did not quite materialise. I stuck it out for five years but in the end, I decided to go', tells Ian. 'Life on the island is twice as tough as on the mainland, especially as far as fishing is concerned. The weather was the main problem. It's far more exposed over on Eigg, a Force 4 can be a problem. Over here on the mainland, it's a doddle, there's always a wee bit of shelter where you can dodge the weather. I'd land five boxes when I can land fifteen now. So when you pile this on top of no house, no social life because we lived in a caravan, and a divided community, you just go! I regret it in a way; there is something special about the freedom of spirit you find on the island, but at the time it did not seem worth it compared with what you could have on the mainland.'

The divide Ian now deplored in the community was linked to the lack of housing and security of tenure. One person would be in a tied cottage, the other would have to make do with a caravan to house his family, even though both worked for the estate. That created a resentment which could be used to play people off against each other. There were those who were dependent on the estate for their livelihood and those who weren't. The former had to be careful not to fall foul of the estate if they wanted to remain on the island. 'It's hard to imagine what it felt like to live under these conditions. People relied on him for so much, he owned the houses, he owned the shop, he owned the hall, he owned the land. I remember thinking, well, he doesn't own me', recalls Natalie Cormack.

However, in spite of the differences which separated the residents of Eigg – work, origin, class, nationality even – and their polarisation in two halves, the community's social dynamic produced enough positive forces to draw them together. The very nature of the relationships within a small community had a crucial role in bridging the gap. Since every individual played several different roles – crofter, farmer, teacher, ferryman, parent, kinsman, friend – relationships existed on several different levels. It was impossible to know only one side of a person and equally impossible to have entirely separate circles of friends since everyone was acquainted or related. The complexity of relationships contributed to defuse any long-term antagonism that might arise. Personalities played a part in that mechanism and qualities of leadership were acknowledged as especially valuable no matter to what side anyone belonged. 'Life here creates its own social obligations', explains Brian Greene philosophically. 'We are a collection of individuals, and there are conflicts sometimes, but this place has a way of rounding off the edges . . . There's so few of us anyway, we can't afford to fall out for long! It's all about a balance in the give and take really, and when there are difficulties, there is a lot of giving.'

Music was one great unifying factor on the island. Everyone, whether they were indigenous or incomers, young or old, liked a good party and a good dance. By the mid-1980s there were enough musicians on the island for it to have its own ceilidh band, its composition reflecting a cross-section of the community, incomers and indigenous islanders playing together for dances on Eigg and locally on the mainland. The island residents had also found out how to access funding to set up their own concerts and dances and within a few years Eigg started to acquire a good reputation as a lively venue for bands which have since made their names on the Celtic music scene. 'It was great, we'd have a brilliant ceilidh in the hall and we'd come back at four or five in the morning, you could see the sun rising on the mainland as we went home, and we'd carry on at Maggie and Wes's house where the musicians generally stayed. They'd be telling jokes and playing more tunes until everybody fell asleep and we'd have a music session at the pier the next day. Then the *Shearwater* would come in and we'd have the traditional farewell drink at the pier and sometimes that would turn into another party', recall the islanders. Having a good time together went a long way towards reinforcing people's sense of a common identity and strengthening their confidence in the community's worth. The children growing up at the time were doing so in an atmosphere so saturated with good music that they themselves started to play an instrument. 'At one time, the island achieved a 100 per cent rate in musical practice for its school-leavers, not a bad record for a bunch of no-hopers like ourselves!' exclaimed Maggie Fyffe, who, like her husband, now played in the island band.

The composition of the island society had changed a lot in the past decade, and the form these changes were taking was somehow affected and shaped by existing cultural patterns. The transmission of tradition was perhaps no longer happening as Hugh MacKinnon had known it, but indigenous islanders did their best to share their knowledge with those who had an interest in the island's history. Some incomers in particular were keen to learn the island's language and traditions, like Davey Robertson, whose ancestors had moved to Glasgow after being cleared from Skye. He considered Gaelic tradition to be his rightful inheritance, one which had been denied him by mainstream education. The Clearances had never been mentioned when he was at school, let alone crofting history. For him and many other islanders, Gaelic culture remained a powerful symbolic force in people's psychological and emotional behaviour. Combined with the bonds established between the seventy-strong community, this allowed a feeling to develop on the island which some would not hesitate to call tribal. This new-found confidence was eventually to change the mood towards the island proprietor from diffidence to defiance.

It was first to manifest itself collectively at the August games of 1988. The island band was to play that night as customary. It had been agreed beforehand, although not 100 per cent confirmed, that there would be an entrance charge for the dance which would go towards the new hall fund, for a full turn-out was expected, the 1988 games being probably Schellenberg's most ambitious effort to date. Following the previous theme of the Jacobites versus the Hanoverians, the theme that year was the Second World War and an international cast of players had been invited, which included Americans who flew to Britain by Concorde to attend the games and the ageing German playboy Gunther Sachs, who descended from his helicopter in full Prussian army dress uniform, his bodyguards garbed in matching ankle-length capes. It soon became obvious at the hall that the guests knew nothing about an entrance fee for the dance. Confrontation was not long in coming as an indignant Schellenberg demanded that the money be given back immediately. The island band walked off the stage, followed by a good many islanders. A furious Captain of Clanranald pursued them outside shouting insults in the dark: 'scum of the earth, half-baked socialists'. 'Some of them are not even British', echoed his friend Keith. By the time the Lodge guests left the island, leaving behind them a huge quantity of yellow tennis balls scattered around the island – their ammunition during the war games – another chapter was added to the growing anthology of Schellenbergiana.

SCHELLENBERG IS FORCED TO SELL

Meanwhile, it appeared that Schellenberg was now taking more interest in his new Georgian mansion in Banffshire than in the progress of Eigg estate. Colin Carr was left in charge of running the farm: 'I was told in 1982 that policy was to keep as many ewes as we could. I suppose sheep then were highly subsidised. All that he was interested in was sheep, the subsidies were very good.' But all was not well between Schellenberg and Mrs Williams, his ex-wife, now remarried. Earlier attempts at settling the amount of money due to her for her half of Eigg had failed.[3] Alarmed by reports about the sorry state of the Lodge, Mrs Williams paid a visit to the island. A few months later, in July 1988, she took legal action against her former husband at the Court of Session in Edinburgh. She accused him of 'mismanagement of their joint assets to the extent that the island was declining in value', and claimed that 'She had not received a penny in revenue from her share of the island or been shown any accounts and she now wanted the island sold so that she could redeem her share'.[4]

Whilst appealing against his ex-wife and hoping to secure for himself the right to manage the business affairs of the island, Schellenberg decided in September 1988 to sell his half-share of Eigg to Cleveland and Island Holdings Ltd. He was now the major shareholder as well as managing director of the family company.[5] The move proved unwise. The following July, the Court of Session ruled that this transaction caused him to lose his proprietary rights to the island and that the sale could now proceed.[6] Undeterred, Schellenberg fought on for another two years. From his point of view, it was 'partly a battle between [him] and the local socialists, men like Brian Wilson'.[7] Brian Wilson, the Labour MP, was one of the founders and columnists of the West Highland Free Press, the radical Skye newspaper which was so consistently outspoken in its criticism of Eigg estate that Schellenberg once tried to ban its publication.[8]

Meanwhile, the islanders were left in limbo, Schellenberg being effectively prevented by the court from having anything to do with the running of the estate. Yet, to all intents and purposes on the island, he still possessed his proprietary rights. In a legislative framework which still required the landlord's consent for a crofter to plant a tree, islanders encountered nothing but obstructions and delays in their attempt to get on with their lives. Transfer of land or decrofting of a building plot for those who hoped to build a home for themselves after years of living in precarious conditions met with countless delays as letters went back and forth between each set of lawyers. 'Eigg is probably the most expensive piece of bracken in the world. Its resilient people will put up with all sorts of weather but this wrangle has worn them down', declared Dr MacLean, echoing the general feeling of exasperation. The islanders who worked for the estate did not know whether they were coming or going with the confusion of rumours about what was happening with Eigg in the course of the lengthy legal battle between Schellenberg and Mrs Williams. But they knew that the eventuality of a sale made their situation more precarious than ever. They could lose both house and job, a state of affairs which worried everyone, as it would have its repercussions on the viability of the shop, the maintenance of existing services, the social and family life. Eventually Mrs Williams and Schellenberg arrived at an arrangement, allegedly at her insistence,[9] whereby the island was split into two farms, with Colin Carr kept as manager of the estate farm and entering into a limited partnership for Kildonnan, which would be leased to him for twenty-five years. The whole thing involved a complicated procedure, consisting of making everyone on the farm redundant so that they could be re-employed afterwards, with Schellenberg selling half his sheep to Colin.[10]

Unlike the farm, the tourist business had ground to a halt when Schellenberg was prohibited from managing the estate after the court decision of 1989. As holiday homes remained empty, the income generated by tourism dropped significantly on the island. Already struggling with the problem of high freight charges, the shop was badly affected. Yet, whilst Schellenberg was spending huge sums of money on lawyers' fees – amounting to half the cost of Eigg by his own reckoning[11] – he was able to say that, on Eigg, he had succeeded in maintaining 'the unspoiled Hebridean atmosphere': 'I love it when people come to the island and say it has not changed in 25 years, I've kept its style slightly run down – the Hebrides feel'.[12]

When Liz Lyon, a friend of his third wife, came to stay at the Lodge, she discovered what exactly 'slightly run down' could mean on Eigg. At the chapel house, one elderly widow was witnessing the building literally falling apart around her. This encounter moved Liz Lyon so deeply that the hospitality at the Big House no longer felt enjoyable. Schellenberg subsequently offered 80-year-old Dolly Ferguson a new home in a vacant house in Cleadale; but, on her return from Eigg, Liz Lyon expressed her concern about the island to Tom Forsyth, who had been instrumental in the regeneration of crofting in Scoraig, an isolated peninsula on Little Loch Broom, north of Ullapool. Forsyth had been to Eigg a few times and he had been struck by the unfulfilled potential of the island from an agricultural as well as a human point of view. Forsyth knew what he was talking about: his efforts and idealism had managed to turn the Little Loch Broom peninsula deserted by the Clearances into a thriving 'neo-rural' community. He felt that Eigg, with its mix of population and its natural assets, could do a lot better than it did and had the potential to become a new Iona. With Tom Forsyth as the driving force behind the project, building stone dykes to raise the necessary funds, Liz Lyon, together with Robert Harris, a Borders farmer with a long experience in community affairs, and Lewis academic Alastair McIntosh, who taught at the Centre for Human Ecology at Edinburgh University, founded the Isle of Eigg Trust, a charitable organisation, in order to put in a bid for the island which was expected to be put on the market at any time. On 24 July 1991, the Isle of Eigg Trust launched a public appeal for £3 million. Its intentions were clearly stated. The trust, which had received its first £100 from the Iona Foundation, aimed to remove Eigg in perpetuity from private ownership, and provide 'a novel approach in landownership' by introducing the idea of 'a viable community held in trust'.[13] The debate on landownership in Scotland was now kick-started back into life. It encompassed a far larger problem than Eigg, but from that time on, Eigg would become one of the test cases in the crucial issue of land reform.

However, although a certain amount of informal consultation with the islanders had been conducted before the launch of the trust appeal, the four trustees still had to grasp the nettle of formal endorsement by the island community. Their plans and ideas had yet to be presented to and approved by the islanders – who were justifiably dismayed to receive the Eigg Trust booklet in the post after the launch rather than before. The first impression on Eigg was that the trust's economic plans were naive and quite removed from their reality. The island had been more or less self-managed for the past four years, and as far as tourism was concerned, the islanders felt they knew the score better than anyone else. After all, the visitors had shifted their allegiance back to the crofters' B&Bs and holiday homes, Kildonnan guest house was run by an indigenous islander, the tea-room by a crofter's wife. The bike hire, the island taxi, the gas supply, all this was now run independently from the estate. The islanders were not really prepared to back another pie-in-the-sky venture, even if it was launched with the best intentions in the world. Opinions were divided after the first formal meeting of the trust and the islanders in October 1991. Angus MacKinnon, like the rest of his generation, was doubtful whether the trust was capable of raising the necessary capital and questioned how it would operate in the event that it succeeded. The younger generations were more receptive to the ecological vision of the trust and its ideals of land restitution but were wary of the influx of urban refugees which it proposed to attract, 'who would want to change everything back to the way of life they were trying to get away from'.[14] There was unanimity on the need for security of tenure to be extended to the whole island and on the positive contribution which islanders could make in the management of the island. When Alastair McIntosh made a special point of emphasising that the trust was really what the islanders wanted to make of it, the idea took a while to sink in – this was after all a very new concept after decades of non-participatory management. But it was an idea which was to take root. The next month, a meeting of the IERA saw a sizeable majority of residents – thirty-five out of forty-eight – voting in favour of ownership by the trust, provided that its constitution was amended to have two island residents on the board of trustees and give the IERA the right to veto any policy or decision which would seriously affect the island community.[15] The islanders clearly felt that the trust offered the best chance to have a say in their future.

Meanwhile, the Scottish Wildlife Trust was tentatively suggesting buying out Mrs Williams' share of the island and entering into a management agreement with Schellenberg. But it was an alternative that many people on the island felt amounted to the preservation of the status quo, although conservation issues now loomed larger than ever before. The SWT, which managed the island wildlife and had had a resident warden since 1986, now found itself facing the bleak fact that a change of ownership could mean the end of its work on the island and a possible threat to the wildlife. 'Eigg has a very special place in the hearts of naturalists because of a tremendous feeling that it has this unspoilt environment,' declared its development officer; 'the island needs a beneficial management system which ensures that it is protected from unsuitable development.'[16] There was no guarantee that a new owner would have conservation high on his agenda, particularly as many landowners in Scotland considered it to restrict management flexibility and reduce the value of the land. Uncertainty loomed large on the horizon, as Karen Helliwell, the

Eigg residents' secretary, explained: 'somebody might buy the island as an investment and put it back on the market in three years' time. That's no help. How much effort do you put into things if you're not sure you're going to live here permanently? At least with the trust, we'll have some say in what we do with the place.' The risk of the island being purchased by an outsider who would have little interest in it was energetically emphasised by the new Regional Councillor for the Small Isles, Dr Michael Foxley, in consideration of the Highland Regional Council's proposed investments for the area. 'Over £1.2 million of public funds are going to be spent on the island. I don't feel like putting that kind of money into the place so that some offshore clown has a more valuable asset at the end of the day', declared the outspoken councillor who had taken the lead in trying to provide better infrastructures and amenities for the island: there were plans for renovation and extension of the pier – a top priority since the 1950s – as well as for a housing development in Cleadale, and the refurbishment of the island school was imminent. Dr Foxley, who had recently succeeded in bringing Ardnamurchan Point into public ownership, wanted to see the same thing happening to Eigg. He saw no reason why the Regional Council could not join forces with the Isle of Eigg Trust in a joint project involving conservation organisations and the community. But his feeling was that, compared to Ardnamurchan, the battle would be harder: 'I don't know if the political will or imagination is there', he stated.[17]

Neither was to materialise when, after months of speculation, the island went formally up for sale in May 1992, expecting to fetch about £2 million. There was not a wide interest in the question of landownership in Scotland or even much awareness of it outwith the Highlands. The Isle of Eigg Trust had mustered a lot of moral support but little financial help, least of all from the National Heritage Memorial Fund, despite the fact that it had evolved from a fund created after the war with a particular brief to restore land to returning soldiers and landless communities. Highlands and Islands Enterprise, which had replaced the HIDB, had financed the trust's feasibility study, but it was no more empowered to help with land purchase than its predecessor had been. The Highland Regional Council was coming round to the idea of supporting or even fronting a community bid but was running out of time: its request to the selling agents for an extension of the closing date for the bids was turned down. The outcome was that on 3 July 1992 the islanders learned that the highest bid for the island was Schellenberg's. No one was really surprised.

THE LAIRD IS BACK

Schellenberg had spent just under £1 million – plus all his lawyers' fees over the years – to buy back the island from himself. 'Being laird [was] a responsibility he could do without, but nobody else who shared his philosophy of island ownership came forward', reported *The Scotsman*, stating his plan 'to take his 1927 Rolls-Royce on a triumphant tour of the island – once it was rendered roadworthy'. 'I could have made some cash from the sale and paid my lawyers, but I could not sit back and watch Eigg becoming a sporting estate or worse still, an example of collectivism', Schellenberg added. 'If there was a Highland family with a name like MacDonald to take over, I would be delighted, but there isn't and I am here because there is nobody else except the trust.'[18]

Disappointed, but undeterred, the Isle of Eigg Trust declared that it would continue as a trust-in-waiting 'with the confident patience that the land will be returned to the people in time'.

In the meantime it would monitor Schellenberg's stewardship of the island. The trustees derived a certain pride from the knowledge that their talk of community ownership had managed to discourage prospective buyers in a property market where islands such as Eigg were regarded as little more than 'collector's items'.[19] Within a year of its launch, the trust had effectively managed to revive the debate about landownership by adding the dimension of community ownership, opening up an alternative to the century-old deadlock between public ownership versus private landowners. With the failure of the conservation bid for Mar Lodge and – closer to Eigg – the case of Knoydart which had been bought, sold and re-sold into lots for vast profits within the space of a few years, the problem of land speculation in the Highlands stood to be exposed. Lochinver Estate in Assynt provided the perfect opportunity.

Formerly owned by the meat baron Lord Vestey, this crofting estate had been acquired by a Swedish investment company which promptly went bust, attempting to sell the land off in seven different lots. This threatened to bring absolute chaos to crofting, with rent going to one landlord for inbye and to another for common grazings, and was totally unacceptable to the community. By June 1992, the Assynt crofters resolved to set up their own community trust, the failed Eigg venture contributing some of the inspiration. For Assynt crofter Ishbel MacPhail, this was 'like the end of a colonial rule – gradually our imagination unchained'.[20] For the chairman of the Assynt Crofters' Union, Allan MacRae, it was the start of a process of land restitution: 'We are very conscious that the land we stand on is in a sense the last stronghold of the native people . . . the remnant of what the natives once possessed'.[21] The Gaelic concept of *duthchas*, of kindness to the land, which people had invoked in vain after 1745 to be allowed to stay on their land, was being re-established. With the support of the Highland Regional Council and development agencies and with donations from all over the world, the Assynt crofters raised £300,000. Unable to attract better offers, the creditors of the bankrupt Swedish company sold out to the community. For historians like James Hunter, the Assynt victory heralded the start of 'a very exciting period when the responsible public bodies along with local interests might change the whole pattern of land ownership in the Highlands'.[22]

In the case of Eigg, a lot of work still needed to be done. When the journalist Lesley Riddoch invited the islanders to take part in a radio debate about landownership prompted by the sale of Eigg, no one apart from Dr MacLean felt confident enough to do so. Fear of retribution was still too strong. Yet everyone on the island was aware that nothing could be the same, Schellenberg as much as everyone else. The islanders found themselves invited to the Lodge, as in the old days, to hear about a new era of cooperation between the residents and the estate. With Schellenberg still reeling economically from the court case and the settlement with his ex-wife, everyone wondered what kind of money he would have left to spend on the island. Marie Carr remembered feeling distinctly uneasy when Schellenberg declared in her kitchen at Kildonnan that 'there were going to be changes and that a lot of people were not going to like them'.

Things seemed to improve at first. A number of repairing leases were given out, enabling one tenant's house to be done up under the grant system which had benefited so many crofters' houses in the past few years. Yet the lease for the shop Fiona Cherry had been waiting for since 1989 arrived back-dated so that she only had three years left out of the five offered to her. 'It was better than nothing, but not exactly what we had hoped for, considering the renovations that were needed.' There was otherwise little sign of any progress. On the farm, Colin Carr was left to patch things up just as before: there was still no money for new equipment, machinery or fencing. 'He now had very little to do with the running of the place, paying wages or checking on progress. In fact he was very rarely there and we now dealt with the new factor, a decent enough bloke from a land agency.' There seemed to be no money to carry out repairs, except at the Lodge which was riddled with dry rot, like Galmisdale where the slates which had been blown from the roof during one winter's gale had never been replaced so that the once prosperous inn was now almost beyond repair.

It was not long before the new honeymoon started to sour. In April 1993, Marie Carr received an offer for a two-year lease for Kildonnan. A little embarrassed, the new factor explained that this would enable them to get Laig up and running as Marie's new guest house, since they already had its agricultural tenancy. For the Carrs, this was a blatant breach of the agreement for the twenty-five-year lease for Kildonnan which they and Mrs Williams had signed before the sale of the island in 1992. They would stay where they were and fight for their rights and for Peggy Kirk's rights in Laig as well. 'It was as if our mother never existed,' recalls Fiona, Marie's sister, 'as if Laig was not her home at all, after thirty-six years there!'

The meeting of the residents and the proprietor which was convened in June 1993 highlighted the defiant mood of a community with a new sense of its own strength. The residents obtained Schellenberg's agreement to lease a site at a peppercorn rent for the new ceilidh hall and to provide the community with a place near the pier where they could install recycling skips for metal and glass. But if they simply ignored his complaints that the regional authorities did not answer his enquiries about funding, alarm bells suddenly rang when he announced plans to start his own Wildlife Trust. This, he explained, would attract funding from nature lovers and Scottish Natural Heritage, the government's newly created conservation adviser. The scheme was unanimously vetoed.[23]

For John Chester – or John-the-bird as his nickname was on the island – Schellenberg's newest brainwave was bad news. A Glaswegian with Highland roots, he had been the SWT warden since 1986 and was largely responsible for the SWT's popularity on the island. He provided advice on grazing policy to help with conservation on the farm, involved unemployed islanders in a rhododendron control scheme, and spent a lot of time allaying the old generation's fears that conservation was another way to restrict land use. In fact the success met in the Outer Isles with the reintroduction of the corncrake in the crofters' hayfields due to the maintenance of traditional practices meant that crofting now appeared to be the most conservation-friendly way to use the land. The warden had also spent the past nine years completing a systematic mapping of all species existing on the island. It was an extraordinary body of data which could now be used to bring about the island's ecological regeneration. He had little intention of leaving a responsible body with a proven track record like the SWT.

Four months later, in October, as the Carr family came back from the first family holiday that they had ever taken, they were shocked to find that Schellenberg had sent people over to gather the estate lambs which Colin Carr had reared, dosed and clipped, ready for sale. Under the terms of his contract, his wages for working the estate farm came from the lamb sales and a proportion of the agricultural subsidies received by Schellenberg for Eigg, out of which he could then reimburse himself for costs and wages paid to the two shepherds he employed to work on the estate. It was an arrangement which depended on mutual trust, and it had worked fine until then. As far as Colin was concerned, that was what farm subsidies were for, to be used to keep people on the land. 'That's the way of farming these days,' he explained, 'that goes for big farms as well as crofts. But where I think it is not right, it's when that money becomes pure profit, without benefiting the land or the people who are trying to make a living out of it.'

This time, Colin did not receive a penny for his 450 lambs, neither from the sale nor from the subsidies. A few weeks later, he saw his job as farm manager advertised in the papers. Shortly afterwards, he received a letter from Schellenberg, dated from Christmas Eve 1993, telling him not to go near estate livestock after Hogmanay and not to use estate machinery. This was a bleak prospect: animals would suffer if not fed, there could be no delivery of wood or gas in the middle of winter, and there would no longer be enough work to warrant employing two people. The islanders who gathered at the ceilidh hall for the bells wished each other a happy New Year but everyone felt that 1994 had started in a bad way and that worse was probably to come.

THE YEAR IT ALL HAPPENED

On Thursday 7 January, as she rounded the pier corner on her morning school run, Karen Helliwell was confronted by the sight of a burnt-out shell emerging from the smoke. Dying flames were still licking the charred metal where the pier sheds had stood with their assorted collection of canoes, dinghies and old bicycles. Nothing was left but a few sheets of corrugated iron and the molten remains of Schellenberg's vintage Rolls, the 1927 shooting-brake with a rare wooden infrastructure, which he had used to drive up and down Pier Hill.

The shock wave went round the island: 'It's going to be very difficult from now on', was the universal thought. The police arrived the next day with Schellenberg, who had been expected for his New Year visit. 'He was hopping mad', recalls Simon Helliwell. 'He was quite scared actually; it was plain that he did not believe it was an accident and that he was wondering what would happen next.' As police enquiries proved inconclusive, Schellenberg's first reaction was to ban the use of the hall: neither the Gaelic playgroup nor the pensioners' Lunch Club would be allowed to use it. Confronted by the local press, he backed out on a threat which he could hardly enforce, but not without blaming 'hippies and drop-outs' for subverting the island traditions with their 'acid-rock parties'.[24] In response, the island's indigenous population sent an open letter to the papers in an unprecedented public indictment. 'We who have been born and brought up on the isle of Eigg would like to refute utterly the ludicrous allegations about the community here, made by Keith Schellenberg. The island has a small but united population of local families and incomers who are between them struggling to develop a community with a long-term future against the apparent wishes of an owner who seems to want us to live in primitive conditions to satisfy his nostalgia for the 1920s.'[25]

It was DJ, the youngest of Peggy Kirk's children, who had instigated the letter: 'I was sick of hearing him waffling on about the white settlers on the island taking over the old traditions: he was talking about my best friends and my relations. It was about time we set the record straight.' In the relationship between laird and tenants, the tables were now definitively turned. Schellenberg himself stated the change, oblivious to what he was implying: 'It is a very worrying climate. It was once the laird's factor who went about burning people out. Now it seems OK to burn out the laird himself.'[26] His response to what he obviously considered to be an attack on his person was to send a seven-page fax vilifying the island residents to every newspaper, radio and television newsdesk he could think of; it was all 'a well organised conspiracy' to try to take his highland farm into so-called 'community ownership' involving the transfer of millions of pounds from the taxpayer 'it was a very serious law and order situation'.[27] As the media machine focused with relish on the scene of such extraordinary happenings, the islanders found themselves in the best position to express their grievances. The chance of confronting their landlord on the issue of the island's future came with a second Speaking Out programme on Radio Scotland to be broadcast live from Eigg on 25 February 1994.

There was a feeling of anticipation and excitement in the island school, the scene of the Land-leaguers meeting a hundred years earlier. Schellenberg turned up late, with his dog Horace, and it took a while for the debate to warm up. Allan MacRae, the chairman of the Assynt Trust, was also present (as he stepped onto the pier, Angus MacKinnon had hugged him for a full minute, speechless with emotion) and he soon got the debate going. 'I can see the proprietor here has no conscience and commitment as far as the people here are concerned. That's what you find with many proprietors in the Highlands and Islands', Allan started after Schellenberg was given his say. 'I think the people here have to take the initiative themselves. This is something that our European counterparts have taken for granted long ago. Here we are in Europe, and we are told to think like Europeans, and yet we still live under a feudal system in the large part of the Highlands and clearly there's got to be changes. Things haven't got to stand still. People can shape the future if they have a will to do it.'[28] By the time the programme had to end, people were pouring out all the things they had kept back all these years. For John Cormack, it was a really cathartic moment: 'I couldn't help it. He had the bloody gall to use me as an example of the people he had helped to get a house! I just couldn't bear it and I had to tell him so – I think he was taken aback by my vehemence – it felt great to have him pinned down, having to listen for once. It was a wonderful, liberating feeling.' It was an experience that a lot of people shared. Getting rid of some of their anger made them feel lighter, more confident about the future. Like Ishbel MacPhail in Assynt, they felt their imagination starting to unchain.

The message which Allan MacRae had expressed so forcefully was not likely to be forgotten. The consensus was that community ownership was now the best way forward. In March, an island delegation was sent to the Highland Forum conference which had 'the people and the land' as its theme that year. They returned full of enthusiasm and inspiration about the way the community could take its own future in its hands. Maggie, Karen, Colin and Marie were moved by the overwhelming support given by every person they met. 'Everyone was so confident that the community would succeed that it gave us a tremendous lift', recalls Colin. The Highland Forum provided that unique opportunity for people from the four corners of the Highlands to compare experiences and exchange solutions and ideas. For remote rural communities such as Eigg, breaking the feeling of isolation was perhaps the most important step towards empower-ment. The next one was the realisation of its own power and strength. In the Shetland island of Foula, this had enabled the islanders to go from 'tribal warfare to total democracy in the space of a few years', pointed out Isobel Holbourn, a Highland Forum director, who always quoted the example of her island. 'If Foula could do it, so could any other communities.'[29]

Meanwhile, the Scottish Wildlife Trust started to look at ways which would ensure that it could continue playing a role on the island. Its proposal was to negotiate a deal with Schellenberg and buy the island, provided that the community would be in charge of the day-to-day running of the island. It did not want to become a landowner in the strict sense of the term. The islanders were confident they could tackle the job but dubious about the success of the SWT's endeavour. They were right, for Schellenberg rose out of a depressive spell when he confessed to feeling 'a bit of liability'[30] to declare emphatically that he would never allow such a thing to happen. Instead, he would sell the island piecemeal, to attract new blood and outside money to the island. Two decaying properties, the Manse and Galmisdale, were portrayed as idyllic Hebridean homes to *Daily Telegraph* readers: 'the crofting township is at the other end, they are far enough away not to be a nuisance'.[31]

The islanders denounced this as asset-stripping, concerned that selling Eigg into lots would turn it into an island of holiday homes, with disastrous consequences for its culture and traditions. They had more constructive ideas. When the Highland Forum came to Eigg in June 1994 to introduce the islanders to its group workshop techniques, the islanders were given their first experience of reaching a consensus of opinion and prioritising the issues facing the community with everyone having an equal say. Everyone enjoyed it. For Katie MacKinnon, it was a welcome innovation. It was the first time she had been able to express her hopes and ideas for the regeneration of land and farming. Her generation knew what the island was capable of producing and she wanted to see it going back to its full potential. For Maggie Fyffe, the most amazing thing about these workshops was the convergence of ideas between the groups: to her it was yet another proof of the remarkable unity of thought and purpose which had emerged lately on the island.

She was part of the new steering committee which had been elected at the SWT's instigation to explore development ideas in the eventuality of a buy-out. 'We were quite a varied collection of people,' explained Maggie, 'but we became a very cohesive group in the process. We certainly learnt a lot about handling the press from Dr Tiarks [the new doctor for the Small Isles]. His political skills proved invaluable.' The islanders fully understood that the only way they could achieve anything was to turn the tide of public opinion in their favour, and they earnestly set out to prove that the community offered the only valid alternative to private ownership.

The time was now ripe for the Isle of Eigg Trust to be handed over to the islanders. For Tom Forsyth, it was very moving to witness on 16 July the materialisation of an idea conceived forty years before. For Alastair McIntosh, it was a historic moment, another step towards what he called 're-empowerment of the minds' in the Highlands. For the islanders, who had elected eight new trustees, six of whom were Eigg residents,[32] it was the launch of a campaign which they hoped would ultimately 'secure the island for Scottish and global heritage'. In their press release they stated their aim to run the island in the interest of the community, achieve security of tenure and sustainable economic growth, and maintain Eigg's cultural heritage and built environment whilst conserving its ecology.

The next step was to raise funds. Alastair McIntosh proposed that the trust should aim for the symbolic sum of £15,000, the price which had been paid when the Chief of Clanranald sold 'his right to the stewardship of the land'. As T-shirts, letterheads and stickers were printed with the motto devised for the trust, *Cuir dochas an Eige* – put your trust in Eigg – a press conference was organised in Glasgow for 15 August 1994. 'There is no point in us just sitting back now and doing nothing. We want to try and get ourselves in a position to bid for the island, should the opportunity arise', announced island delegates John Cormack and Marie Carr.[33] The event was reported on radio and television, making headlines in the local, national and European press. Coverage was in the great majority sympathetic to the islanders' case. This was only the beginning of a lengthy campaign, but the islanders were delighted to have changed their public image from lawless rebels to credible contenders for the ownership of Eigg.

'Ah, here comes the new owner!'

Chapter 13

THE END OF THE LAIRD'S RULE

A GERMAN FAIRY TALE

With the launch of the Isle of Eigg Trust, the islanders were throwing a formal challenge to the old order. Colin Carr, the Steering Committee spokesman, had reminded everyone on 16 July 1994 that there was a far greater and wider issue at stake than the ownership of Eigg. They had to help end the situation of feudalism in Scotland. For an increasing number of people, it was indeed an anomaly that on the eve of the new millennium, the country could retain feudal principles in its legal system when these had been given up long ago everywhere else. The fact was that 100 years after the crofters had managed to force some concessions out of a few large landowners, the residual aspects of the land law's feudal origins still clashed with the comprehensive development framework which post-war governments had introduced. Landowners were in essence feudal superiors who retained and imposed rights on people who, by buying or renting land, technically became their vassals. Among those rights were the right of pre-emption and the right to control and share in the development value of the land.[1] In the 1970s, the success of *The Cheviot, the Stag and the Black, Black Oil*, performed by the 7:84 theatre company, had already brought attention to the problems of landownership in Scotland, which had the most concentrated pattern of ownership in Europe. But the free-market ideology of the 1980s, boosting the confidence of landowning interests, had stalled any attempt to continue the debate in the open. Now events in Assynt and then Eigg brought the debate back to the attention of the wider public.

Schellenberg's reaction to the islanders' appeal was to dismiss it as ridiculous, declaring that he would never consider 'anything so childish or pathetic as the notion of community ownership . . . I own Eigg and I will never sell it'.[2] The following October, Schellenberg's lawyers sent a letter to the SWT, giving John Chester a month to vacate his house, and a letter to the Carr family demanding that they leave by 1 January since they had failed to respond to the proprietor's previous offer. The reasons given to the press were that the assets they occupied were needed 'so that other private sector jobs could be created'.[3]

179

The immediate effect of these threats was to reinforce the feeling of solidarity on the island. Those among the older islanders who had felt uneasy about massive press coverage were now up in arms. The spirit of *duthchas* perhaps demanded that one's birthplace should be kept from dishonourable associations of lawlessness, but that an indigenous islander like Marie, the island registrar, the school bus driver, Donnie Kirk's eldest daughter, should be threatened with eviction with her family, that was going too far. 'The whole thing became completely unworkable from the moment we heard about the evictions', recalls Maggie Fyffe. 'The SWT had run into a complete stalemate with Schellenberg, it seemed inevitable that the island would be up for sale shortly and we all felt we'd better be ready. Our first priority before approaching any funding body was to produce a development plan.' Over a few weekends, using the workshop technique, a preliminary document was produced which expressed in some detail how the islanders envisaged the future: sustainable development at a pace which they would be able to control, focus on ecologically sound agricultural practices, green tourism to capitalise on the island's natural assets, and more involvement in the movement of cultural regeneration which was now spanning the whole of the Highlands. This certainly enabled the islanders to make the most of the 'Planning for real' exercise on Eigg which initiated the consultation process for the Lochaber Local Plan in early November. A few unexpected suggestions were also added to the array of development ideas which they were invited to place on a table-size map of the island. Protest cards were piled on the Lodge, asking for security of tenure. 'The Council should know that Schellenberg is not part of the island's future', spelt some of them.

The story of seventy-three islanders wanting to buy their island was now attracting more and more media coverage, nationally and internationally. Although they found it tiresome, especially the *Whisky Galore* manner in which it was often presented, the islanders put up with the media scrutiny, feeling that they had to adopt the Assynt market-spoiling tactics and make as much noise as possible to discourage potential buyers. Filmed by CBC, the Canadian television channel, the visit of Chief Stone Eagle, invited to Eigg by trustee Alastair McIntosh on his way to the Harris superquarry enquiry that November, was an unexpected morale-booster for the islanders. It was felt to be particularly significant that a Miq'Mac Indian from Nova Scotia, the descendant of the people who had welcomed and helped the people of Eigg fleeing the threat of eviction two hundred years earlier, had now come to Eigg as a gesture of solidarity with the island's own indigenous population. On that front, the intense press coverage certainly had a positive effect. Confronted by an increasing number of journalists, astonished that the story was even attracting international attention, Schellenberg argued that he had never been serious in his intentions to carry out the threatened evictions, people had over-reacted, it had just been a marker.

By the spring of 1995, rumours that a potential buyer was prepared to pay £1.5 million for the island started to circulate, amidst reports that Schellenberg was experiencing renewed financial difficulties through an acrimonious separation from his third wife and losses as a Lloyd's name. A press release was swiftly put together by the islanders on 19 March, deploring the fact that 'the island may have been sold without the community having any knowledge let alone involvement. It typified the problems of landownership in Scotland and gave the community little reassurance.'[4] Shortly before Easter, Schellenberg arrived on the island with his family, ostensibly for the holidays, journalists hot on his trail. Still denying that he had sold the island, Schellenberg was effectively packing his bags. On Monday 27 March 1995, the islanders woke up to hear that he had left at dawn after a night spent shifting furniture and belongings. Excited journalists ran about the island brandishing copies of a fax confirming the sale of the island. Bought for £1.6 million, Eigg was now owned by a mysterious fire-worshipping German artist who went by the name of Maruma, a name he had read in a pool of water in Abu Dhabi.

Eigg had always been the place for surreal moments, and the moment the islanders learnt it was sold was definitely one of them. The island's bush telegraph was buzzing, telephone lines were engaged as relatives phoned to tell the bizarre news. Trustee Katie MacKinnon summed up the general feeling: 'I think we can do without a spiritualist artist.' It took ten days for the sale to be confirmed after vehement denials from the former owner. During that time, the plight of Eigg was brought up in Parliament by Calum MacDonald, Labour MP for the Western Isles. 'Landownership is a speculative market of private investors who buy up the Highlands for the reason they buy jewellery and oil paintings – a tax advantage or a store for spare cash . . . This has got to end. The management of Scotland's wilderness areas, the prosperity and future of Highland communities cannot be left to the whims and vagaries of the speculator and the dilettante.'[5] The Highlands and Islands minister, Lord James Douglas-Hamilton, was asked if he thought it wrong that land, which was the basic economic resource in the Highlands, should be sold to the highest bidder without consultation or the agreement of people who live and work on it, and whether he would be prepared to work with local communities like Eigg to realise their objectives of community ownership. The minister replied that it was better to leave such matters to the free market. Amidst indignation that the reported price meant a staggering and unjustified increase in value, the debate was now firmly placed in the political arena where islanders like Angus MacKinnon had always maintained it belonged.

Whilst the new owner, Marlin Eckhart, alias Maruma, sought to allay islanders' fears by declaring that it was impossible to own a place like Eigg and that the money he had paid was a gift which obliged him to take care and look after the island and help the community improve their opportunities, the islanders' councillor expressed his disgust at the way the sale had been conducted. 'Community consultation is required for an individual to erect the smallest hut,' pointed out Dr Foxley, 'the Crofters' Commission has a statutory obligation to screen a new tenant, yet someone can come in with funds or not his own funds, and there is no assessment or audit of the local community or the wider community. It is completely absurd!'[6] The islanders' reaction was more muted. They felt that due to the uncertain position of those residents who did not have a lease, the whole thing demanded some diplomacy on their part, and they prepared to meet the strange character who now held the key to their future.

Maggie Fyffe was enjoying a well-deserved rest after a particularly lively birthday party when her neighbour came knocking at her door: Maruma's helicopter had landed and Colin was taking him round the island to meet everyone. 'Well, there was a bit of panic to clear the party leftovers of course,' tells Maggie, 'but it wasn't too bad. The whole world came into our house when Colin arrived. Maruma was very polite in a German way, I suppose, shaking hands with everyone. Quite a strange-looking guy, huge, with an unusual kind of stare. He did not say much apart from some wisecrack about the need to start "our own brewery on Eigg" when he was offered a can of beer, and that I looked like the kind of person who would be good at running a pub!' The dozen or so people gathered at the table were trying to gauge the man who created his paintings by some kind of telepathic connection between his imagination and fire and was ready to tap the cosmic energy of the Massacre Cave, as they had read in the papers. Farhad Vladi, the international island dealer who had brokered the sale, was far more talkative, confiding his admiration for the artist, gesturing towards him when one islander asked for more details: 'Why don't you ask him yourself?' Somehow it did not seem an easy thing to do when Maruma was sitting there silent, like some kind of enigmatic buddha, chain-smoking all the time. The old generations, on the other hand, were impressed that the new owner had taken the trouble to introduce himself and visit them in their home: 'it never happened before, it was always the other way around', they remarked. But on the whole, sizing him up from beret to patched cords, they did not think he looked like someone who had an extra £1.5 million to spend on the island as he had told the press.

Maruma showed himself remarkably open to cooperation at first. Everything would be discussed on a regular basis, relationships would be established on a proper legal footing. The island would be his home but he didn't like the Lodge and preferred to turn it into a clinic. He planned to visit every two months and in the meantime, he was willing to pay for the fairly large amount of wrecked cars to be collected and shipped off. As a gesture of goodwill on the community's part, he was presented with a summary of the workshop results to help him get acquainted with the islanders' aspirations. 'Cautious optimism' was the mood of the moment, although nagging suspicions were tugging in people's minds that he might just be a front man. It was all too well primed, too much what the islanders wanted to hear. No one was 100 per cent Maruma'd.

Whatever worries remained were pushed aside for the time being by the feeling of relief and elation which swept the island now that the Schellenberg years were over. But when they found out that their ex-proprietor was planning to remove the map of the island which every other proprietor had seen fit to leave in place, the islanders resolved to make a stand. The map, drawn in 1805 by William Bald, a pioneering Scottish cartographer, provided invaluable information of early settlements and land use on Eigg. Feeling that it represented too important a part of the island's historical heritage to be taken away, the decision was made to take all legal and non-violent means to oppose the map's removal. A disused community bus was pulled against the door of the mothballed craftshop where the map was stored in conditions less than ideal and everyone agreed to be at the pier and park their cars around the bus in time for Schellenberg's arrival the following day.

In spite of the cold drizzle and bitter spring wind, there was a definite festive atmosphere in the air as islanders congregated at the pier after setting out the stalls of the annual fund-raising fair. Journalists arrived first, with a policeman who coincidentally arrived to check the polling station precisely on that day. Children, adults and pensioners were waiting, lined up nonchalantly along the pier, when Schellenberg stepped ashore. As cameras clicked and a video whirred, he caught a glimpse of the crowd and a fixed grin appeared on his face. Making his way slowly up the pier, clutching removal blankets on each arm, he ran the gauntlet of the islanders' ironic gaze, followed by children and dogs. Witnessing his blustering and spluttering when he discovered the bus made up for the humiliations of the past. The islanders were now frankly enjoying the farcical atmosphere as the agent of the law was now informing their ex-landlord that yes, if no one claimed ownership of the vehicle after the thirty-day statutory period, he would be entitled to remove the bus. In the meantime, his suggestion was to get in touch with the island's new owner. 'It was hard to avoid the conclusion that Hamish MacBeth, television Highland cop creation, had come to life after only two episodes', reported a *Scotsman* journalist.[7] Farce reached a pitch as a first helicopter appeared, disgorging more photographers and journalists who proceeded to question an exasperated Schellenberg about the map. 'He is not content with the £1.6 million he received for the sale, he has taken the kitchen sink out of the Lodge, and now he wants the map as well. We interpret it as greed', commented the islanders. 'It's great to see everyone here without any work to do!' taunted the former laird. 'It's Eigg's official holiday', came the reply.[8] Hip-hip-hurraying under the islanders' sarcastic farewells, Schellenberg made his final exit after unloading his game paraphernalia onto the removal boat. 'You never understood me,' he shouted into the wind, 'I always wanted to be one of you.' Another helicopter alighted: the BBC was a bit late. The islanders' home video made the news that night, closing another chapter in island history.

The islanders now busied themselves with taking up the normal thread of their lives. There were preparations for the tourist season to be made and Feis Eige to organise, the island's first traditional tuition festival, the islanders having joined *Feisean nan Gaidheal*, the growing youth tuition festival movement which had started in Barra several years ago and now spanned the whole of the Highlands. The Feis movement was the symbol of the Gaelic cultural renaissance, and the musicians and the Gaelic learners on the island felt Eigg had to have its part in it. Peggy MacKinnon was no longer there, marching onto the stage at ceilidhs to get the whole island to sing its traditional songs, but the islanders would carry on the tradition which she had so jealously guarded. In this buoyant atmosphere, it was also decided that the island would host the Small Isles games for the first time in years. Celebration was the order of the day.

As the inhabitants of Rum, Muck and Soay converged on the island for the Feis and the games in the most glorious weather, the new proprietor arrived to pay his second – and last – visit to the island. Devouring cake after cake in the pier tea-room, he held job interviews whilst the Small Isles games were in progress. The islanders did not think it very polite. They had put a lot of effort in to ensure that the whole event was a success and felt quite annoyed at this diversion on a day which was a festive occasion for all. As meetings carried on into the evening the islanders gathered that the new owner did not like the Isle of Eigg Trust, had no idea of crofting laws, and was intent on following his lawyer's advice and not giving leases for more than five years. Indeed, for Thomson, who had served Schellenberg's interests before becoming co-director of Eigg Island Ltd, the plight of a few islanders was of no great interest. Like estate agents who felt that there was no legal, merely a moral, obligation for a proprietor to look after his tenantry,[9] he underpinned a landownership system which favoured investors interested in short-term profits, not in the stability of the countryside. The next day the full Maruma 'concept' was unveiled to a stunned island audience. Phase One involved the compiling of a database expected to be completed within six months. Phase Two would start with building work within another six months. In the interim period, employment would be created by completing the clearing of the island's rubbish and work in forestry and agriculture. People would be set up as self-employed rather than as estate employees, but eventually more jobs would be created than could be handled by the local community, for Maruma was thinking of increasing the tourist bed capacity from twenty-five to two hundred with recreational facilities, another hall, swimming pool, and a pier development comprising restaurant, coffee-house and shops, maybe a bakery or a brewery. All existing diesel generators would be replaced by an integrated system of wind and solar power backed up by a central generating plant, which would be a great tourist attraction, whilst he would look into buying the pier from the council and getting it done himself, rather than having to deal with all the bureaucracy. Because of his good connections with banks across the world, he would also look at establishing an Isle of Eigg bank within the next two years so that interest-free or low-interest loans would enable all islanders who at present were paying rent, to buy their homes. Residents need not worry. They would be able to voice their feelings at every stage.[10]

As this multi-million-pound development was reported in the press, journalists in Britain and Germany were competing to uncover Maruma's credentials. They succeeded in establishing that his art and architecture professorships were non-existent and that in spite of his claims, he was a complete unknown on the art market although a company called Maruma AG Holding, registered on the Isle of Man, had briefly traded in 1994, offering shares indexed on the value of the owner's paintings.[11] The German magazine *Stern*, which had investigated his credit-rating and found it wanting, questioned whether the mystic mystery which Maruma was wrapping around himself – making him the 'German fairytale prince' of the British popular press, was not in fact a clever device to hide his lack of hard currency.[12] All these revelations confirmed the islanders' doubts. The problem is that people like him could come along, buy a place like Eigg and impose their own personal vision, whilst the community is left dangling, they complained. In just five months, apprehension had replaced optimism.

By October, worry deepened as the press revealed that Eigg had been used as security for a loan of £300,000 at a punishing interest rate of 20 per cent by a German clothing exporter based in Hong Kong immediately after the purchase of the island, a deal arranged by Vladi, the island broker. It was also revealed that Maruma had taken out a substantial bank loan amounting to the value of the island. Meanwhile, the man who had declared in March that he had the connections and the resources to finance his projects on Eigg was now explaining that money was an energy which could be created at will. The story of the Bavarian Walter Mitty was avidly circulated in the media, with for effect a renewal of interest in the glaring anomalies of the landownership system in Scotland; one newspaper's poll indicated that two Scots in three now favoured a regulation of the land market.[13] In that encouraging climate and since none of their communications to Maruma by letter, fax or phone were ever answered, the islanders resumed their work towards a community buy-out.

Chances of mounting a viable bid for a buy-out were now a serious proposition. The SWT, which had grown from small beginnings, fighting a rearguard action for wildlife, to a mature, high-profile Scottish conservation body, was more than ever committed to participate in a joint bid, not only to protect its wildlife on Eigg but to rehabilitate an environment degraded by decades of intensive sheep farming. Together with the islanders, they explored the possibility of bringing the proportion of woodland on the island to 20 per cent, to qualify for Millennium Forest funding towards the purchase of the afforested land. The time-scale was tight, but there was a good chance of success. The next step was to draw a five-year business plan from the islanders' development ideas and a legal framework for a partnership, the necessary conditions for an application to the National Heritage Memorial Fund. If the island was put on the market, this was how the islanders envisaged funding the purchase of the rest of the island. Events proved it to be a timely strategy. Shortly after New Year, the islanders learned that Thomson, Maruma's lawyer, was running out of funds. The end of January arrived without the stockman or the gardener receiving any wages. Maruma had not replied to the islanders' Millennium Forest scheme. It was time for action. A statement of no confidence was issued to the press: 'It is intolerable in a small community like this that people's livelihood can be put in jeopardy by a third party based in Edinburgh or Stuttgart. The community has now totally lost confidence in Maruma . . . He has failed to fulfil any of his initial promises and there has been a complete lack of response to any attempts at communication. There is a sense of *déjà-vu* about this situation and the community is now more than ever convinced that there is no future for the island under the landlord system. It is now clear that the only way forward is through a community-led buy-out.'[14]

Journalists flocked to the island to take pictures of Maruma's only tangible achievement, the pile of rusty wrecks near the pier which risked becoming a permanent feature and which had been quickly daubed the Maruma Centre. The sale of the estate cattle in February, ordered by Thomson to pay wages, including his own, provided another emotional focus on the islanders' plight. With Eigg now constantly in the headlines, the islanders asked all the major political parties for their support. 'The only thing the Scottish Office has to do is either buy the island or allow the local community to buy it', declared Sir Russell Johnston, the local Liberal MP. 'The problems the people of Eigg have faced with a succession of owners highlight the anachronisms of the feudal system that still exists in Scotland . . . The community of Eigg would be far better stewards of the land on which they live and work than a speculator with real or imagined millions choosing the romantic notions of owning an island', underlined Roseanna Cunningham, the MP for Perth and Kinross and the SNP's environment spokesperson. But for the government, there was no question of changing a position it had adhered to since the time of the Crofters' War. 'It's not the Secretary of State's place to [intervene], it's a private matter between the island tenants and their landlord', replied the Scottish Office in March 1996.[15]

This was not a position that the new Highland Council was prepared to follow. Problems of land tenure in the Highlands and Islands were placed at the top of the agenda for the new centralised form of local government which was due to come into effect in April 1996. Within its quasi-parliamentary structure, the Land and Environment Committee – chaired by Dr Foxley – was amongst the variety of select committees charged with investigating a number of important issues. The Highland Council felt its mandate was now to look to the future of the Highlands and Islands within a Europe of regions. It had to break away from feudal legacy and give communities the degree of participation taken for granted in every other European country. There was a feeling of new beginning, of a new mission for a new administration. There was at last some political will and imagination at local government level.

Seeing for herself what services there were for the elderly on Eigg galvanized Lochaber Councillor Olwyn MacDonald into action. Considering the amount of public investment scheduled for Eigg – with the pier, new housing and a day-care centre for the elderly – as well as the help previously given to the crofters of Assynt for their land purchase, was it not time for the Highland Council to pledge its support for a community buy-out on Eigg, she asked. A motion was proposed accordingly by the Land and Environment committee in March 1996 and it was unanimously decided to back the community on Eigg in all possible ways. 'If we didn't help them we would be neglecting our obligation to the people of the Highlands,' declared Peter Peacock, the Highland Council Convener.[16] The council's legal service, its policy, press and public relations departments were called to help. By May, the blueprint for a three-way partnership between the islanders, the SWT and the council was completed, a financial team was assembled to finalise the islanders' business plan and a fund-raising and publicity strategy was under way. Four years after its timid attempt at supporting a community bid, the council was determined it would be ready.

Three months later, on 27 July, Eigg was put on the market for an asking price of £2 million, within eighteen months of its purchase by a man who had bought it after one visit to Eigg in August 1994, so brief that no one had known about it. It was during this visit that, after a night of negotiation, Schellenberg had signed the island away to Maruma on a table napkin, prompted by the approval of his friend, the captain of Clanranald.[17]

PUT YOUR TRUST IN EIGG

A month later, on 27 August, the islanders launched their bid for a community buy-out. There was a sense of historical occasion on the day of the launch and a tremendous feeling of elation that this moment which had been talked about for months had finally arrived. Banners painted with the campaign slogan – Let's crack it, back the Eigg appeal! – were waved at the pier as the ferry arrived overflowing with officials, friends and journalists, and hung in the island hall where the press conference was taking place. The island children had drawn pictures of wildlife and pinned poems to the walls. There were photos and quotes illustrating the journey of the community towards a better future. Journalists were offered some of the 20,000 appeal leaflets printed by the council, ready to be distributed all over the country. Some even bought the campaign T-shirts which the islanders were proudly wearing.

'The pattern of landownership is a fundamental issue affecting the Highlands, and Eigg is one of the most prominent and persuasive examples as to why change is required', stated Highland Councillor Dr Michael Foxley as the Isle of Eigg Heritage Trust was introduced.[17] For the first time a community had joined forces with a conservation body and local government to create a new and innovative partnership. The composition of its board of trustees, with four island representatives, two from the Highland Council and two from the Scottish Wildlife Trust, and an independent chairman,[19] ensured unprecedented participation of the community in the running of an island whose ecological and social future would now be safeguarded. It was anticipated that the bids would be closed before Christmas, and within that period of time the community itself endeavoured to raise at least £800,000, using the Internet to broadcast the appeal overseas. Every donation would be acknowledged, every donor's name entered in a book of Eigg. Lottery funding would be sought through the National Heritage Memorial Fund whilst the Scottish Wildlife Trust would appeal to all forty-seven environmental trusts in Britain for support, and call on all nature lovers in the British Isles to help. As the day wore on, the atmosphere turned from quite solemn to jubilant. 'This is not just a piece of land for someone to pick up,' observed Nick Reiter, the Highland Council's head of policy, 'there is a whole movement here.'

'Then the hard work really started', says Maggie Fyffe, who, as secretary of the Isle of Eigg Trust, was at the heart of the campaign. From her back-bedroom office, she coordinated the sending-out of leaflets from the database compiled by the islanders and conducted dozens of interviews over the phone with journalists and radio stations calling from all over Britain and from America, Canada, Australia and Ireland. The result was overwhelming: within days of the appeal, letters of support and donations began to flood in. This was where the island solidarity came into play. Islanders rallied round to help as the computer boffins on the island got their e-mail and Internet connections fully operational, now that a Scottish company had offered the island its very own website. All of a sudden, the island found itself propelled into the realm of electronic technology: Maggie coordinated all the details of the campaign on her computer powered by the

Fyffe family's brand new hydro-electric scheme. Her 18-year-old daughter Tasha – who was about to make a sponsored parachute jump to raise money through the SWT – helped out in the logging of names, the opening and sorting-out of mail. Mail days now signalled a ritual gathering of people around Maggie's table. As John Cormack brought in the bulging mailbags, everyone joined in the task, the money was only totalled at the very end and the result announced to see if the day had brought a new record. 'It started out at £1,000 per post,' recalls Scruff, the island fisherman, who would call every day on his way home from the fishing, 'and it went up to thirty grand! It was just brilliant, pure magic!' What was almost as magic was the speed and the efficiency with which this staggering amount of letters were processed and answered.

One of the most colourful and successful aspects of the islanders' fund-raising strategy was 'Eigg music aid' which involved ceilidhs, concerts and dances throughout the country and abroad. With benefit concerts taking place from Tyrone to Glasgow, Detroit to Ardrossan, Glenuig and many more places, the climax of Eigg music aid was certainly the 'Not the landowners ball' in Edinburgh on 2 November. Twenty islanders braved the roughest crossing to attend the Eigg benefit at the Assembly Rooms which featured so many favourite musicians: Dick Caughan, Capercaillie's Karen Matheson, Michael Marra and Shooglenifty, whose roots were very much in Lochaber. Not only was it a party to remember but it was one of the high points of the campaign. To see the concert room packed with people who had come to support them renewed their faith in what they were trying to achieve. The islanders need not have worried. By that time, people all over the country had taken on the organisation of fund-raising events. People who had taken pictures of Eigg in their holidays turned them into slide shows, others did car-boot sales, artwork was auctioned off, a relative did a sponsored cycle from the Isle of Man to Eigg. The Eigg story had caught people's imagination in a big way.

Messages of encouragement and hope that the buy-out would succeed kept coming through the post and e-mail. People who had suffered eviction themselves from other estates wrote to say that they wanted to see an end to an unjust system. People who had been inspired and refreshed by their holiday sojourn on the island offered their help. They had enjoyed the unspoilt feeling of the place and its powerful sense of history. They had discovered outstanding wildlife and a friendly community. They put their faith and trust in the islanders as the best custodians for the island.

It was obvious that the island, with its natural beauty, geological uniqueness and undisturbed wildlife, was still exerting the same attraction on people that it had since the earliest days of its history. For urban dwellers in Britain, islands on the north-western fringe of the country offered these very oases of peace which Schellenberg, for one, had sought to provide before his grand plan turned sour. It was important that such places were kept unspoilt and that their wildlife was properly protected. The problem was that in some circles, Eigg's greatest value seemed to be in conservation terms, far more than in social or agricultural terms. But no one on Eigg wanted to live on a reserve or in a theme park. The islanders knew how fragile the security and continuity of their life was, and how vigilant they had to be if a human presence was to be maintained at all. Rum, owned by the Nature Conservancy Council first and now by Scottish Natural Heritage, was proving only too well how difficult it was to maintain a stable community in conditions where nothing had been left of the original culture of the island and where conservation aims dictated over social considerations. In contrast, crofting was now acknowledged as having kept more people on the land in modern times than any other form of tenure in Scotland. From being viewed as simple peasant agriculture, it was now seen as environmentally sound, socially stabilising and economically desirable rural living. The recognition that its traditional methods had the best impact on wildlife protection came as a new system of grants favouring environmentally friendly agriculture was put into place in the early 1990s and gave it a new vigour.[20] On Eigg, as in the rest of the region, crofting was now helping to reverse the population decline. With her nostalgia for the days when 'strings of people could be seen walking up the Bealach Clithe', Marybel MacDonald had rejoiced at each new light appearing in Cleadale as houses were built. Four new entrants to crofting on Eigg meant that a whole crofting tradition could be passed on: one absentee crofter who thought that Eigg was better evacuated like St Kilda seventy years earlier was now more than happy to pass her land to a young incomer. The range of activities which was now available to combine with work on the land was larger than ever, even if some of these, like teleworking, came as a surprise to older generations of crofters. Even Michael Forsyth, the Scottish Office minister, was now acknowledging the importance of crofting and the potential for community trusts to own their land. His breakfast visit to Eigg one cold September morning had given hope to the community that there was some understanding of their social and economical plight at a high level.[21] With the end of Objective One status in sight for the Highlands and Islands which conferred on the region priority European funding for development projects, it was more important than ever that the landownership crisis be resolved as soon as possible. The Small Isles development plan, which included a new ferry for the islands as well as essential structural improvements for their piers, depended entirely for its implementation on European money to match funding from the Scottish Office. When the islanders made their bid to the National Heritage Memorial fund, all these issues hung in the balance, as well as the continuity in conservation policy for an island which presented natural features of national importance. Reflecting the interest aroused by the Eigg campaign, a considerable number of MPs had even signed the Early Day Motion put forward in Parliament in October by Mrs Cunningham.[22] The public had clearly demonstrated its support for the partnership, and was overwhelmingly in favour of lottery money – its money – being donated to effect the purchase. 'Lottery funds could be lavished on a few square feet of canvas to hang in a museum', wrote a supporter to *The Scotsman*'s letter pages. He wanted some of it to be spent to help buy Eigg: 'When you draw your feet along the western shore by Cleadale and hear the sands cry out, when the island peace is torn at night by the screams of the shearwaters, isn't £2 million a bargain?' he asked.[23] Many, many people echoed that thought, and responses to the call for support by the Scottish Wildlife Trust to the members of forty-seven other UK Wildlife Trusts were flooding in. The movement for the defence of wildlife and its habitat in Britain which had grown from strength to strength since the 1930s made this public response an overwhelming plea for action from the powers that be to back the islanders' campaign. A quarter of the sum needed – around £200,000 – had already been collected, showing the sympathy and goodwill the islanders had attracted.[24] It seemed that all these voices had been heard when, on 19 November, eight days from the closing date for the bids, the National Memorial Heritage Lottery Fund agreed 'in principle' to back the buy-out.

'WE DON'T WANT YOUR FANCY DREAMS, WE WANT THE LAND'[25]

The original feeling of elation, echoed through press, radio and TV, was soon tempered with worry. The amber light given by the Heritage Lottery Fund was revealed to be conditional on one crucial change in the composition of the Isle of Eigg Heritage Trust partnership because of concerns 'about the possible conflicts of interest the acquisition could raise between the private benefits of the residents of Eigg and wider public benefits'.[26] An emergency meeting of the Isle of Eigg Heritage Trust directors refused to consider the option of decreasing the participation of the islanders in the partnership to increase the role played by the conservation body. In the light of that decision, the Heritage Lottery Fund answered that the application would be reconsidered at their next meeting.

Time was now running out. 'It got quite tactical at one point. We didn't want any other potential buyer to know through the press how much we had. Secrecy was absolutely essential', recalls Maggie Fyffe. Constantly at the front line of the appeal, she had developed a natural talent for diplomacy which kept the media curiosity satisfied with the details of the day-to-day running of the campaign whilst coping with frantic faxes and phone calls in the background as a mystery donor was offering a very substantial pledge to the islanders' fund. On Thursday 28 November, the islanders had £1.2 million on the table.[27]

Three days later, the selling agents, Knight and Frank, announced that none of the offers had proved acceptable, but that 'Mr Maruma agreed to leave the island on the market to enable those who offered and anybody who might also wish to do so more time to raise the necessary funds to meet the asking price of £2 million'.[28] This created a furore in opposition circles. The islanders' offer was based on professional valuation and represented the actual market price of the island. That their bid was rejected because it failed to reach the asking price – to everyone's agreement a vastly inflated amount – stressed once again the speculative nature of the land market in Scotland. Nowhere else in Europe was the land market so unrestricted and so open to abuse. Calls for compulsory purchase to protect regional investments on the island came from Labour quarters. Scottish Nationalists demanded a land commission to be created on the Irish model which would assess the overall suitability of potential landowners. For the second time, the Eigg question was brought up in Parliament.

On the island, inevitable disappointment was mitigated by the huge relief of finding out that there were few contenders for the ownership of Eigg. The only other serious offer – by a wealthy English farmer – compared with theirs and had been equally turned down. Their greatest fear had been that some investor amongst Farhad Vladi's international clientele would outbid them. 'Buying islands makes such good business sense, their value can only rise', claimed Vladi, who widely advertised Scottish islands as 'the Van Goghs' among the 120 personally inspected islands on his books. 'There is a sense of romance in buying islands . . . It is the ultimate purchase you can make, a complete miniature world of which you can be king', underlined the German estate agent who had already shown the island to an American conservation consortium flown in by helicopter.[29]

The most bizarre twist in the whole Maruma story happened just as the islanders prepared to mount a second bid. A German consultant, Dr Kals, approached the Highland Council in January 1997, claiming to represent Pavarotti, the great Italian tenor, whose foundation was interested in building a European centre of excellence for 3,000 classical music students on Eigg. Highland Council officials nearly fell off their seats but diplomatically pointed out that lack of facilities on Eigg might prove an obstacle, as was the fact that the islanders were trying to buy the island themselves. Reporting the story with relish, the press announced Vladi's news that Maruma and Pavarotti had met to discuss the project and that he no longer thought the island up for sale, even though 'the deadline had been extended a few times and the islanders had been given a fair chance.'[30]

These incredible reports highlighted the absurdity of the situation on Eigg in the immediate aftermath of the final decision by the Heritage Lottery Fund to refuse its help. It announced flatly that not only had the Isle of Eigg Heritage Trust not reviewed its position, but 'furthermore' there was already enough money raised to allow an offer to be made 'at around the amount which the District valuer suggests is the open market value for the island'.[31] To many people, it seemed an easy way out. 'You get the impression the lottery are under huge pressures behind the scenes from certain establishment figures not to give money as it might set a dangerous precedent in landownership patterns in Scotland', declared Peter Peacock, the Highland Council convener. 'The National Memorial Heritage Fund is completely out of touch with the overwhelming wish of the public,' added Dr Foxley, 'and they have lost a marvellous opportunity to show the public that the little guy can also benefit from Lottery funding.'[32] 'If the little guy asks for something, it's a hand-out,' echoed Maggie Fyffe wryly, 'but when it's the big guy, it's a subsidy, a set-aside, or a tax exemption. We'll just have to battle on with the fund-raising.'

She was totally confident that the partnership was in the strongest position to increase their bid with the help of their mystery donor – a woman from northern England who wished to remain anonymous – and the money which continued to come in as people reacted to the lottery let-down. 'We'll get there in the end', she would say confidently, remaining undaunted despite each setback. Like her or Karen Helliwell, the IERA's dedicated secretary, all the women on the island seemed to have an unending amount of energy to pour into the island. Eilean nam Ban Mora – the Island of the Big Women – lived up to its name. Like women the world over, they had a strong sense of continuity and purpose. Many were incomers, but, to them, Eigg was no escapism or Utopia. They knew that living on a small island was not without its drawbacks. It meant accepting parting with one's children at an early age, coming to terms with the lack of privacy of island life, finding the resources to escape tensions or the ennui of repetition. It meant a higher cost of living for fewer services and fewer opportunities whilst coping with the sheer effort of living in a remote area and an unforgiving climate. But it was the life they had chosen and they wanted to defend it for the sake of future generations.

For the island women it was the well-being and the livelihood of people which was at stake. For a group of people in Germany who had never been interested in finding out who they were, Eigg was just 'a place where you could make a development profit as you would anywhere else in the world'.[33] So Dr Kals disclosed in the light of the Lottery statement with its terse reminder about the island's market value. It now turned out that he actually represented one investor out of a group of five Germans who had apparently been led to put up over £2 million towards the purchase price of Eigg and development costs on Maruma's word and without ever seeing the island. From the consultant's own admission, it appeared that the Pavarotti Foundation proposal – with which the singer denied any association whatsoever – had been made to push up the price of the island, ensuring profits and enabling Maruma to pay back his loans. The official valuation of Eigg at £1.2 million left the German investors faced with negative equity and heavy losses if they could not find a way to be reimbursed.[34]

These sudden revelations came as no surprise to the islanders. They only confirmed their suspicions that 'the whole thing had been a scam from the beginning', as Colin Carr put it. To confuse things further, a Luxembourg company with extensive European leisure interests, the

Compagnie de Participation Financière, was now entering the fray, claiming to have plans for a holiday complex which could bring in forty or sixty jobs – and profits to themselves, they bluntly explained.[35] Meanwhile, journalists had also established that the English farmer – whose Surrey-based private bank had gone into administration three years earlier owing over £10 million – had not given up hopes of putting in another bid. Anxious to keep the upper hand in this atmosphere of uncertainty, the Isle of Eigg Heritage Trust placed its revised bid on 6 March 1997, announcing the news in a press release.

On the other side of the world, another of Maruma's creditors – a Hong Kong-based German clothing exporter – decided to act. On 13 March, Hans Rainer Erhardt was granted a decree in Fort William Sheriff Court in respect of the default of Eigg Island Ltd in repaying the £300,000 loan he had made to Maruma on the day Eigg was purchased. It meant that Erhardt held a first-ranking Standard Security on the island and that he could now order the sale of Eigg within twenty-eight days of placing advertisements in the local and national press.[36] 'This was the hardest moment of all', recalled Maggie Fyffe. 'We knew that Erhardt had expressed an interest in our bid, but there was always the risk of a higher bid or that Maruma would pay off his loan! I think it was my three-year-old grandson who kept me sane during the last stage of the negotiations. The phone never stopped ringing, but whenever it would get too much, we'd send him to answer it!'

THE END OF THE LAIRD'S RULE

On Friday 4 April, after a week of nail-biting suspense for the Trust directors, Mr Erhardt's solicitors accepted their offer of £1.5 million. For Colin Carr, who had been waiting all day in Edinburgh with Nick Reiter from the Highland Council and Simon Fraser, the partnership's lawyer, it was pure elation, a moment to savour for ever: 'We cracked it!' On Eigg, birthday celebrations for young Ruairidh Kirk took an emotional turn as the islanders embraced each other, stunned and ecstatic that the day they had dreamt about for so long had finally arrived. 'Well done', commented Katie MacKinnon. 'I want a golden crown', laughed her husband Dougald. As for Maggie Fyffe's grandson, he was greatly puzzled to hear her on the radio whilst he could see her on the phone. 'It is a great day,' declared Maggie with emotion, 'not only for Eigg, but for all communities who live under a landlord's whim. It shows that people in the Highlands and Islands are no longer prepared to be bought and sold like cutlery for their master's table.' 'This is a truly remarkable achievement,' echoed Peter Peacock, the Highland Council convener, 'starkly demonstrating the public's wish to see major reform in the pattern of landownership in Scotland.'[37] The news made the front page of national newspapers and was announced in the local, national and international media, making it to the main news in Australia that day! Congratulation messages and cards flooded in. People who had contributed to the appeal wrote to tell how much this victory of the common man had cheered them up. Politicians spoke of an astonishing victory through people's power.

The other significant victory was to have conquered the doubts which emerged from time to time within the community about the possibility of self-management, particularly from the older members of the community. Self-confidence does not come easily to people who have been told for generations that they could not manage alone without a factor, that there was no future on the islands. 'Too much pessimism doesn't get you anywhere', Angus MacKinnon kept repeating throughout the campaign which he supported with all his heart and soul. Angus, a twelfth-

191

generation islander, knew that some things were gone forever, but he acknowledged that as long as there were people ready to follow or adopt his culture, it would survive in one way or another. Culture, by definition an adaptive mechanism, could not be static. It had undergone countless changes throughout its history, but, over the last dozen years, the Gaelic renaissance had spearheaded a new awareness of roots, culture and traditions. The islanders of Eigg, those who were born there and those who came to live there, intended to carry on playing their part in that renaissance. 'Music and song, laddie, you must have that in you, or the island will lose its soul', said Angus. 'The songs of the fiddle are on every tide, mixing peoples and cultures', Donnie Campbell, the last of the Eigg MacKays, had written in one of his poems.[38] Celebrations to commemorate 12 June, when the island would officially be handed over to the Isle of Eigg Heritage Trust, had to illustrate that in a big way.

Feverish preparations were under way as the date approached. Pier buildings and the hall were brightened up with a new coat of paint. The pier cafe re-opened, taken in hand by two 19-year-old island girls. Vast quantities of food were cooked as the handover day was expected to bring more people to the island than it had seen in a century. And, of course, all hands were on deck to unload the necessary wherewithal for the bar, a huge and memorable tractor-load of crates which included ninety bottles of twenty-five-year-old malt generously provided by Talisker distillery on Skye, founded 150 years ago by the MacAskill brothers from Eigg. To give a lasting symbol of the momentous change in the island's history, the islanders also decided to move the 10ft stone pillar which had lain almost forgotten, save by Dougald MacKinnon, near Sandavore Farm, and erect it on Pier Hill, next to the bronze plaque commemorating the buy-out. The Sgurr pillar – sixty-two million years old – which had presided over island gatherings 5,000 years ago now became *Clach na Daoine*, the stone of the people. In time-honoured tradition, a huge bonfire was lit on the eve of the big day, the orange glow seen from the mainland signalling the end of private landlordism on Eigg.

The new dawn for Eigg started in a cold and misty drizzle but spirits were high as the islanders converged on the pier to welcome over 300 guests. As everyone gathered round the stone in the early afternoon, Dolly Ferguson and Dougald MacKinnon, the two oldest residents of Eigg, unveiled the plaque amidst cheering, clapping, clicking of cameras and blessings by the parish clerics. A piper in full regalia marched the jubilant crowd to the marquee erected on the site of Schellenberg's former tennis court. 'Game, set and match to the islanders', applauded Brian Wilson, the new Minister for the Highlands and Islands. As a long-standing champion of land reform, he had come to share this moment of living history with fellow MPs Calum MacDonald and Charles Kennedy, and a great number of councillors, council officials and friends from all over the Highlands. 'It is always better to light a candle than curse the darkness,' Brian Wilson declared, quoting a Gaelic proverb, 'and Eigg has lit a candle that would ignite a hundred more in the coming years.'[39] As speakers succeeded one another, Maggie Fyffe paying tribute to the thousands of people who had made it all possible, including the island's anonymous benefactress, the island children closed the ceremony with a traditional Gaelic song from Eigg, which Angus MacKinnon, whose grandmother had sung it to Mrs Kennedy-Fraser, had taken great pride in teaching them. This was a day which Professor Christopher Smout, the Historiographer Royal, had felt worthy of attending. The ceilidh which followed was truly amazing. There were more traditional musicians on Eigg that night than anyone had ever thought possible. As the Talisker flowed in countless toasts, the islanders, their friends and supporters danced until the small hours of the morning. The next evening they celebrated again, with a ceilidh improvised in the Fyffes' house, and the next night again, in true Hebridean tradition. 'It was the biggest party ever', Maggie sighed with contentment.

As 12 June became history, the first official steps were taken towards a land reform which the long saga of Eigg had helped to turn into a popular cause. Within a few months, plans were announced for a sweeping review of land tenure to usher in early land-reform legislation in the new millennium.[40] Like Assynt, Eigg had become a landmark in the struggle for communities to free the land they lived and worked on. The challenge now awaiting the islanders was to manage the island for posterity as well as for the good of the community. The road ahead undoubtedly had its difficulties: the buy-out was only the end of the beginning, as Allan MacRae had wisely pointed out at the handover ceremony. Yet, at long last, the people of Eigg could look to the future with a new confidence. For the first time in their recorded history, they held it in their hands.

Watch out: Community management Tiger!

Chapter 14

GRASPING THE TIGER BY THE TAIL

A PIN-STRIPED SUIT FOR EIGG?

Almost a decade after the buy-out, life on Eigg under the Old Regime is already difficult to recall, life without the trust almost impossible to imagine. The Isle of Eigg Heritage Trust, which seemed at first an incredibly radical organisation giving equal power to a bunch of stubborn islanders alongside respectable Highland councillors and established conservationists, has turned into a suitable model for replication, inspiring others to follow suit. When the islanders of Gigha looked into buying their island, put on the market for £4.25 million in 2001, the deciding factor in taking on the daunting challenge was a visit to Eigg. 'We thought, if they can do it, so can we,' said Willie MacSporran, the chairman of the Isle of Gigha Heritage Trust.[1]

In 1997, the purchase of Eigg had signalled the start of a significant shift in status for community ownership. Three years later, the islanders' contribution to the millennium year was to organize their own forum or community ownership as part of the consultation process leading to the land reform proposals events Eigg and Assynt had contributed to put on the table. By 2001, the community right-to-buy had made it to the statute book, with the passing of the Land Reform (Scotland) Act:[2] after 18 years of Conservative rule, Labour was bringing about political reform in Scotland to alter the framework of land tenure, encourage a greater role for communities and change the balance of power in rural development. The focus of policy was firmly on protecting community interest and fostering empowerment. Backed by such political will, a special lottery fund – the Scottish Land Fund – was made available for community land purchases: Gigha was awarded £2.5 million, even though the islanders still had to raise £1 million by themselves.[3] Looking back on this, the Eigg buy-out campaigners reflected how times had changed, since it was their insistence on an equal say for community and conservationists within the trust which had denied them access to the National Memorial Heritage Fund, the public purse providing only 1.2 per cent of the final purchase price (£17,517).[4] That the rules were now changing vindicated the validity of their position. It was equally heartening for them to hear the Community Land Unit publicly acknowledging in its 2004 report that 'the Isle of Eigg Heritage Trust has amply repaid the trust which thousands of well-wishers and donors vested in it.'[5]

For Scotland's radical thinkers, the process of change brought about by the Act was not likely to have a huge impact on the vast tracts of land still under private landownership in Scotland, yet alongside Gigha, another 60 communities throughout Scotland have availed themselves of the right to buy their land since the passing of the act.[6] Not only was the movement spreading beyond the Highlands to the Lowlands, it now appeared that there was a growing commitment to enable greater community ownership and asset management throughout the UK as a whole and not just in Scotland. A team of civil servants, community and voluntary sectors representatives is at present exploring if the community right-to-buy could be successfully be applied to rural and even urban areas of England.[7]

What a change in attitudes and values in the space of ten years! Eigg could congratulate itself for its contribution, its 'steady achievements ably demonstrat[ing] how small communities had the potential to control and manage their own destiny'.[8] Had the islanders succeeded in putting on the pin-striped suit which many thought they would have to wear to gain respectability? Maggie Fyffe thinks otherwise: 'Eigg is not about pin-striped suits. Eigg is about finding another way to look at estate management, away from that kind of thing.' Just an ordinary islander's get-up then, brand new perhaps, but now comfortably moulded to shape.

BUILDING ON THE RUBBLE.

Yet the island's growth in independence and confidence was not achieved without struggles. The islanders bravely grasped the tiger of community management by the tail, not quite sure of what lay ahead, but knowing that they had one thing to prove: that they could do it better than those before them. Many thousands of voluntary unpaid hours – especially on the part of the community directors – went into meeting this challenge, but they did not care, they were 'paid in the economy of Aspiration, minted as Community Achievements',[9] as the chairman of Laggan Forestry Trust – another community trust – elegantly phrased it.

Much of the early work was taken up with property surveys, sorting out insurances, tax issues, financial systems and responsibilities. Getting to grips with these formalities and legal issues was difficult and tedious. For the first three very intense years, board meetings were held every six weeks and initial board meetings would sometimes take 12 hours to sort out the issues. 'It was not unusual to be in a meeting from 5pm to 11pm solid,' remembers Colin Carr.

The first major challenge was the Pier Project. HIE had granted the newly created trust £100,000 of their special funds to build new facilities at the pier on one condition: the building had to be roofed by the spring, with all the difficulties inherent to work in harsh Hebridean winter conditions. It was not so much the building itself but how to find a way to deliver the kind of modern facilities which everyone now expected despite the lack of permanent electricity supply! Fridges, freezers, lights, electric tills on one generator? The solution was to update the old 1920s hydro-electric dam at the Lodge and couple the water-turbine to an inverter and batteries system with a back-up generator. The feeling of satisfaction on opening An Laimhrig, the new pier complex, on 12 June 1998 – the first anniversary of the buy-out – was tangible: here was the first concrete proof that community management could make a difference! Islanders and visitors alike loved it. It was such a fantastic new experience to

195

sit in a spacious, warm, comfortable, rat-free tea-room, looking at the view over Ardnamuchan, or sip a cold beer outside the well-appointed shop, which now sold ice-creams, much to the island children's delight. An Laimhrig soon became the new social focus for the community, especially the younger folk.

The first priorities were the leases, as security of tenure had been so high on the agenda: 'I don't think I ever underestimated the difficulties we faced,' said Karen Helliwell, 'but I am not sure I could have imagined the stress caused by 18 months of intense efforts to sort leases: it was not nearly as straightforward as it looked.' Within a legal system geared to benefit the landlord system, leases off the shelf had to be adapted to suit the new not-for-profit landownership. Once again, the islanders turned to Simon Fraser, the Stornoway lawyer who had been the architect of the trust's structure. (His help as chairman of the trust for two consecutive terms of office was to prove invaluable in many ways.) Fixing the rents was much easier: the valuation was done by a land agent, but the trust substantially lowered the rents to Housing Association levels which people on the island could afford.

At first an executive Group and three more sub-groups were created to tackle all the issues relating to property, farms and woodlands, and the pier project. It did make it a bit easier to square the concept of a voluntary community administration with the requirements of managing a business with a turnover running into hundreds of thousands of pounds. But the pier project made it obvious that complex funding procedures demanding onerous monitoring, required the help of paid staff to share the workload and avoid total burn-out for directors. These people had to juggle their jobs and family commitments and a voluntary role in which they were expected to perform like any management team, being responsible for the running of the company and liable for its legal duties and financial undertakings, all these being very costly in terms of working time. However, there was such a level of activity in the first couple of years that Jacqueline MacDonnell, the young Mallaig graduate appointed as project officer in late 1997, ended up spending too much of her valuable time in administrative tasks. The Community Land Unit responded by awarding funds to create an Administrative Support Assistant post in June 1999 to help to alleviate some of the voluntary time burden and increase local skills. Maggie Fyffe, who until then had worked countless unpaid hours, was the successful candidate: in the space of only a few years, she had graduated from coping with the accounts of her kitchen-counter craftshop to navigating the intricacies of financial software. 'I like seeing all the columns adding up. It gives me a great feeling of satisfaction,' chuckles Maggie, whilst admitting that managing cashflows and start-up costs had been a challenging and at times frightening task.

Housing was the most pressing issue for the majority of people on Eigg: out of the eight tenanted houses now owned by the trust, only one was of tolerable standard. To tackle dereliction in the housing stock, the trust used a number of tactics, the partnership with the council proving very useful in bringing local expertise. Through applying to the local enterprise company and by bringing on board Lochaber Housing Association, the Highland Council and Communities Scotland, 75 per cent grant assistance was accessed from 2000 onwards to renovate four houses for sitting tenants, whilst two more houses were let on secure lease for tenants to carry out their own renovations.[10] The obvious way forward was now for Eigg to have its own building company. The idea was that it could be set up as a trust subsidiary. The trust's legal and financial team set out to work out how this could fit in the overall structure of a charitable trust, which as such was not permitted to trade. 'The trust as an umbrella organisation, a number of subsidiary companies to trade, hold property or carry out renovations with any profits from each company reverting to the trust, this is the best system you can have,' explains Graeme Scott, the radical accountant who helped setting up the subsidiaries. The first was Eigg Construction Ltd, next was Eigg Trading Ltd, the body owning and running the newly built Pier Centre. Eigg Tea-rooms Ltd managed the facilities within as a community business, alongside private enterprises like the Eigg shop and post-office and Eigg Craftshop Ltd, the small craft production and retail cooperative set up by a group of island women.

Expectations were at first that the National Heritage Memorial Fund would help out with a programme of renovation for the island's many historic buildings. In spite of rampant dry rot, the Lodge, for instance, was still perceived as an asset rather than a liability, but funds were required to stabilize the building, as well as doing up all the other principal buildings on the island. Accordingly the trust started out working on an environmental conservation project totalling two-thirds of the purchase price of the island and using the purchase price of the island as sunk funds. However, it soon became obvious that such a project was too ambitious and difficult to administrate and that the way forward was to slice it up in manageable phases and separate funding sources. It was finally decided that the trust would pursue funding for the buildings whilst its conservation partner, the SWT, would apply for environment conservation funds. Bringing community, conservation and local government interests together, the trust's partner-ship approach was coming into its own.

Today the policy on housing has evolved considerably. Pragmatism has dictated that rather than allowing houses for which funding was not identified go further into disrepair, it was better to sell them or rent them on long leases, like Galmisdale, Hulin or Sandavore. At present, the trust is devising a strategy to make plots of lands available. 'We have yet to finalise how it will work,' explains Kenneth Kean. 'Some plots might get held back for young people who want to build houses on the island. We may also pick a couple of plots and sell them on the open market to finance other projects.'[11] With an ever-growing number of properties used as holiday homes in the Highlands, the community has understandable concerns about land speculation: introducing claw-back clauses as burdens on the land for sale is presently considered. Shared equity and shared ownership are also being looked at as ways of providing affordable housing. The result is that today people living on Eigg are secure in the knowledge that they can access a Housing Association house, build their own, or get rented accommodation on the island in one of the trust's houses, according to a point system devised by the community itself which privileges the young, the skilled and the returning islanders. In all these ways, Eigg is making a meaningful contribution to the emerging *social* and *ownership* sector.

During most of 1998, the directors and the community found much of their time taken up with discussions about the new pier: the islanders were finding out that Caledonian MacBrayne officials and Highland Council were extremely difficult to deal with, trying to impose a terminal for a ferry which was built far larger than demand had expected. They had to be very assertive in sticking to their vision in order to avoid being pushed into making unsuitable decisions. As in many other cases, the support of their Highland Council directors proved crucial when they emphatically refused a pier on Castle Island, or to see one of only two Arctic Tern breeding grounds destroyed, proposing instead the compromise of a causeway to the deep-water skerries favoured by Caledonian MacBrayne. This thrawn attitude was repaid with the best deal in the whole of the Small Isles in terms of facilities and equipment as the Scottish Executive dispatched its representatives to the negociating table. Harbour orders for the new pier went in by May 1999, whilst in a visit to Eigg, Donald Dewar, the late First Minister, showed enviable honesty in admitting that the main consideration for the new ferry had had less to do with the Small Isles than a winter link-span for the Mallaig–Skye route.

As all sorts of new skills were being learned – negotiation, management, legal, bureaucratic, administrative, financial – the result was that over the first three years, £200,000 in grant aid[12] was won over, and eight years into the buy-out, a total of £440,000 has been actually invested in housing renovation – some very significant achievements. However, because community ownership of Eigg had resulted in considerable media attention, both positive and negative, these successes were often the butt of recurrent criticism. Why was the fledgling trust incapable of relying on self-generated income: why did it have to rely on public monies? asked the press. The reason was so simple that it often eluded the critics: Eigg was starting from such a low ebb in terms of the local economy and infrastructure, that it would have been impossible to achieve impacts and maintain momentum if it had relied on existing self-generated income provided in the form of rent (and in view of the economic situation on the island) of a limited amount.[13] What was frustrating was that Eigg was demonstrating exactly the high degree of skill which land reformists had predicted empowered communities would acquire to access grant sources open to any community group doing the groundwork in terms of local consultation, planning, costings and submission of applications. 'This type of source existed because communities themselves had fought for this type of provision and people working in the UK development industry had gradually recognised the strong impacts pound for pound which could be achieved via this type of funding at 'grassroots' level,' remarked Issie MacPhail from Assynt.[14] There was undue pressure on community land owners to 'prove themselves' and avoid 'seeking charity'. 'You always have to be whiter than white. How many private organisations have to go through this type of scrutiny?' questioned Maggie Fyffe. Setting up the Friends of Eigg scheme, with its regular newsletter, and the Eigg website contributed much to the badly needed positive marketing and image change. This greatly assisted with project funding and policy initiatives.

The problem with Eigg was that this fledgling trust was breaking even, when many private estate owners claimed it was impossible to run Highland estates without large fortunes to keep them going. Within a debate largely pictured as a struggle of people against privilege, the success of Eigg was causing considerable discomfort in the landowners' camp. It was therefore not that surprising that in the run-up to the passing of the Land Reform legislation, hostile pressure groups tried their hardest to manipulate the media to discredit Eigg since it was one of the highest profile community buy-outs. Unsurprisingly, much of this hostile coverage was found to be coming from friends and associates of Eigg's former owner, Keith Schellenberg. Unfortunately for their cause, and true to character, Keith Schellenberg attempted in 1999 to sue *The Guardian* newspaper under the ludicrous allegation that the Eigg buy-out was a direct result of the paper's biased reporting. The man had bitten more than he could chew: the newspaper took very seriously this arrogant attempt to silence free speech and mustered such a heavy panel of witnesses, including a good number of islanders, that Schellenberg was forced to settle out of court in order to save what was left of his money and dignity. Cheers went up on the island at this news, which firmly relegated the 'Eigg version of Toad of Toad Hall'[15] to a page of history turned long ago.

TACKLING DECADES OF ENVIRONMENTAL NEGLECT

In the meantime, the islanders had more important things to deal with: care and restoration of the environment had been at the core of the buy-out campaign, and from day one, delivering environmental benefits through good conservation practice had been a key objective. The SWT was now taking the lead among conservation bodies in Scotland by working closely with the trust and the islanders themselves to integrate a conservation policy into the general fabric of the island. It was a unique situation among conservation bodies, as the SWT did not actually own or lease any specific areas or reserves on Eigg.

Regeneration of native woodlands and forestry management on the island, were high on the agenda. One of the first issues to be tackled was the problem of uncontrolled grazings: effective stock fencing was almost non-existent and sheep and cattle had virtually unrestricted access, overgrazing botanically rich areas and coastal heaths and inhibiting natural regeneration in the woodlands. Other obvious problems included the general state of many of the woods and a general deterioration of many of the access tracks. Re-stocking Sandavore Farm was essential to bring back the land into good shape. Restoration of the SSSI-listed Blar Dubh Bog, damaged by conifer plantation under Schellenberg, was also an important aim.

'The first step in remedying the situation was to produce a detailed management plan, which had as its broad aims improvements to the natural environment, improved access for visitors and where possible, the creation of local jobs,' explains John Chester.[16] The next step was for the SWT to apply to the Forestry Authority and Millennium Forest Scotland. For the islanders, this meant badly needed jobs, as well as training and machinery they could never have dreamt of accessing themselves. Woodland work being mostly carried out in winter, it was ideally suited to complement crofting activities, and for the six local men who made up the forestry team, this was an income they could now depend on for the next few years.

Miles of stock-proof fencing around the woodlands, conifer clearance at the Blar Dubh bog, Rhododendron control in the 'policy' woods, the creation of wood-chips paths and viewpoints – all this work received a 'highly recommended' certificate from the judges of the 'Scotland's Finest Woodland' competition, at the end of the Millennium forest project in 2001.

Accessing funding was the key to success for conservation, as much as every other aspect of island development. The case for environmental improvements on Eigg was successfully presented as part of the SWT's blanket Heritage Lottery Fund bid in 2001. Another major part of the conservation plan was thus allowed to proceed: ongoing survey, monitoring and species protection, restructuring of the forestry plantations, upland stock fencing, drystane wall repairs and path improvements, most of this again providing much needed local employment and training opportunities.

'At the most basic level, the trust's ownership of the island has allowed wildlife conservation work to graduate, from the merely theoretical to a practical level,' explains John Chester, 'where previously, any management undertaken was by informal agreement only, and extremely limited in scope . . . Through being an active partner of the trust, the SWT is now in the position where it can enter into agreements with the community, in all aspects of land use and management.'[17]

The result is a woodland vastly richer from a bio-diversity point of view, reflects John. 'Hen-harriers bred there for the first time in 2003. Woodland bird species that are nationally declining, such as bullfinches, have seen their number increased on the island. Dragonflies and butterflies are more abundant and we also have the scarce large heath butterflies.' Planting local species – rowan, birch, goat willow – has also given natural regeneration a bit of help. 'I like to think that the children on the island will remember one day how this wood came about,' muses John as he carefully hacks down the bracken preventing the young trees from growing. 'The only problem is bracken; it is on the advance everywhere, not just here, it's to do with the climate change . . .'

FIGHTING DECLINE: ENVIRONMENT-FRIENDLY AGRICULTURE

An important part of the conservation management work on the island was made possible by Sandavore Farm being accepted into the Countryside Premium Scheme. Jumping at the chance of coming back to his native island, Duncan Ferguson had taken over Sandavore farm in a partnership agreement with the trust and put all his energies in trying to put the badly neglected farm in good order, re-stocking it with 500 breeding ewes and 24 cows with followers to graze the hill ground. With heather waist-high in places, extensive controlled heather burning was carried out and Duncan is now working towards a higher ratio of cattle to sheep. 'Duncan is exceptionally good at his job,' remarks Mark Foxwell, one of the SWT directors on the trust board. 'What he has done to put the land back in good heart is remarkable, and the stock he has built up is in top condition.' By allowing more stock fencing to be erected and grazing controls implemented over several areas of botanically rich heathland, much to the benefit of several orchid species, the CPS certainly provided the kind of habitat management that would otherwise not have been viable in the present agricultural climate, particularly with the CAP reform hitting the Highlands and Islands. 'Farming is so hard today that to survive, you must be able to get every environment subsidy that's going, other wise you'll go under.' For Duncan, the difficulties are compounded by what he perceives to be the Isle of Eigg Heritage Trust's main weakness: a lack of initiative in tackling economic growth in general, and agriculture in particular. 'Since we have taken over Sandavore Farm, there has been BSE, Foot-and-Mouth and the £10 lamb. There is an urgent need for forward thinking and capital investment in the old farm buildings, which may have been good when my father was farming 80 years ago, but are unsuitable for today's farming methods. The poor fabric of some of the buildings adds a lot of pressure to the job. There has to be a long term strategy for the agriculture on the island.'

For Duncan, given that the national average age for farmers is 59, part of that long-term strategy should be to encourage younger folk into farming, by making it a more attractive opportunity than it is at present. For 26-year-old George Carr, coming back to Eigg in 1998 after agricultural college, getting his own farm was a start. There was no stock at all on the farm when George approached the trust about taking on the land his grandmother Peggy had held since the Runcimans' time. To make it more viable today, he felt that it needed more hill ground, and proposed taking the farm back to its 1800 boundaries. After a few months' discussion, the area was finalised, and a limited partnership was drawn up between George and the trust. 'Farming is a good way of life, but there is not much money in it just now. I'd love to get on and do stuff, but I have to prioritise. I can't afford to do up the steadings right now. It is good to do all that re-seeding and the infrastructure has improved quite a bit, with a lot of new fencing. I am now down to 100 ewes and 14 cattle, because it is easier to manage, and you've got to wait and see which way it will go. For example, there is no money in sheep at all at present. It's all agri-environment schemes now, so that's why I am involved in two concurrent schemes as part of the Rural Stewartship Scheme.'

The latest environmental scheme on the block, the RSS, is complicated but ultimately rewarding. This Europe-funded scheme is administered by the Farming and Wildlife Advisory Group (FWAG), a voluntary group set up as a charity to facilitate access to such grants. 'FWAG makes your application for you and charges a not inconsiderable amount of money for doing so, but it does save quite a lot of time and effort because the grant applications are incredibly complex, requiring an environment audit and an archaeological survey in the first place,' 'explains Neil Robertson, Eigg Crofters' Grazings Clerk. 'Grants are now more and more environment based and less production based: the aim is to diversify. For instance, last year, I grew oats and kale instead of just doing hay to feed the cattle, and I got money to do that, which was nice. That's what they call extensive cropping. I also left the fields as stubble fields over the winter to encourage wild birds. It's really a return to traditional practices, and it encourages people to look at the land slightly differently . . . If you are environmentally minded, it pays you some of the best grants to do what you would probably want to do in the first place. Take my bottom field for example, it's so boggy that every year, I've had to haul the tractor or the baler out after they sank up to their axles, all that trouble for a return of £150! Now I am getting a management grant of £150 for that field, which means that instead of trying to grow hay in a bog, I can now have ponds there and I can get on with some more productive work elsewhere!'

Encouraging wild birds and bio-diversity is the name of the game for crofting as well as farming; thus encouraging corncrake-friendly habitat has now become a high priority. Croftland was already pretty good for corncrakes, those noisy birds whose peculiar call had kept generations of crofters from the sleep they deserved, but other areas on the islands were not so good. An independent scheme was set up in association with the CPS work to encourage corncrake-friendly management of hayfields and introduce a suitable environment. Much to the amusement of the older crofters, squads of SWT volunteers were drafted in to plant specially fenced areas at Kildonnan, Sandavore and Galmisdale with flag iris and nettles to provide the birds with early cover. The result is that once again, the corncrake's call is part of the summer night on Eigg.

With such new sources of income, crofting on Eigg has now taken a turn for the better, with an encouraging increase in the number of islanders engaged in that activity. The main factor in this improvement has been the re-organisation of crofting which was carried out in 2004 through the Crofters' Commission. The idea for the re-organisation came about as the Eigg crofters were trying to sort out the problems of absenteeism and unused land. The situation was dire at the time of the buy-out: Cleadale had gone down to five working crofts and only four active crofters capable of doing stock management. 'It was getting increasingly difficult to get a bull for the township.' As they approached the Crofters Commission to sort out the problem of Chapel Croft (that piece of land had never been properly registered as a croft), the commission suggested a complete reorganisation, especially as the crofters had already approached the trust about expanding their common grazings by using land from nearby Hulin farm. 'There was a feeling that crofting was coming from such a low ebb, and with crofters now becoming more active, and the number of livestock going up, reorganisation could improve things by providing more common grazing.' All that was required was a landlord in agreement with the scheme and adjacent land available, both conditions being easy to satisfy with the new ownership regime.

The reorganisation also put pressure on absentees to deal with unused land, by subletting, selling or returning to the island. 'Absentees are a big problem in the crofting system because improvements cost money and if you can't get everyone to contribute, it makes it very difficult for the Common Grazings committee to get things moving.' The whole process took two years to come to fruition: the aim was to bring in new blood, new energies into crofting, and help raise the profile of livestock production. And because it was important that people took part in what was already going on, the four new crofts created out of Hulin farm were attributed on a point system designed to be fair yet with a strong bias towards people with experience in stock handling and towards younger people with families. (The reasoning behind the latter was largely based on the Crofter's Entrance scheme, designed to attract younger people by giving them enhanced grants.) There was about a dozen serious contenders, but far from bringing people from outwith the island, the result of the selection process actually went in favour of four people already living on the island: Angus Kirk, born and bred on the island; Kathleen Smith, Katie and Dougald MacKinnon's granddaughter, who moved back to Eigg, a long cherished dream, and started a family; Gwen Sheriff, a capable young Yorkshire woman who came to Eigg as a volunteer to work on Neil Robertson's croft and wholeheartedly embraced the crofting lifestyle; and Pascal Carr, for whom the croft would contribute to the viability of his small holding at the pier.

The new 'Cleadale and Hulin' township can now rely on a total of 11 crofters. In view of the size of holdings on Eigg, crofters will always need to source work outside agriculture, but it is the combination of new grants, cattle sales and diversification which will allow crofting to survive in the 21st century. With his organic 'Eigg eggs' production and an active use of the WOOFER volunteer[18] scheme to bring his vegetable garden to full production, Neil feels that at last he and his family are getting to be more self-sufficient. The crofting lifestyle is certainly a lot more sustainable than it has been in the last decade. Yet Neil has doubts about the the current free-market ideology expressed in a new Crofting Bill. He too thinks that it may very well lead to the disappearance of crofting in its present form. Farming and crofting may well be 'a way of life' as Colin Carr philosophically puts it, but it seems a way of life that is becoming endangered, just like the species agri-environment grants are trying to protect.

EIGG, A MICROCOSM OF HIGHLAND HISTORY

A chance conversation on Rum between a Royal Commission archeologist interested in 'nailing the Small Isles' and an Eiggach of French origin with a passion for history resulted in an entirely new archaeology survey, part of the SWT major HLF bid in 2000. By its completion in 2002, Eigg could 'reasonably claim to be one the best archaeologically and environmentally audited and surveyed community land initiatives in Scotland'.[19]

Steve Boyle, who led the Royal Commission on the Ancient and Historical Monuments of Scotland team, was impressed with 'the extensive and often spectacular archaeology of the island,' where the team was able to identify and map over 1,150 individual structures. As in Canna, many of which were situated in heather moorland or other rough pasture, well above the limits of post-medieval cultivation, which is why they have survived so well. Much less survives on Muck, where there is very little unimproved or uncultivated ground, or on Rum, where 'locations suitable for settlement have presumably always been restricted to the same few niches around the coast, densely settled and heavily cultivated into the early 19th century'.[20]

The survey did much to fill the gaps in Eigg's early history, as three more Iron Age forts were discovered on the island, two in Grulin and one above Laig, all bearing visible remains of circular house-platforms. High up in the hills, towering over basalt cliffs, the Laig fort in particular occupies a spectacular site overlooking the sound of Rum. For an Iron Age chieftain, it was a visible demonstration of power and a testimony to the large following he would have been able to command sometimes between 700 BC and 500 AD. On the other hand, the stone wall which protects the Sgurr, cutting off the only approach to the summit, led to the enclosed area being re-evaluated as either a temporary refuge or a focal point for Iron Age islanders, perhaps used for gatherings and festivals at particular times of the year. 'It is not difficult to imagine that the dramatic outline of the Sgurr, instantly recognisable for miles around, may have lent it some symbolic importance,' remarked Steve Boyle,[21] much as it still did when 19th-century proprietors ordered bonfires to be lit there! Yet it was another Iron Age prehistoric site which was deemed to be the most impressive of all. 'It stands amongst a jumble of gigantic boulders beneath the cliffs on the north-east coast, in many respects the most remote corner of the island. Here, a substantial platform has been constructed, on top of which there are the remains of a thick-walled circular enclosure. Opening from the interior there is the entrance to a large boulder cave that runs westward beneath the enclosure wall. The main chamber of the cave measures about seven metres in length and there are other, smaller, chambers opening off to either side and at the end. The cave entrance and the sides of the chamber have been modified by the insertion of rough walling, and a thick deposit of midden material covers the floor, including animal bones, shells and broken hammerstones, some of which have a concretion of crushed shell on their points . . . The sense that this has been a "special place" is inescapable. Moreover, it is difficult to argue the case for an ordinary defensive or domestic function for the site. It is evidently a secluded spot, hidden away in the scree, over 400m of difficult terrain separating it from the shore. There are easily accessible shieling-huts and fragments of enclosure walls on grassy terraces close by, but to reach the enclosure involves a tricky scramble and the use of all four limbs. We know next to nothing about Iron Age religious practices in western Scotland, but it is tempting to speculate that this may be some prehistoric "eremitic" site.'[22] If it was such a site, or perhaps an even older site of initiation for rebirth and naming rituals inside the bowels of Mother Earth, it may also have been re-used by more modern islanders as a refuge in times of trouble or a handy shelter at shieling times.

Another discovery has brought yet more speculation. Above the shore at Laig, below the farmhouse, what appeared at first to be field clearance heaps were finally interpreted as a cemetery of at least 15 square cairns, undoubtedly pagan, quite possibly Pictish, certainly rare in the Hebrides, the largest of this kind recorded on the west coast. Was such a cemetery to be associated with the beautiful hunting scene carved on a slab of pink sandstone which was alledgedly found at Kildonnan? The anomalous vertical orientation of the hunting scene had long intrigued specialists, who compared the ringed cross and key patterns in raised relief on the other side with the type of carving associated with the heartland of the Pictish kingdom in Eastern Scotland. It seemed to suggest that originally, the slab had had another use, for a type of shrine structure when the orientation was horizontal. The slab would then have been re-used later on for an upright cross-slab, probably taking advantage of the plain dressed surface which would have been the inside surface of the shrine.[23] Whatever the details of the story, this made it plain that in Dark Ages Scotland, Eigg was in the hands of a secular elite, an important site on the western marches of Pictland, and Laig had long been a place of high status, dominating and guarding the fertile northwest part of the island. It was a reminder that in that mid-first millennium AD, Eigg was very much part of the frontier territory between Pictish and Dalriadic peoples.

Like the small coin of French silver found on the Sgurr, chance discoveries sometimes do much to help explain the mystery of the past, especially if the discoverer is observant enough, like the late Brigg Lancaster.[24] Brigg liked to find things and apart from a copper button from a 19th-century coat in the Massacre cave, he had failed to find a real treasure, but that day in May 2001, when he dug into deep ground behind his house in Galmisdale, he knew that the deep turquoise bead which crumbled between his finger was something extraordinary. More careful digging brought to the surface strange clay pieces, which he recognized straight away as something to do with smelting. As he dug, more clay fragments surfaced. Whatever they were, Brigg knew they would be very old. The discovery was extraordinary enough for the Royal Commission staff to alert the National Museums of Scotland, and an excavation was immediately started in Scotland, there are no more than a handful of sites offering substantial evidence for metalworking. Brigg's hunch was right: he had found the remains of moulds and a crucible used to produce socketed axes, a knife and a pointed tool. The site had been the temporary workshop of a Late Bronze Age smith, probably an itinerant craftsman, either working under chiefly patronage or, more prosaically, serving the needs of the local community.[25] Today, another young newcomer, Karl Harding, with a love of wood, bloodstone and metal work, is nursing the ambition of reproducing knives and daggers, rediscovering old welding techniques.

For some of the islanders, old stock or new stock, such discoveries had the power to make Eigg suddenly come alive, fuelling their imagination and fostering a sense of belonging. As it had been successfully argued throughout the buy-out campaign, Eigg *was* a microcosm of Highland history and deserved to be looked after in the best possible way. The Royal Commission survey had shown how, amongst the monuments of types familiar from other parts of Highland and Hebridean Scotland, 'there are still others which are more unusual, even unique – a reflection, no doubt, of the island's position on the western seaways, which has exposed it to a wide variety of influences throughout prehistoric and historical times'.[26]

The islanders have also started to interpret their history themselves. Painting and refurbishing the old 1940s corrugated-iron shop and post office that had served the islanders so well until the opening of the modern pier centre, provided an opportunity for gathering the flotsam and jetsam of older generations and harnessing the imagination of the island's children to tell the story of Eigg to the public. Another initiative was the setting up of Comunn Eachdraidh Eige, the Isle of Eigg History Society, taking as its symbol the Pictish rider of the hunting scene carved on that intriguing slab of pink sandstone. By systematically collecting island photographs and organizing them in an outstanding collection of over 3,000 photographs, the society has helped to preserve the islanders' past for the present and future generations. As the generation of older islanders who had borne with them the torch of island tradition dwindled away, it became a momentous and timely task.[27]

As soon as images of the island's past were published on the internet, enquiries started to pour from all over, especially America and Canada, about origins and genealogies. Descendants of Eigg people came to visit the land of their ancestors and many moving stories emerged, which, like the discoveries made by the Royal Commission, help to fill a bit of more of the colourful puzzle of Eigg history. Here is Dorothy's story from Canada: 'Our ancestors were Robert McCormick, born in Cleadale in 1760, and Oireg Stuart . . . The family history says that Oireg was of 'royal' blood. But it is very possible that the story was embellished as my people had a highly romanticized view of Highland history: Bonnie Prince Charlie was a hero, the '45's a glorious war fought for noble motives, etc . . . Oireg's family did not approve of the match because his station in life was much lower than hers. So, in 1790, when he decided to go to the new world, her family forbade her to sail with him. Yet by that time they had three children, John aged six, Mary aged three, and Catherine aged one year. According to family tradition, just as the ship was about to sail, Oireg placed Catherine in Robert's arms. She hoped that by doing so, her family would soon consent to her and their two other children joining Robert and Catherine in the New World. But it took years before he was able to fetch Oireg and the children from Scotland . . . It was sometime before 1801, because in that year, she bore Robert another son in Canada. The sad thing is that she died shortly after that, and with such a young child to look after in what were rough circumstances, Robert soon married again. The bride's name was Catherine MacDonald. In 1802, they had their first child and named her Oireg, a name which has remained in the family for generations, although it was anglicized to Harriet. Today, there are still McCormicks in Glengarry County, Ontario, and the place where they first settled is still called Eigg Road.'[28]

Other stories tell of dispersal in the large Lowland cities, in other islands, like this islander who found work as a laundress in Bute and sent word to relatives and friends that there were good opportunities to be had, so that a little Eigg settlement was recreated there. All these tales help foster the sense of belonging for a community whose make-up has changed in the past few years as dramatically as the system of ownership.

MANAGING CHANGE

Visitors who had been coming to Eigg for years frequently commented on the way the new ownership regime had changed the whole feel of the place: to them, it felt as if the island was buzzing with activity. The huge achievement of the buy-out had generated a positive mindset throughout the community with each anniversary celebrating some new progress in the island's infrastructure. 'I hope and pray this community hall will be a symbol which links the past, and the present and the future of this wonderful experiment which you brought into being on the island,' said Ann Schukman, Lord Runciman's grand-daughter, on 12 June 2005 when she came to open the beautifully renovated community hall originally built by her family. She could not help but comment again on how different the island felt, liberated from that feeling of dependency which had been so widespread in the old days.

It was at the level of the community's involvement that the changes were perhaps more tangible: 'Eighteen years ago, when I started as secretary,' reflects Karen Helliwell, 'the Eigg Residents' Association used to meet three or four times a year, and, from one meeting to the next, people would forget all about it. There is now an interest in knowing what is going on, in being involved in the decision-making and making sure the community's voice is heard. The Eigg Residents' Association is now asking for a much larger role.'

It did take a while for the community to reach that stage. Lack of communication was at first a problem between the trust and the community as the board took some time to adjust to a new style after the secrecy which went with the nature of the buy-out campaign. As in Assynt, where initially insufficient or inefficient communication between the small group of people actively involved in the management and the rest of the community had been a problem,[29] the Eigg community directors learnt the hard way that they 'had to bend over backwards to be as open and transparent as possible'.[30] To their bafflement and frustration, they realised that the suspicion towards power-holders, which was once directed at the landowner, now found itself directed at the trust. It was proving a little difficult for some folks to adjust to having their affairs run by their neighbours down the road. 'It was a lot harder than we thought to get people to grasp the idea that this was *their* trust, that they were part of it.'[31] The difficulty was to overcome the suspicion that power was not used for the select few, but for everyone's benefit, an issue that each community land initiative has had to deal with in a culture where the concept of democratic representation is still relatively new.

These were problems which Andrew Binnie, the trust's second project officer, tried his best to address: 'Although the community through the mechanism of the trust had already achieved a great deal, I felt it was important to involve people in the daily work of the Trust and so set up a number of voluntary positions including fundraiser, office assistant and conservation volunteer co-ordinator. This was partly to demonstrate the trust's transparency and openness to new ideas, partly to share the workload which was considerable and partly to build skills and confidence on the island. When I left I recommended that the job title was changed to Development Co-ordinator to emphasize the community's role in the development of the island and get away from the idea of the project officer being some kind of new age factor working for a new age landlord.'

Issuing minutes of the fortnightly meetings held by the community representatives on the trust board, the administration secretary and the project officer also went a long way towards keeping the community in the picture and alleviating fears. Another way of improving the situation was to define the relationship between the trust and the community representative body in a more structured and formal way. The system now in place ensures that the Eigg Residents' Association meets to discuss the trust agenda before each quarterly full board meeting. The issues raised at this meeting are presented to the trust as a series of recommendations to inform any decisions taken by the board.

For Kenneth Kean, who served as ERA chair and trust director, the way the system works is like a triangle. 'The trust is at the top and the community is at the bottom of the triangle. Any of the decisions at the top are always made through the Residents' Association. It can be quite a slow process sometimes, when perhaps a decision has to be taken quite quickly, but it is as democratic as you can get . . . It gives everybody an input, and we have to have a majority for certain types of things, the big sales like the Lodge, that type of things . . . All these decisions go back to the community for approval and it is the people of Eigg who take the decision whether to go forward with it or not.'

The meetings were also meant to ensure that the trust answered the expectations of those living on the island. These expectations were themselves changing. At first, there was an expectation that the trust had to provide direct employment opportunities, much as in the paternalistic regime it had replaced. But it was soon realised that the scope for direct employment opportunities by the trust was limited. It was rather as a facilitator that the trust could best function to help with job creation, providing opportunities and giving the islanders the support necessary to realise these opportunities through the provision of training. From IT to accountancy, from first aid and communications to tourism and forestry skills, capacity-building has been an important part of the trust's strategy.

Today the problem exercising community leaders is that participation at meetings is hard to maintain at the level it was when the islanders embarked on their buy-out campaign. The natural process is often that after getting themselves organised in a cohesive group to respond to a threat, individuals tend to draw back when the crisis is over. But there are also more complex reasons. Centuries of feudal repression do not make way to participative democracy overnight; the cultural reluctance to express one's opinion in a public forum rather that an informal social occasion such as the weekend pub session will take time to change and evolve into a culture of debate,[32] a problem not restricted to Eigg. What it requires is self-confidence (lack of which being the perennial Scottish problem), maintaining a congenial atmosphere where people can feel comfortable in the possibility of expressing a differing opinion, and a good deal of chairmanship skills. When these conditions are lacking, there is a strong risk that those who hold a different opinion feel disaffected and lose their incentive to participate. And when the views of any significant minority are not taken into account, tensions can develop which can become hard to manage. Moreover, participation depends on how much individuals feel that they are stakeholders in the organisation. On Eigg, encouraging the Residents' Association to deal with management decisions rather than taking the final decision away is helping a great deal.

There is also the question of the organisational stage reached by the community, as it goes through adaptation, goal attainment, integration and pattern maintenance. On Eigg the situation is particularly complex because the community is actually experiencing all development stages simultaneously. These are characterised by a strong return of individualism, some fear of change, a feeling that in view of the successes achieved there is no need to invest further, and at the same time a continual drive to move forward. And it does take time for people to make sense of their new reality, to realise the new emerging capabilities. Yet, once confidence is established, it is then that members are increasingly willing to invest their time in the group itself. For Mairi MacKinnon, Eigg's Small Isles Community Councillor and former ERA Chair, the important thing is to remember that 'the community can only go forward at the speed of the slowest cog in the wheel. There has been so many changes in such a short time that we need to give people the time to digest all that is happening! What's needed, really, is on-going training.' What is becoming evident is that 'development is a totality, an integrated cultural process, comprehending values such as natural environment, social relations, education, consumption, production, well-being. Development can only come from within a society which defines its vision and strategy in total sovereignty and has to count first and foremost on its internal strengths.'[33]

Interestingly, one of the difficulties over this process of integration has been an increased complexity in self-imposed procedures. Being used to deal with things informally or on an *ad hoc* basis during the long vacuum of power of the Schellenberg–Maruma era had given the islanders a good grounding in running their own affairs, but in some kind of no-man's land where it was possible to believe that you could escape bureaucratic red tape. This was a feeling of liberty from mainland constrictions which many found appealing. Now they found themselves in a situation where they actually brought bureaucracy upon themselves and they were not quite sure if they liked it. 'The more efficient we try to make this organisation, the more we end up like the mainland,' reflects Karen Helliwell. 'The harder we try, the more we create something that is different from what attracted us in the first place.' The increase in red tape did produce quite a lot of frustration, and in reaction, ways of circumventing it, sometimes quite successfully! To some, this means that the new Eigg lacks a sense of order. 'I find it frustrating to see that if some of us do decide not to do something, we can flaunt the rules . . . If rules and regulation are not being adhered to, when they have democratically been arrived at, what are they worth?' For others, what seems a lack of consistency at times is attributable to the difficulties inherent to island life, which entails a number of survival strategies – not generally goal-oriented. 'To survive in the face of all the obstacles that conspire to make life difficult on an island, there is a tendency to adopt a mañana approach. It's a way of coping with life, of remaining happy instead of hitting your head against a brick wall. In any case it has served people well.'

In common with the rest of the Small Isles, Eigg also has the problems associated with the small size of the community. The potential pool of directors is necessary limited. Finding enough candidates for election as director or office bearer is proving difficult. 'The way the trust is set up, it requires direct community participation,' reflects Pascal Carr, a current trust director. 'If people are not prepared to put in any kind of time, then the trust's structure fails to deliver what it originally proposed to deliver . . . People really don't appreciate that they have to be involved. They have to take responsibility because otherwise the trust will not work. We don't quite know how it is that we are going to do to encourage people to take on these kind of responsibilities. Perhaps, if we were able to attract more people, there would be a bigger number of people from which to choose or who would like to take on those responsibilities.'

Yet one of the successes of the trust was that the island's population has actually increased, or at least maintained itself at a stable level through major changes in its demography, with 18 new inhabitants since the buy-out. The decade 1995–2005 has certainly witnessed a complete reversal in the proportion of indigenous islanders to incomers. 'We were lucky enough to have been on Eigg when the old stock was active, these things have gone on the mainland, we managed to hang on them an extra thirty years, but it is eroding.'[34] Angus MacKinnon, Allie MacDonald, Dougald MacKinnon, Dolly Ferguson, those familiar, venerable or iconic figures in the crofting community have now gone. Morag Campbell, Janet and Sheena MacDonald, their brother Duncan, whom people knew and related to as and identifiable people in the island genealogies, have gone too. To be an indigenous islander today no longer has the same meaning; it means being born of a family residing on the island, and being brought up on Eigg. It no longer necessarily means being related by blood ties to island families.

The islanders' feeling of identity is now bound to the social cohesion achieved through the process which led to the buy-out and sustains it. Much as in the old days, people were politely excluded until it was felt that they had sufficiently 'mucked in', people must signal an interest in the concerns of the community to be fully included. The question of when to allow newcomers the right to vote at residents' meetings was a case in point. It was the subject of much debate, the conclusion being that there had to be a process of adaptation and learning to acquire the 'necessary knowledge' to take part in the decision-making. Incomers can listen and participate, but cannot to vote for the first eighteen months of their life on the island. This is the most formal process by which the community protects itself from a take-over by incomers, especially if they display 'the middle-class values of assertiveness, explicit style of communication and formal methods of decision-making', which are often lacking in island communities, and in the Highlands in general. Such would-be leaders may be called upon to take their turn in serving the community, and often fulfil a valuable role, particularly as they are seen as more 'impartial', but not before the community is satisfied that they have integrated some of the values which they feel are at the core of their cultural make-up. These are the values of mutual aid, neighbourliness and hospitality. As generations of incomers the world over have experienced, putting these into practice helps overriding differences between locals and incomers and reinforces the shared sense of community solidarity.

Through this evolution, boundaries have now changed in the island's socio-cultural space. People who were born and bred there but left to make a living away have not found themselves necessarily automatically included on their return, as the ethnic make-up of the community has become more heterogenous. Social inclusion tends to depend on the attitude to the new ownership. This has a potential for creating a good deal of tension, as feelings of exclusion and discrimination arise, and can created a polarisation of extremes in the community, each becoming suspicious of the other. The only way to strengthen one's sense of identity is then by defining oneself in opposition to the other, through the spread of derogatory gossip (some of which finds its way to a press always hungry for sensational tit-bits) or the exclusion from the social discourse where the stock of knowledge which binds islanders together is elaborated. In this process, roles are established which become almost impossible to change as stories become part of the collective mythology and are bound-up with a sense of identity. This is perhaps one of the burdens of life in small communities which is most difficult to cope with. 'You are part of a tiny community of people, unified on some issues but often divided along different lines on others. Like most of the west of Scotland, the community is made up of people from a wide variety of backgrounds and countries, and expectations vary accordingly.'[35]

What makes it hard for the community to find a satisfying solution for such tensions, is that it remains in the continual gaze of public scrutiny, 'because as part of a nationwide movement towards community land ownership, the Isle of Eigg Heritage Trust is much more than simply the owner of the island. It is the vehicle for the aspirations of the community and their partners the Highland Council and the Scottish Wildlife Trust. As such, it will always have a political and leadership role in how best to effect community land management. It was a clear sense of purpose in gaining control of the land which brought the community together and again it will be a well understood purpose, or vision, for the future development of the island, that will keep the community motivated, dynamic and cohesive.'[36]

TOWARDS A GREENER FUTURE

As well as being a symbol of nationhood, land in Scotland is also a tool of economic and social development.[37] For that reason, land ownership and management will remain central political issues for a long time to come. Yet, rather than the re-awakening of the political drive for reform, it was the pressure from the public demanding more environmental benefits which led to the present system of land management coming under closer scrutiny. The changes witnessed now are really a result of developing environmental awareness. As local communities and conservation groups emerge as significant forces in the land market, the partnership approach which brings conservation and community interests together, as successfully pioneered on Eigg and then in Knoydart, has become an enviable model. Even on Rum, where, after many vicissitudes, community development is now taking place, the mighty SNH appears to have come round to the fact that conservation of the environment is best secured by the maintenance of a viable community structure.[38]

The key to the future for Eigg is therefore to capitalize on this environmental awareness both in the public and on the island itself. The one pressing issue has always been the provision of reliable and cheaper power. Frugality bred out of necessity may have made the average islander a lot more aware of energy issues than most people on the mainland, but for the time being, the islanders still spend a huge amount of their time looking after diesel generators, maintaining private hydro-systems, checking gas levels for converted petrol generators, just to acquire enough power for their daily needs. Grid-type electricity supply is one common fervent wish on the island. It has also been identified as indispensable for the economic well-being of the community. Taking into account the Muck experience where two windmills are contributing to energy needs, and after experimenting with setting up two local hydro-power systems,[39] the trust has taken the lead in commissioning a highly innovative renewable energy system based on 98 per cent renewable power coming from wind, hydro and solar sources and only 2 per cent from diesel in the form of back-up generators.[40] 'If and when hydrogen generation technology becomes more-user friendly, perhaps ten years from now, the back-up generators in the system could be replaced by hydrogen cells, and that would mean an island totally run on green power,' enthuses Ian Leaver, Eigg's third project officer, who masterminded the energy project. With costs of about £1.4 million – still vastly cheaper than bringing a cable from the mainland – this ambitious and far-sighted renewable energy project is mainly funded by Lottery, European and government money. Indeed, for Eigg Electric Ltd to be able to deliver 24-hour power on the 10th anniversary of the trust in 2007, as is scheduled at present, is a tremendously fitting return on all the energy deployed on Eigg since the buy-out!

Apart from green energy, green tourism remains a highly desirable goal, not only for Eigg but also for Muck, Rum and Canna, since it makes economic sense for the Small Isles to market themselves together in their variety and diversity as well as what they have in common – their cultural and environmental dimensions and the determination of their inhabitants to survive against the odds. Their combined strengths may well succeed in overcoming the disadvantages of their remoteness and small populations. Proposals for a regional geopark are on the table, the Small Isles are already part of a National Scenic Area, and Fort William has become the 'Outdoor Capital' of the UK. Opportunities are there to develop tourism in a way which will help sustain economy and population growth. Kildonnan Farm Guest House, entirely renovated in partnership with the trust, serviced by hydro-power, offering good wholesome fare and traditional hospitality, is one of the island businesses which has gone from strength to strength, and as visitor numbers steadily grow, others are following.

In this perspective, organic food production on Eigg is slowly becoming a more viable proposition. Over the last five years, the organic garden Pascal Carr and Catherine Davies have created at Shore Cottage has proved increasingly popular with locals and visitors. 'We just did it bit by bit, each year adding more, making new beds. Four-foot beds for the vegetables so that we don't have to stand on the soil. The first year, after preparing the beds, we double dig them, and every year on, we just add the seaweed and the worms come up and take it down and the soil never has to be dug again. We grow flowers that the birds and the insects like and then they pollinate the vegetables, and they all work together to make a complete system.' So far north, Pascal and Catherine have successfully managed to grow a whole range of Mediterranean vegetables, including aubergines and charantais melons. Selling some of their production to visitors, they found that as well as delivering vegetables with a great deal more flavour than

210

people are used to, their garden actually fulfils an important educational need: 'The tourists come here and ask if we have tomatoes and cucumbers in March or May, out of season. They don't understand seasonal eating anymore. People have lost touch with how things grow, where things come from. When we sell vegetables, we invite people up to see them growing because most people have never seen a cucumber vine. You show people something and they say: "Well, it does look like the one we get in the shop!" . . They just don't understand how long things take to grow or anything about the growth cycle of the food they eat. And so in a way, we try and help educate people by allowing them to see what it is they are eating.' Yet, for Pascal and Catherine to make a living from their growing skills or for Neil Robertson's Eigg eggs business to remain viable, the financial return on organic production needs to improve. The other irony is that the islanders live in an environment where high-quality meat is being produced, yet it is well nigh impossible to consume it locally. In today's global world, as in the days of the kelp boom, communities like Eigg find themselves subordinated to the power of impersonal market forces and of far distant bureaucratic decision-making. The effect is that the range of economic options open to local producers is substantially restricted. However, encouraging signs are that the balance is shifting in favour of locally produced food. Initiatives such as the mobile slaughter-house on Mull are providing replicable and adaptable models. Farmers' markets are now developing on the mainland or larger islands like Skye, yet for peripheral isolated communities such as Eigg, the market will remain frustratingly limited unless consumer numbers grow or freight costs decrease.

Most of all, it is the closeness to nature and the elements in an increasingly urbanised world, and a slower pace of life in its goal-oriented, frenetic pace, which are amongst the finest qualities small islands can offer. As networking between small islands of Europe develops, an island philosophy[41] is emerging, encapsulating the value of slow living, of taking time, of caring for each other, of working with nature and not against her, things which are becoming increasingly attractive to a wide range of people. Thus, as in many other islands, as in other times, a new generation of pilgrims is rediscovering Eigg's attraction as a contemplative sanctuary for the well-being of body and soul. In silence, far from the crowd, on island beaches, 'the narrow ribbon of sand between land and ocean is a perfect place to understand the mind of wisdom',[42] the 'seashore mind' expressed in all its spontaneous joy through the lively mouth music Eigg women sang as they went down to the shore to gather shellfish . . .

> Mac'il leo ro
> Hao ri o huo
> Mac'il leo ro
> Ho ri a bho bho
> A bhotachan, a bhrilaicheag, a bhrilaicheag, a bhrilaicheag
> Mac'il leo ro
> Hao ri o huo
> Mac'il leo ro
> Ho ri a bho bho
> A bhotachan, a bhrilaicheag, a bhrilaicheag, a bho bho![43]

In his fundraising days to set up the original Eigg trust, this was very much the vision that Tom Forsythe had held for the island: 'You see, [an oak seedling's] taproot is bigger than the growth

211

above ground. Human culture's the same. The taproot of some trees remains even after the top has been shaved off by sheep. What we've got to do in the world, what we're trying to do on Eigg, is to graft on a scion, a new shoot, to that taproot. We've got to make for modern times new growth that's rooted in ancient spiritual bedrock!'[44] For Aidan MacEoin, an Irish poet and playwright who has finally settled on Eigg after life on Knoydart and Rum, it is something even simpler: 'There is a sense of freedom on the island that makes it a congenial place to write; that's why I like it here.' As for Eddie Scott, another Irishman, it is even simpler: ' I just like the smell of the island; it smells like home used to smell. And now it's home.'

For all those who opted for island life, the natural environment and its inherent quality of life rank high in their motivation to live on Eigg. This concern for the environment and interest for a more holistic way of life can probably also explain why opportunities to volunteer on conservation projects has become an important growth area on the island and stands to be developed further. Not only does it improve the young islanders' social life, but it provides a steady pool of candidates for island life as well as providing the 'sweat capital' much needed to carry out a whole range of labour intensive activities like rhododendron or bracken cutting. This is something the island's latest business wants to capitalise on. 'Earth Connections', set up by Centre of Human Ecology graduates, Bob and Norah Wallace, has already seen 50 volunteers in its first year, including a group from Russia and young people from Denmark, America and Nigeria.

Bob, a marine engineer for Greenpeace, and Norah, a wildlife ranger, had actually spent two years travelling around the west coast on their old ex-Royal Navy harbour launch to look for the right place to live and build their sustainability centre before coming to Eigg. A phone call telling them that there was a need for new people on Eigg got them up for a visit and this how they found the Lodge. 'We were originally thinking of a new build, but with lots of rooms and a central place where people can get to, surrounded by beautiful woodland and nature, the Lodge was perfect for what we had in mind. We thought that retro-fitting an old building in an ecologically sound way would be an exciting and interesting challenge for us. And because part of what we want to do is to try and help people re-connect with nature, we wanted somewhere with lots of different habitats, and Eigg is just fantastic for that; it was the perfect place.'

The Wallaces put a proposal to the trust and eight months and a few changes later, the proposal was finally accepted. 'It went to the residents to be voted on and it was unanimous, apart from one person who was asleep. We like telling that story!' For Kenneth Kean, ERA chair at the time, this decision illustrates perfectly the way Eigg works. 'The community had been at a loss about what to do with the Lodge ever since the buy-out. We had been through several process to find a use for the Lodge, and we were eventually unable to find a use that was viable financially, so it almost came down to demolishing it or giving it away to somebody to see if they could do something with it. And that's when Bob and Norah came into the picture. They came up with an offer for the Lodge and an outline of what they planned to do. We decided that it was as good a project as we could imagine that we'd like to see happening in the Lodge. Nobody really wanted to see it demolished, I think. Although as a building it is a bit out of place on the island, it still means quite a lot to people, just because of the visual impact it has, but that was not the basis of the decision that was taken. It was because of Bob and Norah's ideas of what they wanted to do with it. The fact that they had two children was also important in the decision we took. That's just how it works. You have to look at everything overall to see what the advantages are. Maybe we did not make huge financial gains out of the lodge, but we made gains in other ways.'

'Gaining in other ways' is precisely what it means: increasing the island's social capital, the number and variety of its inhabitants. Ten years of community ownership on Eigg has shown that social well-being is just as important as economic and environmental well-being for the future of a community: taking care of that balance is what social landownership is about in all of Scotland's community-owned land. It is no easy task, it is no utopia, but it is a task that ultimately engages people in what is fundamental in human lives.

Today, the island has a greater diversity of people and talents than ever before. The challenge is to bring out these talents to benefit the local economy and continue to ensure the future, a goal encapsulated in this confident statement: 'We will remain a vibrant, inclusive, enterprising, community, in harmony with the natural and cultural environment.'[45] There is also a growing awareness than in order to achieve this vision, it is essential to keep up the unspoken indigenous ethos, and maintain its time-tested culture of reciprocity and mutual help to create an environment where everyone is happy to play their part. 'We share a pride in our island community and in the value of integrity, cooperation, and respect for each other and our heritage,'[46] declare 'old' and 'new' islanders.

And it still is the musical aspect of this heritage which provides much of the social cement which binds people together. 'Music and song, laddie, you must have that in you, or the island will lose its soul,' Angus MacKinnon had always said. With the second-generation islanders playing the button box, fiddle, whistle or banjo, and Feis Eige now nurturing the third generation's musical education, music-making plays as strong as ever a part in the island's social life. It has even inspired a novel concept, the 'ceilidh-croft,'[47] and a new cultural enterprise, the 'ceilidh studio,' run by Donna MacCulloch, who met Angus MacKinnon at a Feis dance and stayed on to learn some pipe tunes. She never left, like many others who have come under the spell of island life, and has now become Eigg's piper in residence.

As to the epic festivities that are gathering Eigg's friends and well-wishers every year since that first 12 June, they have now become a regular date in the Highland folk music calendar. 'It is one of those events that has grown organically, chiefly by word of mouth,' tells a happy party-goer, 'not a festival as such, but a highly musical gathering, given its popularity among the Highland folk community'.[48] A good couple of hundred folks make the trip for the 'Anniversary' each year, arriving via Cal-Mac, the *Sheerwater* and an assortment of boats large and small from neighbouring communities, Knoydart, Arisaig, Glenfinnan or Glenuig, pitching their tents along the shore and around the pillar-like monument that commemorates the buy-out before heading for weekend revels that last way past sunrise. Every year, like at so many other times in its history, the island becomes once again a great gathering place.

POSTSCRIPT

Big green footsteps, small carbon footprint

On 1 February 2008, the Isle of Eigg entered a new era with the switching on of the island electrification project, which made 24-hour power available for the first time to all residents and businesses on the island. Until then the island had been entirely dependent upon making its own power; now it had leapt to the forefront of electricity generation using renewable energy resources. Its solar, wind and hydro power generation scheme has become a world leader in the integration of multiple renewable energy sources into a grid system to supply an isolated and scattered small community. Conceived and driven by the enthusiasm of the whole community, the island electrification was the culmination of 10 years of achievement since the purchase of Eigg in 1997.

This complex project, which was paid for with £1.6 million of European and other public funding, and which brought together a large team of designers, contractors and islanders,[1] won a number of awards, amongst which was *Best Community Initiative* at the 2008 Scottish Green Energy Awards, making Eigg a shining example of Renewable Energy success of international reputation.[2]

On the strength of the island's electrification, the community on Eigg entered the Big Green Challenge, a competition to find new and better ways to tackle climate change, run by the National Endowment for Science, Technology and the Arts (NESTA). By September 2008 they were the only Scottish finalist. They then spent two years' hard work to reduce use of fossil fuels and make the most of the island's natural assets and its woodland in particular. The islanders feverishly embarked on a round of house insulation, promoting solar water heating and transport alternatives, reducing waste and also food miles with polytunnel vegetable-growing, a community orchard and a farmer's market. By January 2010 their efforts were crowned with success: the Isle of Eigg community won joint first place – and £300,000! A few months later, the Scottish public voted for Eigg to win the Environment category of the Glenfiddich Spirit of Scotland Awards. 'It was an amazing feeling to win this award,' recalls Tasha Lancaster, one of the two Eigg BGC project workers. 'This time there were no judges, no questions to answer, no reports to write; simply the good wishes and appreciation of people who had taken the time to recognise what we've achieved by registering their vote. Thank you to everyone who voted for us. [Their] belief in what we've done, and will continue to do, means a lot.'

Within the ranks of Community Land Scotland, the umbrella body for community land owners, Eigg is now making the case for more community-owned land in a Scottish landscape where the pattern of ownership is still very slow to change. The island and its people have shown indeed how communities that are incentivised, empowered and supported can become a powerful vehicle for social and environmental change.

Eigg
From where I sit in the
late summer solitude
I can see the track
that leads to Kildonnan House
and the sea beyond
gathering its strength
in readiness
for the coming winter season
that's inevitable.
In the fields, the hay is cut, baled and stored
the silage wrapped in black
contrasting with the golden yellow
meadow upon which it lies
in readiness, until needed
there is an urgency of preparation
on the island
borne from generations of
experience that belie the toil
the islanders embark upon
as each season approaches
the soil yields
to the hands that tends it.[3]

Appendix I

Census of the Small Isles
1764–1765 (transcribed by Alan Blair and Catherine MacInnes)

List of all the men, women and children of the parish of Eigg taken by Neil McNeill, Catechist in the said parish, in November and December 1764 and January and February 1765 with a true account of their age and religion, the number of families in each of the islands and the number of protestants in each island and the same observed the number of papists

The island of Eigg is for [the] most part inhabited by papists (Catholics). [In] the year 1764, there was no protestants families on the isle there, but 3. The island then and before had 3 principal papist families on it by which the priests had access to come to the place and stayed in those families for some weeks. The protestants then had no rest but the priests and the rest of the inhabitants would be so troublesome to them by arguing with them with regard to religion that times the priests gained two of them to his side, but [the] more years passed, two of those principal papists died and left no heirs to succeed them in any manner or way. The third of them sold the land he had to Clanranald and left the place so there is no papists of any account on the place but poor tennants now. There are at present 13 protestant families on the island, the minister excepted. The protestants here at the time come some of them from Skye when the minister came there to live, the rest from Rum and Isle of Muck. There is half a dozen of the papists of Eig that come to hear the minister preach when the priest is not upon the island. I was present to them doing the same in January last [of the] 1765 year.

Neill McNeill, Cstst

217

LIST OF THE PROTESTANTS IN THE ISLE OF EIGG

1	Kenneth McCaskill	64	8	Donald McKay	50
	Ann McLeod, his wife	50		Florance McKinnon, his wife	32
	Petter McCaskill, his son	23		John McKay, his son	2
	Marion McCaskill, his son	15		Roderick McKay, his son	$\frac{1}{4}$
	Doanld McCaskill, his son	12			
	Mary McLean	24	9	Hector McLean	30
	Margrat McCaskill	$\frac{1}{2}$		Marion McLean, his wife	27
				Donald McLean, his son	8
2	John Campbell	51		Charles McLean, his son	4
	Donald Campbell, his son	22		Ann McDonald	28
	Margrat Campbell,	24		Angus McDonald	60
	Mary Campbell, his daughter	18		Donald McGillireach	20
	John McCaskill, his son	2			
			10	John McKay	29
3	John McCaskill, elder	37		Mary McKay, his daughter	4
	Marion Cameron, his wife	36		Margrat McKay, his daughter	2
	Kenneth McCaskill, his son	9			
	Caristin McCaskill, his daughter	7	11	Donald McMillan	60
	Ann McCaskill, his daughter	4		Malcum McMillan, his son	30
	John McCaskill, his son	1		John Camron	12
	Marion Camron, widow	76			
			12	Donald McDonald	47
4	Neill McGnish	21		Janet McNivan	22
	Cathrina McLean	36		Isabell Stewart	27
				Cathrina McDonald, convert	60
5	John Funlayson	30		Donald McDonald, convert	21
	Ann Funlayson, his daughter	6		Marion Camron	12
	John Funlayson, his son	4			
	Mary McDonald	21	13	John McDonald, junior	70
				John McDonald, his son	32
6	Malcum Stewart	32		Cathrina McCall, his wife	30
	Cathrina McDonald, his wife	28		Donald McDonald, his son	5
	Ewn Stewart, his son	$1\frac{1}{2}$		Allan McDonald, his son	3
	Effie Stewart, his daughter	$\frac{1}{3}$		Rachel McDonald, his daughter	7
	Mary McMillan, servant	18		Cathrina McDonald, his daughter	2
	Marion Stewart	12		Allexander Ferguson	62
			13		
7	John McGnish	52		Margrat McKinnon, convert	50
	Donald McGnish, his son	12		AlexanderMcLeod,herson,convert	18
	Rory McGnish, his son	10		ArchibaldMcLeod,herson,convert	16
	Marion McGnish, his daughter	3		Ann Funlayson	32
	Donald Campbell	25		Mary Beaton	26
	Duncan McCalluman	21		Mary McLean	27

HERE FOLLOWS A LIST OF THE PAPISTS IN EIGG

1	Donald McDonald	40		2	Marion McDonald, widow	50
	Mary McDugall, his wife	37			Catriona McDonald, widow	58
	Angus McDonald, his son	21				
	Rory McDonald, his son	18		4	Donald McKinnon	50
	John McDonald, his son	12			Mary McKay	47
					Donald McKinnon	16
3	John McKinnon	30			John McKinnon	21
	Anna McDonald, his wife	27			Neil McKinnon	9
	Ewn McDonald, widow	76			John McKinnon	7
					Anna McEachen, servant	24
					Donald Henderson	20

GALLMISDELL (GALMISDALE) IN EIGG, PAPISTS

5	Kathrin McLean	52		9	Mary McGnish	80
	Mary McDonald	30			Mary McGnish junior	36
					John Mcallpin	10
6	Ewen Camron, widow	30			Mary Mcallpin	7
	Ann Camron	20		10		
					Malcolm McKinon	29
7	Mary MacDonald	40			Peter McKelled	30
	Mary MacDonald junior	18			Marion McDonald	40
	Neill McErick	18			Ranald McDonald	13
	Mary McDonald	40			Allan McDonald	10
8	Margrat McMillan	27				
	Mary McKay	4				
	Margrat McKay	9				

GRULINE ON EIGG, PAPISTS

11	Angus Johnson	60		17	John McGnish	36
	Mary McDonald, his wife	40			Mary McDonald, his wife	32
	Flory McDonald	18			Alexander McGnish	12
					Donald McGnish, his son	9
12	Cathrina McDonald	40			Angus McGnish, his son	7
	Jannet McLean	12			Allan McGnish, his son	4
	Allexander McLean	10			Marion McGnish, his daughter	5
					Margrat McGnish, his daughter	$1\frac{1}{2}$
13	Allexander Beaton	23			Margrat McLean, widow	72
	Mary Beaton, his sister	27				
	Cathrina McLeod, widow	67		18	Neil McGnish	70
	Allexander Johnson, servant	20			Mary McDonald, his wife	60

14	John McDonald	35	19	Malcolm Johnson	40
	Margrat McDonald, his wife	22		Mary Johnson, his wife	10
	Marion McLean	18	20	Marion Johnson, his daughter	36
15	Angus Johnson	40	21	Cathrina John, widow	40
	Donald McDonald	60		Donald Scott, her son	10
				Marion McGnish, servant	36
16	Allexander McDonald	72			
	Mary McDonald, his wife	50		John McLeolan	40
	John McDonald, his son	24		Ann McGnish, his wife	32
	Donald McDonald, his son	27		Macolm McLeolan, his son	9
	John McDugall, servant	28		Angus McLeolan, his son	7
	Lauchlan McLean	12		John McLeolan, his son	4
				Donald McLeolan, his son	2

LAIG TOWN

22	James McDonald	60	24	Donald McLean	57
	Cathrina McDonald	50		Mary McKinnon, his wife	50
	Kett McLeolan	25		Catrhrin McLean, his wife	21
				Neill McLean, his son	12
23	Duncan Swann	37			
	Cathrin McLeolan, his wife	36			
	Mary Swann, his daughter	12			
	Donald Swann, his son	9			
	Effie Swann, his daughter	7			
	Ann Swann, his son	6			
	Malcolm Swann, his son	2			

LAIG IN EIGG, PAPISTS

25	Donald McLeolan	32	29	Andrew McDonald	50
	Marion Campbell, his wife	30		Carilina Swann, his wife	45
	Anguss McLeolan, his son	3		Rachel McDonald, his daughter	9
	Cathrina McLeolan, his daughter	¾		Cathrina McDonald, his daughter	6
	Marion McLean	60		John McDonald, his son	6
				Rory McDoanld, his son	4
26	Duncan McIsaack	35		Mary MacDonald, his daughter	3
	Mary Swan, his wife	27			
	John McIsaack, his son	7	30	Marion McDonald, widow	70
	Donald McIsaack, his son	4		Cathrina McDonald	20

27	Donald McQuary	56
	Cathrina McIsaack, his wife	50
	Laughlan McQuary, his son	22
	Donad McQuary, his son	16
	John McQuary, his son	12
	Cathrina McQuarry, his daughter	14

28	Donald McKay	27
	Mary McKinnon, his wife	32
	John McKay, his son	2
	Ewn Mckay, his son	1½

31	Anna McLeollan, widow	36
	Malcum McAllpin, her son	9
	John McAllpin	7
	Florance McLeolan	80

CLAIDILT (CLEADALE) IN EIGG, PAPISTS

32	Ann McDonald	60
	Anna McDonald, her daughter	30
	Allexander McDonald, her son	19
	Cathrina McPherson, servant	36
	John McKinnon	36

33	Donald McDonald	40
	Florance McDugal, his wife	34
	Rachel McDugal, servant	24
	Angus McDonald, his son	7
	Cathrina McDonald, his daughter	5
	Mary McDonald, his daughter	3

34	Mary McLeod, widow	58
	Allexander McDonald, her son	22
	Margaret Brown, servant	27

35	John McDonald	40
	Florance McLeolan, his wife	36
	Anna McLean, servant	27
	Marion McDonald, his daughter	8
	Rorry McDonald, his son	8

36	Donald McDonald	32
	Ann McDonald, his wife	29
	John McDonald, his son	3
	Cathrina McDonald, widow	40

43	Donald McCormick	29
	Cathrina McDonald, his wife	27
	Robert McCormick, his son	8
	John McCormick. his son	2
	Kett Fergusson, widow	60

44	Angus McDonald	60
	Cathrina McKinnon, his wife	60
	Mary McDonald, his daughter	28
	Anna McDonald, his daughter	23

45	Donald McCormick	35
	Anna McEachern, his wife	27
	John McCormick, his son	9
	Lauchlan McCormick	2
	Mary McGnish	10

46	John McPherson	30
	Mary McDonald, his wife	26
	Mary Brown, servant	14

47	Duncan McLean	24
	Cathrina Campbell, widow	56
	Cathrina McLean, her daughter	16
	Kett Scott, widow	40
	Mary McKinnon	22

37	Lauchlan McKinnon	29
	Marjory McDonald, his wife	26
	John McKinnon, his son	7
	Malcolm McKinnon, his son	2
	Mary McDonald, servant	27
38	Donald McDonald	80
	Mary McDonald, his wife	70
	Ranald McDonald, his son	27
	Angus McDonald, grandson	7
39	Allan McDonald	36
	Mary McFarlan, his wife	32
	Rorry McDonald, his son	4
40	Angus Campbell	60
	Marion Campbell, his wife	52
	Lauchlan Campbell, his son	20
	Mary McDonald, grandchild	7
41	Hough McKinnon	55
	Flory McKinnon, his wife	24
	Donald McKinnon, his son	4
	Mary McKinnon, his daughter	3
	Neil Mckinnon, his son	1
	Cathrina Campbell, servant	22
42	George McDonald	57
	Margrat McDonald	52
	Ranald McDonald, his son	19
	Dugall McCormick	67
	Mary McDugall, his wife	40
	Marion McCormick	6

48	Donald McEachern	51
	Florance McDonald, his wife	42
	Janny McEachern, his son	7
	Angus McEachern	5
	Margrat McEachern, his daughter	7
	Kett McDonald	19
49	John McLeod	28
	Marion McDonald	27
50	Finlay McLeod	60
	Marion McEachern, his wife	50
	Marion McLeod, his daughter	12
51	Mary McLeod, widow	40
	Florance Donald	16
	Margrat McDonald, widow	40
	John Brown, her son	9
52	John Swann	60
	Marion McQuary, his wife	50
	Florance Swann, his daughter	24
53	John Ross	32
	Kett Brown, his wife	40
	Ewn Ross, his son	12
	Donald Ross, his son	9
	Angus Ross, his son	2
	Mary Ross, his daughter	1

TOLAND (HULIN) IN EIGG, PAPISTS

54	Allan MacDonald	40
	Ann McDonald, his wife	36
	Carl McDonald, his son	13
	Anna McDonald, his daughter	10
	Mary McDonald, his daughter	7
	Kett McDonald, his daughter	5
	Angus McDonald, his son	½
	Florance Livingston, servant	20
	Cathrina McGuary, servant	19
	Mary McDonald, widow	74
	Allexander McLeod, hand	17
55	Allan McDonald	30
	Mary McLeod, widow	55
	Dugall Livingston, servant	57
	Margrat Livingston	17
	Cathrina McDonald	27
56	Neill McLeod	56
	Donald McLeod	30
	Cathrina McLeod	7

57	Donald McKinnon	27
	Mary McGuary, his wife	23
58	Neill McLeod	30
	Doanld McLeod	60
	Cathrina McLeod	4
59	Neill Mcleod junior	26
	Mary Campbell, his wife	30
	Ann McLeod, his daughter	3
	Ewn McLeod, his son	8
	Cathrina Ross	8
60	John McDonald	29
	Caristina Swan, his wife	26
	Ann MacDonald, servant	26
	Mary Mc\Edam, his mother	61
	Allexander McDonald	27

FIVE PENNIES IN EIGG, PAPISTS

61	Cathrina McPherson, widow	45
	Cathrina McLeod, her daughter	5
	Florie McLeod, her daughter	2
62	Florie McDonald, widow	40
	Archibald McDonald, her son	14
63	Donald McLeod	36
	Margrat McDonald, his wife	24
	Florie McLeod, widow	45

64	Neill McSwine	52
	Rebecca McDuphie, his wife	50
	Marion McSwine, his daughter	24
	Evan McSwine, his son	15
	Duncan McSwine, his son	22
	Archibald McSwine, his son	16
65	Donald McKinnon,	32
	John McKinnon	29
	Lauchlan McKinnon	19
	Effie Brown, widow	65

SAND MOR (SANDAVORE) IN EIGG, PAPISTS

66	Ranald MacDonald	36
	Ann MacEachen, his wife	28
	Mary MacDonald, his daughter	5
	John MacDonald, his son	4
	Florance Campbell, servant	19
67	Ewn McDugall	50
	Cathrina McDonald, his wife	64
	Anna MacDonald, servant	13
68	John McDonald	50
	Mary McPherson, his wife	36
	Mary McDonald, his daughter	17
	Malcum McDonald, his son	12
	Margrat McDonald, his daughter	5

69	Angus Smith	40
	Cathrina McLeolan, his wife	36
	Marion Smith, his daughter	9
	Donald Smith, his son	7
	Malcum Smith, his son	5
	John Smith, his son	3
	Mary Smith, his daughter	½
70	Malcum Beaton	60
	Cathrina McGuary, his wife	63
	Lauchlan McKinnon	21
	Marion Beaton, his daughter	24
	John McKinnon	2
	Ranald McKinnon	70

SAN BEG (SANDAVEG) IN EIGG, PAPISTS

71	Ranald McDonald, major	60
	Mary McDonald, his wife	59
	Mary McLean, servant	19
72	Donald McDonald	40
	Mary McDuphie, his wife	38
	Anna McDonald, his wife	12
	John McDonald, his son	9
	Angus McDonald, his son	4
	Mary McDonald, his daughter	2
	Jannet McDonald, widow	60
73	Lauchlan McKinnon	24
	Caristin McDonald, widow	50
	Cathrina McKinnon	21
74	Angus McLeolan,	50
	Cathrina McDonald, his wife	45
	Donald McLeolan, his son	21
	John Mcleolan, this son	15
	Donald McDugall, servant	40
	Ann McLean, maid servant	25

77	John McLeolan	40
	Mary McDonald, his wife	27
	Mary McLeolan, his daughter	3
78	Mary McLeolan, widow	72
	Mary McLeolan, blind	27
79	Donald McLeolan	50
	Cathrina McDonald, his wife	54
	Archibald McLeolan, his son	18
	Donald McEachen	24
	Marion McLeolan	21
	Mary McLeolan, widow	72
80	Donald Campbell	32
	Mary McDonald, his wife	30
	John Campbell, his son	12
	Donald Campbell, his son	9
	Cathrina Campbell, his daughter	4
81	Donald McKinnon	61
	Cathrina McLeod, his wife	59
	Effie Campbell, very old	89

75	Florie McDonald, widow	55
	Donald McLean, her son	18
	Ewn McLean, grandchild	4

76	Angus McPherson	47
	Florance McDonald, his wife	36
	Allexander McPherson, his son	7
	Jannet McPherson, his daughter	5
	John McPherson, his son	2
	Ranald McPherson, old man	76

KILDONNAN, IN EIGG, PAPISTS

83	Allexander McEachen	30
	Mary McEachen, his wife	30
	John McEachen, his son	5
	Anguss McEachen , his son	4
	Donald McEachen, his son	3
	Beaig McEachen, his daughter	9
	Mary McEachen, his daughter	1
	John McEachen, his fayer	79
	Anna McEachen, his sister	29
	Cathrina McEachen, servant	12

84	Anna McSwine, widow	52
	Malcum Brown, her son	9
	Margrat Brown, her daughter	16
	Marion Brown her daughter	13

82	Mary McDonald, widow	60
	Marion McDugall, widow	50
	Kett McSwine, widow	49
	Peggie McGnishe, widow	50

85	Neill McIsaak	50
	Donald McIsaak, his son	10
	Lauchlan McIsaak, his son	2
	Allan McIsaak, his son	7
	Caristin McIsaak, his daughter	5
	Margrat McIssaak, his daughter	3

86	Donald McSwine	50
	Anna McDugall, his wife	57
	Caristin McSwine, his daughter	29
	Beaig McSwine, his daughter	24

87	Mary Johnson, widow	68
	Mary McDonald,	12
	Margrat McKinnon, widow	52

| 88 | Marion McEachean, widow | 60 |
| | Archibald McSwine | 17 |

Appendix II

EIGG PRISONER LIST
AND PASSENGER LIST

LIST OF EIGG PEOPLE CAPTURED AT OR AFTER CULLODEN ON BOARD THE *PAMELA* IN SEPTEMBER 1746

MacCormick Robert	Farmer at Clatill (Cleadale)	transported
MacDonald Angus	Farmer at Grulin	transported
MacDonald James	Farmer at Grulin	transported
MacDonald John	Farmer at Clatich (Cleadale)	released
MacDonald John	Farmer at Galmisdal	transported
MacDonald John	Farmer at Houlin	transported
MacDonald Roderick	Farmer at Kirktown (Kildonnan)	transported
MacDugall John	Peddlar at Galnashel (Galmisdale)	transported
MacKinnon Donall	Farmer at Clatill (Cleadale)	died
MacLean Angus	Farmer at Laig	transported
MacLean John	Gardener at Laig	transported
MacQuarry Donald		transported
MacQuarry John	Farmer at Galmistill	transported
MacQuarry John		transported
Quilly Donald	Farmer at Houlin	died

Source: J. Gibson, *Ships of the 45's*, Hutchison & Co., London, 1967

LIST OF EIGG PASSENGERS ON THE *LUCY*

Name	Occupation	Township	adults	12–8	8–6	6–4	4–2	under 2
Alexander MacDonald	peddlar	Galmistle	6	–	–	1	1	1
John MacLean	tenant	Kildonnan	5	1	1	1	–	–
Angus MacDonald	Howlun		2	–	–	–	–	1

LIST OF EIGG PASSENGERS ON THE *JANE*

Dugald macCormick	peddlar	Grulin	1	–	–	–	–	–
Donald MacDonald			2	–	1	2	–	1

LIST OF EIGG PASSENGERS ON THE *BRITISH QUEEN*

Name	Occupation	Township	adults	12–8	8–6	6–4	4–2	price paid (£ s d)
Peggy MacDougall	tenant	Cleadale	1	–	1	1	1	4.12.4½
Allan MacDonald	tenant	Cleadale	4	2	–	–	–	7.15
Donald MacDonald	tenant	Cleadale	2	–	–	–	1	7.15
John MacKinnon	tenant	Cleadale	1	–	1	1	1	2.1
Lachlan MacKinnon	tenant	Cleadale	4	1	2	2	2	15.9
Lachlan Campbell	tenant	Cleadale	3	–	–	1	1	4.8½

Appendix III

GENEALOGY OF THE LAIG AND CNOC OILTEAG MACDONALDS

source *The Island of Eigg* by Duncan Ferguson

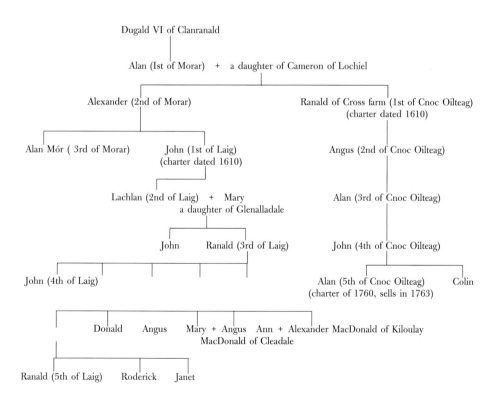

NOTES

INTRODUCTION

1. C. Jedrej and M. Nuttall, *White Settlers, the Impact of Repopulation in Scotland*, Edinburgh, 1996, p. 124.

CHAPTER 1

1. C. R. Wickham-Jones, *Scotland's First Settlers*, London, 1994, pp. 46, 84.
2. N. MacPherson, 'Notes on the Antiquities of Eigg', *Proceedings of the Society of Antiquaries*, Edinburgh, 1878, vol. 12, pp. 590–1.
3. S. Wade-Martin, *Eigg, an Island Landscape*, Countryside Publishing, 1987, p. 9.
4. James Robertson, in Alexander Carmichael, unpublished notes (Eigg), Edinburgh University Library archives.
5. W. D. Lamont, 'House and Pennylands in the Highlands and Islands', *Scottish Studies*, vol. 25, Edinburgh, 1981, p. 65.
6. K. MacLeod, *The Road to the Isles*, Edinburgh, 1927, p. 90.
7. S. Heaney, *Sweeney Astray*, London, 1984, pp. 3–5. Suibhne, the Ulster king cursed with madness for striking the saint who had come to build a church on his land, was turned into a bird and came to roost for six weeks in the cave of Donnan on Eigg during his flight from tree to tree, from one hill to the next until death finally delivered him.
8. I. Fisher, first draft for *Early Medieval Sculpture in the West Highlands*, Edinburgh, 1998.
9. K. MacLeod, *The Road to the Isles*, p. 90. W. F. Skene, *Celtic Scotland*, vol. 1 (49), p. 152.
10. H. Miller, *The Cruise of the Betsey, or a Summer Holiday in the Hebrides*, Edinburgh, 1870, pp. 33, 49.
11. Rev. D. MacLean in *The Statistical Account of Scotland*, vol. XX, Edinburgh, 1794–5, p. 287.
12. M. Martin, *A Description of the Western Isles of Scotland, Circa 1695* (4th edn), Stirling, 1934, p. 304.
13. A. P. Smyth, *Warlords and Holy Men*, Edinburgh, 1984, p. 108.
14. This is inferred from the name of a well in Grulin, Tobar nam Ban Naomh, literally 'the well of the holy women', although 'Ban Naomh' does also mean 'nuns'. According to Hugh MacKinnon, tradition ascribed healing powers to this well which could not be used for washing.
15. A. P. Smyth, *Warlords and Holy Men*, p. 108.
16. I. Fisher, first draft for *Early Medieval Sculpture in the West Highlands*, RCAHMS.
17. B. E. Crawford (ed.), *Scandinavian Scotland*, Leicester, 1987, pp. 45–51. A. W. Broger, *Ancient Emigrants, a History of the Norse Settlements in Scotland*, London, 1929, pp. 114–15.
18. B. E. Crawford (ed.), *Scandinavian Scotland*, p. 123.
19. N. MacPherson, 'Notes on the Antiquities of Eigg', *Proceedings of the Society of Antiquaries*, vol. 12, pp. 590–1.
20. Rev. C. M. Robertson, 'Topography and traditions of Eigg', *Transactions of the Gaelic Society of Inverness*, vol. 22, Inverness, 1897–8, pp. 193–7.
21. D. Ferguson, *Notes on the History of Eigg*. According to oral tradition, Castle Island is the corruption of 'Eilean Thathasdal' – Thathasdal's island – and not Eilean Chasteil.

231

22. D. J. MacDonald of Castleton, *Clan Donald*, Edinburgh, 1978, p. 47. The use of a davoch is interesting here, as this Pictish land measure was now replacing the Norse merkland. A davoch was equivalent to an ounceland.

23. B. E. Crawford (ed.), *Scandinavian Scotland*, p. 39.

24. H. MacDonald, 'A History of the MacDonalds', *Highland Papers*, Edinburgh, 1881, vol. 1, p. 24.

CHAPTER 2

1. N. Banks, *Six Inner Hebrides*, London, 1977, p. 189.

2. W. F. Skene, *Celtic Scotland*, Edinburgh, 1886, vol. 3, p. 433.

3. Dr Walker, *A Report on the Hebrides of 1764 and 1771*, Edinburgh, 1980, p. 225.

4. A. MacDonald and A. MacDonald, *Clan Donald*, Highland Papers, Inverness, 1900, vol. I, p. 321. The two families amongst the cadets of the Morar family were associated with Eigg. The line of the MacDonalds of Knockeiltag started in 1610 when the tack of Knockeilteach – or Cnoc Oilteag in what is now Cleadale – was bestowed on Ranald, the cadet son of Allan I of Morar, son of the infamous 6th chief. The line of the MacDonalds of Laig started when Allan's successor, Alexander II of Morar, provided for John, his cadet son, by leasing him the farm of Laig out of their remaining Eigg lands. Grulin remained the property of the MacDonalds of Morar until 1771, when it was sold to the chief of Clanranald against the remittance of some outstanding debts (Scottish Record Office GD 201/5). Closest in rank to the chief of Clanranald, MacDonald of Laig acted as his baillie on Eigg. According to Hugh MacKinnon, succeeding baillies were Ranald MacDonald of Cross, also from the Morar family, in the late seventeenth century, who held the tack of Sandavore, his son Ranald MacDonald, then Angus MacDonald of Laig, the grandson of the poet Alasdair mac Mhaighstir Alasdair, and Dr MacAskill, Angus's son-in-law.

5. R. C. MacLeod of MacLeod, *The MacLeods of Dunvegan*, Inverness, 1929, pp. 76–9.

6. According to the Eigg tradition, the rhyme told by the old woman was:

Biolaire bog 's dulus an tuig   The soft watercress from the hollow
'S deoch do Thobar mor Tholain, A drink from the big well at Holin,
'S fognaidh sud.   And that will be enough.

7. J. L. Campbell, 'Sad is the climbing' ('S trom an direadh), *Hebridean Folksongs*, Oxford, 1977, pp. 88–91.

8. R. C. MacLeod of MacLeod, *The MacLeods of Dunvegan*, p. 78.

9. W. F. Skene, *Celtic Scotland*, vol. 3, p. 433. I. F. Grant, *The MacLeods*, 2nd edn, Spurbooks, Edinburgh, 1981, p. 136.

10. H. Miller, *The Cruise of the Betsey*, p. 25.

11. Register of the Privy Council of Scotland, Edinburgh, 1881, vol. 4, p. 342.

12. M. C. MacKenzie, *History of the Outer Isles*, Edinburgh, 1974, p. 178.

13. D. Ferguson, *Notes on the History of Eigg*.

14. R. Pitcairn, *Ancient Criminal Trials in Scotland*, Bannatyne Club, Edinburgh, 1833, p. 20. 'Enviring', which means encircling in Old Scots, was the Gaelic way of showing respect to the person of the chief, whilst 'chapping handis', clasping hands, represented the swearing of feudal obedience to the chief, and the commitment to live and die in his service.

15. A. MacDonald and A. MacDonald, *Clan Donald*, 1900, vol. 3, p. 252.

16. D. Morrison, *The Morrison Manuscript: Traditions of the Western Isles* (ed. Norman MacDonald), Stornoway, 1975, pp. 104–5.

17. Clanranald Papers, GD 201/3, Scottish Record Office, Edinburgh.

18. J. L. Campbell, *Canna, the Story of a Hebridean Island*, Oxford, 1984, pp. 46–50. Of a post-medieval design common throughout the Hebrides, the new church, thought to be built in the mid-fifteenth century, was rectangular in plan, with a round arch doorway in the south, a narrow lintel window opening to the east and a recessed tomb on the north wall. Such tombs were built for the burials of chiefs when Iona stopped being their last resting place, and were a feature of Hebridean churches. The recessed tomb on Eigg bears the Clanranald armorial shield but the date of 1641 sculpted on it can only indicate that the stone was placed on the wall for a burial posterior to the date of the church.

19. Clanranald Papers, 201/3, Scottish Record Office.
20. M. Martin, *A Description of the Western Isles of Scotland, Circa 1695* (4th edn), Stirling, 1934, p. 302.
21. Ibid., p. 303.
22. Ibid.
23. J. L. Campbell, *Canna*, p. 57.
24. M. Martin, *A Description of the Western Isles of Scotland*, p. 345.
25. J. Fraser, 'A Treatise on the Second Sight', *Miscellanea Scotica*, vol. 3, Glasgow, 1820, pp. 70–2.
26. J. L. Campbell, *Canna*, p. 87.
27. D. Thomson, *An Introduction to Gaelic Poetry* (2nd edn), Edinburgh, 1989, p. 148.

CHAPTER 3

1. Clanranald Papers, GD 201/5 1257/3, Scottish Record Office, Edinburgh.
2. Ibid.
3. Dr Walker, *A Report on the Hebrides of 1764 and 1771*, Edinburgh, 1980, p. 196.
4. J. L. Campbell, *Canna, the Story of a Hebridean Island*, Oxford, 1984, p. 125.
5. Ibid., p. 129.
6. D. Ferguson, *Notes on the History of Eigg*.
7. Ibid.
8. A. MacDonald, 'Proceedings on Eigg', in R. Forbes, *The Lyon in Mourning*, Edinburgh, 1895, vol. 2, pp. 86–8.
9. J. Gibson, *Ships of the '45s*, Hutchinson & Co., London, 1967, pp. 51–3.
10. A. MacDonald and A. MacDonald, *The Poems of Alexander MacDonald*, Inverness, 1924, pp. 151–3.
11. Clanranald Papers, GD 201/5, Scottish Record Office.
12. J. Hunter, *The Making of the Crofting Community*, Edinburgh, 1976, p. 13.
13. Dr Walker, *A Report on the Hebrides of 1764 and 1771*, Edinburgh, 1980, p. 225.
14. Clanranald Papers, GD 201/2, GD 201/5, Scottish Record Office.
15. Clanranald Papers, GD 201/5, Scottish Record Office.
16. Ibid.
17. D. Ferguson, *Notes on the History of Eigg*.
18. Letter of Alexander MacDonald to John Geddes, 11 May 1790, *Blair Papers*, Scottish Catholic Archives, Edinburgh.

CHAPTER 4

1. Petition from Mr Donald McQueen to the presbytery of Skye, 1729, CM1/2/59, f. 44.
2. F. Tolmie, *Journal of the Folksong Society*, vol. 16, London, 1911, pp. 143–8.
3. H. MacKinnon, *Tocher* 10, pp. 70–5.
4. Ibid.
5. Ibid.
6. Clanranald Papers, GD 201/5, Scottish Record Office, Edinburgh.
7. Clanranald Papers, GD 201/2 2a. Presumably Ranald MacDonald was the same Ranald MacDonald who received the tack of Sandavore – both inn and farm – from Clanranald in 1761. D. Ferguson, *Notes on the History of Eigg*.
8. D. Ferguson, *Notes on the History of Eigg*.
9. C. MacDonald, *Moidart or Amongst the Clanranalds*, Oban, 1889, p. 250.
10. J. Boswell, *The Life of Johnson*, vol. I, London, 1960, p. 534.
11. K. MacLeod, *The Road to the Isles*, Edinburgh, 1927, pp. 74, 75.
12. Necker de Saussure, *A Voyage to the Hebrides*, Geneva, 1810.
13. H. Miller, *The Cruise of the Betsey, or a Summer Holiday in the Hebrides*, Edinburgh, 1870, p. 217.
14. T. Pennant in J. L. Campbell, *Canna, the Story of a Hebridean Island*, Oxford, 1984, p. 111.

15. K. MacLeod, *The Road to the Isles*, p. 140.
16. R. Black, 'The old wife and the crippled goat', in 'Seasons', *West Highland Free Press*, 22 October 1987.
17. James Robertson in A. Carmichael, *Carmina Gadelica*, Edinburgh, 1971, vol. 3, p. 278.
18. Ibid.
19. D. Ferguson, *Notes on the History of Eigg*.
20. Rev. C. M. Robertson, 'Topography and traditions of Eigg', *Proceedings of the Gaelic Society of Inverness*, vol. 22, Inverness, 1897–8, pp. 193–7.
21. K. MacLeod, *The Road to the Isles*, p. 206.
22. Ibid., p. 201.
23. Eigg tradition.
24. M. Martin, *A Description of the Western Isles of Scotland Circa 1695* (4th edn), Stirling, 1934, p. 348.
25. K. MacLeod, *The Road to the Isles*, p. 233.

CHAPTER 5

1. H. MacKinnon, *Tocher* 10, pp. 40–7.
2. D. Ferguson, *Notes on the History of Eigg*.
3. H. MacKinnon, *Tocher* 10, pp. 40–7.
4. Ibid.
5. Rev. D. MacLean in *The Statistical Account of Scotland*, 1794–5, vol. XX, p. 231.
6. J. L. Campbell, *Canna, the Story of a Hebridean Island*, Oxford, 1984.
7. M. MacLean, *The People of Glengarry*, Montreal and Kingston, 1991, pp. 109–13.
8. Rev. D. MacLean in *The Statistical Account of Scotland*, p. 231.
9. Rev. D. MacLean, *State of Emigration from the Highlands of Scotland, its Extent, Causes and Proposed Remedy*, London, 1803, p. 124.
10. Ibid.
11. Fr James MacDonald, 12 October 1790, *Blair Papers*, Scottish Catholic Archives, Edinburgh.
12. J. M. Bumsted, *The People's Clearance*, Edinburgh University Press, Edinburgh, 1982, p. 239.
13. A. MacDonald and J. MacDonald, *Fair is the Place*, Nova Scotia, 1980, p. 19. John MacDonald – or Iain mac Dhomhnall mhic Raonuill mhic Uilleam mhic Challum as was his patronymic – was probably a nephew of the tacksman of Laig. Leaving with his wife Effie and their four grown-up children, John, a blacksmith, Donald Ruadh, Ronald and Mary, and his younger brothers Angus and Rory, John first settled near Arisaig, Nova Scotia. After his wife's death, he married another Eigg emigrant, Annie Flora MacKinnon, who bore him another four children, and the whole family then moved to Judique, Cape Breton. Other Eigg emigrants who settled nearby were Donald and John MacKinnon, two brothers who had arrived in Pictou in 1791, moved to Cape Dore and Parrsboro before finally settling in Antigonish. John married Eunice, the daughter of another Eigg emigrant, Neil MacLeod, the progenitor of all the MacLeods of Antigonish County and of some in Inverness County. Colin Francis MacKinnon, the son of John and Eunice MacKinnon, who was born in 1810, became Bishop of Antigonish and was the founder of St François Xavier University, Nova Scotia.
14. Fr James MacDonald, 12 October 1790, *Blair Papers*.
15. J. M. Bumsted, *The People's Clearance*, pp. 240, 243.
16. M. MacLean, *The People of Glengarry*, pp. 119–20, 182–3.
17. Rev. D. MacLean, *State of Emigration from the Highlands*.
18. H. MacKinnon, *Tocher* 29, p. 329.
19. From the oral tradition of Dougald MacKinnon.
20. Clanranald Papers, GD 201/5 1, Scottish Record Office.
21. Ibid.
22. D. J. Rankin, *A History of the County of Antigonish, Nova Scotia*, Toronto, 1922, p. 5. Amongst these emigrants were Angus MacDonald who settled at Fox Brook, Pictou; Donald MacDonald the tailor; John Ban MacDonald who came in 1819; Neil MacIsaac, the progenitor of all the MacIsaacs of Georgeville, Mount Pleasant; Ronald Fraser who settled in Eigg Mountain like Rory MacIsaac, and his

three sons John, Malcolm and Lauchlin, as well as Archie MacLellan, who came to Eigg Mountain in 1825 and married a MacIsaac.

23. J. Hunter, *The Making of the Crofting Community*, Edinburgh, 1976, p. 24.

24. Ibid., p. 19.

25. Ibid., p. 17.

26. Clanranald Papers, GD 201/8 87, Scottish Record Office. The Hulin/Cleadale boundary used to be at Lon na Gruagaich, and the high turf march dyke which marked it can still be seen stretching from the cliff all the way down to the sea.

27. H. MacKinnon, *Tocher* 15, pp. 256–61.

28. 1819 rentals, Clanranald Papers, GD 201/5, Scottish Record Office.

29. J. Hunter, *The Making of the Crofting Community*, p. 36.

30. C. MacDonald, *Moidart or Amongst the Clanranalds*, Oban, 1889, p. 163.

31. Clanranald Papers, GD 201/5/ 1235/1, Scottish Record Office.

32. J. Hunter, *The Making of the Crofting Community*, p. 39.

33. From the oral tradition of Hugh MacKinnon from Muck.

CHAPTER 6

1. Clanranald Papers, GD 201/5, Scottish Record Office, Edinburgh.

2. Rev. N. MacLean in *The New Statistical Account*, vol. 14, Edinburgh and London, 1845, p. 145.

3. 1831 census, Isle of Eigg Archive.

4. J. L. Campbell, *Canna, the Story of a Hebridean Island*, Oxford, 1984, pp. 87–90.

5. 1831–1841 census, Isle of Eigg Archive.

6. From the oral tradition of Duncan Ferguson.

7. H. Miller, *The Cruise of the Betsey, or a Summer Holiday in the Hebrides*, Edinburgh, 1870, p. 18.

8. H. MacKinnon, *Tocher* 3, pp. 73–7.

9. C. MacDonald, *Moidart or Amongst the Clanranalds*, Oban, p. 163.

10. H. MacKinnon, *Tocher* 10, pp. 51–3.

11. Ibid.

12. H. Miller, *The Cruise of the Betsey*, pp. 92–3.

13. J. Hunter, *The Making of the Crofting Community*, Edinburgh, 1976, pp. 94–6.

14. H. Miller, *The Cruise of the Betsey*, pp. 90–1.

15. D. Ferguson, *Notes on the History of Eigg*.

16. *Report on Destitution in the Highlands Down to the Year 1841*, Parliamentary Papers, 1841, VI, p. 61.

17. H. Miller, *The Cruise of the Betsey*, p. 30.

18. Captain Baynton to Coffin, *Correspondence Relating to the Measures adopted for the Relief of Distress in Scotland*, Parliamentary Papers, 1847, LIII.

19. Dr MacPherson to Coffin, ibid.

20. N. Banks, *Six Inner Hebrides*, London, 1977, p. 92.

21. From the oral tradition of Duncan Ferguson and Angus MacKinnon.

22. Peterkin, *Board of Supervision for the Relief of the Poor in Scotland*, Annual Reports, 1847, p. 76.

23. From the oral tradition of Duncan MacKay.

24. H. MacKinnon, *Tocher* 10.

25. Ibid.

26. More details about the MacQuarries of Eigg can be found in D. J. Rankin, *A History of the County of Antigonish, Nova Scotia*, Toronto, 1922, p. 5. John MacQuarrie was related on his mother's side to Colin Francis MacKinnon, Bishop of Antigonish, who advised the family to settle in Nova Scotia rather than Upper Canada where they had originally intended to go.

27. A. Carmichael, *Carmina Gadelica*, Edinburgh and London, 1971, vol. 1, p. 284.

CHAPTER 7

1. M. P. Edgeworth, Diaries, 1857, 1858, 1862, 1863, 1877, 1881, unpublished. (Courtesy of N. Banks.)

2. N. Banks, *Six Inner Hebrides*, London, 1977, p. 87.

3. M. P. Edgeworth, Diaries, 1857, 1858, 1862, 1863, 1877, 1881.
4. Ibid.
5. J. Hunter, *The Making of the Crofting Community*, Edinburgh, 1976, p. 121.
6. F. Tolmie, *Journal of the Folksong Society*, vol. 16, London, 1911, pp. 143–8.
7. A. Carmichael, *Carmina Gadelica*, Edinburgh, 1971, vol. V, pp. 61–3.
8. Ibid.
9. M. Chapman, *The Gaelic Vision in Scottish Culture*, London, 1978, p. 119.
10. J. Hunter, *The Making of the Crofting Community*, 129, pp. 136–7.
11. T. C. Smout, *A Century of the Scottish People, 1830–1930*, London, 1969, p. 65.
12. Ibid., p. 74.
13. J. Hunter, *The Making of the Crofting Community*, p. 129.
14. Ibid., p. 133.
15. Ibid., pp. 143–4.
16. *Report of the Commissioners of Inquiry into the Conditions of the Crofters and Cottars in the Highlands and Islands of Scotland*, 1884, XXXII.
17. C. Fraser-Mackintosh, *Antiquarian Notes*, Second Series, Inverness, 1897, p. 261.
18. J. Hunter, *The Making of the Crofting Community*, p. 163.
19. H. R. Mackenzie, *Yachting and Electioneering in the Hebrides*, Inverness, 1886, p. 51.
20. J. Hunter, *The Making of the Crofting Community*, p. 162.
21. *Royal Commission (Highlands and Islands), Report and Minutes of Evidence*, 1895, XXXVIII. The western part of Canna and the eastern part of Muck were also recommended for division into crofts as well as the northern part of Rum, from Guirdil to Kinloch, to be shared among those victims of the Skye clearances who were now populating Bullough's shooting estate. These recommendations were never implemented.

CHAPTER 8

1. N. Banks, *Six Inner Hebrides*, London, 1977, p. 103. D. Ferguson, *The Island of Eigg*.
2. From the oral tradition of Iain Campbell.
3. From the oral tradition of Duncan MacKay.
4. N. Banks, *Six Inner Hebrides*, p. 103.
5. M. E. M. Donaldson, *Wanderings in the Western Highlands and Islands*, Paisley, 1927, p. 225.
6. Ibid.
7. M. Kennedy-Fraser, *Songs of the Hebrides*, London, 1909, pp. xvi–xvii.
8. Ibid.
9. H. MacKinnon, *Tocher* 10, p. 63.
10. D. Murchison, *The Gaelic Prose of Kenneth MacLeod*, Gaelic Text Society, Edinburgh, 1958, pp. xxxv–xxxviii.
11. M. Kennedy-Fraser, *Songs of the Hebrides*, p. 23.
12. K. MacLeod, *The Road to the Isles*, p. 74.
13. A. D. Cameron, *Go and Listen to the Crofters*, Stornoway, 1986, pp. 118–19.
14. Minutes of the Board of Governors, Small Isles Schoolboard, 1906–13. Inverness Library Archives, Inverness.
15. C. Connel, *The Scottish Naturalist*, 161, September–October 1926.
16. H. MacKinnon, *Tocher* 36, pp. 364–77. This issue gives the full-length account of how shinty was played on Eigg.
17. Ibid.

CHAPTER 9

1. N. Banks, *Six Inner Hebrides*, London 1977, p. 103; D. Ferguson, *The Island of Eigg*.
2. Ibid., p. 39.
3. J. Urquhart, *Eigg*, Edinburgh, 1987, p. 142.
4. J. Hunter, *The Making of the Crofting Community*, Edinburgh, 1976, p. 199.
5. From the recollections of Ann Schuckman.

6. Ibid.
7. Minutes of the Small Isles Parish Council for the Poor Law, 1897–1924. Inverness Library Archives.
8. Conversations with Dr MacLean.

CHAPTER 10

1. N. Banks, *Six Inner Hebrides*, London, 1977, p. 104.
2. R. Kirk, 'Eigg in the Hebrides', *Yale Review*, 1951, p. 533.
3. J. Hunter, *The Claim of Crofting*, Edinburgh, 1991, p. 59.
4. F. F. Darling, *West Highland Survey: an Essay in Human Ecology*, Oxford, 1955, pp. 50, 170–2.
5. R. Kirk, 'Eigg in the Hebrides', p. 524.
6. Ibid., p. 529.
7. G. Scott-Moncrieff, *Scottish Islands*, London, 1952, pp. 198–9.
8. Lachie's party piece was the telling of an adventure which had happened to him as a child on Muck. He and his brothers had been away on the shore for so long that their parents had come out to look for them. The children were found safe and sound, and claimed that 'little tiny people dressed in green had come ashore in a tiny boat and had offered them tiny little biscuits, the size of a penny'. They had with them a tiny dog and wanted the children to come with them in their boat, they would make them as small as they were. The children had declined the offer but they were so enthralled by these little people that they forgot about the time. The story had even been recorded by an Edinburgh lady and Lachie was sure she had made a lot of money from it!
9. R. Kirk, 'Eigg in the Hebrides', p. 529.
10. Fr A. Ross, 'Hugh MacKinnon's obituary', *Tocher* 10, pp. 37–9.
11. R. Kirk, 'Eigg in the Hebrides', p. 523. According to the *Third Statistical Account*, 1955, vol. 14, p. 440, Gaelic had virtually ceased to be the language of the community, but if it was true of Rum and Muck, Eigg and Canna were still largely Gaelic-speaking.
12. G. Scott-Moncrieff, *Scottish Islands*, pp. 198–9.

CHAPTER 11

1. J. Hunter, *The Claim of Crofting*, Edinburgh, 1991, p. 149.
2. Conversations with Gavin Scott-Moncrieff.
3. Conversations with Peter Findlay, the engineer who had helped his brother-in-law, Gavin Scott-Moncrieff, to formulate his business plan.
4. J. Grassie, *A Highland Experiment, the HIDB*, Aberdeen University Press, Aberdeen, 1983, pp. 36–7.
5. Conversation with Fred Longrigg.
6. Conversations with Barry Austin.
7. Conversation with Fred Longrigg.
8. D. Morgan, *The Isle of Eigg: Land Reform, People Power*, unpublished Ph.D. thesis, Department of Politics, Edinburgh University, 1998.
9. *Press and Journal*, 7 August 1976.
10. J. Grassie, *A Highland Experiment, the HIDB*, 88.
11. *Glasgow Herald*, 7 August 1976.
12. Conversations with Angus Kirk.
13. K. Schellenberg, *Holiday Accommodation Guide*, 1979.
14. Ibid.
15. Ibid.
16. Conversations with Angela Blom.
17. *Scotland on Sunday*, 12 July 1992.
18. *West Highland Free Press* (WHFP), 23 February 1994.
19. H. Porter, 'Scrambled Eigg', *Harpers & Queen*, October 1991.
20. *Daily Mail*, 29 January 1995.

21. K. Schellenberg, 'The sporting life on Eigg', letter to the editor, *Glasgow Herald*, 11 September 1984.
22. J. Urquhart, 'Meeting the challenge of Eigg', *The Field*, 15 March 1986.
23. *Harpers & Queen*, October 1991.
24. *Glasgow Herald*, 7 August 1976.
25. *Harpers & Queen*, October 1991. D. Morgan, *The Isle of Eigg: Land Reform, People, Power*, pp. 75–85.
26. *WHFP*, 3 July 1992.
27. *The Field*, 15 March 1986.
28. *Harpers & Queen*, October 1991.
29. K. Schellenberg, 'The sporting life on Eigg', letter to the editor, *Glasgow Herald*, 11 September 1984.
30. Ibid.
31. *WHFP*, 10 May 1991.

CHAPTER 12

1. J. L. Campbell, *Canna, the Story of a Hebridean Island*, Oxford, 1984, p. 195.
2. Letter from K. Schellenberg to A. Jackson, Lochaber District Council, 2 July 1987.
3. D. Morgan, *The Isle of Eigg: Land Reform, People, Power*, unpublished Ph.D. thesis, Department of Politics, Edinburgh University, 1998, pp. 75–85.
4. *The Scotsman*, 15 July 1988.
5. *The Scotsman*, 29 June 1989.
6. *The Scotsman*, 15 July 1989.
7. H. Porter, 'Scrambled Eigg', *Harpers & Queen*, October 1991.
8. *West Highland Free Press (WHFP)*, 11 August 1989.
9. D. Morgan, *The Isle of Eigg: Land Reform, People, Power*, pp. 75–85.
10. This action was current practice at the time in farming circles. It actually allowed Schellenberg to keep the maximum subsidy for his sheep, the Scottish Office having introduced a maximum headage on the quotas allowed for sheep subsidies, whereby these decreased markedly by about a thousand sheep.
11. *WHFP*, 31 July 1991.
12. *WHFP*, 10 May 1991.
13. *Glasgow Herald*, 24 July 1997.
14. *The Scotsman*, 16 May 1992.
15. Minutes of IERA meeting, 8 November 1991.
16. *WHFP*, 14 December 1990.
17. Ibid.
18. *The Scotsman*, 10 July 1992.
19. A. McIntosh, A. Wightman and D. Morgan, 'The Scottish Highlands in Colonial and Psychodynamic Perspective', *Interculture*, 124, University of Montreal, Summer 1994, p. 31.
20. Ibid., p. 33.
21. Ibid., pp. 32–3.
22. *WHFP*, 12 June 1992.
23. IERA minutes, 11 June 1993.
24. *WHFP*, 21 January 1994.
25. *WHFP*, 21 January 1994. The letter was also sent to the *Oban Times* and the *Press and Journal*.
26. *The Independent*, 28 January 1994.
27. Ibid.
28. *The Future of Eigg, Have Your Say*, Speaking Out, Radio Scotland, 25 February 1994.
29. *Getting Involved, Report on the 1991 Highland Forum Conference*, HIF, Inverness, 1991, p. 11.
30. *WHFP*, 21 January 1994.
31. *Daily Telegraph*, 23 May 1994.
32. The new trustees were: islanders Fiona Cherry, Katie MacKinnon, Peggy Kirk, Barry Williams, Dr Christopher Tiarks who assumed the function of secretary of the trust until he stepped down to be replaced by Maggie Fyffe, and Duncan Ferguson with Alastair McIntosh from the Centre for Human Ecology and journalist Lesley Riddoch.
33. *The Scotsman*, 16 August 1994.

CHAPTER 13

1. A. Wightman, *Who Owns Scotland*, Edinburgh, 1996, pp. 6, 190–1.
2. *Daily Record*, 20 August 1994.
3. *Glasgow Herald*, 2 November 1994.
4. Isle of Eigg Trust press release, 19 March 1995.
5. *West Highland Free Press* (*WHFP*), 24 March 1995.
6. *WHFP*, 31 March 1995.
7. *The Scotsman*, 5 April 1995.
8. *The Scotsman*, 5 April 1995.
9. C. Dudgeon from Savills, a well-known Scottish estate agent, *Observer*, 6 April 1997.
10. IERA minutes, 2 July 1995.
11. *The Sunday Times*, 15 October 1995.
12. *Maruma, the Fog-maker of Eigg* (trans. Robert Melohn), *Stern*, 31 July 1995.
13. *Scotland on Sunday*, 29 October 1995.
14. *The Scotsman*, 31 January 1996.
15. *Press and Journal*, 2 February 1996.
16. *WHFP*, 1 March 1996.
17. *Faobhar*, at BBC2 in Scotland, 6 November 1997.
18. *WHFP*, 30 August 1996.
19. The four islander directors are now Maggie Fyffe, Colin Carr, Karen Helliwell and Donald MacLean, the SWT directors are David Hughes Hallett and Sir John Lister-Kaye and the Highland Council directors are Councillors Dr Michael Foxley and Charlie King, with Simon Fraser as independent chairman. The help given by this Stornoway solicitor and crofting law specialist, who had assisted the Assynt crofters in the setting-up of their trust, was crucial in setting up the partnership and negotiating the last stages of the Eigg buy-out.
20. Scottish Crofters' Union, *Crofting and the Environment*, Inverness, 1992, pp. 28–9.
21. *The Scotsman*, 26 September 1996.
22. Roseanna Cunningham, Early Day Motion 1237, 14 October 1996. The EDM proposed by Mrs Cunningham went as follows: 'That this house supports the Isle of Eigg Trust, in its efforts to raise the finances to enable the community in partnership with the Highland Council and the Scottish Wildlife Trust, to buy and run the island, notes with dismay that successive absentee landlords have allowed the island to deteriorate, recognizes that vagaries of the private landlord system have left the islanders facing an uncertain future, further recognizes that a sustainable future for the community and the environment on Eigg can only be possible with community ownership and control, and hopes that the situation on Eigg highlights an urgent need for radical land reform across Scotland to overhaul the medieval system of land tenure which tolerates land misuse and abuse.'
23. Diarmuid Cameron Mowat, letter to *The Scotsman*, 17 August 1996.
24. The SWT's membership brought in 108,000 donations, the islanders' appeal 90,000 (*The Scotsman*, 19 November 1996).
25. This was the famous answer of the Lewis crofters to Lord Leverhulme, in J. Hunter, *The Making of the Crofting Community*, Edinburgh, 1976, p. 198.
26. Heritage Lottery Fund, press release, 22 January 1997.
27. The islanders' mystery benefactor, a woman from the north of England who wished to remain anonymous as the condition of her gift, pledged the sum of £900,000, which under the government's gift aid scheme increased to £1,000,000, as tax on that sum could be claimed back by the islanders for their appeal.
28. *Press and Journal*, 3 December 1996.
29. *Daily Express*, 11 April 1997; *Geographical Magazine*, October 1996.
30. *The Scotsman*, 24 January 1997; *Daily Mail*, 24 January 1997.
31. Heritage Lottery Fund, press release, 22 January 1997; *WHFP*, 24 January 1997.
32. *The Scotsman*, 5 April 1997.
33. *Press and Journal*, 31 January 1997.
34. Ibid.
35. *Press and Journal*, 6 March 1997.

36. *WHFP*, 28 July 1997.
37. *The Independent*, 5 April 1997; *The Scotsman*, 5 April 1997.
38. D. Campbell, *Spark*. Quoted by kind permission of his mother, Barbara Campbell.
39. *Glasgow Herald*, 13 June 1996.
40. *WHFP*, 7 November 1997.

CHAPTER 14

1. *Gigha prospers after community takes the lead, a case study*, www.hie.co.uk/strengthen-your-community.htm.
2. Key aspects of this legislation are:
    i. The 'right to buy' is restricted to communities that live on, or in close proximity to, the land in question.
    ii. The price to be paid is determined by a government-appointed valuer and based on the current market value.
    iii. A Scottish Land Fund created from the proceeds of the National Lottery helps communities meet the valuation price. Grants and loans at favourable rates and worth up to a £1 million are available.
    iv. Communities are given time to raise the additional funding by introducing a minimum period between notice to sell and the closing date.
    v. The 'right to buy' is backed up by a new power of compulsory purchase that will be used if the owner attempts to evade community purchase, for example by gifting land or by trading in shares.
3. *Gigha prospers after community takes the lead, a case study*, www.hie.co.uk/strengthen-your-community.htm
4. Issie MacPhail, *Eigg, a case study*, draft report, 2003, Highlands and Islands Enterprise.
5. Donnie MacKay, *Isle of Eigg Heritage Trust: The First Seven Years of Community Ownership, Progress Report*, April 2004, Community Land Unit, Highlands and Islands Enterprise.
6. Private landowners own more than 16 million of Scotland's 19 million acres, with public bodies owning over 2 million acres. But the growing not-for-private-profit sector, which includes communities, charities and conservation bodies, now owns or manages about 700,000 acres, having increased by over 21 per cent in the past five years, John Ross, *The Scotsman*, 19 November 2005.
7. Andy Wightman's blog, *Land reform for England and Wales 2*, 14 October 2005.
8. Donnie MacKay, *Isle of Eigg Heritage Trust: The First Seven Years of Community Ownership, Progress Report*, April 2004, Community Land Unit, Highlands and Islands Enterprise.
9. Roy Tylden-Wright, The Dynamics of Partnership, A personal review of the workings of the Laggan Forest Partnership at the start of a new Millennium, March 2000, www.caledonia.org.uk /socialland.
10. Issie MacPhail, *Eigg, A Case Study*, draft report, 2003, Highalnds and Islands Enterprise.
11. Kenneth Kean, IEHT director.
12. Issie MacPhail, Op. Cit. 43 per cent of IEHT income has been from project grants, 28 per cent from grants for woodland and access work, 8 per cent from grants for house renovations and 10 per cent from rents.
13. Ibid.
14. Ibid.
15. Jamie Wilson, *Laird who deluded himself with an action for libel*, The Guardian, 20 May 1999.
16. J. Chester, 'Wildlife recovery on Eigg', in *The New Landowners, Scotland's Experiments*, ECOS, vol. 23, issue 1, p 19.
17. Ibid.
18. Voluntary Workers on Organic Farms. This international scheme, introduced on Eigg by Sue Hollands, Neil Robertson's wife, has brought a steady number of volunteers from all over the world to the Robertsons' croft, improving their garden and enhancing the variety of their social interaction. Currently, another three islanders have joined or are thinking of joining the scheme.
19. Donnie MacKay, Isle of Eigg Heritage Trust: The First Seven Years of Community Ownership, Progress Report, April 2004, Community Land Unit, Highlands and Islands Enterprise
20. Steve Boyle, *Eigg and the Small Isles*, RCAHMS interim report, www.rcahms.gov.uk/highlight-eigg.html.
21. Ibid.

22. Ibid.
23. Comunn Eachdraidh Eige newsletter, issue 3, 2003.
24. One of Eigg's dynamic young newcomers, Brigg Lancaster married Tasha Fyffe in 2000 and died tragically in a fatal car accident in 2003.
25. Trevor Cowie, *A Preliminary Report on the Discovery of Late Bronze Age Metal Working Debris at Galmisdale, Isle of Eigg*, Department of Archaeology, National Museums of Scotland, January 2002.
26. Steve Boyle, Op.Cit.
27. Most of the credit for this task must go to Peter Wade-Martins, the Norfolk archaeologist who did much to investigate the island's archaeology prior to the RCAHMS survey. To sample the Eigg archive collection, go to history society in the Eigg website, www.isleofeigg.org.
28. Dorothy 'Babbit' Thrower.
29. H. Chenevix-Trench and L. Philip, *Community and Conservation Ownership in Highland Scotland, A Common Focus in a Changing Context*, Aberdeen Papers in Land Economy, Department of Land Economy, University of Aberdeen, October 2000, p. 7.
30. Karen Helliwell.
31. Ibid.
32. C. Dressler, *Taking charge on Eigg'*, in *The New Landowners – Scotland Experiments*, Ecos, vol. 23, issue 1, p 12.
33. Steven Clarke, *Social Work as Community Development: A Management Model*, p. 147.
34. Karen Helliwell.
35. Andrew Binnie.
36. Ibid.
37. H. Chenevix-Trench, and L. Philip, Op.Cit., p. 2.
38. The Rum Community Association, spearheaded by Sandy Fraser and Fliss Hough, organised its first very successful music festival the Sound of Rum in 2005 which saw 500 people coming over for a weekend of traditional music on an island which normally has a population of 20 people; an amazing achievement.
39. The Lodge hydro-power system, an upgrade of the 1930s hydro-power turbine dating back to the Runcimans, which now powers the hall and the pier buildings, and Kildonnan, where a new hydro-power system powers five houses.
40. The plan is to have most of the power produced renewably with five small (and discreetly sited) wind turbines between Galmisdale and Grulin, 30-kW solar panels behind the telephone exchange, the two hydros and a new one on Laig burn, more powerful, and to have two large diesel generators as back-up power.
41. Presentation at the European Small Island Network (ESIN) meeting in Bere Island, Eire, on 13–16 November 2005.
42. Deng Mingdao, 365 *Tao, Daily Meditations*, p. 41.
43. Marjorie Kennedy-Fraser, *Songs of the Hebrides*, vol.1, p 47. Mouth music uses words and syllables to make rhythms, without necessarily needing any meaning.
44. Alastair McIntosh, *Soil and Soul*. p 176.
45. Working with Winners strategy workshop. 4–5 December 2005.
46. Ibid.
47. As in 'Wes and Maggie Ceilidh Croft', a tune composed by button-box player Leo McCann, which is now widely played.
48. Sue Wilson, 'The Isle of Eigg Anniversary Ceilidh', *The Scotsman*, 14 June 2005.

POSTSCRIPT

1. In this project, the islanders were led by John Booth, the retired scientist who put three years of voluntary work on the electrification scheme before the much needed renovation of Galmisdale farmhouse, his home on Eigg.
2. http://www.communityenergyscotland.org.uk/userfiles/file\Case studies\Isle of Eigg electrification case study.pdf.
3. Aidan MacEoin, 'Eigg', from a forthcoming new poetry collection due for publication in 2006, following in the footsteps of *In the Boat I Don't Yet Have* his first poetry collection and a debut album *Rustic*, mixing poetry with traditional music and contemporary beats. (www.phatcontroller.co.uk).

BIBLIOGRAPHY

Banks, N., *Six Inner Hebrides*, David and Charles, London, 1977.

Bingham, C., *Beyond the Highland Line*, Constable, London, 1991.

Boswell, J., *Journal of a Tour to the Hebrides with Samuel Johnson* (ed. R. W. Chapman), Oxford University Press, Oxford, 1924.

Boswell, J., *The Life of Johnson*, Heron Books, London, 1960.

Boyle, S., *Eigg and the Small Isles*, RCAHMS interim report, 2003, (www.rcahms.gov.uk/highlight-eigg.html).

Brøger, A. W., *Ancient Emigrants, a History of Norse Settlements in Scotland*, London, 1929.

Bumsted, J. M., *The People's Clearance*, Edinburgh University Press, Edinburgh, 1982.

Cameron, A. D., *Go and Listen to the Crofters*, Acair, Stornoway, 1986.

Campbell, J. L., *Hebridean Folksongs*, Clarendon Press, Oxford, 1977.

Campbell, J. L., *Canna, the Story of a Hebridean Island*, Oxford University Press, Oxford, 1984.

Carmichael, A., *Carmina Gadelica*, vols 1–6, Scottish Academic Press, Edinburgh and London, 1971.

Chapman, M., *The Gaelic Vision in Scottish Culture*, Croom Helm, London, 1978.

Chenevix-Trench, H. and Philip, L., *Community and Conservation Ownership in Highland Scotland, A Common Focus in a Changing Context*, Aberdeen Papers in Land Economy, Department of Land Economy, University of Aberdeen, October 2000.

Clarke, S., *Social work as community development, a management model for social change*, 2nd ed., Aldershot, 2000.

Cohen, A., *Whalsay, Symbol, Segment and Boundaries in a Shetland Island Community*, Manchester University Press, Manchester, 1987.

Cohen, A., *The Symbolic Construction of Community* (2nd edn), Routledge, London, 1989.

Connel, C., *The Scottish Naturalist*, issue 161, September–October 1926.

Cowie, T., *A preliminary report on the discovery of late Bronze Age metal working debris at Galmisdale, isle of Eigg*, Department of Archaeology, National Museums of Scotland, Edinburgh, 2002.

Crawford, B. E. (ed.), *Scandinavian Scotland*, Leicester University Press, Leicester, 1987.

Darling, F. F., *West Highland Survey: an Essay in Human Ecology*, Oxford University Press, Oxford, 1955.

Deng, M., *365 Tao: Daily Meditations*, HarperSanFrancisco, New York, 1992.

Dodgshon, R. A., *Land and Society in Early Scotland*, Oxford University Press, Oxford, 1981.

Donaldson, M. E. M., *Wanderings in the Western Highlands and Islands*, 3rd edn, Alexander Gardner, Paisley, 1927.

Dressler, C., 'IEHT, the first 18 months,' in Boyd, G. and Reid, D. (eds), *Social Land Ownership: Eight Case Studies from the Highlands and Islands*, vol. 2, Not-for-Profit Landowners Group, Inverness, 1999.

ECOS, *The New Landowners: Scotland's Experiments*, vol. 23, issue 1.

Fenton, A., *Country Life in Scotland: Our Rural Past*, John Donald, Edinburgh, 1987.

Ferguson, D., *Notes on the History of Eigg*, unpublished manuscript.

Fisher, I., First draft for *Early Medieval Sculpture in the West Highlands*, RCAHMS, Edinburgh, 1998.

Forbes, R., *The Lyon in Mourning*, vol. 2, Scottish Historical Society, Edinburgh, 1895.

Foster, S., *Picts, Gaels and Scots*, B. T. Batsford/Historic Scotland, 1996.

Fraser, J., 'A Treatise on the Second Sight', *Miscellanea Scotica*, vol. 3, George Wylie & Co., Glasgow, 1820.

243

Fraser-Mackintosh, C., *Antiquarian Notes*, 2nd series, A. & W. Mackenzie, Inverness, 1897.

Gastie, J., *Democracy in small groups*, New Society Publishers, Philadelphia, 1993.

Gibson, J., *Ships of the '45s*, Hutchinson & Co., London, 1967.

Grant, I. F., *Highland Folkways*, Routledge & Kegan Paul, London, 1961.

Grant, I. F., *The MacLeods*, 2nd edn, Spurbooks, Edinburgh, 1981.

Grassie, J., *A Highland Experiment, the Story of the HIDB*, Aberdeen University Press, Aberdeen, 1983.

Grigor, I. F. *Highland Resistance*, Mainstream, Edinburgh 2000.

Heaney, S., *Sweeney Astray*, Faber & Faber, London, 1984.

Henderson, G., *The Norse Influence on Celtic Scotland*, J. Maclehose & Sons, Glasgow, 1910.

Hubert, H., *The History of the Celtic People*, Bracken Books, London, 1992.

Hunter, J., *The Making of the Crofting Community*, John Donald, Edinburgh, 1976.

Hunter, J., *The Claim of Crofting*, Mainstream, Edinburgh, 1991.

Jedrej, C. and Nuttall, M., *White Settlers, the Impact of Rural Repopulation in Scotland*, Hardwood Academic Press, Luxembourg, 1996.

Johnson, S., *Journey to the Western Islands of Scotland*, R. W. Chapman (ed.), Oxford University Press, Oxford, 1924.

Kennedy-Fraser, M., *Songs of the Hebrides*, vols 1 and 2, Boosey & Co., London, 1909.

Kirk, R., 'Eigg in the Hebrides', *Yale Review*, Yale University, 1951.

Knox, J., *A Tour through the Highlands of Scotland*, J. Walter, London, 1787.

Lamont, W.D., 'House and Pennylands in the Highlands and Islands', *Scottish Studies*, vol. 25, Edinburgh, 1981.

Land Reform Policy Group, *Identifying the Problems*, Edinburgh, Scottish Office, 1998.

MacDonald, A. and MacDonald, A., *Clan Donald*, vol. 2, The Northern Counties Publishing Company, Inverness, 1900.

MacDonald, A. and MacDonald, A., *Clan Donald*, vol. 3, The Northern Counties Publishing Company, Inverness, 1904.

MacDonald, A. and MacDonald, A., *The Poems of Alexander MacDonald*, The Northern Counties Publishing Company, Inverness, 1924.

MacDonald, A. and MacDonald, J., *Fair is the Place*, Sydney, Nova Scotia, 1980.

MacDonald, C., *Moidart or Amongst the Clanranalds*, Duncan Cameron, Oban, 1889.

MacDonald of Castleton, D. J., *Clan Donald*, MacDonald Publishers, Edinburgh, 1978.

MacDonald, H., *A History of the MacDonalds, Highland Papers*, vol. 1, Scottish History Society, Edinburgh, 1881.

McIntosh, A., Wightman, A. and Morgan, D., 'The Scottish Highlands in Colonial and Psychodynamic Perspective', *Interculture*, issue 124, University of Montreal, Summer 1994.

McIntosh, A., *Soil and Soul*, Aurum Press, London 2001.

Mackay, D., *Scotland's Farewell, the People of the Hector*, Scarborough, Ontario, 1980.

MacKay, D., The Isle of Eigg Heritage Trust: The first seven years of community ownership, *Progress Report*, April 2004, Community Land Unit, Highlands and Islands Enterprise.

Mackay, I., 'Clanranald tacksmen in the late 18th century', *Transactions of the Gaelic Society of Inverness*, XLIV, Inverness, 1964.

MacKenzie, M. C., *History of the Outer Isles*, James Thin, Edinburgh, 1974.

Mackenzie, H. R., *Yachting and Electioneering in the Hebrides*, privately printed, Inverness, 1886.

MacKinnon, H., *Tocher 3*, 10, 15, 29, 36, Journal of the School of Scottish Studies, University of Edinburgh, 1973–1982.

MacLean, D. (Rev.), *State of Emigration from the Highlands of Scotland, its Extent, Causes and Proposed Remedy*, London, 1803.

MacLean, F., *A Concise History of Scotland*, revised edn, Thames & Hudson, London, 1993.

MacLean, M., *The People of Glengarry*, MacGill-Queens University Press, Montreal and Kingston, 1991.

MacLeod, K., *The Road to the Isles*, R. Grant & Son, Edinburgh, 1927.

MacLeod of MacLeod, R. C., *The MacLeods of Dunvegan*, privately printed, Clan Society, Inverness, 1927.

MacMillan, D., Thomson, K. and Slee, B., *Land Reform in Scotland, An economic commentary on the community right to buy land*', Department of Agriculture and Forestry, University of Aberdeen, 2001.

MacPhail L. I., *Eigg, a case study*, draft report, Highlands and Islands Enterprise, 2003.

MacPhail, I. M. M., *The Crofters' War*, Acair, Stornoway, 1989.

Martin, M., *A Description of the Western Isles of Scotland, Circa 1695* (4th edn), Eneas MacKay, Stirling, 1934.

Miller, H., *The Cruise of the Betsey, or a Summer Holiday in the Hebrides*, 8th edn, William N. Nimmo, Edinburgh, 1870.

Morgan, D., *The Isle of Eigg: Land Reform, People, Power*, unpublished Ph.D. thesis, Department of Politics, University of Edinburgh, Edinburgh, 1998.

Morrison, D., *The Morrison Manuscript: Traditions of the Western Isles* (ed. Norman MacDonald), Stornoway, 1975.

Murchison, D., *The Gaelic Prose of Kenneth MacLeod*, Gaelic Text Society, Edinburgh, 1958.

Murray, W. H., *The Islands of Western Scotland*, Methuen, London, 1973.

Necker de Saussure, L. A., *A Voyage to the Hebrides*, Geneva, 1810.

The New Statistical Account of Scotland, vol. 14, William Blackwood & Sons, Edinburgh and London, 1845.

O'Driscoll, R. (ed.), *The Celtic Consciousness*, Canongate, Edinburgh, 1981.

Pennant, T., *A Tour of Scotland in 1769*, Melven Press, Perth, 1979.

Pitcairn, R., *Ancient Criminal Trials in Scotland*, vol. 3, Bannatyne Club, Edinburgh, 1833.

Porter, H., 'Scrambled Eigg', *Harpers and Queen*, October 1991.

Proceedings of the Society of Antiquities, vol. 12, Edinburgh, 1878.

Rankin, D. J., *A History of the County of Antigonish, Nova Scotia*, Toronto, 1922.

Report of the Royal Commission on Ancient and Historical Monuments (Scotland), *The Outer Hebrides, Skye and the Small Isles*, HMSO, Edinburgh, 1928.

Richards, E., *A History of the Highland Clearances*, Croom Helm, London, 1982.

Robertson, C. M. (Revd), 'Topography and traditions of Eigg', *Transactions of the Gaelic Society of Inverness*, vol. 22, Inverness, 1897–1898.

Schellenberg, K., *Holiday Accommodation Guide*, Isle of Eigg, 1979.

Scottish Crofters' Union, *Crofting and the Environment, a New Approach*, Inverness, 1992.

Scott-Moncrieff, G., *The Scottish Islands*, B. T. Batsford, London, 1952.

Shaw, F. J., *The Northern and Western Isles of Scotland, their Economy and Society in the Seventeenth Century*, John Donald, Edinburgh, 1980.

Skene, W. F., *Celtic Scotland*, vols I, II and III, 2nd edn, David Douglas, Edinburgh, 1886.

Smout, T. C., *A History of the Scottish People, 1560–1830*, Collins, London, 1969.

Smout, T. C., *A Century of the Scottish People, 1830–1950*, Collins, London, 1986.

Smyth, A. P., *Warlords and Holy Men*, Edinburgh University Press, Edinburgh, 1984.

Somers, R., *Letters from the Highlands after the Great Potato Famine of 1846*, 2nd edn, Melven's Bookshop, Inverness, 1977.

The Statistical Account of Scotland (ed. Sir John Sinclair), vol. XX, William Creech, Edinburgh, 1794–1795.

Streits, J., *The Sun and the Cross*, Floris, Edinburgh, 1977.

Third Statistical Account of Scotland (ed. Hugh Barron), vol. XVI, Scottish Academic Press, Edinburgh, 1985.

Thomson, D., *An Introduction to Gaelic Poetry*, 2nd edn, Edinburgh University Press, Edinburgh, 1989.

Tylden-Wright, R., *The Dynamics of Partnership, A personal review of the workings of the Laggan Forest Partnership at the start of a new Millennium*, March 2000, (www.caledonia.socialland.org.uk).

Tolmie, F., *Journal of the Folklore Society*, vol. 16, London, 1911.

Urquhart, J. 'Meeting the challenge of Eigg', *The Field*, March 1986.

Urquhart, J., *Eigg*, Canongate, Edinburgh, 1987.

Wade-Martin, S., *Eigg, an Island Landscape*, Countryside Publishing, 2004.

Walker, Revd J., *A Report on the Hebrides of 1764 and 1771* (ed. M. MacKay), John Donald, Edinburgh, 1980.

Wickham-Jones, C., *Scotland's First Settlers*, B. T. Batsford/Historic Scotland, London, 1994.

Wightman, A., *Who Owns Scotland*, Canongate, Edinburgh, 1997.

UNPUBLISHED RECORDS

Blair Papers, Scottish Catholic Archives, Edinburgh.
Carmichael, A., Manuscript Collection, Edinburgh University Archives.
Census 1841–1891, Isle of Eigg Archive copy from the Scottish Record Office, Edinburgh.
Clanranald Papers, GD/201, Scottish Record Office, Edinburgh.
Isle of Eigg Heritage Trust, Draft Management Plan, 2000.
Isle of Eigg Heritage Trust, Progress Report, November 2001.
Isle of Eigg Heritage Trust, Sustainability Strategy, 2004.
Minutes of the Isle of Eigg Residents' Association, 1990–2005.
Minutes of the Isle of Eigg Heritage Trust, 1998-2005.
Minutes of the Board of Governors, Small Isles Parish Schoolboard 1906–1913, Inverness Library Archives.

OFFICIAL PUBLICATIONS (Parliamentary Papers)

Board of Supervision for the Relief of the Poor in Scotland, Annual Reports, 1847.
Correspondence relating to the Measures Adopted for the Relief of Distress in Scotland, Parliamentary Papers, 1847, LIII.
Register of the Privy Council of Scotland, H.M. Register House, Edinburgh, 1881, vol. 4.
Report of the Commissioners of Inquiry into the Conditions of the Crofters and Cottars in the Highlands and Islands of Scotland, Parliamentary Papers, 1884, XXXII.
Report of the Royal Commission on the Conditions of the Crofters and Cottars of the Highlands and Islands of Scotland, Parliamentary Papers, 1884, XXXII.
Report on the Destitution in the Highlands down to the Year 1841, Parliamentary Papers, 1841, VI.
Royal Commission (Highlands and Islands), Report and Minutes of Evidence, Parliamentary Papers, 1895, XXXVIII.

NEWSPAPERS AND PERIODICALS

The Field Magazine
Glasgow Herald
Geographical Magazine
Press & Journal
The Scotsman
Tatler
West Highland Free Press

INDEX